THE INVENTION OF CELEBRITY

THE INVENTION OF CELEBRITY

1750–1850

ANTOINE LILTI

Translated by Lynn Jeffress

polity

First published in French as *Figures publiques. L'invention de la célébrité. 1750–1850*, © Librairie Arthème Fayard, 2015

This English edition © Polity Press, 2017

Polity Press
65 Bridge Street
Cambridge CB2 1UR, UK

Polity Press
350 Main Street
Malden, MA 02148, USA

ISBN-13: 978-1-5095-0873-0
ISBN-13: 978-1-5095-0874-7 (pb)

A catalogue record for this book is available from the British Library.

Typeset in 10 on 11.5 pt Sabon by Toppan Best-set Premedia Limited
Printed and bound in the UK by CPI Group (UK) Ltd, Croydon

The publisher has used its best endeavours to ensure that the URLs for external websites referred to in this book are correct and active at the time of going to press. However, the publisher has no responsibility for the websites and can make no guarantee that a site will remain live or that the content is or will remain appropriate.

Every effort has been made to trace all copyright holders, but if any have been inadvertently overlooked the publisher will be pleased to include any necessary credits in any subsequent reprint or edition.

For further information on Polity, visit our website: politybooks.com

CONTENTS

ACKNOWLEDGMENTS

This book has been a work in progress for almost ten years, and since its first formulation I have had time to accumulate numerous debts, which I here have the pleasure of acknowledging. Many of my colleagues and friends had the patience to listen to me or read me, discuss my hypotheses, suggest examples or readings. This permanent dialogue that allows one to avoid the stumbling blocks one encounters when working alone is an essential aspect of the constant pleasure I find in doing research.

There were several drafts of this work on celebrity, the first focusing on the issue of Rousseau, and then by progressively enlarging on the questions in several seminars and symposiums. I had the good fortune to be invited to the Maison Française d'Oxford and the following universities: Cornell, Johns Hopkins, Berkeley, Stanford, Bordeaux III, Cambridge, Peking, Grenoble, Créteil, Geneva, and Montreal, including several seminars at the École des Hautes Études en Sciences Sociales (EHESS). I want to thank everyone who made these meetings possible as well as all the participants. I owe much, also, to those in my own seminars at the École Normale Supérieure and then at EHESS who patiently listened to me construct the principal chapters of this book. I must admit I often tested ideas on them first and they sometimes convinced me of their point of view.

Among the many colleagues whom I have the pleasure of thanking, I want to acknowledge Romain Bertrand, Florent Brayard, Caroline Callard, Jean-Luc Chappey, Christophe Charle, Roger Chartier, Yves Citton, Dan Edelstein, Darrin McMahon, Robert Darnton, Pierre-Antoine Fabre, Carla Hesse, Steve Kaplan, Bruno Karsenti, Cyril Lemieux, Tony La Vopa, Rahul Markovits, Renaud Morieux, Robert Morrissey, Ourida Mostefai, Nicolas Offenstadt, Michel Porret, Daniel Roche, Steve Sawyer, Anne Simonin, Céline Spector, and Mélanie Traversier. The following showed great benevolence, or friendship, in reading whole chapters, sometimes even the entire book, and helped me avoid many errors: Étienne Anheim, David Bell, Barbara Carnevali, Charlotte Guichard, Jacques Revel, Silvia Sebastiani, Valérie Theis, and StéphaneVan Damme. I thank each of them.

From the Canal Saint-Martin to the hill of the Pincio and back again, Charlotte was always there, and this book owes more to her than I can ever say. Juliette and Zoé will perhaps read it in a few years, remembering that I was not always available as much as they would have liked. Or maybe not.

I am very glad that my book has now been issued in English, and I would like to heartily thank John Thompson for making this publication possible. Many thanks, too, to the whole editorial team at Polity, especially Paul Young and Justin Dyer. I am grateful, finally, to Lynn Jeffress, who had the patience to translate my French prose into English.

INTRODUCTION

Celebrity and Modernity

"Marie-Antoinette is Lady Di!" On the set where his daughter Sofia was making her film on the French queen, Francis Ford Coppola was struck by the parallel between the two women's destinies.[1] This comparison is strongly suggested by the anachronistic angle taken by the film: Sofia Coppola presents Marie-Antoinette as a young woman today, torn between her thirst for freedom and the constraints imposed by her royal station.

The film's music, which mixes baroque works, 1980s rock groups, and more recent electronic pieces, deliberately emphasizes this interpretation. After the enigmatic and melancholy young women of *The Virgin Suicides* and *Lost in Translation*, Marie-Antoinette at first appears to be a new incarnation of the eternal adolescent girl. Then another theme emerges that Sofia Coppola took up overtly in her following films: celebrities' way of life. Like the actor of *Somewhere*, holed up in his luxury hotel, where he is dying of boredom but does not envisage leaving, Marie-Antoinette is confronted by the obligations associated with her status as a public figure. She can have anything she wants, except perhaps what she really wants most: to escape the exigencies of court society, which appears as a prefiguration of the "society of the spectacle" (Guy Debord). One scene in the film shows the young crown princess's astonishment and embarrassment when, having awakened after moving into her quarters at Versailles, she finds herself surrounded by courtiers staring at her like modern paparazzi scrutinize the private lives of celebrities. Rejecting the choice between condemning and rehabilitating the queen, Sofia Coppola presents a futile young woman whose historical role seems to consist in a long series of luxurious parties. Filming Marie-Antoinette's life at Versailles as if she were filming the amusements of Hollywood stars, the director foresees a world in which the royal family is no different from that of show business stars.

In general, historians don't like anachronisms. However, it is worth considering this image of Marie-Antoinette as a celebrity *avant la lettre* who is forced to live constantly under the eyes of others, deprived of all privacy, hobbled in her quest for authentic communication with her contemporaries. It is true that this parallel leaves out an essential element: the court ceremonial. This ceremonial placed sovereigns under the permanent observation of the courtiers and was very different from the modern mechanisms of celebrity. It was not the result of a vast audience's curiosity about the private life of famous people, but instead fulfilled a political function following from the theory of royal representation. Whereas the culture of celebrity is based on the distinction between an inversion of the private and the public (private life being made public by the media), monarchical representation presupposed their identity. In the time of Louis XIV, the *lever du roi* was not that of a private individual, but rather that of a wholly public person who incarnated the state. Between the political rituals of monarchical representation and the media and commercial apparatuses of celebrity, a profound change made the former obsolete and the latter possible: the conjoint invention of private life and publicity.

Nonetheless, there is something singularly right in Sofia Coppola's view of the queen's condition. At the end of the eighteenth century, Versailles was no longer the isolated space of monarchical representation. The court henceforth lived in Paris's orbit, and it was deeply affected by the changes in the public sphere, the multiplication of newspapers and images, the development of fashion, shows, and the commercialization of leisure activities. Under Louis XIV, protocol placed the monarch's whole life before the public and made manifest the radical separation between the sovereign's grandeur and his subjects, but this protocol was completely controlled by the king. In the course of the eighteenth century, it was gradually emptied of its meaning; courtiers, preferring the amusements of the capital, reduced their stays at Versailles to the strict minimum; sovereigns themselves gradually ceased to play a game in which they no longer really believed and developed a private life separate from the ceremonial; in the end, this privacy was intensely scrutinized and exposed. Whereas Louis XIV was attacked for his politics, Louis XVI and Marie-Antoinette were attacked for their sex lives, supposed or real.

Granted, by projecting her favorite themes and no doubt part of her personal experience onto Marie-Antoinette, Sofia Coppola was not claiming to do the work of a historian, but she makes clear the changes that were then affecting court society and the status of the queen under the impact of the nascent culture of celebrity. In the course of the eighteenth century, something happened that has to be accounted for. This is where the rights of the historian come into play.

But the historian has to exercise these rights. Whereas today celebrity is a characteristic trait of most societies, historians hesitate to take an interest in it. Stars are everywhere, in the periodicals devoted to them and in the general media, on movie screens and on television, on radio and on the internet. Specialists in the media and popular culture have devoted numerous studies to them, dealing with their audiences, their fates, and the meaning of the fascination they exercise. There is a semiology and a sociology of celebrity, and even, more recently, an economics of celebrity – a sign that the theme is beginning to gain legitimacy.[2] But historians have shown little interest in the origins of this phenomenon. Where did they come from, these stars who colonize our screens and our imaginations?

In the absence of genuine historical works on celebrity, two opposed interpretations share the market of received ideas. The first asserts that celebrity is a universal phenomenon, which is found in all societies and periods. Leo Braudy provided a persuasive illustration of this view in a massive general study, *The Frenzy of Renown*, which traces the history of celebrity and the desire for fame from Alexander the Great down to our own time.[3] As is often the case with such an undertaking, one can admire the effort taken to produce a synthesis or the accuracy of certain analyses while remaining skeptical about the result: what is the use of such a broad conception of celebrity, one that lumps together in a single word phenomena as disparate as the glory of the Roman emperors and the celebrity of contemporary actresses? Inversely, a second interpretation of celebrity sees it as a very recent phenomenon connected with the rise of mass culture, with "the society of the spectacle," and the omnipresence of audiovisual media.[4] This kind of celebrity is defined by its most extreme manifestations: the fans' hysteria; the endless multiplication of celebrity images; the stars' exponentially increasing incomes; their eccentricities; TV reality shows; and the success of the celebrity press. These two interpretations are strangely compatible. They feed a critical, conservative, and now very conventional discourse that goes more or less this way: there have always been very well-known people; they used to owe their notoriety to their adventures, their talents, and their deeds, whereas now they are famous only in proportion to their exposure in the media, and they have no other "claim to fame." Celebrity is supposed to be only a degenerate form of glory, a tautological media phenomenon, whose formula was defined by the American historian Daniel Boorstin: celebrity designates people "well-known for their well-knownness," individuals without talent and without achievements, whose sole merit is to be on television.[5]

3

These interpretations are not satisfactory. They are based on definitions of celebrity that are too broad or too reductive, and they do not allow us to understand either its origins or its meaning. When they extend to all forms of fame, it prevents an examination of the specificity of the phenomenon's contemporary mechanisms. Conversely, when they reduce celebrity to the current excesses of the star-system, they fail to see that the phenomenon has its roots in the very heart of modernity, in forms of public recognition that appeared, as we shall see, during the Enlightenment. So it is not surprising that studies of contemporary celebrity struggle to escape these confusions. Celebrity is presented sometimes as the foundation of a new elite endowed with a capital of visibility and benefiting from privileges, and sometimes as a mechanism of alienation that binds famous people to the desire of an all-powerful public. In some authors, it appears as a modern substitute for religious beliefs and myths: the "cult of the stars" is supposed to be an anthropological variant of the cult of saints and heroes, a modern idolatry. "Worshipped as heroes, divinized, the stars are more than objects of admiration. They are also subjects of a cult. A religion in embryo has formed around them," Edgar Morin wrote in 1957, in one of the first essays devoted to movie stars.[6] This hypothesis, which at that time had the merit of being new, has now become a commonplace. For other writers, celebrity is, on the contrary, a completely secularized consequence of the economy of the spectacle and the culture industry, whose peculiar logic consists in concentrating prestige and income on a few individuals. Celebrity, disenchanted, is now simply a question of marketing.

Coincidentally, all these elements are fused in a disconcerting whole, as in Chris Rojek's book *Celebrity*, published in the United States in 2001 and accompanied in the French edition with a preface by Frédéric Beigbeder, a French novelist and TV host.[7] The latter, both a protagonist and an observer of the culture of celebrity, and in that respect in a position to talk about it, manages to juxtapose in two pages all the apparently incompatible clichés. Celebrities are a caste of privileged, rich, and arrogant people who get the best tables in restaurants and live in palaces, but they are also the victims of fanatical admirers who make their lives impossible by subjecting them to permanent surveillance. This contradiction results in the expected unveiling of a kind of merchandise omnipotence, the motto of inoffensive criticism: "Celebrity, like publicity, is a dream that serves only one end: selling." Let's be honest: these contradictions themselves have a long history. They lead us toward a difficult question: why is celebrity such an ambivalent and contested value?

I propose to start from a definition of celebrity that cannot be reduced to the simple fact of being very well known. There are too many ways of

4

being well known. If we want to make the notion of celebrity analytically effective on the sociological and historical level, we have to distinguish it from other forms of notoriety, such as glory and reputation. Glory designates notoriety acquired by someone who is judged to be extraordinary because of his or her achievements, whether these are acts of bravery, or artistic or literary works. It is essentially a posthumous designation and flourishes through the commemoration of the hero in the collective memory. Reputation, for its part, corresponds to the judgment that the members of a group or a community make collectively regarding one of their own: is he or she a good spouse, a good citizen, competent and honorable? It results from the socialization of opinions by way of conversations and rumors. It can be completely informal or more formalized. If glory is reserved for a few individuals considered to be exceptional, every individual, by the simple fact of living in society, is the object of the judgment of others and thus has a reputation, which varies depending on the places and the groups concerned.

The opposition between these two forms of notoriety, glory and reputation, is a long-standing aspect of European history, sometimes masked by the great range of vocabulary available for naming these phenomena. In French, for example, there are the words *renom*, *renommée*, *estime*, and *reconnaissance*. Every language obviously contains a large number of such terms. In English, "fame" has, as we shall see, many different meanings that overlap with those of "reputation" and "glory." The use I make of the terms "glory" and "reputation" is first of all analytic: it provides us with tools for distinguishing different social and cultural configurations. Glory concerns heroes, saints, illustrious men – all the figures whose glorification has played a major role in Western culture, including their modern avatar, the "great man" – *grand homme* – dear to Enlightenment philosophers; reputation belongs to local mechanisms of social judgment, of *fama* and honor. Because they have not distinguished between these two forms of notoriety, most historians, taken in by the imprecision of the vocabulary, confuse them, even though they are based on very different social mechanisms. Today, the difference between the two forms of notoriety is still manifest. On the one hand, the glory of great heads of state, artists, scientists, and even sports champions: Charles de Gaulle, Pablo Picasso, Marcel Proust, Marie Curie, Pelé, to mention a few. On the other hand, an individual's reputation based on qualities, private or professional, evaluated by those who know and spend time with him or her. One can be a reputable physician in one's city or a scientist well known to his or her peers without claiming to have achieved glory. And who does not know that Vincent Van Gogh, whose posthumous glory has been so great, was known to only a few people during his lifetime?

But the specificity of modern societies has to do with the appearance of a third form of notoriety: celebrity. At first sight, the latter takes the form of a very extensive reputation. The celebrated individual is not known simply to his family, his colleagues, his neighbors, his peers, or his customers, but to a vast group of people with whom he has no direct contact, who have never met him and will never meet him, but who frequently encounter his public image, a whole set of images and discourses associated with his name.[8] In other words, a celebrated person is one known by people who are not directly involved in making a judgment regarding his personality or his competencies. The celebrity of a singer begins when his name and his face are known to those who do not listen to his songs; that of a soccer player when he is recognized by those who never watch soccer games. As a celebrity, he is no longer concerned with colleagues, admirers, customers, or neighbors, but rather with an audience.

Are we now getting close to glory? Isn't celebrity only a stage on a continuum of notorieties that stretches from (local) reputation to (universal) glory by way of (extended) celebrity? This hypothesis has been advanced in the form of concentric "circles of recognition" that lead in the worlds of culture, for example, from the judgment of peers to that of fans and critics, and then to the public at large.[9] This model, however, underestimates the differences between reputation, glory, and celebrity. Glory is essentially posthumous (even if it may be sought after), and concerns posterity, whereas celebrity is based on the contemporaneousness of a person and an audience. Celebrity is not commemorative; instead, it espouses the rapid rhythm of current events. Whereas glory designates a community's admiration for an individual considered to be exemplary, a dead hero who incarnates certain intellectual, physical, or moral virtues, the source of celebrity is quite different: it is the curiosity elicited among contemporaries by a singular personality. This curiosity is not always admiring and rarely unanimous: there are celebrated criminals and scandalous or controversial celebrities.

At the other end of the spectrum, despite appearances, celebrity is not simply an extended reputation. By enlarging to the extreme the circles of recognition, the mechanisms of publicity open onto a specific reality. First of all, celebrity becomes autonomous with regard to the criteria that govern reputations. When a writer, an actor, or a criminal becomes celebrated, the curiosity they elicit is no longer evaluated by a standard of criteria specific to their original activity. They have become public figures who are no longer judged solely with respect to their competencies, but rather with respect to their ability to capture and maintain curiosity on the part of the audience. This explains the salient characteristic of the culture of celebrity: it levels out the status of those who have come from very different spheres of activity. During the sometimes short period of their notoriety, actors and politicians, writers and the protagonists of fleeting news items are treated on the same level, like the stars of a media spectacle.

A second characteristic distinguishes celebrity from reputation: the curiosity it arouses carries with it a particularly lively interest in the private life of famous people who become the object of collective interest. The extension of the notoriety well beyond close family and peers does not translate, as one might think, into a distant relationship, timid and vaguely curious, but, on the contrary, by a sometimes very emotional attachment, often very powerful, and for which the figure of the *fan* is the incarnation. This attachment is inseparable from an intimate, personal bond, even if it is most often a distant intimacy, fictitious and unilateral, whose workings must be understood. Between reputation and celebrity, as between glory and celebrity, the distinction is not just quantitative, not simply a matter of the number of people who know a person.

Even so, it would be absurd to plead for an absolute division between reputation, celebrity, and glory. It is essential, instead, to identify a group of issues: why is it that certain people, actors, writers, politicians, or even "celebrities of the moment," accidental heroes of some newsworthy event, arouse so much curiosity, in some ways independent of their merit or their actions? How does this curiosity transform the conventional forms of recognition established in specific worlds, such as the worlds of culture and that of politics? Why has celebrity always been treated with suspicion and disdain, including among those who avidly seek it? All research into celebrity must begin with the question: what is the nature of this curiosity which makes us interested in the lives of certain of our contemporaries whom we have never met?

In order to answer this, we must understand the first manifestations of this curiosity. Celebrity appeared during the eighteenth century, at a time of profound change in the public sphere and when leisure was first being commercialized. Since that time, celebrity has undergone considerable change proportional to the expansion of the media sphere. But the principal mechanisms that characterize it were already perfectly identifiable at the end of the eighteenth century. Many authors have written detailed descriptions of it, seeking to understand the new social being, the celebrity, who could not be viewed as a known quantity, nor as a hero -- and yet in the process of being reborn with the traits of a great man of genius – nor a good and honest man with an excellent reputation, nor an artist recognized by his peers. The development of specific mechanisms of celebrity was thus accompanied by *the topic of celebrity*. I include in this the discourse, anecdotes, and stories which, although not forming a unified body of knowledge, testify to a collective effort to think about a new phenomenon and provide the foundations, narrative or linguistic, with which individuals tried to navigate the strangeness of the social world. Not only did the word "celebrity" in its original meaning appear in the eighteenth century, but the practices it designated aroused a flood of observations aimed at recognizing the phenomenon and making sense of it.

To study celebrity in its infancy, so to speak, when its expression was not yet manifest in all the various cultural institutions (magazines, television programs, fan clubs, etc.), allows one to better show the ambivalences which characterize it: a symbol of social success, sought after for the advantages which seemed associated with it, celebrity was never really legitimate. Always suspected of being ephemeral, superficial, indeed excessive, it was the subject of endless criticism, endless ironies. This paradox associated with celebrity, both sought after, as a modern form of social prestige, and decried as a media artifice, corresponds to the ambivalence of collective opinions found in democratic societies. To understand it, one must undertake to describe the practices and the behaviors which shape this celebrity culture, as well as the discourse which tirelessly makes them an object of study.

Therefore, the image of the public sphere during the Enlightenment is itself transformed. Since the work of Jürgen Habermas, it has been thought of as a sphere of critical and rational discussion where private individuals make public use of their reason. For Habermas, the public sphere of the eighteenth century, middle-class, enlightened, and broad-minded, was built on the ruins of the public sphere of representation, where each individual was defined by a social status and political communication extended only unilaterally, from those in power to their subjects. But this critical public sphere, identified as the legacy of the Enlightenment, entered into crisis during the nineteenth century and disappeared in the twentieth century, as a result of two effects: mass media and the commodification of society, leaving room for the public sphere to be dominated by political propaganda, the culture industry, and marketing. Public opinion from then on was no longer a tribunal of criticism carrying with it the ideal of freedom, but a passive entity easily manipulated. Even the concept of "publicity" was totally subverted. It no longer related to a demand for the submission of the secrets of power to a collective critical discussion; it became another name for "advertising," a way to condition minds to accept commercial products or politicians.[10] Whether or not they agreed with the proposition, numerous authors shared the idea that there was a golden age of the public sphere. It allows the denunciation of alleged vulgarity and emptiness in our age, dominated by spectacles and merchandise, by political storytelling and the invention of ephemeral stars. The opposition between publicity thought

8

of as a requirement for the critical use of reason and publicity understood as commercial media manipulation is normative rather than historical fact. It is entirely based on a political ideal, that of public deliberation, projected on to the golden age of the Enlightenment in order to better analyze everything in our modern world that has diverged from such an ideal.[11] It completely idealizes the eighteenth century, but above all, and more seriously, it creates an obstacle to our understanding of what a public entity is.

Studying the mechanisms of celebrity reveals that the public is not solely an instance of literary, artistic, or political judgment; it is rather an entire group of anonymous readers who all read the same books and, more and more in the eighteenth century, the same newspapers. The public is defined not by rational arguments, but by sharing the same curiosity and the same beliefs, by being interested in the same things at the same time and by being aware of this simultaneity. From this arises the ambiguity of the public, interested in political debates as well as the private life of celebrities and rarely reaching the expectations placed on it by political philosophers and ethicists. Most of the authors we will look at in this study were convinced of this. The success of Habermas's reexamination of the Kantian definition of the public hides an important fact: throughout this period, numerous definitions of the public emerged, some more sensitive to its ambiguities. Starting in the second half of the eighteenth century, the idea of the public was always seen to be a problem, of which public opinion was only one aspect. This question of the public was inseparable from the theory of communication as it was understood a century after Immanuel Kant by the sociologist Gabriel Tarde, author of the theory of social imitation. It was the "sensation of being in" – the realization and the pleasure of being interested in the same things as one's contemporaries – that created the unity and the force of the public, thought of as "a dispersion of individuals who are physically separated and whose cohesion is entirely mental."[12] This cohesion, due primarily to periodicals, but also to the fashion world or to literary triumphs, is based on the effect of collective imitation, individuals influenced from a distance by the realization that they make up a public, which means they are interested in the same thing at the same time.

One understands, then, that *publicity* is inherently ambivalent, if one means by publicity that audiences are always created by the distribution of discourse and images thanks to printed matter and other forms of media. It appears fundamentally democratic, in the sense that it opposes secrecy, the control of information by small groups, and seems to favor a bigger, more egalitarian broadcasting of political discussion and cultural works. But in the eyes of the elite, publicity is often marked by vulgarity because it clashes with their categories of cultural distinction and their conviction that they possess political expertise. Publicity carries with it sudden mass infatuations, sometimes ephemeral, which seem irrational (the success of bestsellers, popularity maintained by opinion polls, celebrity cults), the result of the mechanism of long-distance imitation, collective hypnosis, which stems from the very essence of the public itself. This is not simply a matter of discourse; emotions are also involved. The result is that publicity is a means for exercising collective criticism, an instrument for market capitalism, and the basis of mass culture. This plural conception, an alternative to Habermas's rationalist construct, enables us to avoid the narrative of degeneration, a facile resort of conventional criticism, and to insist instead on the essential ambivalence of publicity as a practice.

Considering celebrity from the point of view of publicity allows its most important characteristics to be recognized, which are often left unexplained or appear contradictory. Thus, attachment to famous people is experienced in a much more personal and subjective way when it is shared by many people. The more a star is famous, the more his or her fans are easily convinced that they have an intimate relationship with that star. Publicity both encourages and rejects individuation: the individual is most singularized at the very moment that he or she becomes part of a public. These are the paradoxical workings of mass culture. But there is also an inversion of private and public which is operational in the culture of celebrity. The most private aspects of the celebrity's life, the most intimate aspects, are subject to the curiosity of the public. The very dynamics of celebrity imply the exposure of private facts about the celebrity and reveal the star to be unique, but also weak and fragile. This dynamic is one of the most complex aspects of the curiosity aroused by stars, as well as the empathy that is awakened. A public figure is both great by way of his or her celebrity and also similar to common mortals in his or her weaknesses and imperfections.

This mixture of curiosity and empathy in the eighteenth century was found in a fast-growing literary genre, the novel, and in particular the love story, whose success accompanied the nascent culture of celebrity. Readers learned, in *Pamela* or in *La Nouvelle Héloïse*, to be excited by the life of characters who resembled them, who recounted in detail their daily life and their emotional ups and downs. At the same time, the most celebrated individuals of the period became true public persons whose lives were recounted like serialized novels. In both cases, admiration and pity, these traditional passions, were supplanted by curiosity and sympathy, two profound bases of identification when social conditions are such that each person, for better or worse, can identify with others. The modern *moi*, the self, was curious and sensitive. It recognized in others, in spite of social distance, a fellow creature. Thus the rise of celebrity in the eighteenth century was linked to these two phenomena: the development of publicity and a new concept of self. Far from being opposite, these two evolutions constituted the two sides of modernity.

But can one still seriously entertain the notion of modernity? After being a central idea in the social sciences in the twentieth century, the idea today is greatly suspect. It is accused, pell-mell, of implying a teleological concept of history, one entirely oriented toward the present, promoting an occidental perception of history, naïvely progressive or cynically polysemous, dealing only with blurred and normative content, in short being from another age when historians or sociologists felt they were authorized to contrast the moderns, that is, themselves, with everybody else: ancients, medievalists, primitives, all ensconced in their traditions and their beliefs. It is, however, difficult to ignore the notion, but it is helpful to be precise about its usage. By modernity, I mean two things. First, a group of profound transformations that affected European societies, varying in timing and method, whose epicenter, at least for occidental Europe, was between the middle of the eighteenth century and the start of the twentieth. The principal traits are known, prioritized according to personal interpretation: urbanization and industrialization; division of labour; the increased political role of the people and erasure of judicial inequalities – creating other forms of inequality, however; affirmation of instrumental rationality; and "disenchantment with the world." These developments have often been the subject of detailed discourse called democratization, the industrial revolution, the end of civilization, secularization. We could discuss and critique these forever. It is difficult to totally reject them. Given the framework of this book, two elements less often mentioned will be focused on: the development of long-distance communication techniques, from the printing press to radio and television; and the ideal of the authentic individual, the apogee of which was Romanticism. The development of "media communication" had profound social and cultural consequences in the way it favored new forms of social interaction, very different from traditional face-to-face societies, and the spread of cultural property that became merchandise.[13] If telecommunications in the twentieth century accelerated this change, its origins go back to the invention of the printing press and the intensification of its use in the eighteenth century. News reports, exposés, and images circulated among a public that was more and more indeterminate, potentially unlimited; this phenomenon profoundly transformed the way an individual could be known by contemporaries. The ideal of an authentic self, in opposition to all these social representations which made up the public face of an individual, was in large part, as we will see in the case of Jean-Jacques Rousseau, a reaction to this new media environment.

11

But modernity is also a relationship to the times, a narrative that moderns invent about themselves, the confirmation of a specificity, the conviction of having broken with the past, an ever-growing worry about clichéd responses. Historiography as we have known it for the last two centuries is entirely dependent on this modern relationship to the contemporary moment, allowing the present to seize upon the past as an object of knowledge in order to either keep it at a distance or allow it to point out what we owe it and what about it concerns us. For my part, I do not conceive of the past as a different world, peopled with astonishing inhabitants, insisting on the differences which separate them from us moderns. I discover in the past familiar practices and beliefs, even though they are dealt with differently; I recognize the environment in which contradictions develop and which we continue to discuss. To the ethnographic principle which increases the distance between cultures, I prefer a genealogical principle, not in order to claim reassuring origins or to trace a linear continuity, but in order to grasp what is at stake for modernity at the precise moment the issues arise.

Thus, the thesis of this book is the following: celebrity is not something new that has arisen in the twentieth century, which proves the decline of culture and the public sphere, or even the forgotten promises of freedom that modernity sets forth; celebrity is a characteristic trait of modern societies, a form of greatness that corresponds to them, an almost impossible greatness, always threatened with illegitimacy. To show this, I will attempt to describe the first age of celebrity, whose initial signs appeared in Paris and London in the middle of the eighteenth century, took shape in the course of the century, and reached a zenith in Western Europe and the United States in the first half of the nineteenth century. This chronology, which unites the Enlightenment and Romanticism, is not familiar to historians because it casually crosses the sacrosanct line of the French Revolution. It does, however, correspond to a slow and cohesive transformation in Western European societies. Crisis in the social order, the first developments of a market and cultural economy, at least in theory, and the principle of popular sovereignty: these principal traits of modernity are put in place. Two important historical aspects of celebrity include the appearance of public opinion, as a principle and as a reality, and the new ideal of self, based on the demands of individual authenticity. Such a history as this obviously does not lend itself to strict dates. Nevertheless, the appearance of Jean-Jacques Rousseau on the public scene in 1751 and the spectacular concert tours of Franz Liszt around 1844, which created a veritable Lisztomania from Paris to Berlin, offer convenient points of reference. From the one to the other, the lines which cross are much more numerous than one would ordinarily imagine.[14]

Rousseau rightly occupies a place of importance in this book, since he was at the center of my desire to write it. In certain ways, *The Invention of Celebrity* was conceived in the beginning as a long detour in order to resolve certain contradictions in his work, contradictions which appeared insoluble given that celebrity has never been accepted as a veritable subject of historical study with all its concurrent weight and ambiguities. As the first real European celebrity, Rousseau is also and above all the first to describe the experience of celebrity as a burden and alienation. An entire chapter will be dedicated to him, but before that we will plunge into the heart of the celebrity mechanism. We will discover that many of the characteristics of our hypermedia societies began in the eighteenth century: big money focused on a few stars; advertising mechanisms; the business of celebrity images; scandal sheets; fan mail. We will begin the study with an event of great symbolic importance: the crowning of Voltaire at the Comédie-Française in 1778, which had a much more ambiguous meaning than historians normally give it. Far from being the apotheosis of a great man, the ceremony made clear to contemporaries the ambivalence of celebrity (chapter 1). Thus immune to unequivocal interpretations, we will begin a discovery of the world of spectacle that produced the first public figures, actresses, singers, and dancers (chapter 2), and we will see the main vectors of celebrity, the reproduction of images, the new uses of biography, and the role of scandal. It is the public sphere which will be the center of this analysis (chapter 3). It is important to understand how these new mechanisms were described and analyzed, creating a veritable interrogation of the new forms of publicity (chapter 4).

After the pages dedicated to Rousseau (chapter 5), we will return to the consequences of this new culture of celebrity in the political domain. We will look at Marie-Antoinette again, and also see how new figures of democratic power such as George Washington and Mirabeau had to contend with the imperatives of popularity and how Napoleon's prestige fused the traditional mechanisms of glory and of celebrity. And we will investigate the growing celebrity culture as it is introduced into political life, seeing that perhaps far from being a sign of contemporary depoliticization and pervasive vulgarity, it might be the concession of charisma to modernity (chapter 6). Finally, a last chapter will show the full development of the mechanisms of celebrity in the Romantic era, incarnated by the figure of Lord Byron, but also by others less well known today, like Jenny Lind, who crossed the whole of the United States during a triumphant tour (chapter 7). This will lead us to the beginning of a new phase in the history of celebrity, one marked by photography, the cinema, and the pulp press, for which the tools of mass reproduction of images play a more and more important role.[15]

— 1 —

VOLTAIRE IN PARIS

In February 1778 Voltaire, then eighty-five, returned to Paris after a thirty-year absence. This visit created enormous excitement. Any Parisian considered to be a writer made an effort to celebrate the Ferney patriarch, while the elite class outdid itself in finding clever ways to catch a glimpse of the man whose name was on people's lips all over Europe. Visitors in greater and greater numbers flocked to the home of the Marquis de Villette, where Voltaire was staying. The Académie Française received him with great pomp. Benjamin Franklin solemnly asked him to bless his grandson. These tributes culminated in an improvised ceremony at the Comédie-Française where Voltaire attended the production of his tragedy *Irène* and in front of a wildly excited audience his bust was crowned with laurels, while an actor recited poetry in his honor. This is generally cited as the symbolic sanctification of the writer, the moment when Enlightenment philosophers gained social and cultural prestige, liberating them from their traditional role and giving them instead secular and spiritual power that reached its zenith in the age of Romanticism.[1] The crowning of Voltaire's bust seems to prefigure the official ceremony in 1791 that accompanied the transfer of Voltaire's remains to the Panthéon, the first celebration of its kind, a public tribute to a great man. And this is the way that literary historians have interpreted the episode, as a "triumph" and an "apotheosis."[2]

But is this interpretation so absolutely obvious? The scene is almost too good to be true. And in fact, the canonical story repeated for the last two and a half centuries has inspired writings by Voltaire admirers who have given the episode a flattering appearance.[3] However, some witnesses to the event mocked it. Adversaries of the Enlightenment philosophers, annoyed by the success of their old enemy, were vocal in their anger.[4] Other members of French cultural life, although they did not have religious or political motives, were still skeptical and sarcastic, even openly hostile. Louis Sébastien Mercier, a distinguished connoisseur of theater life, wrote in his *Tableau de Paris*: "This famous coronation was simply a farce in the eyes of anyone with good sense."[5] Far from being impressed by the show, he saw only its clownish aspect, orchestrated by enthusiastic fans, which dimmed Voltaire's prestige by throwing him pell-mell into the limelight. "An epidemic curiosity made people rush to catch sight of Voltaire's face, as if the soul of a writer were no longer in his writings but in the way he looked." Instead of an apotheosis or triumph, Mercier only saw vaguely grotesque buffoonery during which the great writer was overwhelmed with frantic applause and signs of unseemly familiarity. What most displeased Mercier was not the tribute rendered Voltaire but the form it took, reducing the author of *Oedipe* to the level of a public curiosity, celebrated like an actor with much more excitement than true admiration.

Indeed, the theater might appear to be an ambivalent setting for an apotheosis. If it was the place par excellence where the glory of heroes was represented in tragedies, of which Voltaire was the uncontested master and had been for decades, the theater was also the place where reputations of actors and authors were made and unmade by public acceptance or rejection, depending on how good the intriguing partisan claques were or how loud the derisive catcalls. The theater was as much a social gathering place for the rich as it was a place of merrymaking for the common people, so much so that the police had to be on their toes to keep order. And above all, theaters were the principal arena for the new culture of celebrity, where actors were the main protagonists, despite their lack of social status. Far from being an official, solemn ceremony, the performance on March 30, 1778 was very much an exuberant party, almost a kind of costume ball, and it is not known if Voltaire particularly enjoyed himself. It appears that he was conscious of the potentially ridiculous nature of the situation; despite the applause, he immediately took off the crown of laurels that the Marquis de Villette had placed on his head,[6] questioning, perhaps, if it were really appropriate to be celebrated in this way while still alive?

The crown of laurels recalled another famous episode in literary history very much on the minds of Enlightenment philosophers: the coronation of Petrarch on the grounds of the Capitoline in Rome in 1341.[7] But Petrarch had been crowned by Robert of Naples, the king's representative, one of the most powerful patrons of his time. This alliance between the glory of a sovereign ruler and the renown of a poet, powerfully manifested throughout European courts up until the reign of Louis XIV, was now in crisis. And Voltaire knew this better than anyone. Could the excited public at the Comédie-Française really substitute for a prince? Didn't public homage risk discrediting the author? Wasn't this parody of a coronation more like the tributes paid to actresses and singers than the consecration of a great poet?

What happened on that particular day had to do with the difficult alignment of various aspects of Voltaire's personality: highly respected author of the *Henriade* and *Oedipe*; a celebrated writer exiled to Ferney whose comings and goings were known throughout Europe; and the great man he already was for his admirers and the classical author he would become. Because Voltaire embodies for us a great writer of the Enlightenment, the first author admitted into the Panthéon, we see in this episode simply the first step towards posthumous glory. But for his contemporaries and for Voltaire himself, the stakes were more ambiguous. Was it possible to transform the intense public scrutiny focused on his person into an anticipation of his glory? This process was more complicated than it might seem in hindsight because it supposed a solution to the thorny problem of how the fame an individual enjoys while alive relates to the image that posterity eventually receives, the one image that alone assures eternal glory.

"The Most Famous Man in Europe"

Voltaire's celebrity in 1778 was unchallenged. It had largely surpassed the narrow framework of the literary world, the recognition that came from peers and critics. Even those who had never read his books had heard his name. Newspapers detailed his activities. In the *Mémoires secrets de la République des lettres*, a popular chronicle of cultural life, his name appeared over and over again. Voltaire knew like nobody else how to keep his name in the news through literary polemics and political engagement, through his wit and his brilliance. He had for some time been not only an admired writer but also a public figure who excited curiosity. Beginning writers and those less well known looked for ways to profit from his fame, and as early as 1759 a young Irish writer, Oliver Goldsmith, published the fake *Mémoires de M. de Voltaire*, playing on the curiosity of the public in order to launch his own career with a stock of anecdotes that were more or less true and others that were totally invented.[8] The lawyer Jean-Henri Marchand amused himself for over thirty years parodying and publishing works such as the *Testament politique de M. de V**** (1770) and the *Confession publique de M. de Voltaire* (1771).[9]

Voltaire did not need anyone to orchestrate his celebrity. A trip to visit him, exiled now and living in Ferney, became obligatory for all travelers.

It was not enough to read his work; one had to see this great figure of contemporary Europe in person. Voltaire greatly enjoyed these visits and jubilantly welcomed visitors with a ceremony, a cross between theater and court ritual, encouraging visitors to spread picturesque anecdotes about the life of the great writer they had just seen.[10] Nonetheless, these visits were also a constant source of embarrassment, a waste of time and energy, and he never hesitated to dismiss importunate people who came to see him out of curiosity and from whom he had nothing to gain. Charles Burney reports on the bad treatment received by some English visitors who were asked by Voltaire: "Well, gentlemen, you now see me, and did you take me to be a wild beast or a Monster that was fit only to be stared at, as a show"[11] There was not a lot of difference between a celebrity and a circus animal. This was a comparison that would be encountered in the work of other writers as well, a common thread, but suffice it here to underscore the ambiguities of public curiosity. Curiosity for a celebrity was both a resource and a menace: at any moment it could transform the famous man into a simple object on display.

Curiosity did not concern only the elite, nor simply newspaper readers. Voltaire's name was a publicity strategy that fanned the greed of publishers and encouraged forgeries. The philosopher was well aware of this and played a complex and crafty game with the world of publishing, denouncing publishers who pirated his works while at the same time using their services. He openly invoked the consequences of his "unhappy fame," for example, in order to complain that someone had just published a phony collection of letters written in his name: "There will always be some copies that escape. What can you do? It's the sacrifice one has to make for this unhappy celebrity, which it would be so nice to exchange for peaceful obscurity."[12] There was no doubt a tongue-in-cheek element in this disdain he claimed to have for his celebrity, and that he actually kept alive through being the great publicity agent that he was. Nonetheless, the attitude became broadly shared and his correspondents fell in line. When François Marin suggested that Voltaire put together a volume of his private letters in order to get even with the "cursed booksellers" in Holland who published anything bearing his name, he immediately said as if it were a commonplace: "That is one of the misfortunes attached to being a celebrity."[13] This wasn't just a simple matter of one's reputation, but a social condition with all its servitude, which included the watchful eye of the curious, the nosiness of printers, and the maneuvers of unscrupulous publishers. Already in 1753, even though Voltaire was not yet the patriarch of literature crowned at the Comédie-Française, he was the most celebrated writer of his time, whose complex relationship with Frederick II helped pay for the writing he was publishing. His niece, Madame Denis, wrote to Georges Keith: "It is sad that my uncle's fame means he cannot lift a finger without having all of Europe watching. He definitely has decided to find a retirement area far away and so forgotten that perhaps they will let him die in peace."[14] Fame is both greatness and enslavement, given that it makes of the famous person a public figure, imposing obligations such as being exemplary and having to justify oneself publicly. According to Jean Robert Tronchin, Voltaire had to be ready to defend himself against accusations of impiety: "The more celebrated a person, the more he must show great delicacy when attacked in such a sensitive area."[15]

Clearly what distinguished Voltaire from other great writers was the fact he was not just a famous name; he was also a famous face. There were numerous portraits of him, as well as busts and engravings, and they had increased since 1760.[16] One artist in particular specialized in images of Voltaire: Jean Huber, a master of *découpure*, a technique consisting of representing the silhouette or the face of someone by cutting it out of fabric.[17] After having painted many portraits of Voltaire and having represented him in a number of *découpures*, in 1772 Huber created a series of small paintings showing him doing everyday things: drinking coffee, playing chess, taking walks around Ferney. The journal *La Correspondance littéraire* mentioned the success of these paintings "representing diverse scenes in the private life of the most famous man in Europe," and reported that Voltaire criticized Huber for coming too close to caricature.[18] When one painting showed him getting up in the morning and clumsily pulling on his pants, all the while dictating to his secretary (Fig. 1), and then the painting was copied and engraved and put up for sale by all the engraving merchants in Paris and London, Voltaire got angry. Huber cleverly retorted that the very essence of celebrity was an invitation to play with a subject's public image, introducing "a bit of ridicule" in order to excite public interest, without for all that tarnishing his prestige. "The fervor of your idolatrous Public for everything that represents you, well or badly, forces me to vex you constantly. I feed the public's idolatry through my images, and my Voltairianism is incurable."[19] This was a valuable insight because it came from an artist who was particularly sensitive to the changes in visual culture.

Images of a famous person geared to public curiosity about that person's private life, including its most commonplace aspects, distinguished celebrity images from representations of glorious sovereigns or even great writers. Voltaire was not represented as a writer in the midst of all the symbols of his intellectual activity, as in traditional images of writers who were surrounded by books and paper and pen and ink. He is shown in a very "domestic scene," whose interest lies in seeing what constitutes the life of a writer when he is not writing, when he is being an individual like other individuals. The appeal of this image is less in an admiring distance than a desire for intimacy at a distance, curiosity about the famous man as a special individual, both different from others because of his fame and at the same time familiar. A bit of the ridiculous is not bad, either; in fact, it humanizes the public man, making him more accessible.

Public clamor for images showing Voltaire in his private life at Ferney was all the more surprising because this series of paintings had initially been commissioned by Catherine II. But infatuation with Voltaire was such that art merchants, smelling success, had the images engraved. Other scenes painted by Huber were also reproduced in quantity, notably *Voltaire Playing Chess*, *Voltaire Receiving a Visitor*, or *Voltaire Whipping a Rearing Horse*, making the gaunt face of the patriarch of Ferney a familiar image, partly smiling, partly grimacing.[20] It was neither a classic look nor a true caricature. Huber's series of paintings fed the feeling of paradoxical intimacy which the public desired to have with Voltaire, keeping a distance because of his prestige, his age, and his exile, and at the same time intimate because the public could see him doing ordinary things like getting up, getting dressed, eating, and exercising. The success of the *Lever de Voltaire* was in large part due to the spontaneous nature of the sketches, which appeared to take him by surprise, as if the viewer had the power to surreptitiously step into the bedroom with the great writer.

Intimate images of a famous man, stolen and then reproduced by unscrupulous merchants for a curious and passionate public whose idolatry was confined to voyeurism: there is no need to push this description any further to see a familiar mechanism at work today. Add to this Voltaire's anger and Huber's reaction to his anger and one can see that the effects were intriguing. Did circulation of these kinds of images improve the standing of the Ferney philosopher or did it tarnish his reputation? Two well-known engravings from the *Lever de Voltaire*, one French, one English, include ironic verses, giving the impression that the images were interpreted as caricatures.[21] However, the same images were sought after by both the fans of Voltaire and those who wanted to make fun of him. Above all, people were interested in them mostly because of the illusion they gave that through these images the viewer could gain access to and observe the philosopher's most intimate moments. Huber wanted to make money from this market demand and encouraged his English correspondents to announce that the engravings were "the only way to see the real Voltaire in every possible aspect."[22] The public didn't want stereotyped images that could be interchanged with similar ones; they wanted images of Voltaire that allowed them to see a unique individual.

19

Voltaire and Janot

This two-sided aspect of celebrity, curiosity and admiration, was prevalent at the time of Voltaire's visit to Paris. He was recognized at the gates of Paris the minute he arrived: "My God! It's Monsieur de Voltaire," one guard apparently shouted.[23] Once it was known he was in Paris, his presence created a sensation. "The appearance of a prophet or an apostle could not have caused more surprise and admiration than the arrival of Monsieur de Voltaire. For a short while, nothing else was of interest except this new prodigy," wrote the *Correspondance littéraire*, entirely won over by him.[24] The *Journal de Paris*, the first French daily, created the year before, described the sensation caused by the presence of Voltaire in the capital: "In cafés, at plays, in society, he was the only one talked about. Have you seen him? Have you heard him?" Provincial newspapers avidly reported the tiniest details and witticisms of his Parisian visit.[25] Taking advantage of this general curiosity, François de Neufchâteau publicly boasted of having spent a wonderful hour with Voltaire, while, in the name of a discretion too often abused, refusing to divulge any secrets. "Celebrity has the disadvantage of creating around the famous person a kind of spying on his words, his thoughts,"[26] Neufchâteau wrote in a tone that seemed to chastise the publishers of the *Journal de Paris*, showing that celebrity had become a cause to be debated. Madame du Deffand noted with irony that "all of Parnassus, from the gutter to its exalted heights," was hurrying to see Voltaire.[27] She herself could not resist the desire to see him again.

Voltaire incited unanimous but also ambiguous curiosity. The coronation at the Comédie-Française had created a new model, the glorification of a great man. The ceremony sought to produce a consensual posthumous image among Voltaire's contemporaries, as if they could see posterity's view of him, as though he were already dead. "They want me to die,"[28] Voltaire allegedly said, focusing on all the excessive honors given the living while at the same time seeing a dangerous proximity of these same honors to posthumous glory. Jean-François Ducis said something similar but with more solemnity when he succeeded to Voltaire's chair at the Académie Française the following year: "Alive, he witnessed his own immortality. His century paid in advance the debt that centuries to come would owe him."[29] In a way this was also the meaning of the nude statue Pigalle sculpted of Voltaire a few years earlier. Public opinion was shocked, but this nudity clearly expressed a singular message: the emaciated body of the writer anticipated his death and authorized the portrayal of him as an ancient hero. Voltaire was already a great man, so he was permitted, a little in advance, the honors that posterity would render unto him in the future.

The coronation evening at the Comédie, on the other hand, was somewhat dubious, marked more by excitement than by solemnity. This was seen in even the most favorable reviews, like that in the *Correspondance littéraire*, which focused on the excitement, the disorder, the jostling. "The whole room was filled with dust caused by the rising excitement of the agitated crowd. This enthusiasm, this kind of universal delirium, lasted more than twenty minutes, and it was only with great difficulty that the actors were able to begin the play."[30] Consequently, the most severe critics wrote ironically about the theatrical, disorderly quality of this supposed apotheosis. That this coronation took place on stage in a theater, with the star role played by an actress disguised as a maid, only added to the almost parodic character of the evening. A few weeks later, the nearly clandestine burial of Voltaire showed that his moment of official recognition had not yet come and that celebrity did not lead directly to glory. "The vulgar homage he was accorded while alive deprived him of funeral honors," Mercier remarked ironically.

This iconoclastic interpretation deserves closer investigation. After targeting the coronation's disrespectful clowning, Mercier puts forward a less biased view by comparing Voltaire's success with an even greater one, that of the comic actor Volange at the Variétés-Amusantes, one of the new boulevard theaters. The clamor aroused by Voltaire's Parisian visit was, in fact, soon eclipsed by the prodigious success of Volange and the figure Janot that he played in a low-class farce. The play *Janot ou Les battus paient l'amende* was very far from the tragedies of Voltaire. In the most famous scene, the contents of a chamber pot were thrown over the head of Janot and he wondered what the liquid could be. "Is it? Isn't it?" This response made Paris laugh for months and was repeated in conversations everywhere. There were several hundred performances of the play and the leading actor became very fashionable. "He not only amuses the public on stage but also in society. He is invited to every party and creates much merriment. Recently, when he came down with a cold his house was inaccessible because of the carriages sent by high society women to find out how he was doing, and the most distinguished lords came themselves for news of his health. There is no telling how long this delirium will last,"[31] wrote the editor of *Les Mémoires secrets*, disconcerted by this collective infatuation. The *Correspondance littéraire* mentioned the prodigious success of the Janot character, now "a national icon," and contrasted the public enthusiasm for Volange with its loss of interest in Voltaire's tragedies only weeks after the coronation event. "While there have been enormous audiences for the hundred and twelve performances of *Battus paient l'amende*, not even two box seats

21

have been sold for the opening of *Rome sauvée* by M. de Voltaire, and a third of the theater is empty."[32] Public admiration is an invaluable resource, sought after constantly by celebrities. Mercier pushes the comparison even further, going to the very heart of celebrity culture: "In the end, Janot has been modeled in porcelain as much as Voltaire. Today, the vaudeville actor sits on every mantelpiece."[33]

This wry remark makes an essential point: celebrity puts a great writer and a popular actor on the same level; a tragedy equals a vaudeville farce. On the applause meter, how does one distinguish between a great man with indisputable talent and the ham actor whose slapstick quips are loved by the audience; an author whose works are admired by posterity and the man whose success is short-lived? Mercier's irony is bitter. While he rails against novelty shows that are put on the same level as works of greatness, he points to an astonishingly modern political reading: "There is no need to persecute a living celebrity. When someone like Voltaire comes to the fore, there will always be a Jeannot [*sic*] to set against him." What is at stake is the very capacity of a public figure to be heard. Voltaire's fame did not rest solely on his tragedies, but rather on the battles he fought for a quarter of a century through polemical pamphlets combating religious fanaticism and prejudice, incarnating in the eyes of all Europe the new militant and critical philosophy of the Enlightenment. To take to the public stage was a philosophical strategy, a way to fight for the truth, a way to change minds and manners.[34] But what happens if public speech is a cabaret show, if the philosopher is simply an entertainer who could just as well be replaced by a circus performer?

Seen in this way, the coronation of Voltaire has another meaning, much more complex than the one usually attributed to it. It is not merely a step on the ineluctable journey from Ferney to the Panthéon, but rather the spectacular and ambivalent manifestation of Voltaire's celebrity. A controversial celebrity, however: was the coronation necessarily a sign of his genius, as admirers and others who stood with him in his struggles wanted to see it? Or was it perhaps just a sign of what was fashionable, of moral decadence, as his adversaries believed? Or was it, as Mercier suggested, proof that the changing moods of the public held sway and the public's "epidemic curiosity" transformed the greatest writers into mere performing artists at the expense of their life's work and their commitments? Another observer, Simon Linguet, a former lawyer turned journalist and pamphleteer, addressed the same issue and reproached the public for transforming the writer into a "theatrical hero." For him, the coronation ceremony was simply a farce, "a childish pantomime the audience should have been ashamed of, a marionette show far beneath the quality of street theater for the rabble [*populace*]."[35] There is a

22

marked difference between the "public" and the "rabble." If manifestations of celebrity are so quick to be criticized, now as in the eighteenth century, it is because the audience itself is so controversial and its judgments can so easily be dismissed.

Historians have quite rightly pointed to the work of public validation and "public opinion" in the eighteenth century. It is certainly true that today public opinion is sought after, whether it is a matter of evaluating the merits of a theater piece or denouncing political injustice. However, this elevation of the public to a reasoning critic is unfinished. The public is easily suspected of being manipulated, of becoming unthinkingly enthusiastic about ephemeral issues, of judging by pleasure and not by reason, of yielding to curiosity and the line of least resistance. Newspapers that denounced the public excitement over Voltaire reminded readers of the calm judgment of posterity: "A powerful claque has risen up among us. What won't it do to seduce the vulgar, to impose its opinion on a multitude of idiots and to attain its ends? [...] Stripped of all ambition, passion, or bias, posterity alone can assign a writer his place in history."[36] Two very different attitudes are at work here. The contemporary world prefers fan clubs and the "multitude of idiots," while glory can only come from the serene judgment of posterity embodied by "cultural institutions and people of good taste."

It is not simply a single step from the reputation of a writer cherished by a nation's literary world and the posthumous glory of a great man. Celebrity opens a new area between practice and discourse, fed by the indiscretions of the media, by a widespread circulation of images, and by the curiosity of the public, which, intrigued, wants to know what the fuss is all about. The surprising comparison (to our mind) of Voltaire and Volange-Janot, of a great writer and an entertainer, shows that celebrity does not concern the literary or artistic world alone. The theater is a perfect milieu for it, constituting the privileged arena of this new culture of celebrity. It is here that the investigation must begin.

— 2 —

SOCIETY OF THE SPECTACLE

Urban societies of the Ancien Régime were governed by the requirement of ceremonials. The exercise of power necessitated performances, rituals, and complex staging, from royal entrances to court celebrations. Aristocratic culture, still hegemonic, implied that the value of an individual was indistinguishable from his or her public standing: both the courtier and the average law-abiding person were aware that they were playing roles, that they incarnated a certain status, and no one would think of comparing their public appearance with an interior reality, a truer, more authentic one. The idea of this social game was summed up in the metaphor of the *theatrum mundi*, the world stage: life is a performance, a permanent spectacle where each person plays the role that he or she has been given. Urban growth in the eighteenth century, the emergence of densely populated cities like Paris and London, as well as Naples and Vienna, where inhabitants had to continually interact with unknown people, served in the beginning to reinforce this development: the theory that a social being was an actor, preoccupied above all by the effect produced on an audience, and the repetition of this effect. The *theatrum mundi* was no longer a play performed for a God watching from afar, but a spectacle that men and women performed for each other.[1]

If everyone was acting, however, some were acting more than others: they made it their career. Theatrical productions were no longer passion plays performed by devout Christians on the steps of churches at the time of religious celebrations, or plays reserved for elite courtesans who circled around the prince; they had become urban entertainment par excellence. Starting in the middle of the seventeenth century, in all the large European capitals and more and more in big provincial cities, permanent theaters multiplied. Operas, comedies, comic operas, and also carnival shows attracted enormous audiences in Paris that were sometimes a mix of nobles, bourgeoisie, and even common people, all

24

together in the stalls at the Comédie-Française. In eighteenth-century Europe, spectacles had become an essential mark of urban culture.

Two criticisms were heard in reaction to this generalized spread of theater: the first questioned the artificial and inauthentic nature of a social life in which everyone was role playing; the second denounced the corruption provoked by the success of the theaters. Although the criticisms dealt with specific issues, they converged around the idea of the deleterious effect of big cities. The new ideal of personal authenticity, based on feelings and sincerity, permitted an attack on the emotional separation caused by professional actors in urban settings, paid to act feelings they weren't experiencing, and passive spectators who were fascinated by these imitations. The most eloquent critic of these spectacles was Jean-Jacques Rousseau, who contrasted urban theater with that of village celebrations, where everyone participated in a collective outpouring of feeling.[2]

As it turns out, this criticism of theatricality and spectacle in the name of an ideal of authenticity has lasted a long time. It was seen in the Romantic period. Then the development of audiovisual media in the twentieth century lent renewed vigor to the criticism of theatricality because of the separation created between the spectator and the images that were shown to him or her. The most radical formulation of this criticism was provided by the work of Guy Debord, a striking mix of neo-Marxism and dark romanticism. In classical prose, which often seems a parody of the seventeenth-century moralists, at times taking on Rousseau-like accents, his critique of the "society of the spectacle" recycles Marxist denunciations of fetishistic merchandising which uses media images. Celebrity, the heart of the modern system of spectacle, is a characteristic trait. Stars are the "spectacular representation of a living human being," even a negation of the individual; stars embody lifestyles, personality types, forms of human fulfillment, that have become inaccessible to the alienated spectator reduced to a poor and fragmented life.[3]

Today, given the magnitude of celebrity culture, criticism of the society of the spectacle, often separated from its anti-capitalist substratum and reduced to a slogan, has become pretty much a cliché. However, the formula works as far as it is a reminder that media economy, which invests the public sphere with celebrity figures, had its origins in the eighteenth-century world of urban spectacle which produced the first stars. Actors, singers, dancers, were created by performing in public and owed their social existence to these performances. Those with the highest exposure became veritable public figures, even outside the theater hall: their names became known, their faces reproduced, their private lives the object of curiosity. To understand the social and cultural transformations which allowed stars to emerge is the aim of this chapter.

The Birth of Stars: The Economics of Celebrity

The term "star," though slightly later in theatrical usage, indicates the development of an economics of spectacle. The French word *vedette* designates, in military language, a sentinel in an elevated position, as well as, in the eighteenth century, the words written in large fonts on a poster. Then, at the beginning of the nineteenth century, the word "star" was used metonymically to mean the most important artist in a spectacle, and thus the phrase "star billing." This development happened gradually, and contrasted with the traditional habit of referring to the entire troupe as a collective entity. This apparent minor modification in fact revealed a major transformation: starting in eighteenth-century London, and then in Paris, Naples, Vienna, and Berlin, and in other large European cities, the economics of the theater were profoundly changed because of the urban public that emerged along with new commercial practices. Theater, but also music and dance, freed itself from the model of court audiences and privileged theater performances entirely controlled by the governing powers. Spectacles, frequented by a more diversified public, from worldly elites to the new middle class, became associated with the city. Culture was no longer solely shared by courtly elites grouped around the prince or the king, but became an object of consumption. London's Drury Lane theater could seat 2,360 spectators and more than 3,000 after it was enlarged in 1792. That was almost the same as its rival, Covent Garden. New urban spectacles mobilized the energy and the capital of private investors, who did not hesitate to use varying publicity techniques in order to recoup their investments.[4]

Theater directors had every reason to headline actors who were successful. Besides financial strategies, the entirely new system associated with the commercialization of leisure encouraged the culture of celebrity, and in particular the rapid growth of a specialized press for theater productions and cultural advertisements, the sale of celebrity portraits, the existence of mixed space used for theater, entertainment, and business, on the model of Vauxhall Gardens in London, created in the 1730s, where visitors could dance, eat, go to concerts and plays, and stroll about. A few years later, the Ranelagh Gardens in the Chelsea quarter of the same city, inaugurated in 1742, immediately became a very "in" place.[5] In Paris, the role of privileged theaters, institutionally tied to the court (the Comédie-Française, the Opera), was still important, but private theaters, notably along the boulevards, new areas for strolling and entertainment, developed in the 1750s. Marionette shows and animal trainers were seen there, as well as the theater of Jean-Baptiste Nicolet, a gymnastics group which came from the Saint Laurent Fair and whose success did not diminish until the Revolution. It was along the boulevard that Nicolas Audinot set up his Ambigu-Comique (Theater of Comic-Ambiguity) in 1769, Louis Lécluse founded the Variétés-Amusantes (vaudeville shows), and Volange triumphed with his Janot series.[6]

The economic transformation of spectacles accentuated the hierarchy that existed within the acting troupes themselves. An enormous gap grew between the money earned by ordinary actors and those the public and the theater directors considered irreplaceable. Not only did the latter receive higher salaries, but they were also given advantageous benefits. At the beginning of the eighteenth century, the practice of "benefit nights" was inaugurated, and the gross ticket sales were given to an actor or actress whose name was well known enough to attract the public. The first actress to benefit was Elizabeth Barry in 1708. At the end of the century, Sarah Siddons' contract guaranteed two benefit nights per season, which meant a considerable income. David Garrick, certainly the biggest star on the English stage in the middle of the century, managed to amass a fortune estimated at his death to be £100,000.[7] In France, the commercial success of boulevard theater rested on the talent of name actors who attracted audiences thanks to some recurrent character they played. This was the case with Toussaint Gaspard Taconet, in the middle of the century, at the Nicolet Theater, and also Volange. After his success in the role of Janot, well-known writers (Dorvigny, Beaunoir) wrote plays specifically for him, not simply a series of Janot pieces (*Janot chez le dégraisseur, Ça n'en est pas, Le Mariage de Janot*), but also as the Pointu series (*Jérôme Pointu, Boniface Pointu, Les Bonnes Gens*), shows about a middle-class family that allowed Volange to give free rein to his talent for cross-dressing. He often played different characters, much to the delight of audiences, enraptured by the performance of this star actor.[8]

At the Comédie-Française, the acting company was organized in a more collective way and theoretically more egalitarian. Nonetheless, the new star-system emphasized the differences. Lekain, one of the biggest male actors, maintained his celebrity by touring in the provinces and gaining a financial advantage.[9] As for tragic actors, Hippolyte Clairon was so popular that her mere presence could fill a theater. "Mlle Clairon is always the heroine. She just has to be announced and the house is full. As soon as she comes on stage, applause interrupts everything. Her admirers have never seen her like before and they will never see it again."[10] Throughout the eighteenth century, a veritable European actors' market was put in place, as well as a market for singers and dancers. Circulation of the most famous actors resulted from stringent competition in the courts and European aristocracies, where the best actors were sought. Italian musicians were wanted all over Europe, while the finest French actors, to the dismay of the monarchy, were greatly solicited by

27

foreign countries.[11] Then, more and more, London theaters, no longer under the patronage of the crown but always trying to draw bigger and bigger audiences, sent agents around Europe and offered advantageous contracts to those actors they wanted to attract.

Augustin Vestris was among those actors widely sought out. His father, Gaétan, one of the most famous dancers of his time, the self-proclaimed "god of dance," exercised his talent in the different European courts. With his son's generation, the performance conditions for professional dancers began to change and London theaters offered an alternative to court spectacles, and even alternatives to the Parisian stage. After being recruited by the Paris Opera when he was only twenty, in 1779, Vestris immediately signed for a six-month engagement at the King's Theatre in London, where he was an enormous success. London was submerged in a wave of "Vestris-mania," in the words of historian Judith Milhous, who saw in this the beginning of Britain's enthusiasm for dance, which up until then had been overshadowed by theater and opera.[12] This enthusiasm owed less to new ballet techniques, of which Vestris and his father were ambassadors, than to the person of the dancer himself, who was young, talented, and handsome, and thus enthusiastically received by London audiences.[13] The newspapers, usually laconic when writing about the ballet, were tireless in recounting anecdotes about Vestris' visit and didn't hesitate to spread rumors about his feminine conquests. As soon as he arrived, his salary was revealed in the press and a controversy arose: Was it fair that an actor should be paid such a sum? How could a circus performer earn more in one night than an honest laborer his whole life?[14] This did not, however, stop the public from rushing to his benefit night, which, according to Horace Walpole, brought in £1,600, but which also ended in a riot, the theater taken by storm because the crowd was too numerous, forcing authorities to close its Haymarket entrance.

The controversy surrounding the income of Vestris was obviously only the beginning of a long series of debates about the economics of celebrity, about the enormous salaries that were authorized, about the sometimes impressive income gap between those the star-system favored and those it did not. In our day, the trading of soccer players and the income of film actors regularly feed the polemic about "star salaries." Economists and sociologists search for reasons to explain why varying talent, sometimes uncertain and often difficult to measure objectively, can produce such income gaps, a result of the cumulative effects of fame and recognition, but also due to the logic attached to the commercialization of show business.[15] These debates originated in the eighteenth century when start-up newspapers specialized in news about spectacles and began to compare box office receipts among different performances, weighing the prestige

28

of actors and their capacity to make money for the theater, at the same time criticizing earnings that appeared to them excessive.

The response to this was the development of charity nights, when the most famous actors performed not for personal profit but for the Theatrical Fund, charged with aiding actors in need, the poor, and the elderly. In this way, a star as well known as Garrick could polish his popularity with the public, appear as a protector of the English stage, and show how selfless he was. Thanks to this philanthropic posture, he made up for the growing inequalities at the heart of the spectacle world and at the same time reaffirmed his superiority, because it was his celebrity, in fact, which guaranteed the success of these performances. Rather ironically, in a few years this philanthropy became a sort of moral obligation which stars could not avoid without consequences. Sarah Siddons gained a reputation for avarice after her early success because she missed a few of these benefit performances, and the notoriety followed her tenaciously, almost bringing down her career.[16]

The new celebrity of actors, singers, and dancers also included a discrepancy. Although they were offered advantages, notably financial, this in no way guaranteed them an honorable social position in the Ancien Régime. Even more so than with writers, one saw to what extent celebrity could be at odds with the social order. The tension was particularly strong in France, where actors were theoretically relegated to a dishonorable social status, even though some among them were extremely popular. Even in England, where actors did not suffer the same indignities, the celebrity of female actors remained ambivalent. If celebrity was a tribute to their talent, it also transformed them into an object of desire for the public. Comparison with courtesans was inevitable, and the fame of certain actresses as early as the seventeenth century rested on the troublesome curiosity of the public for their supposed escapades. Celebrity, very far from the admiration that underscores glory, came in part from the erotic fascination for libertine actresses whose private lives aroused rumors and gossip. The actress, as a public woman, seemed mixed up in the mind of the male public with the courtesan or prostitute. It was the same in France, with dancers from the Opera who had the reputation of being kept by rich lovers and leading a dissolute life. Marie-Madeleine Guimard, inevitably referred to in the press as the "celebrated Guimard," is the perfect incarnation: the litany of her lovers and protectors was commented on much more than her exploits on stage. If her initial success was due to her qualities as a dancer, her striking rise in society was due above all to her talents as a courtesan, to the generosity of the tax collector Laborde and the Prince of Soubise, as well as to the libertine parties she organized, which fed the gossip columns with hearsay, probably exaggerated and perhaps invented.[17]

Recent historiography has insisted on this point, sometimes to an excessive degree.[18] In reality, a celebrated actress was not merely the projection of desire on the part of the spectator. The new culture of celebrity also offered actors and actresses enormous leeway to manage their careers, excite the curiosity of the public, and make the most of their notoriety. This was particularly the case with actresses who practiced "puffing" or "puff pieces," which consisted of asking newspapers to insert laudatory articles about them. This equivocal situation permitted spectacular social climbing. In England, the model of the actress turned courtesan was incarnated in exemplary fashion at the beginning of the Restoration by Nell Gwyn, mistress of King Charles II, to whom she gave two children.[19] Less spectacularly, the role was played by several different actresses in the following century. Frances Abington, having started as a flower seller and street singer, became a great success on the stage, notably after her visit to Dublin between 1759 and 1765, where she was a star in the local community. On her return to London, she acted in a series of successful roles at Drury Lane. Joshua Reynolds painted her portrait numerous times, the most famous representing her in the role of Miss Prue, in which she scandalized the public with her latent eroticism. Famous for perfectly pulling all the strings of "puffing," she was also known for her many affairs, in particular the one she had with Lord Shelburne, the future prime minister.

A successful career in the theater did not only lead to the bedroom of aristocratic elites. Other trajectories were possible, such as that of Kitty Clive, considered among the best comic actresses of her time, who triumphed as a singer in the role of Polly in John Gay's *Beggar's Opera*, one of the great successes of the English stage throughout the eighteenth century. She progressively diversified her repertoire (she sang popular ballads as well as arias by Handel), but also her activities: she partnered with Garrick to create the Drury Lane theater, wrote comedies, joined with Samuel Johnson and Walpole, and, at the end of her life, seemed very well integrated into polite London society. Other paths were even more complex, such as that of Mary Robinson. Following her great success at the end of the 1770s in the role of Perdita, which stuck to her like glue, she became the mistress of the Prince of Wales, the future George IV, who lived the high life and whose dissolution fed the newspapers.[20] After paying off the show chroniclers and the gossip columnists with her success on stage and her numerous lovers, and having gained a pension by agreeing never to publish the letters she received from the heir to the throne, Robinson retired and started a second career dedicated to literature, publishing novels and poetry. Several of her biographers wanted to see in her an ambitious woman starved for fame, seeking out notoriety in every possible way.[21] In fact, having been plunged very early into the heart of the success system and public recognition, Robinson had a very ambivalent attitude toward it, conscious of the desirable effects and the risks.[22] In her *Memoirs* she acknowledged that the success of her first novel, *Vancenza* "owed its popularity to the celebrity of the author's name."[23] But in other texts she assumed a more complex position, criticizing the uncivilized pursuit of celebrities. She was one of the first to complain explicitly about being recognized in the street and the embarrassment she felt being gawked at by the curious. When she went out shopping, she could not enter a shop without being surrounded by a crowd trying to get a look at her and block access to her coach.[24] Her *Memoirs* nevertheless testify to the excessive attention she never ceased to give to her public appearances: dozens of years later, she could still remember the outfits she wore on each occasion.

The celebrity of actors and actresses rests on the interweaving of their person and the characters they play on stage. They are often represented by their iconic roles, and indeed Mary Robinson kept the nickname "Perdita" all her life.[25] In polite society, the fame of certain actors, which makes them sought after, does not necessarily mean personal recognition. This has to do with a phenomenon often experienced by film actors today, who note with a mixture of satisfaction and resentment that spectators confuse them with the characters they incarnate. It was a situation not unknown in the eighteenth century, and Volange had a bitter experience with it. While the success of his character Janot had opened many doors of polite society to him, and he had regaled those in attendance at social evenings with his famous burlesque retorts, he had the idea that he would like to diversify his repertoire and liberate himself from the role to which he owed his celebrity. When he was invited to the home of the Marquis de Brancas, he was announced as "Janot" and felt he had the right to correct the introduction: "I am now M. Volange," which drew a scathing reply: "All right, but since we are only interested in Jeannot [*sic*], M. Volange will be seen to the door." The *Mémoires secrets pour servir à l'histoire de la République des lettres*, which reported this anecdote, did not refer to the insolence of Brancas' rude remark, but to the arrogance of Volange, this presumptuous actor who thought he could be received into polite society like a gentleman.[26]

That was an extreme case, one in which the fame of the actor was completely engulfed by the character he played, at least in the eyes of polite society, which delighted in slumming at the circus but was not willing to embrace a circus actor as one of its own. Generally, the relation between an actor and the character he or she plays is more complex. When the public image of actors is confused with the characters they play, the curiosity of the public for the actors' private life grows. The split between a public character who stands apart from the real person and the private person whose personal life is difficult to hide is at the heart of the celebrity system. This is exacerbated with actors, because theater audiences delight in the possible differences between a character and the person who is playing that character. Thus, at the beginning of Mlle Raucourt's career, she aroused public curiosity even more because she rejected all love affairs in her personal life while playing a character who was carried away by her passion. This excited the fascinated admiration of the audience. Later, after becoming famous for her role playing great tragic characters, she kept the gossip columns busy in the capital recounting her debts, her high life, and her sexual preferences. Her taste for women, called at the time *tribadisme*, referring to the excitement aroused by lesbian sex, created so much satire that Marie-Antoinette, who held her in great esteem, had to publicly stand up for her. This mediation was not, however, anodyne for an actress, since their social distance from the queens they played on stage was an important and ambiguous element surrounding their public image. What was the nature exactly of an actress's prestige whose talent drew audiences to the theater to watch her publicly play the greatest characters and yet who herself only came from a lowly social status?

Three examples will make it easier to understand the system of celebrity which transformed the world of spectacle throughout eighteenth-century Europe. These concern three different trajectories: an Italian castrato making his career and causing scandal in London; an English tragedian who gained a veritable cult following; and a French actor whose celebrity took on a highly political tone, in a revolutionary context.

Scandal at the Opera

The international success of castrati in the eighteenth century rested on their exceptional vocal performances as well as their fascinating physical appearance, especially since castration was practiced clandestinely in Italy and was officially condemned throughout Europe.[27] The best Italian castrati were sought out by the European courts and by London producers, who did not hesitate to send agents to Italy to recruit promising talent. The spectacular rise of Farinelli is well known: how he immediately became the talk of the town from his first concerts in Naples at the beginning of the 1720s and afterwards in Bologna, Milan, and Venice, where he was enthusiastically applauded by English tourists.[28] When they returned to England, they clamored to have the prodigy brought to London, where he had a huge success in 1734 and over the next three seasons. His "benefit nights," which were advertised in the press (in the

Daily Advertiser, the *London Daily Post,* and the *General Advertiser),* attracted polite London society and earned him thousands of pounds.

Nevertheless, Farinelli's London success was accompanied by a whiff of scandal that fanned the curiosity of the public, producing outrage along with high praise. Public infatuation with his unusual voice, the result of a practice often deemed "barbaric," seemed to a number of critics excessive and dangerous, threatening the social, moral, and sexual order. The contestation began initially at the opera and then with Italian singers performing in England, a country where the break with the papacy was an important point of cultural identity. But the scandal was above all fueled by sexual ambiguity. In the eyes of moralists and satirists, the castrati were corrupting English taste, confusing sexual identities, and causing bizarre audience reactions with strong erotic overtones in both women and men. Hostage as Farinelli was to the public, pamphlets multiplied railing against him, charging him with affairs with some of the most famous London courtesans, insisting on the unnatural seduction he exercised, and accusing him of corrupting the young. A satirical poem castigated him for "ruining whole families" and "cuckolding half the Nation."[29]

At this price, the sweet charm of celebrity seemed less appealing. No doubt tired of the incessant criticism which rained down on him, and perhaps conscious that the public infatuation wouldn't last forever, Farinelli quit London at the end of three years, and after a summer in Paris he left to pursue his career with the court in Madrid. There he became a court performer, the favorite of Philip V, who monopolized his talents and bestowed on him the privilege of direct access to his private rooms.[30] In this way, Farinelli knew how to use his fame to assure himself a position at court, both more stable and more peaceful, far from attacks by the London public and from the demands of public life.[31] He had opted for a classic form of honor in the personal service of the king, preferring this to the more ambivalent prestige of a public figure. After the death of the king in 1759, he returned to Italy and settled down in Bologna. His reputation among lovers of music remained considerable – Charles Burney was witness to this when he made an emotional visit to see the singer in 1770 – but Farinelli had stayed away from the public scene for too long.[32] His celebrity would only have lasted a few years.

The following generation was won over by the seductions of the marketplace rather than the comforts at court. A number of castrati began to build their careers around the flexibility and the dangers of celebrity. One of the most famous, Giusto Fernandino Tenducci, arrived in London in 1758 and rapidly knew resounding success. In just a few years he became one of the most popular singers on the London concert scene and one of the best paid. He sang regularly in the principal theaters

(Haymarket, Covent Garden, Drury Lane, King's Theatre), but also in Ranelagh Gardens, where he had immense success giving recitals of popular English songs. The songs were then sold as little books and reproduced in the *London Magazine*. Tenducci played different roles: he was a great Italian opera singer, beloved by the sophisticated upper classes, but thanks to the English folksongs he became very popular with a new and emerging public, more socially mixed, who often came to the Ranelagh Gardens. The cosmopolitan musician doubled as someone who was also associated with English national culture, which had sprung up everywhere. And at the height of his celebrity, he made an appearance in contemporary novels, for instance in *The Expedition of Humphry Clinker* by Tobias Smollett, whose heroine supposedly falls in love with Tenducci after hearing him sing in Ranelagh Gardens.[33]

Like Farinelli before him, Tenducci aroused both fiery praise and biting satire. Success as a celebrity did not result in a unanimous judgment but rather in a simultaneous expression of both enthusiasm and reprobation. The singer excited passionate responses from his public, which were in no way limited to the admiration that enthusiasts felt for him. The seduction, both musical and erotic, raised intriguing questions and worries. Tenducci's career was dotted with polemic, which reinforced his public personality. From the beginning he was accused of corrupting morals and English taste when it was learned that a woman from the upper classes had sent him a series of love letters. A few years later he fled with a young Irish woman and married her, to the great dismay of her family. It was a complete scandal. On the one hand, it was an unauthorized marriage, which damaged the family, and, on the other, it was unnatural, raising questions about the kind of relationship a castrato could have with his wife. It also focused attention on the ambiguous fascination the singer exercised over his public, causing social and moral disorder. Tenducci was arrested, judged, and freed. He and his wife finally returned to London, where they lived openly as a married couple, causing snide commentaries in all the European newspapers.[34] The birth of a child excited curiosity and caused a wave of jokes and parodies, in polite society as well as in the lower classes in London, and even among seasoned travelers.[35] When Casanova, who himself was no stranger to hocus-pocus, met Tenducci, the singer told him a bizarre story about a third testicle that had been spared castration. The spellbound Venetian hastened to add this story to his memoirs.[36] The mysteries and questions about Tenducci's virility became a public matter, openly debated during the annulment of his marriage, which was finally asked for by his wife.

There could be no more fitting image to show the workings of celebrity and how it ends by making the private life of famous people, including the most intimate details, the object of public curiosity. In this case the judicial proceedings were only an additional detail. They accelerated the publicizing of the controversy surrounding Tenducci's sexual nature by giving it the characteristic form of a court case.[37] There certainly have been famous cases in which the married life of a couple, up until then unknown, is debated in public because of a lawsuit that excites public opinion. But the difference here is that Tenducci's intimate life had already for some years been the object of public discussion and debate, an essential aspect of any public figure. Such fascination for the sexuality of celebrities in show business was not reserved only for castrati, as has been shown, but it was more intense in their case since their sexuality seemed so mysterious and thus troubling. Was their singularity a weakness or an advantage, an infirmity or a blessing, a handicap or a strength? This ambivalence, which makes a strength out of weakness, is a characteristic trait of the curiosity aroused by celebrities, where admiration is never pure and unequivocal, as it is for heroes and great men; it is often mixed with compassion or, to the contrary, with disdain or repulsion. It is why celebrity is often linked to scandal, an extremely efficient tool for becoming famous or staying famous, but an almost inherent consequence of such a status. In the eighteenth century, as in our day, certain artists made use of provocation and scandal to promote themselves publicly, but the link between fame and scandal is not simply a strategy, it is something more substantial.

For some time, anthropologists have shown that scandal has an important function in more or less homogeneous societies in the sense that it reaffirms the status quo and shared values of the group, drawing the community together by often excluding the troublemaker.[38] In the case of scandals concerning public figures in modern society, the effects are more complex. There is little doubt that the increase in debates about Tenducci's sexuality was a sign of conservative tension at a time when mores were changing in London society, in the second half of the eighteenth century, concerning a redefinition of masculinity. But essentially what concerns us here is something else. Scandal is by nature a public event, its dynamic is linked to the configuration of the public. One of the first researchers to be interested in the sociology of scandal put it this way: "There is no scandal without an audience, without public diffusion of the scandalous event which contributes to its nature, without *mass communication.*"[39] This means that scandal does not simply depend on the public dimension; the public participates in its formation. It is through debates around fascinating and scandalous people that the public becomes aware of itself, not as a tribe, according to the old metaphor, but as a group of curious spectators, excited or shocked, enthusiastic or reproving, adherents or skeptics, yet all interested in learning more about their contemporaries. But although local scandals generally end with the guilty party being punished, sometimes even excluded, media scandals amplify the subject's celebrity to such an extent that the person can come out of them both dishonored and greater than ever.[40] As with the case of Tenducci, this type of scandal tends to be focused on the link that the public has with the star. This therefore explains the paradoxical nature of media storms, which stir up and maintain unhealthy curiosity and then denounce the effects which are produced. In reality, what is scandalous in the castrato is less his sexual life than his celebrity.

It is hard to know to what extent Tenducci voluntarily encouraged the scandalous dimension of his sexual and family life, or if he simply accepted the publicity as an inevitable price to be paid for celebrity. It is certain, in any case, that his career hardly suffered. It is even possible that the public exposure was actually beneficial, stirring up curiosity and mass interest. After the court case and annulment of his marriage, the end of his career was extremely brilliant. Considered one of the greatest living singers, he continued to give concerts in London but traveled more and more, spending time in Paris, for example, where Mozart composed music for him. His celebrity was such that he did not hesitate to publish corrections in newspapers when he was displeased by an article about himself. In the 1780s, when his voice started to weaken and he did not have the same prowess, he cleverly used his celebrity to give music lessons to members of polite society in London. He thus used his name and the publicity as tools to maintain his career, notably by publishing announcements in the *Public Advertiser*.[41]

During these same years, in the 1780s, when Tenducci's star was beginning to fade, a young actress was just having her first stage success in London. Sarah Siddons, after a number of years spent playing secondary roles with acting troupes in the provinces, won immense fame for her role as Isabella in *The Fatal Marriage*, by Garrick, which played at Drury Lane. Three years later she won great acclaim as Lady Macbeth, a role that she would play over and over again throughout her career and one which seemed to fascinate the public, in particular the famous sleepwalking scene where Lady Macbeth desperately tries to wash the blood off her hands.[42] Siddons was then thirty and would reign on the English stage for another three decades.

"Something Idolatrous"

Whereas Tenducci, in spite of his talent, appeared to be a strange and foreign star, wicked and scandalous, Sarah Siddons incarnated a highly legitimate figure in British culture. She soon specialized in tragic roles, notably the great Shakespearean ones, and often played queens – in

36

particular Queen Katherine in *Henry VIII*. She led a peaceful family life, marked by a number of pregnancies, and acceded rapidly to the status of a cultural icon, not only because of her success but also because of the multitude of portraits of her that the English could admire. With her first great role, when she played Isabella, she posed for William Hamilton and carriages formed a line in front of the artist's studio to see the painting.[43] Between 1780 and 1797, eighteen portraits of her were shown at the Royal Academy, the most famous of which was painted by Reynolds in 1783 and represents her as the muse of tragedy. Reynolds' painting was enormously successful and he decided to keep it and make copies instead of selling the original. When Siddons gave lectures, she often struck the melancholy pose of the painting, as though Reynolds had painted a real image and she was just imitating it. These multiple portrait sessions led to a frequent, although implicit, association between Sarah Siddons and the wife of George III. At the beginning of 1789, Thomas Lawrence was inspired by Reynolds' portrait of Siddons to paint a portrait of Queen Charlotte. With age, the parallel between the two women would nurture Siddons' celebrity, making her a sort of substitute queen at the moment the English royal family was choosing to withdraw into domestic life, making few public appearances. Like a queen, Siddons' celebrity cut through the various social categories: she was immensely popular with London commoners, who mobbed her after each performance, but she was also beloved by social elites. Siddons was a friend of Garrick, of Burke, of Johnson and Reynolds, and thus perfectly integrated into the little world that controlled cultural life in the capital.

Thoughtful reflection about the passion she aroused appeared in newspapers. One of her most fervent admirers, the renowned literary critic William Hazlitt, dedicated a long article to her in 1816 in which he compared the Siddons cult to a form of idolatry. This passage which is often cited merits further investigation.

> The homage she has received is greater than that which is paid to Queens. The enthusiasm she excited had something idolatrous about it; she was regarded less with admiration than with wonder, as if a being of a superior order had dropped from another sphere to awe the world with the majesty of her appearance. She raised tragedy to the skies, or brought it down from thence. It was something above nature. We can conceive of nothing grander. She embodied to our imagination the fables of mythologies; of the heroic and deified mortals of elder time. She was not less than a goddess, or than a prophetess inspired by the gods.[44]

This grandiose text, often misunderstood, should be read in light of its publication date. At the time Hazlitt wrote it, Sarah Siddons, who bid farewell to the theater four years earlier, had just decided to return to the stage at the official request of the royal princess. Hazlitt challenged her decision, which seemed unreasonable to him, and he criticized it again a few months later in a criticism he wrote of her performance when she once again played Lady Macbeth, her iconic role.[45] He reproached Siddons for not holding to her original decision, since she was no longer capable of the full plenitude of her talent. He preferred that the mind's eye of her public be fixed forever on her great performances. He remembered seeing her play Lady Macbeth twenty years earlier; not only did the new performance seem less impressive, it weakened his memory of the first one, threatening to destroy the ideal image he had of it. It should be noted that Hazlitt in these two articles invoked the "reputation" of Siddons and her "glory," but never used the words "fame" or "celebrity." He hardly valued the system of celebrity, too much tied as it was to the public mood, preferring instead the classical conventions of glory. He reproached Siddons for not being content with her past glory, by virtue of which she now belonged to her public. Not her contemporary public, the "enormous crowds" who came to cheer her at Covent Garden when she returned to the stage and only half the crowd could get into the theater; rather, she belonged to the public of the years of her perfection, when she was "tragedy personified." This then explains the use of the past tense in his text when Hazlitt invokes the idolatry which accompanied her triumphs. It was a way to better explain that the Siddons cult wasn't a personality cult built around the private person of Siddons, now only a great actress in retirement, but rather the way her appearances in the past indelibly marked the spirit of the spectators. "To have seen Mrs Siddons was an event in every one's life; and does she think we have forgot her?"[46] Even more specifically, Hazlitt writes that Siddons was not only the idol of spectator crowds but also the "solitary worker" whose interior life was nourished by the memory of this exquisite emotion.

In the end, Hazlitt saw very clearly the nature of the star's celebrity, and in particular the prodigious attachment of the English public to Siddons: an emotion both collective and individual that was felt by all those who were lucky enough to be present in person at one of her performances. Siddons was not a mythic hero whose legendary exploits were recounted, nor even an illustrious woman from the past whose exemplary life could inspire virtue: she was a contemporary presence who changed the life of all those who saw her on the stage. But Hazlitt wanted this relationship to remain pure, almost abstract, wrapped in the memory of the original feeling directed not at Siddons as an individual but Siddons as the incarnation of the actor's art. For this he would have preferred that she be immortal, not subject to the passage of time, always capable of repeating the same performances, or that she would have agreed to let her posthumous glory spread over her while still alive, and in that way hide from the eyes of the world that she was only the shadow of the actress that she had been. "Players should be immortal [...] but they are not. They not only die like other people, but like other people they cease to be young and are no longer themselves, even while living."[47]

Nevertheless, this argument, with every mark of the melancholy aesthete, is blind to what really makes up celebrity: admiration for the talent of the actress, to the point of intense curiosity about her person, both her public life as an actress and her private life. After Siddons, the history of spectacle, theater and then films, but also sports, will be marked by innumerable attempts by former stars at "come-backs." It is easy to see how impossible it is for those who have known public success to be satisfied with a life in retirement, always feeling a need to prove that they are still alive and in demand. But if these come-backs are willingly orchestrated by the cultural industry, it is because the public is so fond of them, and one can hypothesize that the pleasure in such a phenomenon comes more from curiosity than from a sense of loss. In contrast with Hazlitt, the public was less interested in finding Siddons unchanged and more interested in what she had become. The personal and artistic (or athletic) challenge implied in every tentative come-back is the fascinating and sometimes morbid attraction that they arouse. What appeared almost sacrilegious to Hazlitt about Siddons' return, the weight of years, the combining of the public and private, the confusion between the actress that Siddons was and the private person she had become but which she was no longer content to be – all of this was just what attracted crowds to Covent Garden for her return to the stage.

Hazlitt knew this confusedly, even if he didn't have, as we do now, the advantage of two centuries of celebrity culture to understand it. In comparing Siddons' long and triumphal past with the cult of idols and goddesses, he did not seek, as other essayists did after him, to interpret the star cult as a form of modern and secular religion. Instead, he contrasted the grandeur reserved for heroes and goddesses, which arose from the wondrous and the glorious, with the celebrity reserved for exceptional artists: passionate interest in their risqué lives, where all grandeur faded in the glare of the footlights, publicity, and spectacle.

A European Celebrity

The career of François Joseph Talma offers an interesting parallel to that of Siddons. His first big success took place in the autumn of 1789, in *Charles IX* by Marie-Joseph Chénier, just after the young Talma, twenty-six, had joined the Comédie-Française. The play, which had been accepted before the Revolution but had not yet been staged, became both a theatrical and a political event, appearing to be a denunciation of both absolute monarchy and religious intolerance. After this striking success, Talma came to symbolize revolutionary theater.

His popularity immediately came into conflict with the collective logic of the acting troupe. As early as 1790, the actors suspended him for his individualistic attitude, his refusal of collective discipline. He responded by insisting on his revolutionary zeal and his concern for the audience, but also playing on his closeness to high-ranking political figures such as Mirabeau, and at the same time accusing the actors of reacting like an administrative body of the Ancien Régime, demanding that he obey the king. Consequently, and no doubt as Talma expected, the quarrel quickly became public, with a series of publications and then a petition in favor of him.[48] From then on, he was one of the most famous actors in Europe, conscious of both the political and commercial link he had with the public: "When my name is announced on a poster, I am the one the public wants to see, it is my voice it wants to hear."[49]

Talma's celebrity reached its zenith under the Consulate and the French Empire, owing, as the public saw it, to his very special relationship with Bonaparte. On stage the heroes whom the actor played seemed to evoke the consul and then the emperor. Once, under the Consulate, during a performance of *Iphigénie en Aulide*, the announcement of a victory for Bonaparte was made and Talma entered the scene proclaiming, to great enthusiasm, the lines: "Achille va combattre et triomphe en courant" ("Achilles goes to fight and triumphs at once").[50] Napoleon never missed a chance to let his esteem for Talma be known. The relationship the two men had, besides common popularity, was mysterious; it fascinated contemporary society as well as historians, certain people imagining that Talma gave the emperor lessons in diction and bearing. But Napoleon himself, from Saint Helena, tried to nullify this less than flattering interpretation.

Talma's celebrity was not simply political, however, and it survived Napoleon's fall. In 1822, the announcement of his retirement excited great controversy; the government was accused of not doing everything possible to see that Talma continued acting. The *Courrier des spectacles* did all it could to keep him from retirement, no matter what the cost might be. An early article mentioned his international reputation: "To arrive at this degree of celebrity where his name is known all over Europe, as well as at such an eminence that it is impossible for anyone to be compared to him, Talma can go on doing the great job he has done up until now." The next day a second article dwelt on the economic aspects: the celebrity of a great actor draws tourists from all over Europe, and this alone can swell box office receipts at the Comédie-Française. No matter what one thinks of his last performances or his political engagements, there is no doubting the "utility of such a famous actor."[51]

His celebrity was both national and international. A major figure at the Comédie-Française, a tragic actor of great classical roles from Racine and Corneille to Voltaire, associated in the mind of the public with Napoleon, Talma belonged profoundly to French culture and political life. Given that the zenith of his career came at a moment when French theater was being seen all over Europe, he could not help but be noticed in foreign countries. Having grown up in England, he admired English theater and shared this admiration with his friend and accomplice the writer Ducis, the pre-eminent importer of Shakespeare into France. Ducis adapted several plays in which Talma was the principal actor; this worked so well that in the first years of the nineteenth century the actor appeared to embody a French theater open to European influences, Talma having distanced himself from the frozen aspect of the classical tradition. This image was one of the basic reasons for his renown in Germany and England. An enthusiastic letter from Humboldt to Goethe contributed ultimately to the international reputation of the actor. Mme de Staël give him a powerful write-up in De l'Allemagne, describing Talma as the archetype of acting genius, but also the renovator of the European stage, capable, by his way of declaiming lines, of combining both Racine and Shakespeare.[52] Stendhal, who did not like Talma, commented perfidiously: "This eloquent woman took it upon herself to teach fools the terms in which they had to speak of Talma. Needless to say, Talma's name became European."[53]

In England, his celebrity arrived early and did not seem to have suffered from the English hostility to the French Revolution. Talma's father, who lived in London, often complained in letters to his son that he learned more about him in the English newspapers than from his letters: even the announcement of his marriage came by way of the press. In 1796, he wrote that in spite of the war, "our English newspapers" continued to speak about Talma and to sing his praises. In this way he experienced the public scrutiny of his son and the immense distance between an ordinary person and a famous one. "I am often asked if I have a relative who is an actor. They are very surprised when I say that Talma is my son."[54] After the fall of Napoleon, Talma undertook several tours across the Channel, notably in the first years of the Restoration, and then again in 1824. His English success showed the tensions between the international aspect of his celebrity and cultural patriotism. In 1817, on his return to London, Talma was obliged to defend himself in the newspapers for reproaches "made against him publicy."[55] The controversy had to do with a celebration in honor of the great English actor John Kemble, who was retiring from the stage. Talma gave a speech at the time praising the English theater. The newspapers wrote about the speech and gave it a political dimension; Talma felt forced to declare his patriotism. He justified himself by saying that he was simply responding to a toast in honor of "Talma and the French theater."

Another line was crossed, on the English side, during Talma's second tour in 1824. An article published in the English newspapers, recalling the personal relationship between Talma and Bonaparte, forced the affirmation of his nationality by wrongly stating that he was born in London and praising his perfect English pronunciation: "One generally forgets that this great tragedian, who was hired by Mr Kemble to play in Covent Garden for twelve nights, is English."[56] The ambiguity from that point on was total. Talma, whose career had been so strongly associated with the French Revolution, to the point of embodying a kind of theatrical Bonapartean alter ego, found himself, in a way, without a nationality. This capacity for famous people, in spite of their strong national ties, to be denationalized and to see their image circulate largely in a transnational sphere is the consequence of the incredible extent of the bonds of notoriety and media intervention that separate the famous person from his or her celebrity. Posthumous glory often took on the work of renationalizing celebrities.

Talma's death on October 19, 1826 was of course an important event, both culturally and politically, especially since the actor had wanted to be buried with no religious ceremony, in spite of the efforts of the Archbishop of Paris, who came to visit him just before he died. While friends of Voltaire, a half-century earlier, had to give up trying to have him buried in Paris, the burial of Talma caused a veritable public event, with eighty thousand people walking behind the funeral procession from his house to the cemetery. Of course this response must be placed in the context of the intense politicization of funeral ceremonies which marked the Restoration,[57] but it is certainly the celebrity of Talma that provoked such an emotional outpouring. The *Mercure de Londres* declared itself to be "in mourning" and put a black border around the edge of the paper for three months. Newspapers specializing in literary or theater news dedicated their headlines, and sometimes an entire issue, to the death of the actor. One issue of *La Pandore, Journal des spectacles, des letters, des arts, des moeurs et des modes* was completely reserved for the event with a black border around the front page and the title all in capitals: "THE DEATH OF TALMA."[58] The general press did not ignore the story either. The *Courrier de Paris* devoted long articles, issue after issue, to the illness and then death of the tragedian. As early as October 18 the newspaper claimed that "the public" was caught up "in the painful news about the illness of the great actor they might lose."[59] Two days later, October 20: "Talma is gone!!! Death which cannot be disarmed by the most virtuous people, or the most gifted, has struck down the great actor in his sixtieth year of life, who, before our very eyes, made live again the wonders with which Roscius long ago astounded the Romans."[60] Then on October 22, a very long article filled almost half the newspaper relating the funeral service in great detail. By focusing on the dignity of the speeches, the event was given an obvious political dimension and the secular funeral procession offered "a great example of the extent to which public reason and tolerance had grown." But the newspaper also described a veritable apotheosis, the passage from celebrity to glory as seen in Talma's death and the mass funeral procession. "Talma, whose life was marked by so much glorious success, has achieved the greatest triumph that a people can award a renowned individual."[61]

The *Journal des débats* and the *Journal de Paris* announced in unison the death of Talma. As for the serious and liberal *Constitutionnel*, the most important French daily, it dedicated a long obituary to him, categorically affirming his European and almost universal celebrity: "Talma's renown spread throughout Europe; it crossed the seas; his name was that of one of the greatest celebrities of his time."[62]

The Invention of the Fan(atic)

What goaded thousands of Parisians to follow Talma's funeral procession and readers from all over Europe to read in the newspapers the accounts of his last days and all the details of his career? Most of them had never seen him on stage, but they knew his name and bits of his biography, and they knew, mostly from the press, that his death was an event. Although it is difficult to know to what extent his death affected them, it made news: they were interested in it, and by following the procession or by simply being spectators they affirmed that they belonged to a collective, to a public. Celebrity is indissoluble from the existence of the mass of readers and spectators who learn the same news at the same time in the same newspapers, taking an interest in the same events and feeling the same emotions when they read the same books. But celebrity is distinct from simple success in that it goes beyond the work or the performance to focus directly on the author or the artist, in this case the actor. The public was not content just to appreciate the voice of Tenducci, or the acting of Siddons or Talma; they were interested in the details, the particularities of their lives, including the most intimate aspects of their existence. This interest took various forms, from the rather superficial curiosity of newspaper readers up to the enthusiasm of admirers who wanted to catch a glimpse of the stars, own their portraits, perhaps meet them. Public interest in the life of celebrities was often ambiguous: one part a sort of game and assumed futility, the other a profound desire for intimacy and imitation.

The sometimes superficial character of affective demonstrations toward a celebrity, which was already perceived and denounced in the eighteenth century, should not hide the fact that a part of the public had a relationship with the famous person that was based on a desire for intimacy with him or her from a distance, and sometimes the conviction that they had it.[63] This desire in which the unknown person made an imaginary friend of the celebrity, even a family member, can evolve into a fictive love affair, the extreme form of this fantasy. But generally it remains virtual, fantastic, or shared only with a few intimate friends, although it sometimes leads to writing directly to the famous individual or paying a visit. There is also a dark side that is seen when an extreme form of curiosity arises, a desire to know everything about the famous man or woman. At that point it is sometimes difficult to say how the alienation works: is the fan a victim of a celebrity media mirage, mesmerized by an artificial image, hostage of an illusory relationship which can become a mania, or, to the contrary, is the celebrity a victim of harassment by indiscreet fans, reduced to an object of desire created by the media?

This desire for closeness exposes a paradox at the heart of the modern system of celebrity: the most massive media events do the best job of creating this illusion of long-distance intimacy. This paradox, well known by specialists of contemporary mass culture, rests on two factors. The first is the capacity of the media to fictitiously erase the distance between individuals who are geographically and socially apart from each other. This power is particularly evident with modern media such as television, which allows the image and voice of stars to enter the private space of ordinary individuals. This was already the case to some degree when the newspapers of the eighteenth century wrote articles about the private lives of writers, actors, or socially prominent celebrities whose pictures could be bought for a few *sous*. In fact, the essence of media communication is to allow what is sometimes called "mediated quasi-interaction," which is often intense, between individuals who do not meet directly.[64] A second factor involves a rather astounding mass cultural phenomenon: certain widely distributed cultural products can cause very personal reactions, feeding a singular kind of subjectivity, even if these reactions are shared by thousands of readers or spectators. Again, this is a phenomenon that is well known to cultural sociologists, but which could already be observed in the eighteenth century. It is only necessary to mention the two bestselling novels of the century which provoked in many readers a highly subjective emotional experience: *La Nouvelle Héloïse* and *The Sorrows of Young Werther*.[65]

The conjunction of these two mechanisms makes it possible to understand that celebrity is expressly different from mere reputation; it is not only a matter of recognition. The more an actor, a writer, or a musician is known by a lot of people, the more he or she excites powerful emotional reactions among the curious and the admirers. Unknown individuals are convinced they have a special relationship with the celebrity, and they become *fans*. The term is obviously anachronistic. It did not appear until the second half of the twentieth century in order to designate sports enthusiasts (*fan*atics). And if the eighteenth century did not have the numerous and sometimes spectacular developments concerning fan culture, its institutions and its legends,[66] there were numerous instances of readers and spectators who did not just admire stars or show their curiosity; they actually developed an emotional attachment to a celebrity which helped them orient and define themselves.

One long-lasting practice which has characterized the reaction of fans is letter writing. Fan mail is a well-known celebrity phenomenon in the present day. Historians often see the origins of fan mail as beginning with letters sent to Rousseau by readers, with further development of the practice in the first half of the nineteenth century. Historians see it as characteristic of Romanticism and also a specific response to the power of fiction, to the "promise of literature" that incited readers to create images of the social world through an exchange with authors.[67] This analysis perhaps focuses too much on literature in particular, and not enough on the mechanisms of celebrity. Starting in the middle of the eighteenth century, not only authors like Rousseau and Bernardin de Saint-Pierre, but also actors and actresses like Garrick and Siddons, received a lot of mail: anonymous individuals felt authorized and even encouraged to pick up a pen and write to celebrities, either to comment on their work or their life, to solicit a friendly and ongoing relationship, to ask for financial subsidies or advice, or even to declare their love. An anonymous woman admirer of Garrick's who came to London to see him in the role of Lear wrote and asked him to get her a ticket.[68]

For a fan, writing to a famous person, feeling authorized to get in contact with the celebrity, is a way of establishing reciprocity. Fundamental to celebrity is the fact that media communication is unilateral, as opposed to the real-time communication one has in face-to-face conversations. It is aimed at an indeterminate public and does not call for a response. Even so, the public is not passive; each reader works hard to appropriate and interpret texts and images, thus creating a private image of the artist and an imaginary relationship with him or her. This work is not necessarily done alone; it is often social, done in discussion with friends, other fans. To pick up a pen and write to a star is to cross a line, establishing reciprocity, an attempt to enter into direct communication.

Let us look again at the case of Talma. The archives at the Comédie-Française include a set of letters received by the tragedian. In certain of them one finds occasional verse and praise, often pompous, addressed to Talma by his admirers. The actor kept the letters and sometimes copied them, indicating the level of interest they held for him. A young English girl of fourteen sent him a "hesitant tribute and proof of her admiration" and begged his indulgence.[69] Another made a poem out of the list of roles that Talma had played.[70] For certain letter writers, expressing their admiration was not enough. They constructed little narratives aimed at attracting the attention of Talma, but also giving the writer an active role in the relationship. One admirer from the provinces took a friend of his, prejudiced against Talma from having read articles by the critic Geoffroy, to see the actor in *Britannicus*. The narrative, very detailed, became the story of a conversion, where admiration, once again, turned into "ardor," a stupefied fascination and almost love at first sight: " 'What features! What talent! What a voice!' the friend cried out at every instant, animated with admiration. His mouth hung open, his eyes were fixed on Talma with a sort of cupidity, and he was afraid that words would fly out of his mouth." These are the words of a convert and they describe the passionate character that defines the relationship of the public with a celebrated actor: "I feel that once one has seen Talma, one immediately wishes to see him again, to always see him because one never tires of admiring him."[71]

One admirer who wrote to the famous actor presented himself as a fan who was sharing his enthusiasm with everyone around him. Other writers wanted to start a dialogue with the famous person. Between 1799 and 1802, Talma received a great deal of correspondence from an individual who called himself "Anonymous from the Stalls," whom he never met and who only much later revealed his identity (M. de Charmois). M. Charmois critiqued Talma's performances in long letters where praise was the rule but where criticisms also appeared. "Anonymous from the Stalls" was a very knowledgeable amateur whose passion for the theater centered on Talma; he was a spokesman for the public, noting, for example, in June 1800, "the unanimous and universal enthusiasm with which the Public welcomes your entrance on stage."[72]

If "Anonymous from the Stalls" liked to discuss and critique the performances of Talma, others wrote above all to express their admiration and their attachment. One correspondent used a discussion he had had with some friends as a pretext to write a laudatory letter concerning the pronunciation of the word "respect" used by Talma in *Athalie*, full of dithyrambic sentences about the actor's performance and the passion it aroused. The letter cleverly noted the constraints the anonymous writer was under and his desire to have a personal relationship: although he said that he preferred to remain anonymous in "the crowd of your admirers," he brought up his "strong desire not to be anonymous" and pleaded for a response (he gave the address of a friend, which was perhaps his own). The letter's form of address itself, "Monsieur, or Talma," played with the idea set down by social convention of the objective distance which separates two individuals who have never met and the personal tie which unites the public with the celebrity, addressing him by his first name, the line between respect and familiarity. The rest of the letter ranged between admiration for the actor expressed by the theater buff and a more affective register that placed the admirer's feelings above everything else: "I feel a need to tell you about even the tiniest bit of deep emotion that you have so often stirred up in my soul." This deeply felt emotion surpassed the evaluation of the actor's talent; even the area of hyperbolic admiration created an emotional bond between the author of the letter and Talma. The function of the letter was to express and, if possible, transform this bond into an affective relationship.[73]

Other writers did not so much address themselves to the great actor as to a famous man from whom one could solicit favors, usually subsidies. Some of the requests had a connection with the theater. A certain Beauval, from Limoges, recommended his nephew, author of a tragedy, and sent the letter to "Monsieur Talma, celebrated artist and resident at S.M., in Paris." Another, Beurtez-Delancourt, calling himself "a Man of Letters," printed and sent to Talma "Thoughts on the urgent necessity in which I find myself and my need to ask for help." A man named Delhorme from Grenoble said that he was writing to Talma to explain about a somber legal proceeding and asking for his assistance. He pressured him in letter after letter to keep his promise. And someone else, a certain Lagache, wrote from Clermont in the department of Oise, introducing Talma to a certain "method of playing roulette" based on mathematical calculations and said he was ready to "fly" to Paris if he got a favorable response from him.[74] Talma's fame in this case was not the basis for an affective and personal relationship, but the status of a public figure one imagined to be rich and powerful and who attracted numerous people soliciting favors from every part of France. Most of the time the two elements came together, at least in the writer's rhetoric. Ouvrard, a professor of writing at Bordeaux, asked Talma to help him find an apartment in Paris, where he could focus on his passion for the arts without sacrificing the presence of his four children: "How fortunate these children are that they can still reach out to the God of Drama, whom France honors even in his lifetime and of whom it is said no one has ever been refused when they asked him for help."[75]

To write to a famous man is one thing; to meet him is still more fascinating. We have little evidence of this in regard to Talma, but one

letter offers a very significant expression of a desire to see the famous
man, a necessity both touristic and ritualistic. A writer from Rouen told
Talma that she and some friends were coming to Paris and dreamed of
meeting the famous actor. Her pompous request began this way: "You
understand, Monsieur, that to go to Paris without seeing Talma is worse
than going to Rome without seeing the pope."[76]

It's regrettable, of course, that there is no trace of this visit. We
do not even know if Talma was flattered by this desire to see him or
embarrassed by the prospect of an importunate visit. On the other
hand, Sarah Siddons did leave a record of her intrusive admirers. In
her *Reminiscences*, written when she knew she was dying, she openly
admits to having sought celebrity. But celebrity is presented in a rather
somber light, because of the social obligations implied, the continual
requests made of her, which left little time for her work as an actress or
for family life. Her ambition as an actress as well as her personal well-
being were threatened by the "ardor" with which every new celebrity
was solicited in order to be put on show. One evening when she had
accepted an social invitation, having been promised that there would
only be a dozen people present, she found herself caught in a real "trap,"
surrounded until dawn by dozens of guests ready to climb up on chairs
in order to see over the shoulders of their neighbors.[77] The hostess had
even encouraged her to come with her baby in order to make the whole
event more interesting, "more for effect than for her beautiful eyes,"
Siddons commented bitterly.

This image of the young actress surrounded by a crowd of unknown
people climbing on chairs to get a glimpse of her and her baby is striking. Siddons gives another example, even more amazing. Although she
had gotten in the habit of locking her door to keep out unknown people
attracted to her solely out of curiosity, some did not hesitate to force an
entrance. One day she had a visit from a woman of very high standing
whom she did not know and who showed up uninvited.

> She was a person of very high rank. Her curiosity had been, however, too
> powerful for her good breeding. "You must think it strange" said she "to
> see a person entirely unknown to you intrude in this manner upon your
> privacy; but you must know I am in a very delicate state of health, and
> my physician won't let me go to the Theatre to see you, so I am come to
> look at you here." So *she* sat down to look, and *I* to be looked at, for a
> few painful moments, when she arose and apologised.[78]

Whether this anecdote is true or partially fiction, it functions as a metaphor about how aggressive the public can be in their desire to see a celebrity, even to the point of depriving them of their privacy. The unknown
person was seized by a sort of voyeuristic impulse which pushed her to

observe the famous actress. But how is this to be interpreted? One may see celebrity as a new form of social prestige. The upper-class person has forgotten the exterior signs which govern her social place, notably her manners, and she is reduced to a mere silent admirer, mesmerized to the point of watching the silent tragedian without saying a word. But Siddons focuses on the uncomfortable, almost violent, aspect of this intrusion. She herself is reduced to an object of desire by this female spectator, who is incapable of distinguishing between the time and place where the actress publicly plays a role in the theater and the rest of her social life where she has a family and children. As in the previous scene, Siddons, outside of the theater, is obliged to submit to the gaze of others. That a great aristocrat personifies the public is not insignificant. Anonymous and unknown to Siddons, she is simply an indiscreet admirer, without a personal story. But her social standing suggests that the social and symbolic domination that aristocrats exercised over actors, even when they admired and protected them, was transmitted to the public, without losing much in the translation. Far from socially liberating actors, celebrity subjugated them to other constraints, no less demanding.

The fan can be distinguished from the admirer or the disciple, two figures considered more classic in the traditional spectator–celebrity relationship. The fan has two sides which illustrate the ambivalence of celebrity. The passionate interest that the fan has for a certain public figure can come from a sincere desire for intimacy, aroused initially by artistic or intellectual admiration, or even empathy with the unhappiness of individuals (writers as well as criminals), as has been reported in the press. But it can also darken into an excessive curiosity, almost obsessive, a type of voyeurism, a desire to possess the celebrity by denying him or her any autonomous existence outside of a public life. The fan, an exaggerated incarnation of the relationship that the public maintains with celebrities, is not part of a cult, nor is he or she a simple spectator; the fan is a more worrisome person whose motives are intriguing. This individual only makes sense when one considers the new configurations of publicity, which profoundly transformed the very constitution and reputation of public figures, whether actors, artists, or writers.

— 3 —

A FIRST MEDIA REVOLUTION

Talma found a letter from an anonymous correspondent along with a portrait of Garrick in his mail. The letter praised the high quality of the picture, contrasting it with the mediocre images that had been around during the career of the great actor: "We have painted an infinite number of Garricks. The most insignificant doodler in the Academy wanted the support of the English Roscius."[1] It was not an exaggeration: Garrick had in his lifetime become a demotic icon, in England, most of all, but also in France. There were more than two hundred and fifty different images of him, painted or engraved, sometimes numerous examples of the same image (Fig. 12). Garrick had himself painted in his favorite roles, as theater director, as a gentleman, in casual conversation with friends, in a *tête-à-tête* with a woman. There was a Garrick for every taste and every purse, and this intense iconographic offensive revealed the importance that the actor accorded his public image. He has been called the "first media personality,"[2] given that he knew how to portray himself as a public figure, immediately recognizable, using this visual strategy in the service of his artistic ambitions as well as in his great desire for recognition. He profoundly impressed himself on the minds of everyone in Europe; Denis Diderot, who had rarely seen him on the stage, thought of him when he wrote *Paradoxe du comédien*. Talma was painted many times during his career and his image was widely distributed. That the images of famous actors were so often reproduced is not insignificant. It was a new phenomenon which showed to what extent the theater was important in eighteenth-century urban life. It was also part of a larger transformation in visual culture.

It is often thought that modern celebrity is linked to the massive reproduction of images characteristic of the twentieth century. New image production and reproduction technologies, starting with photography, then film and television, supposedly transformed the history of celebrity, making "visibility" the dominant form of renown.[3] There is no denying that these technologies considerably transformed the media world as well as the relationship to media images. Today, photos of stars are available everywhere, stills or moving images, close-ups or telephoto shots. Nonetheless, a transformation in the visual culture had already taken place in the eighteenth century: it rested on innovative techniques, like burin, copper engraving, and etching, which allowed better and better likenesses and large print-runs that were impossible with wood engraving. But the changes were above all social and cultural. In large cities, portrait images were more and more visible in every medium, painted portraits were exhibited during academy shows, porcelain figurines had become fashionable gifts, and numerous engravings were sold in merchants' stalls.

But celebrity cannot be reduced to visibility and the presence of images: it is nourished just as much by stories, discussions, texts, as seen today in the "people" magazines. Changes in printed matter were decisive during the eighteenth century. Public literacy grew considerably and the relationship to books and reading greatly altered. Formerly a scholarly activity, reading now had a new status demonstrated by the success of inexpensive novels, and above all newspapers, which multiplied at the end of the seventeenth century throughout Europe. Literary journals and political gazettes have attracted the greater part of attention from historians. Journals were the source of intellectual communication among scholars, along with private correspondence that structured the literary world during the First Republic. Political gazettes inaugurated a new age of political information when it no longer circulated uniquely through written correspondence and rumors but also through newspapers.[4] Theoreticians of public space speculate that it was through social gatherings and a collective reading of newspapers that open public speculation and commentary were exercised during the Enlightenment. When Kant in his book *What Is Enlightenment?* described *Aufklärung* as a process of individual and collective emancipation that allowed for the use of reason by each person "who was a reader," he was obviously referring to those who read newspapers, an idea that appeared in his well-known text published in the *Berlinische Monatsschrift* in 1784 during a debate on the issues involved in religious marriages. A few years later, Hegel went so far as to write that reading a newspaper in the morning was the modern man's prayer.

Nevertheless, alongside the scholarly and political newspapers that reported diplomatic and political news, surveyed the latest literary and scientific news, or welcomed intellectual debates, there also existed other newspapers in the eighteenth century, many of them interested in social and cultural news in a broader sense. They offered readers news about spectacles and literary publications, about literary and political events, but also reported salient news events and a growing number of anecdotes about the public and private life of famous people. Although historians have little studied these periodicals, many readers in the eighteenth century were interested in them and they had a decisive influence on shaping the public consciousness of the urban middle class, those who constituted the public sphere. News was fed as much by gossip and scandal as by treaties and battles.

These various transformations marked the beginning of a new media age that one historian jokingly proposed calling Print 2.0, to indicate that it was a veritable turning point in the history of printed matter, usages, and effects.[5] Information filtered through the media, distributing texts and images to an ill-defined and potentially limitless public, became the standard for society news and competed with traditional forms of information based on word of mouth, physical presence, and reciprocity. Even the conditions of celebrity were profoundly changed: networks that created reputation expanded and it became more and more common to be confronted with the name or image of someone one had never met in person. The fame of well-known individuals was no longer confined to traditional circles (the court, the salons, the theater, universities, and academic circles) but instead was projected into the public sphere through a series of representations – discourses and images – aimed at undefined and anonymous readers and consumers, who were curious as well as admiring. This potentially unlimited and unverifiable circulation of representations constituted the world of public figures.

The Visual Culture of Celebrity

Where were portraits of living people seen before the eighteenth century? On pieces of money which carried images of the sovereign, in palaces where courtesans could admire portraits of the king, in aristocratic mansions where nobles readily had their portraits painted and hung up alongside their ancestors. It was a matter, above all, of representing power, political or social. The portrait of the king was a facsimile of power in that he possessed the leverage to represent it, to be, in a way, power itself, by his force and his prestige, in the same way that socio-political forces emanated from the portraits of aristocrats.[6]

Of course, seventeenth-century portraits of some writers did exist, like those of Corneille or Molière, but, on the other hand, there was not one portrait of Rabelais during his lifetime.[7] The reign of Louis XIV had seen a rise in portraiture, with the creation of a painting and sculpture academy where portraitists were admitted, and with the success of Pierre Mignard and then Hyacinthe Rigaud. However, portraits remained essentially linked to the courtly world and high nobility, where they had a political and emotional function. It was very difficult to copy them.[8] Up until the beginning of the eighteenth century, the existence of portraits signaled the access by a few rare cultural figures to an exceptional social position, notably in the area of academia. Portraits only circulated in inner circles and they almost always had to do with personal relationships. To possess the portrait of someone was an honor related to the distinguished nature of the model, but it also demonstrated a direct link to the model, familial or amicable. When Samuel Sorbière, who admired Thomas Hobbes and contributed a great deal to the distribution of his work throughout Europe, wanted to obtain his portrait, he had to personally ask for authorization to make a copy of the existing portrait which belonged to Thomas de Martel: "Please, I beg you with my whole heart, hoping that you will kindly consider my request and be so good as to forgive my boldness."[9] In 1658, he wrote once again saying that his greatest pleasure was being able to talk about Hobbes and his work with friends and to look at "the portrait in my collection." The portrait takes the place of the absent friend, it is part of a regimem of familiarity, affection, and admiration. Its presence honors Sorbière because it shows that he has direct and amicable links with the model. In 1661, Hobbes agreed to pose in Samuel Cooper's studio for his great friend John Aubrey as a way to thank him for making it possible for him to enter the good graces of Charles II. Aubrey himself was extremely grateful, qualifying the gesture as a "great honor."

A few years later, Isaac Newton would use his own portraits as recompense in exchange for vows of allegiance. Pierre Varignon, a French mathematician with whom he had ties, asked him several times over the years for a portrait. Newton only accepted at the end of his life during negotiations for a deluxe edition of *Optics* with which he wanted Varignon's help. The same thing happened when Varignon asked Newton for a portrait on behalf of Johann Bernoulli. Newton saw Bernoulli as an ally of Leibniz and made it a condition that in exchange for a portrait Bernoulli would publicly acknowledge the priority of Newton's work on infinitesimal calculus.[10]

One sometimes found the portrait of an author on the cover of his work, but this portrait was an indication of authorship rather than the singularity of the person.[11] Up until the sixteenth century, moreover, the resemblance of the author was not the point; a sort of stereotyped image was the goal.

Portraits were at that time rather rare and seldom seen publicly. Saint-Simon recounts a story that indicates how difficult it was to obtain the image of someone. It is an exceptional case, of course, because it concerns the Abbé de Rancé, the famous founder of the Trappists, whom Saint-Simon greatly admired and whose portrait he wished to have. Knowing that the modest Rancé would refuse to have his portrait painted, Saint-Simon invented a strategy: he came to visit him with the painter Hyacinthe Rigaud, who, he said, was a relative. Rigaud observed Rancé in order to paint him later from memory. The portrait was such a success that the artist could not stop himself from boasting about it. Soon a number of people asked for a copy; thus, Saint-Simon's secret was out.

> I was very angry with all the gossip this caused but I consoled myself by having attained an image of someone so dear and so illustrious and by being able to pass on to generations the portrait of such a great man, so accomplished and so famous. I never dared to tell him about my petty theft, but when I left La Trappe I told him the whole story in a letter and asked his forgiveness. He was extremely saddened, touched and distressed.[12]

This episode is revelatory of the social usages of portraiture at the beginning of the eighteenth century. The desire to have the painted portrait of a great contemporary, to own it and to pass it on, was at odds with the scarcity of images, and it forced Saint-Simon into lies and trickery. But already the demand pushed the painter to produce copies and create engravings of the portrait, making the image public. Even a man as shy and reserved as the Abbot of Rancé had become so "famous," as Saint-Simon put it, that his admirers wanted to have a portrait of him by any means possible.

In the eighteenth century, portraits of famous men multiplied and gained in stature. First, there was the distribution of painted images, which were much more frequent and, most importantly, were shown publicly. The annual exhibits of works by artists from the Academy in Paris (starting in 1699) and in London (after 1761) became important events drawing large crowds. In Paris, the number of spectators never ceased to grow, with the salon of 1787 having almost sixty thousand visitors. At the same time, competing events developed in an attempt to break the academic monopoly.[13] In London, exhibits took place in the Great Room at Spring Gardens, then later on Pall Mall starting in 1769, and after that in Somerset House in 1789, welcoming thousands of visitors. At the same time, paying exhibits were taking place in urban entertainment centers like Vauxhall.[14] All these exhibits, and in particular those of the Academies, were public events of great importance, profoundly transforming the world of art, controlled, albeit contested, by academic standards in France, and at the center of a more commercial culture in England.[15]

Portraiture occupied a dominant place. In France, where the ideals of historic painting remained powerful among critics, and the Academy held sway through its model of royal portraiture, this profusion of private portraits was criticized, sometimes virulently. Classical criticism, formulated in the Renaissance, reproached portrait artists for their overweening attachment to likeness to the detriment of the imagination and the idealization of the real, and they added a political critique of the democratization of the portrait. Étienne La Font de Saint-Yenne, in his reports of the salons from 1747 to 1753, complained of portraits being too "obscure" and " too indifferent to the public." He denounced "this group of obscure men, without a name, without talent, without reputation, even without a face, all these people whose only merit is to exist [...] giants in their own eyes and nobody in the eyes of the public." He contrasted them to those with merit, worthy to be painted, among them famous men: "There is no one who does not ardently desire to see the face of an excellent citizen, a great writer or a person who is famous for his deeds."[16] Political merit, literary talent, and celebrity were the three elements which, in the eyes of the critic and in the name of public interest, authorized a portrait. Celebrity had to be justified by "deeds" that corresponded to the political and moral ideal set forth by the Academy. Twenty years later, the editor of the *Mémoires secrets* used the same irony when he invoked "the multitude of portraits that I see everywhere" and which constituted more than a third of the exposed work. "The salon will bcome imperceptibly a gallery of portraits," deplored the author, and continued: "It would almost be acceptable if they showed us important men of status or celebrity, or pretty women, at least, or remarkable faces with great character, but what do we care about Mme Guesnon de Ponneuil, Mme Journu la mère, M. Dacy, M. Le Normand du Coudray..., etc.?"[17] On the contrary, criticism of the democratization of the portrait, which allowed larger areas of the population to be represented, rested on three principles which the author thought legitimate: the social-political principle ("men who are important because of their status"), the aesthetic principle (pretty women and faces fit for medals), and the principle of "celebrity." This latter, it should be noted, was empowered by "deeds."

In London, where portraiture had an even greater success and was less contested, it served to feed the new culture of celebrity.[18] Joshua Reynolds, the most important painter of the period, took marvelous advantage of this. He exhibited a large number of celebrity portraits, literary stars or socialites, and linked his own reputation to the fame of his models. Most of his paintings could be seen in his studio, which became a famous art space in the English capital. Reynolds very consciously played on the fame of his models and the stories which circulated about them in the press, exciting public curiosity and helping build his own reputation as a fashionable artist.[19] Money was also at stake; the prices asked for his work could be very high and the gossip that accompanied them attracted new clients.

The portraits that Reynolds exhibited were often linked to news events. In 1761, he painted the portrait of Laurence Sterne, whose *Tristram Shandy* had just been successfully published. The year before Sterne was an unknown, a minister from the provinces without any contacts in London. His book, having been refused by London publishers, was published in York, paid for by himself. He sent a few copies to London and managed, with the help of an actress, to gain Garrick's support. The book was an immediate success and a few weeks later Sterne arrived in the capital proclaiming with effrontery: "I wrote, not to be fed but to be famous." He then posed eight times for Reynolds, and he took the painting, barely finished, to an engraver he had solicited: "I shall make the most of myself, & sell [my head] both inside and out."[20]

Reynolds did not only exhibit portraits of popular writers (Samuel Johnson, Oliver Goldsmith), but also other public figures: persons known to high society, actors or young women who excited public curiosity. The following year, 1762, he exhibited the portrait of Garrick, whom he was associated with and whom he painted on numerous occasions, but also the famous courtesan Nelly O'Brien, the new mistress of Lord Bolingbroke, which the *St James's Chronicle* had made public some months earlier. Exhibiting on the same wall simultaneously portraits of writers, politicians, great aristocrats, and courtesans was not without consequence: such socially different figures were seen at the same level in the eyes of the public. Reynolds, given his taste for the paintings of courtesans, agreed to be associated with the libertine world along with its cosmopolitan, and slightly scandalous, sexual celebrity, which was good publicity.[21] And this did not stop him from also being the portraitist of aristocracy, as well as the royal family, especially after the 1780s. Whether it was Samuel Johnson, Frances Abington, Georgiana Cavendish, or the Duchess of Devonshire, he only painted portraits of celebrities.[22]

When Reynolds exhibited a portrait of the Prince of Wales, at the salon of 1785, the young heir to the throne was talked about the whole winter, his tumultuous party life, his affairs, his passion for the races and for women. On the opposite wall, Reynolds hung the portrait of Laetitia Derby, "Mrs Smith," a famous courtesan who was known to be the mistress of Lord Lade, a great friend of the prince. A few days before the opening of the exhibit, the *Morning Post* published a rumor that the prince had allegedly had sexual relations with Mrs Smith in Lord Lade's own carriage.[23] One can imagine how the visual presentation of the two portraits, one facing the other, excited the curiosity of visitors and created a good deal of talk.

Public Figurines

Exhibitions only lasted a few weeks, but the reproduction of works through engraving allowed for a massive distribution of celebrity portraits and assured their permanent presence in the public sphere. The portrait of Garrick that Reynolds exhibited at the Academy in 1762 was engraved by Edward Fisher, one of Reynolds' official engravers, then copied thirteen times by other engravers. It circulated widely in England but also on the Continent. Thanks to the progress being made in this technique, engravings could faithfully reproduce the image of the subject and produce large print runs, thus allowing the cost to be reduced, which varied according to the quality and the size of the print. Portraits called "posture size," ten inches by fourteen, could be sold for a shilling.[24] These works represented art world assets that admirers and the curious could acquire quite easily, whether they were attracted by the quality of the original painting or by the famous figure who was represented. This spectacular development in the engraving market multiplied the presence and availability of portraits, but also their usage for publicity. Garrick's fame was put to profitable use by clever salesmanship, tobacco or bookstore merchants using his picture to decorate their business cards.[25]

In France, too, the portraits of famous people began to be objects of mass consumption. Since the seventeenth century, engravings were more than inserts in printed books, but by the eighteenth century they had become a veritable object of consumption because of their unprecedented commercial development.[26] Sixty percent of estate inventory after Parisian deaths, with all social categories mixed together, mentioned engravings. Some authors, like Louis Sébastien Mercier, protested this profusion of engravings, declaring a trivialization of images and excessive reproduction: "There has been a ridiculous abuse of engraving in our time. [...] This miserable and continual translation of every painting and every face creates a boring monotony in houses, since one finds in one house what one has seen in another."[27]

Newspapers constantly announced new print arrivals: roughly seventy-two a year between 1764 and 1782, generally a thousand copies of each one. In the last years of the Ancien Régime, more than a hundred new prints appeared every year. Of these, portraits took second place after scenes from life. Portraits appearing in-folio, engraved with a burin, were starting to disappear and be replaced by little medal portraits done as etchings. Notably, there were more and more engravings reproduced from drawings rather than from paintings, and thus drawings were being created directly for the engraving market, which was free. The engravings could be sold by the engraver himself, by a print merchant who had a shop, or by retailers who spread their engravings along the quays and were called "street hawkers." Often the prices were not high, but there was a great difference in quality between the beautiful engravings made by reputed engravers from paintings by masters which could sell for as much as 16 *livres*, and ordinary engravings, which sold for between 1 and 4 *livres*.[28]

The demand was such that certain engraving merchants specialized in the production and sale of cheap little portraits for the general public. Merchants Jacques Esnault and Michel Rapilly set themselves up as specialists for these little portraits. Arriving from Normandy, they began as street hawkers in 1768, selling their merchandise on the quays of the Seine, then moving to a boutique in 1770 on rue Saint-Jacques, under the name La Ville de Coutances, where they began to publish numerous small-size portraits of celebrities that sold for 12 *sols*, or *sous*. An inventory of their stock made in 1790 showed 155 "small portraits engraved by the most famous engravers of this kind of art." Among the portraits, next to the royal family, the pope, and the principal European heads of state (Joseph II, Catherine of Russia) were a few rare writers from the past (Montaigne, Molière, and Bossuet) and a profusion of cultural or political celebrities from the Enlightenment (Beaumarchais, Buffon, d'Alembert, Linguet, Rousseau, Voltaire, Necker, and even the Chevalier d'Éon, the opera star Mme de Saint-Huberty, and her rival Rosalie Duthé, who had become one of the most famous Parisian courtesans). Foreigners were not absent either, notably soldiers, politicians, and explorers, such as the "famous Admiral Kepel," English heroes of the Seven Years' War, Captain Cook, and even George Washington.[29]

This explosion of the portrait engraving market created greed and encouraged suspect commercial practices in a market that was not well regulated. Esnault and Rapilly, as well as their competitors, required their engravers to produce portraits more or less resembling the subject, but sometimes they ended up reproducing existing portraits without authorization, changing only a few details. These kinds of forgeries caused complex legal problems. How could someone say they owned the face of a famous man? From the moment the resemblance became principally a business matter, much more than a matter of the artistic quality of the portrait, how could the intellectual property of the images be assured? How could anyone be stopped from copying them?[30]

Among 380 portraits registered in the *Journal de la Librairie* between 1764 and 1788, 84 percent were of contemporaries, linked to current affairs: kings and people at court, but also a number of writers, scientists, and artists (25 percent), actors (9 percent), and several celebrities of the moment: Mesmer, Montgolfier, Cagliostro, Bergasse.[31] Unfortunately, it is difficult to know to what purpose these portraits were put or who the buyers were. We have the catalogue of sales of an engraving dealer, Vallée, for 1787/8. Out of 216 customers, 97 were not merchants themselves. It was a varied lot, including aristocrats, the elite from the Third Estate, doctors, artists, but also a more disparate group. Vallée sold portraits that included one of Benoît Louis Henriquez, painted in 1786, much sought-after portraits of Voltaire and Rousseau, and those of current political figures: Bergasse, again, particularly in light of the Kornmann trial, which made him famous, Necker, and the Duc d'Orléans. The Bergasse engraving, put up for sale in December 1788, was bought by a wine merchant and a carpenter, that of Necker by a clockmaker, a bookseller, a bishop, a carpenter, and a journalist.[32]

Besides engravings, the faces of famous men and women were seen in various art forms toward the end of the century, from traditional sculpture to new cultural art objects: medals, figurines, cups. Although statues had been reserved up until then for sovereigns, a number of sculptors specialized in the production of busts, like Augustin Pajou or Jean-Baptiste Lemoyne, and most importantly Jean-Antoine Houdon, a renowned sculptor of cultural and political celebrities of the period. His debut had not, however, been easy. Born in 1741, he was denied major royal commissions in the 1770s by Angiviller, who did not like him and would not give him, from his list, any busts of great men to sculpt. He was competing with the established success of Pajou and Jean-Baptiste Pigalle, as well as with the hostility of Jean-Jacques Caffieri, his great rival. Houdon found a way around all this, playing on the commercial success of portraiture. Each year he sent busts of famous people to the salon (Sophie Arnould, Voltaire, Franklin) and exhibited his sculptures all year in his studio; a Swiss assistant was put in charge of showing people around when Houdon was not there. This strategy drew the hostility of his competitors but raised the interest of portrait enthusiasts, which led to numerous private sales. At the height of his career, during the Consulate, Houdon's studio was immortalized by a Boilly painting showing the sculptor at work, surrounded by dozens of busts of cultural and political celebrities; among those easily recognizable were Voltaire, Sophie Arnould, Buffon, Franklin, Washington, Gluck, Cagliostro, Jefferson, Rousseau, Lafayette, and Mirabeau.[33]

Houdon was perfectly conscious of the commercial stakes attached to a large production of plaster cast copies, molds made from busts created initially in marble or terracotta, and he tried hard to reserve the copyright for making these in his studio. At the 1775 salon he exhibited a marble bust of Sophie Arnould after her huge success in two Gluck operas, *Orphée* and *Iphigénie en Aulide* (in fact Houdon exhibited the bust that same year). Arnould, who was much acclaimed for her triumph by the Dauphine Marie-Antoinette in person, wore the headband of Diane in her role of Iphigénie and flowers in her hair. Houdon was not one to sacrifice his art to allegorical constraints, which was often the case when making representations of actors. His bust was above all expressive, faithful to the physiognomy of the singer, but it also reminded the spectators of the role in which Arnould a few months earlier had thrilled the public. So it was a matter not of preserving the memory of a great artist or representing, through her, the greatness of the music, but rather concentrating on the event itself, letting the public see the face of the most famous singer of the time, who, after making news by her relationship with the Duc de Lauragais and her witticisms, had just had an even more legitimate success.[34] In the end, this allowed Arnould to turn her success to good account among her many admirers and for Houdon to associate himself with it. He contracted to sell 355 plaster copies to admirers of the opera singer.[35]

Three years later, during Voltaire's visit to Paris, Houdon made a bust of him bare headed that took three modeling sessions and was a great success: "All of Paris came to M. Houdon's studio to see the Voltaire bust, which was no doubt the best likeness of the patriarch out of all the portraits ever made of him."[36] This statue of Voltaire was in its turn reproduced in bronze and in plaster, but also as an engraving, much to the displeasure of Houdon, who complained of these forgeries.[37]

Models of celebrities also became part of mass culture, notably with the appearance of the first wax museums. Wax sculptures had been around since Antiquity and served in the Middle Ages and then in the Renaissance for the funeral effigies of kings.[38] In the modern period, the realism achieved through wax made it useful for royal portraits and for anatomy courses. Its usage as entertainment dated back to 1668, when Antoine Benoist was given design patents allowing him to exhibit his "royal circle," a representation of the French court and several ambassadors, in his studio on rue des Saints-Pères.[39] Later, it was still the court being represented, and Benoist's studio was mostly frequented by aristocrats. Furthermore, Benoist was accepted into the Royal Academy of painters and sculptors, creating a wax portrait of Louis XIV in 1705. Nevertheless, his studio marked the beginning of an evolution in wax sculpture for urban spectacles, playing on the hyperrealism of its representations. La Bruyère was not wrong when he referred to Benoist as a "puppeteer."[40]

Commercial usage of wax statues dates back to the arrival in Paris of Philippe Curtius, who founded the first wax figure museum in 1770 on the Boulevard Saint-Martin. He then moved to the Palais-Royal and finally, in 1782, to the Boulevard du Temple, next to the Théâtre de Nicolet, the new center for urban entertainment. Like Benoist, Curtius had a room where the entire royal family was represented having a meal, but he presented the public with other celebrities as well: Voltaire, Franklin, Necker, Mesmer, Linguet, and even Janot. He also created "a great thieves' cavern," which showed models of criminals and to which he regularly added new wax sculptures according to what was happening in the news. The entrance fee was two *sous*, which made it a cheap show and no doubt extremely popular, since Curtius, if one is to believe Mercier, made up to 100 *ecus* a day, which supposed three thousand visitors daily, probably an exaggerated estimate.[41] After the death of Curtius, in 1794, his student Marie Grosholtz married François Tussaud, and in 1802 left for England, where she permanently set up her famous wax museum in 1835 on Baker Street.[42] The fad for wax statues existed across Europe. In Vienna, at the end of the eighteenth century, the court sculptor Müller-Deym developed a wax museum in which the entire imperial family was represented, as well as the principal sovereigns of Europe.[43] In a working-class area of theaters and carnival stalls in Naples, next to the little San Carlino Theater, one could find wax statues. In 1783, alongside the pope, the emperor and some crowned heads of state, Napolitanos could admire the effigy of the popular poet and librettist Metastasio, as well as statues of Voltaire, Washington, and Rousseau.[44]

One of the most important technological and commercial innovations at the end of the eighteenth century was the development of ceramic figurines. These already existed, but they were considered luxury items, requiring the delicate application of a varnish and selling in only small numbers. Between 1750 and 1770, however, several innovations modified figurine fabrication. "Biscuit firing," without color or varnish, offered a better likeness and cost less, and then the development of porcelain in "hard paste wax" allowed studios to produce numerous identical copies of sculptures, and especially busts. In France, while Sèvres remained, above all, the manufacturer of decorative porcelain and especially tableware, it nonetheless made a business of copying the busts of "illustrious men," commissioned by the monarchy, and produced a series of original busts of contemporaries, among them writers and artists, such as Voltaire in 1767, then Rameau, Diderot, Rousseau; actors, such as Préville, after his triumph in the role of Figaro, Dazincourt, and even Janot, whose bust in 1780 was the "fashionable New Year's gift"[45] and scientists and politicians, such as Franklin and Washington. However, this practice remained somewhat limited.[46]

In England, to the contrary, the ceramics revolution was developed by the entrepreneur Josiah Wedgwood, an emblematic figure in the

61

commercial development taking place at the end of the eighteenth century.[47] In the 1760s, Wedgwood developed a kind of ceramic made with black basalt, the "famous jasper body." With the help of the sculptor John Flaxman, he developed a catalogue of figures and established a line of ceramic portraits. Contrary to the royal Sèvres line, Wedgwood chose from the start to orient his work toward the public, by adapting himself to its interest in images of famous people and by widely distributing his catalogues and his collections and offering attractive prices. Statues of foreign writers were also available, notably French ones, such as the fraternal enemies Rousseau and Voltaire, in different sizes and at different prices. For each figure, the ceramic image was made to accord with the person's fame and with the expectations of the English public. When Wedgwood found a drawing of Rousseau planting herbs in the gardens at Ermenouville, he decided to make a statue of it but worried the image of a writer as botanist might disconcert the public.[48]

Besides the busts and statues, the price of which could often be relatively high and thus targeted at a middle-class or aristocratic public, Wedgwood took advantage of the culture of celebrity to develop a series of porcelain cameos, in a series called "Heads of Illustrious Moderns," listed in his catalogue of 1773.[49] At that period, there were not many contemporary figures and they were listed side by side with Shakespeare, Milton, and Newton. But by 1787 the collection had grown immensely with separate categories; one could find European celebrities Joseph Priestley and Franklin along with Rousseau, Voltaire, and Sarah Siddons.[50] The catalogue was translated into many languages, notably French, attesting to the fact that the market for images of famous people was now European.[51] These cameos, in various formats, could be collected, but also made into rings, or worn as bracelets or pendants.

Idols and Puppets

Another man was to be found in the catalogues of both Wedgwood (Fig. 10) and Sèvres next to Voltaire and Rousseau: Benjamin Franklin, whose wax figure was one of the attractions at the Curtius show. Franklin was, in fact, one of the most represented men in the last quarter of the eighteenth century. When he moved to Paris in 1776, he was already famous throughout Europe, for his work on electricity, but also as the author of *Poor Richard*, a successful almanac.[52] In France, where he had spent time previously on two different occasions and where he had friends (he was an associate member of the Academy of Sciences), an edition of his work was published three years earlier. His arrival at the port in Nantes, announced in the papers, "caused a sensation," as Beaumarchais said.

The celebrity of Franklin, which continued to grow, was accompanied by a wide distribution of his portrait.

Franklin was extremely careful about his public image. He quickly had his portrait painted by Duplessis, a painting that became famous, representing him without a hat, dressed very simply, his jacket casually open; Franklin used it to have a number of engravings made. But it was also copied in other forms: medals, ceramic figurines, terracotta pendants, wax statues. In 1783, Duplessis painted a new version of the portrait, this time with Franklin in a gray suit and tie; this in turn would be recopied many times (Fig. 4).[53] Franklin also had himself sculpted by Caffieri and then by Houdon, two marble busts, of which there were numerous plaster copies (Fig. 5). These representations were in one sense official portraits, authorized by Franklin, and which he wanted distributed because they corresponded to the image he wanted of American insurgents: a simple man, dressed without ostentation, far from European courtly manners. These images were in contrast to the portraits of Franklin during his long visit to England, where he posed in a velvet suit like the British aristocracy. The new image distanced Franklin from French fashion, which he certainly knew how to respect, however, when he was received at court and in polite society.

Franklin well understood the political uses that could be made of his celebrity in favor of the American cause, playing as he did on the public infatuation with his person. But it is striking to see how his image became a fashionable icon to be found in a number of mediums. Jacques-Donatien Le Ray de Chaumont, steward at Les Invalides in Paris, set up a ceramics factory in the Château de Chaumont and commissioned Jean-Baptiste Nini to make a number of terracotta medallions representing Franklin, with variations (with and without glasses, with and without fur cap), which were produced in great quantity and were very successful, many still existing today in numerous collections (Fig. 7). More valuable objects were available, such as ceramic miniatures that were used to decorate candy or snuff boxes, like the one made by François Dumont in 1779 using a portrait painted by Duplessis (Fig. 8). Earthenware and porcelain factories used the Franklin theme not only on miniature statues and cameos, but also on dishes. The Victoria and Albert Museum has a Sèvres cup decorated with the portrait of Franklin (Fig. 9). These objects attest to the popularity of Franklin as an iconic theme since it was now possible to drink tea in a cup or a bowl (Fig. 11) decorated with the face of the great scientist.

Nonetheless, engravings had contributed the most to this diffusion of his image in large sections of the population. The engraving office in the Bibliothèque Nationale de France (BNF) has more than fifty engravings from the eighteenth century with images of Franklin, some beautifully created, sometimes even in color, and others barely a likeness, made using low-cost printing for a market that was growing phenomenally. Here is a list of most of the engravers specializing in portraits of celebrities with strong market potential. Pierre Adrien Le Beau, author of at least a hundred engravings for Esnault and Rapilly, notably several portraits of Marie-Antoinette, but also portraits of writers, artists, actors, and a little portrait of Franklin engraved during the first year of Franklin's visit to Paris. It was announced in the *Gazette de France* on September 22, 1777, and put on sale for twelve *sous* with this simple caption: "Benjamin Franklin, born in New England, Boston, January 17, 1706," and the address of the merchants, "À la Ville de Coutances" (Fig. 6).[54]

This multiplication of Franklin's image astounded him and he wrote to his daughter in June 1779, sending her an engraved medallion made by Nini, saying that his face had become as famous as the face of the moon:

> The clay medallion of me you say you gave to Mr. Hopkinson was the first of the kind made in France. A variety of others have been made since of different sizes; some to be set in lids of snuff boxes, and some so small as to be worn in rings; and the numbers sold are incredible. These, with the pictures, busts, and prints (of which copies upon copies are spread everywhere) have made your father's face as well known as that of the moon, so that he durst not do any thing that would oblige him to run away, as his physiognomy would discover him wherever he should venture to show it. It is said by learned etymologists that the name *Doll*, for the images children play with, is derived from the word *IDOL*; from the number of dolls now made of him, he may be truly said in that sense, to be *i-doll-ized* in this country.[55]

Franklin was amused, certainly, but his lucid and ironic commentary is very interesting. The most immediate result of this massive distribution of portraits and copies of portraits is that they escaped the control of the model. It was no longer, or not just, a case of using images for political propaganda, as with the portraits of royalty. It was the consequence of a new urban culture where the images of celebrities were avidly sought and became a consumer product. By proposing his imaginative etymology linking the idol to a child's toy with a human face, Franklin was joking, but he made clear a public desire to transform the image of a person into multiple objects, even into a toy. He hinted also at an ambiguity: Was the multiplication of his image a compliment or a worrisome threat? It was not an idle thought. He was echoing criticisms of certain contemporaries worried by seeing the portraits of others reduced to the level of a toy or a trinket. A few months earlier, the *Mémoires secrets* had written: "It is fashionable now to have an engraving of M. Franklin on one's mantel-piece," but added: "as one formerly had a puppet: thus, the portrait of this serious person is being derided – a little like the useless trinket which served as a toy thirty years ago."[56] Most of the iconographic studies of Franklin see the distribution of his portraits as a sign of his popularity and a perfect mastery of public communications. However, his peers, like Franklin himself, were very conscious that it is a very thin line between a fashionable image and a toy, the difference between a public idol and a child's doll. Celebrity was an object of both fascination and derision.

This new urban culture of the image had another side which pushed the derision much further: the strong development of caricature throughout the eighteenth century. It not only targeted famous individuals. It readily focused on social and religious types, as in William Hogarth's anti-Jesuit caricatures, without sparing, of course, famous figures in cultural and political life. England, again, had a more rapid development in regard to images. Hogarth gave satirical caricature its respectability, but an entire deluge of satirical images, often crude and carnivalesque, descended on London in the second half of the century.[57] Politicians, aristocrats, and celebrated cultural figures were all openly mocked, their physical faults ridiculed, their sexual indiscretions, real or supposed, the object of rather tawdry jokes. James Gillray and George Cruikshank were two of the most famous caricaturists whose work delighted the English public.

Emma Hamilton, born Emma Lyon, illustrated the double-sided nature of visual culture in regard to celebrity. Nothing predisposed this young woman from a poor family, who began her career as a prostitute in a London brothel, to become one of the most represented women in England at the end of the century. After serving as a model for James Graham, a charlatan who organized spectacles and lectures about sexuality, she became the mistress of several gentlemen from polite society. In 1782, her then lover, Charles Greville, had her portrait painted by George Romney, Reynolds' great rival. The portrait, entitled *Sensibility*, met with immense success, as did the reproduced engraving. From that moment on, Hamilton posed more than two hundred times for Romney who created in following years a number of other famous paintings portraying her as Circe or as a weaver (Fig. 2).[58] Unlike actresses, Emma was not painted because she was famous, she became famous because she was painted. Her face was her fame before being a name.

The second phase of her notoriety dates from her affair with Lord Nelson. After marrying Lord Hamilton, the ambassador to Naples, in 1791, Emma frequented the court of the Bourbons, and then became the mistress of Nelson, whom she met in Naples two years later. Caricatures multiplied after that, mocking the strange *ménage à trois* that included her husband, an old ambassador, and her lover, a national hero. After the death of Nelson and the progressive decline of Lady Hamilton, many caricaturists ridiculed her plumpness. Friedrich Rehberg in 1794 published a series of portraits of Emma Hamilton in different poses representing statues from Antiquity, showing her beauty and her grace; thirteen years later, James Gillray published twelve cartoons parodying those images and in which Emma Hamilton is shown as obese and totally deformed (Fig. 3).[59]

Although traditional political caricature, that created by the political enemies of Louis XIV, for instance, was fundamentally antagonistic to the official iconographic forms, the caricatures which targeted celebrities had a more complex relationship to the model. Sometimes, as with Gillray, the caricatures were brutally satirical. But they could also simply reinforce the meaning of positive images: for example, in the case of actresses and courtesans whose portraits played on their beauty and the desire they aroused, the caricatures revealed, sometimes crudely, the implied erotic burden. Inversely, when the transgression was slight in regard to the classic modes of portraiture, it was sometimes difficult to know when the imagery was favorable or satirical. This was the case with the series of nude portraits made of Voltaire, painted by Huber, which was disliked by the patriarch of Ferney, because he saw in it an unpleasant satire whereas Huber meant to humanize his model and nourish his celebrity. The multiplication of celebrity portraits, notably those made in less elegant mediums, wax statues or everyday objects, threatened at any moment to make celebrities objects of derision.

Caricature thus had an ambivalent relationship to celebrity. Even today, for a public person in France to have his or her figure on the *Guignols*, a satirical television program, is both a trial and a consecration. Puppet shows representing famous people began, in fact, in the middle of the eighteenth century, under Samuel Foote. He himself had become famous by doing imitations in his Haymarket shows, at the end of the 1740s. His success rested on the celebrity of the persons he imitated: he played on their status, notably by having his shows written up in newspapers and by accompanying them with jokes, never hesitating to make fun of his subjects, joking about how short Garrick was and his well-known taste for celebrity.[60] Some did not relish the consequences of their celebrity: Samuel Johnson supposedly threatened to beat Foote if he put Johnson in his show as he had intended to do. In 1773, Foote produced a puppet show representing famous celebrities of his time, which aroused great public enthusiasm according to *Gentleman's Magazine*.[61] According to a letter from Horace Walpole, Garrick supposedly paid Foote to leave him out of the "puppet show," which nonetheless did not stop Foote from saying to a woman who asked if the puppets would be bigger than life: "Oh dear Madam, no [...] not much above the size of Garrick!"[62] Foote also attacked famous London aristocracy, putting on stage the Duchess of Kingston, whose trial for bigamy was all over the London newspapers.

Caricatures of famous people only made sense in regard to all the representations, visual or textual, which circulated in the public sphere making up their public personalities. Kitty Fisher, one of the most famous English courtesans of the eighteenth century, whose portrait was painted many times by Reynolds between 1759 and 1765 and whose face was so sought after it even decorated the little round watchpapers placed between the inner and outer cases of pocket watches, was, at the same time, the object of dozens of satirical pamphlets, such as *The Juvenile Adventures of Miss Kitty F...R*, *The Adventures of the Celebrated Miss Kitty F...R*, or *Miss Kitty F...R's Miscellany*. These developed, sometimes as a game and sometimes shamelessly, the sexual innuendos that the portraits of Reynolds suggested and which had made of her a figure in popular culture, a woman whose name still exists in nursery rhymes.[63] As early as March 1759, even before the paintings of Reynolds had been shown publicly, she published in the press and in engraving shops an announcement denouncing the public exhibit of paintings with her as a subject. "She had been abused in the public papers, exposed in Print shops, and to wind up the whole, some Wretches, mean, ignorant and venal, would impose upon the public, by daring to publish her Memoirs."[64] One might wonder if this protestation was sincere or if, at this early date, it was a publicity trick aimed at publicly jump-starting her budding and potentially scandalous celebrity.

"Heroes of the Hour"

In England, a number of newspapers were dedicated mainly to cultural and high society news. The prototype was the *Gentleman's Magazine*, first published in 1731 and made up of reprinted newspaper articles, literary and political news, and rumors about fashionable people. Its complete title, *Gentleman's Magazine, or the Tradesman's Monthly Intelligence*, made clear its readiness to connect with a hybrid public, both the elites of society and the merchants and traders who made up a large part of the new middle class in London.[65] Along the same lines, starting in 1769, *Town and Country Magazine* was published, a thick monthly review in which readers could find, all jumbled together, a quick survey of politics in Europe, some educational articles about history or culture dedicated to great historical figures, announcements for coming shows and books, letters from readers, and a number of anecdotes about London life. One of the established specialties of *Town and Country Magazine* was the revelation of secret love among members of polite society. Each issue contained what the magazine called *tête-à-têtes*, portraits side-by-side of a man and a woman whose affair was then recounted in detail. Names were partially hidden thanks to a process of leaving out several letters but in such a way that most readers could identify them. The magazine played on the connection between the image and the text, on the fame of the people from polite society and those from the world of spectacle, as well as the sulfurous nature of the news story. In January 1780, the annual issue of the review appeared with a frontispiece representing a woman, outraged, holding a copy of *Town and Country Magazine* that had just revealed her love life, under the mocking regard of Mercury and Momus, thus making the link between news and satire.[66]

The political press and the news in general did not escape this development; they made more and more room for rumors about the personal life of those in the public eye. Contemporary newspapers, which had few journalists in the modern sense of the term, counted on news furnished by readers, contributors paid by the paragraph or by people interested in giving their opinion about current scandals or announcing an overnight success. Most newspapers thus offered a mix of public announcements, rumors, and disparate viewpoints, with some attempting to sway opinion. Far from publishing discourse specifically for readers produced by professionals and news experts, the press was instead a large public sounding board consisting of myriad conversations which provided London society with food for thought.[67] In this way, the press managed to give such stories credibility and an apparent objectivity, which meant publicity. Whereas word of mouth circulation of the news, indiscretions, and rumors from within the heart of polite society assured credibility among the upper class, the publication of rumors in the press meant public readership, by both actors and spectators of the news event.

The English situation could be considered a specific case, in the sense that the press was more developed there than in the rest of Europe and benefited from greater editorial freedom. In France, for reasons of censorship, the principal cultural magazine, *Mercure de France*, prudently stopped at announcements of official events, publication of poetry, and extracts of new works. Numerous newspapers were published outside the kingdom in order to bypass the censors, but they were primarily publishing political news. In 1777, publication of the first French daily, the *Journal de Paris*, did not greatly change things, in spite of its success (there were immediately two and a half thousand subscribers, then five thousand, who received a news sheet every morning, printed during the night). Connected as it was to governmental and reformer groups aimed at both upper-class society and middle-class merchants and professionals, the newspaper wanted a kind of "casual conversation" with Parisians, as well as to cover the news. In their leaflet which appeared in October

1776 the editors announced their wish to publish news about famous people. But after the first issues got a stormy reaction (the newspaper folded at the end of a few weeks and did not appear again until after being subjected to heavy censorship), the *Journal de Paris* returned to a more standard formula, much more prudent, filled with literary news, advertisements for new businesses, announcements of spectacles, and edifying anecdotes.

Given these conditions, news of famous people had to find another way of circulating, mainly in the form of handbills. The public was eager for such news, as attested by the remarkable success of the *Mémoires secrets pour servir à l'histoire de la république des lettres*. These bulletins, published early in 1777 and up until the Revolution, have intrigued historians for a long time, revealing numerous anecdotes found in the thirty-six volumes covering the years 1762 to 1787. Recently, the volumes have been studied more systematically.[68] The nature of their publication remains mysterious. First, falsely attributed to Louis Petit de Bachaumont, who in reality had no part in them, they seem to have been in fact published by two polygraphers, Pidansat de Mairobert and then Mouffle d'Angerville, starting out with "handbills," written texts circulated secretly in Paris. One of the strangest aspects of the first *Mémoires secrets* volumes is that they were published fifteen years after the events they related. Published in 1777, they covered the years from 1762 to 1775. Readers who hurried to buy these first volumes were reading news that was singularly out of date. The gap narrowed and the following volumes appeared about a year after the events. The time difference remains surprising for a work that was based on the distribution and a summary of the news. This did not, however, hinder the success of the *Mémoires secrets*, which revealed both the keen interest of the French public, which did not have at its disposal the same resources as the English public, and also the time difference in respect to the news compared to what we have become accustomed to with contemporary media. Moreover, one of the fundamental aspects of the *Mémoires secrets* was describing the societal and cultural life of the capital in terms of "fashion." It showcased, ironically, passing fads, both passionate and short-lived, for objects, for practices, for people, and it is possible that the publication's lag-time paradoxically reinforced the charm of these gazettes. The ambivalence that the editors showed in regard to fashion, which was both an object of criticism and at the same time a source of interest for readers, was enriched by the slight temporal distance: readers were reading fashion articles about things that were no longer in fashion and news about celebrities who were sometimes already forgotten. The effect of social mimicry, accelerated in a large city like Paris, was thus put in perspective by the delay in publication.[69]

One of the great charms of the *Mémoires secrets* was giving readers the – sometimes scandalous – news about the lives of celebrities which they did not find in official publications like the *Mercure* or even in the *Journal de Paris*. Editors justified this editorial practice by arguing that the people they wrote about were already famous and they wanted even more publicity. So it was in no way transgressive to contribute to their desire for publicity:

> We only highlight people who are already ridiculous or who have triumphed by their vices; and then, by offering to posterity, for their instruction, their follies and atrocities, we are simply serving their strongest wish, it would seem, to make a splash, to be talked about, to be an overnight success, in a word, to become famous, by whatever means possible at whatever price.[70]

This reasoning anticipated that of contemporary tabloids, which readily affirm that they only mirror a culture of exhibitionism and celebrity while maintaining a very ambiguous relationship with the stars whom they affect to disdain while simultaneously writing about their private lives for a curious public.[71] The vocabulary used for the new topic of celebrity was very revealing, and clearly distinct from the topic of glory: celebrities aroused public curiosity, desiring above all to be talked about, to generate gossip. Their notoriety was a media phenomenon, totally disconnected from actual merit, which the *Mémoires secrets* records, feeds, and critiques. The ironic expression "overnight success" clearly denoted the displacement between celebrity and the heroic model, the latter meant to be lasting, while celebrity was a simple, fleeting event. The expression also registered the ambiguity inherent in these publications, which were both complicit in and critical of the budding culture of celebrity, pretending to denounce the practice and at the same time encouraging it.[72]

This ambivalence reveals the inadequacy of one Enlightenment definition of public space as "criticism." The success of the *Mémoires secrets* was based less on the public use of critical reason than on the emergence of public curiosity and consumerism, for which the life of famous people, their images as well as anecdotes about them, had become objects of consumption, merchandise. In the *Mémoires secrets*, this merchandising of the public face of famous people had the effect of putting short stories, political scandals, and anecdotes about polite society on the same level. Criticism of the Academy's painting exhibits went hand-in-hand with literary anecdotes, miscellaneous news stories, numerous rumors about theater life, and, in particular, the love affairs of currently popular actors and actresses. Until the death of Voltaire, the *Mémoires secrets* offered a sort of journal of his life, the works he published or those that were attributed to him, the visitors he received. He was, by far, the most quoted person, with 668 references, twice as many as anyone else.

Listing those individuals who were the most often cited gives a good idea of the most famous people of the period, who included personalities from various levels of society. Among the fifteen individuals mentioned more than a hundred times, one finds writers, and in particular those who took pleasure in provoking scandal, like Rousseau or Linguet – the latter having the advantage of also being a lawyer and being involved in a number of court cases about which the *Mémoires secrets* reported the vagaries; politicians like Necker or Maupeou, princes like the Duc d'Orléans or the Comte d'Artois, an ecclesiastic (the unfortunate Cardinal de Rohan, caught up in Marie-Antoinette's tortuous "necklace affair" – see chapter 6), and actors, like Mlle Clairon. On the other hand, men or women who played an important role in Parisian cultural and society life but were not in the public eye, for example housewives who maintained the main salons of the capital, are rarely cited. Mme Geoffrin and Mme Necker only appear about twenty times in the whole series, many fewer times than Mlle Clairon (103 mentions), the singer Sophie Arnould (97 times), or the actress Mlle Raucourt (71 times).[73]

The presence of actresses (and also actors, but to a lesser degree: Lekain appears roughly fifty times) is not surprising. It confirms the role that they played in the budding celebrity culture. In the *Mémoires secrets*, they provided a permanent source of news for the culture chronicle, that of new shows, and for scandal sheets, the secret loves of actresses. Mlle Clairon and Mlle Raucourt were given praise for their public performances and a detailed, though non-verifiable, account of their private escapades.[74] This double curiosity indicates the interest that the public had in actresses. But it encouraged, or at least accompanied, a permanent passage from admiration to voyeurism.

For newspapers, the death of famous people is obviously one of the most notable events. Famous people are those whose deaths are announced in newspapers. But there is another aspect to the question: Since when have newspapers announced the death of celebrities and not just that of sovereigns and men of state? As a journalistic genre, necrology first appeared in England in Restoration journals, where the memory of the faithful servants of the Stuarts was saluted, and then at the beginning of the eighteenth century, in a curious periodical entitled *The Post-Angel*, where one of the four rubrics was dedicated to recounting the life and death of those who had just died, whether it was Queen Marie or Captain Kidd, the famous Scottish pirate hanged in London in 1701.[75] *The Post-Angel* existed for only two years; it was after 1730 that the necrology genre really developed, in particular in the *Gentleman's*

Magazine, which gave the genre respectability by every month offering its readership a highly colorful article about the life of famous people who had just died.

A new periodical was founded in France in 1767 entirely dedicated to necrology, aptly titled *Nécrologe des hommes célèbres de France*. Its editor, Charles Palissot, who became famous a few years earlier through his attacks on Enlightenment philosophers, was intent on preserving the memory of great contemporary individuals: "Poets, orators, historians, etc., artists, sculptors, musicians, architects, etc., famous actors and actresses, all individuals in fact who during their life merited the attention of their century will receive in this journal a tribute of homage and sadness, capable of arousing emulation by those who might want to copy their example and distinguish themselves in the same careers." Presented in this way, an obituary appears to resemble a eulogy for great individuals, but it is distinguished by its insistence that the famous individuals who had just died were contemporaries of the public, embodied in the readers and the publishers of *Nécrologe*. Soliciting family and friends of the dead to furnish the journal with "anecdotes" about the dead person's life, Palissot commented: "Know that we were the contemporaries of these famous individuals we have written about; that we personally knew most of them; that we were witness to the different emotions produced by their work."[76] There is a difference here between the classical model of illustrious men, where emulation is much stronger because of the distance in time which caused the individual to grow in stature, thus making him a model, and modern celebrity, which relies on temporal proximity and even contemporaneousness. The death of a famous individual became a news element, in the Gabriel Tarde sense: a collective consciousness of being part of a public by concentrating collective attention on the same event. For readers, what drew them to the obituary of a famous person was not so much his or her exceptional life, but rather the retrospective narrative of the article, the moment a celebrity who had marked his or her era died and whose brilliant life focused public curiosity ("we were witness to the different emotions produced by their work"). A victim of its success, the *Nécrologe des hommes célèbres de France* was bought in the 1780s by the *Journal de Paris*, which up until then had a rubric "Burials" with a list of the deceased but no real obituaries.

Necrologies came at a meeting point in history for different forms of notoriety. They were dedicated to artists, scientists, actors, who, while alive, were reputed in their fields and in death were considered to be major intellectual and cultural figures, potential candidates for posthumous glory. Some, like Rousseau or Voltaire (included in the 1770 volume of the *Nécrologe*), do in fact attain this glory. Others (Antoine de Laurès and Mme de Marron, for instance, in the following volume) are overshadowed and forgotten. The publication of these obituaries in the press distinguished them from academic eulogies which the Academy pronounced at the death of an academician. What qualified someone for an obituary notice in the press was not that he or she belonged to a scientific group, nor that he or she had a certain reputation within that group, nor the personal judgment of the editor about his or her talent, but rather an assumption that the readers already knew the person's name and would be curious to read an article about that person's life when he or she died. Newspapers did not publish obituaries about great artists and great scientists; they published obituaries about those the paper had talked about when they were alive. The only requirement was that the public already knew these "famous people."

The obituary is basically linked to the press, in the sense that it rests on the idea of an article that is immediately distributed. It is clearly distinguished from the epitaph, another kind of writing which has long been associated with death.[77] The epitaph is intended to be visible for a long time to the limited readership of those who are physically present at the tomb where it is engraved. Inversely, the obituary has a much larger distribution, but a shorter life span, printed in an ephemeral medium, the newspaper. The epitaph is aimed at posterity; it concisely summarizes the exemplary aspects of a life for those who come later. The obituary, in a narrative, addresses a contemporary public curious to learn details about a life the principal traits of which are already known, and to share this communal event.

Private Lives, Public Figures

With the advent of obituaries, the press left the area of anecdote and daily chronicles and entered the domain of biographical writing. This type of writing, in fact, was profoundly transformed by the culture of celebrity. Up until then, the writing about lives, those of kings, of saints, of illustrious men, was ruled by a principle of excellence in line with the idea of glory. It was a matter of recounting glorious lives through exploits and heroic deeds. The genres associated with these biographical writings (the panegyric, hagiography, eulogies, funeral orations) had in common that they were based on a series of edifying stereotypes and interchangeable events.

At the end of the eighteenth century, a new way of recounting the lives of great people emerged. The word "biography" was found in the writing of John Aubrey, who edited a series of short biographies about his contemporaries.[78] But Aubrey did not publish *Brief Lives*, the title given to the text by editors a century later. It was actually in the eighteenth century that biographical writing changed, as both a literary and an editorial genre, accompanied by deep reflection on the way to write about a human life. This new form of biography was no longer reserved for great historical figures, but concerned all sorts of individuals whose lives were of interest to the reader. The narrative was not limited to public actions, but included a variety of private anecdotes, even intimate ones, which were chosen not for their edifying instruction but because they brought to light what was usually hidden from the public. The chief novelty adhering to biography was that it focused on the singular trajectory of a unique individual, the contradictions in his or her personality, and thus arrived, one way or another, at that person's subjectivity.

This new writing was tied to the emergence of the modern novel, which was based on the assumption that all lives, even the most humble, were worthy of being related.[79] We know that this development evolved in a very significant way through a change in the word "hero," which designated the main character in a novel, even when this character was not heroic in the traditional sense of the term. Distinguishing itself from classic literary genres, which were based on the exemplary actions of their characters, the novel assumed that readers were interested in the details, *a priori* insignificant, of the life of an ordinary individual who resembled them. With the romance novel, which was a success in France as it was in England, and then throughout Europe, from Richardson to Goethe by way of Rousseau, the idea that readers could access the intimate feelings of a character whose life was being told to them instilled itself as a new imperative at the heart of European culture. This had been prepared for in the second half of the seventeenth century with works like *La Princesse de Clèves*, which was based on public interest in the psychological questions and feelings of a particular character.[80] With the success of *Clarissa*, *La Nouvelle Héloïse*, and *The Sorrows of Young Werther*, the phenomenon became much larger: thousands of readers identified, sobbing all the while, with characters in novels, with their domestic miseries and their emotional tribulations. Diderot would put forth this theory in his "Éloge de Richardson."[81] The evolution of the novel, a major development in eighteenth-century European cultural history, fed the culture of "sensibility" which deluged European elites. It also helped familiarize readers with narrative forms they would later enjoy in historical tales and biography.[82] One author embodied this new biographical writing: Samuel Johnson, author of the remarkable *Lives*, who became himself the object of a famous eighteenth-century biography, *The Life of Samuel Johnson*, by James Boswell.

As an author, Johnson began with a masterpiece in 1744 when he published *The Life of Mr Richard Savage*, a poet and playwright with whom he had been friends and who had recently died in great poverty.

In spite of his poetic talent, Savage was known above all for his dissolute life, his abuse of alcohol, for murder, and for excessive debts which put him in prison. He was an iconic figure in bohemian London, half-way between poet and criminal; there was nothing of the illustrious man about him. Johnson's aim was not to offer an example; to the contrary, he made no effort at all to hide or play down Savage's faults, his mistakes and his vices. Instead, it was a matter of paying tribute to the memory of his friend, his companion in drunken nocturnal wanderings, and also to seize the implacable complexity of a destiny like that of Savage's, whose talents had led to his degradation. Of course the moral perspective was not absent. Savage's life exemplified the ambivalence of a human life, nourished by both talent and weakness, made up of success and failure, right up to the unhappy end. It was also written to put into question the capacity of a biographer to make judgments. No one could judge Savage, and there was no more sense in judging a great man than a criminal. Savage, Johnson wrote, was, above all, a biographical eccentric whom one wanted to understand, someone who could interest and move readers, who would not leave them indifferent. Johnson himself insisted on the personal link he had with the man whom he had decided to write about, the intimate knowledge on which his writing was based. *The Life of Mr Richard Savage* was the result of documents that the author had patiently collected, but most of all direct and personal knowledge that gave his account credibility.

Johnson emphasized several times the importance in biographical writing of anecdotes drawn from private life. The moral interest of biography had not disappeared, but the real value of an individual was now to be sought in the "the minute details of daily life,"[83] those more viable indications of his personality and his merits. This important development, ripe with consequences, stresses the idea that private life is more authentic, more interesting, than the public accounts of an individual. In the spirit of Johnson, this inversion of the public/private hierarchy corresponds to speculation about what constitutes the value of a human life. Part of the success of biographies throughout the centuries was this increase in domestic anecdotes that responded to the public's desire to get as close as possible to the private life of celebrities, through the aegis of witnesses.

Johnson was taken at his word. His most faithful disciple in this regard was none other than his friend and biographer James Boswell, who became his friend, it so happens, just so he could become his biographer. For twenty years, Boswell lived as a member of the Johnson entourage, scrupulously noting his acts, his gestures, his declarations, and anecdotes about his daily life, to the point that his biography was "a perfect literary copy of his life, faithful to a dizzying degree."[84] Born into a very good Scottish family, Boswell was capricious and appealing, afflicted with a depressive and romantic temperament, willfully narcissistic and shameless, and always looking for admirable figures he could be close to. After being educated in Edinburgh, he took a grand tour of Europe, during which he never missed the chance to visit celebrities associated with Enlightenment Europe, from Voltaire to Rousseau. Through flattery, he bonded with Rousseau, identifying with him to such a degree that he seduced Rousseau's woman companion, Thérèse Levasseur. Then he left for Corsica, attracted by the patriotic insurrection, whose merits Rousseau had been praising. There he met Pascal Paoli – who at first was suspicious of this young Scot who noted down his conversations and whom he suspected of being a spy – later becoming friends with him and his most ardent defender. On his return to the Continent, Boswell published his first book, which became an international success: *An Account of Corsica* was the history of an island, a travelogue and eulogistic portrait of Paoli.[85] Boswell perfected a biographical form that came close to reportage, not hesitating to put himself in the scene, and helping to make Paoli known throughout Europe.

On his return to England, Boswell found in Johnson a friend and a subject, which allowed him to bring together his fascination for famous people, his sentimentalism, and his taste for quasi-ethnographic observations of the new urban culture which was spreading through London.[86] His *Life of Samuel Johnson*, published in 1791, was a masterpiece. It represented both a monument raised to the memory of the writer and testimony to their friendship. Boswell avoided the panegyric and sought above all to give an account of the personality of Johnson, without hiding his dark side. He plunged the reader into the daily life of the writer, including long conversations. He did not hesitate to put himself in the scene as friend and biographer, becoming himself a historical person being written about, but also a researcher who completed his memoir by sounding out those who had known Johnson well. Thus, the intimacy he maintained throughout was the legitimate basis for his writing, because this life of Johnson was not written from a place of moral objectivity, nor in the name of a grateful community, but was the testimony of a man who had admired and lived closely with him. When Johnson died in 1784, Boswell was already pushing to publish his journal of their voyage to the Hebrides. Although Johnson had written up successful geographical, literary, and philosophical thoughts about the trip, Boswell's account was more a journal about their voyage, based on the recounting of daily events, and with a biographical perspective, reconstituting the totality of a singular life. This was based obviously on Johnson's celebrity and on public curiosity, to which Boswell explicitly addressed himself, but it did imply a profound transformation in the concept of biographical writing.

The *Life of Samuel Johnson* became a major literary work. But this *chef-d'oeuvre* should not hide the increase, throughout the century, of biographies about famous individuals. which became a veritable publishing genre. Once again, English actors were at the forefront. At the beginning of the seventeenth century the first biographies of actors appeared. But it was especially after the 1730s that biographies of great stage figures, sometimes romanticized, knew a huge success, in writing often linked with satire and scandal.[87] In France, because of the return of censorship, this type of writing clearly belonged in the libelous category. Mayeur de Saint-Paul, himself an actor, published several collections of anecdotes in his *Chroniqueur désoeuvré* (1781), then *Le Vol plus haut, ou l'espion des principaux théâtre de la capitale* (1784), whose subtitle promised readers *a short history of actors and actresses from these same theaters, enriched with philosophical observations and amusing anecdotes.*

Besides actors, another category of famous individuals became the subject of biographical writing in spite of coming from a lower, even infamous, social level: criminals. Public curiosity for the life of brigands and criminals was not new, but it now veered away from one-off write-ups.[88] Consider Cartouche, arrested and executed in 1721 by the Parisian police. Between his arrest and his death, he spent six months in prison, during which time he managed to escape before being caught again, and numerous articles and images about him circulated in the press. Interest in Cartouche was largely due to how the police behaved and their efforts to build an entirely negative image of him, that of a dangerous gang leader, the head of organized crime. Parisians, to the contrary, seemed to react by inventing a positive brigand, courageous and generous, handing out money stolen from the rich and rebelling against the police. One could see the traditional mechanisms of the rumor mill at work based on a common culture of opposition to power, but the Cartouche story revealed above all new forms of public celebrity developing in Paris at the time of the Regency. During Cartouche's trial, while he awaited his judgment in prison, two plays were enacted in Parisian theaters. On October 20, the Commedia Italiana put on a little play, *Arlequin-Cartouche*, whose text no longer exists but which consisted no doubt of a series of improvisations about the figure of the brigand, relying on the public's familiarity with his persona. The *Mercure de France* commented: "We have so often talked about Cartouche that everyone knows that his name refers to a young man about twenty-six years old, head of a band of robbers, famous for the number of his thefts and murders, and even more so for his cleverness, his courage, and his tricks for evading the law."[89]

The next day, the Comédie-Française staged *Cartouche ou les Voleurs*, a play by Marc-Antoine Legrand that was published at the same time.

The play attracted "an astonishing crowd," according to the attorney Barbier, until it was stopped by the police after thirteen performances. How can this tardy censorship be explained? It is possible that the play from the start was an initiative by the authorities, who wanted to show Cartouche in a negative light and also show their efficiency in arresting him, and who were then surprised by the enthusiasm and sympathy demonstrated by the audience.[90] How to understand this turn of events, this empathy by the public for a felon presented as a dangerous criminal? Some historians read this in terms of political culture, which made the big-hearted bandit a symbol for the public's refusal of police order imposed by monarchs in all big European cities.[91] But this does not explain why public infatuation with criminals affected all categories of the Parisian population, according to numerous witnesses, including those who had everything to gain from police protection. On the other hand, one might hypothesize that Parisian interest in the figure of Cartouche came less from an acceptance of criminality than from a mix of curiosity and empathy which celebrity aroused. An extract from the *Mercure* points out the cumulative and self-sustaining character of the narratives about Cartouche. Spectators hurried to see the plays because he was already much talked about. One of the mainsprings for the success of these plays, but also the success of various texts about his life, was that they encouraged the feeling that Parisians constituted a public which was interested in the same things at the same time, read the same news, and attended the same plays. At the end of 1721, the *Histoire de la vie et du procès de Cartouche*[92] appeared along with engravings representing his arrest and showing him in his cell. Some of the engravings simply reused the old portraits of brigands, but in order to convince buyers it was implied they were a "true portrait of Cartouche drawn from life in his cell."[93] The most spectacular image and the most authentic is doubtless that of the body of Cartouche, exhibited to the public by the executioner himself, for a price. A wax mask was made by M. Desnoue which was also put on public display.[94]

Cartouche's celebrity was not restricted to Paris, or even to France. Portrait engravings were made in Germany. Legrand's play was translated into English and Dutch. The Cartouche story fit perfectly with the new criminal literature in England, emphasizing the role of individualized brigands, as opposed to traditional literature about beggars that focused on the collective nature of robber bands. Jack Sheppard and Jonathan Wild were the two greatest criminal figures in England during the 1720s. The first, arrested for theft, became famous after several escapes from Newgate prison. The English newspapers chronicled the arrest of Sheppard in October 1724 and the next month the *Evening Post* announced the sale of two engravings (six pence each) representing him in prison, as well as the itinerary of his escape. After the second arrest, he was executed, aged twenty-two, in November 1724. The day of his execution, a brochure, edited no doubt by Daniel Defoe, was published entitled *A Narrative of the Life of Jack Sheppard*.[95]

Starting in 1750, the lives of criminals became a successful publishing genre. The year of the arrest and execution of Mandrin, in 1755, a number of biographies of the smuggler appeared, as well as a play, *La Mort de Mandrin*, performed in Marseille in August, less than three months after his torture in Valence.[96]

Criminal lives, sometimes very admonitory, sometimes more empathetic, played on the reader's fascination with a life of crime and misery as well as on the expectations aroused by the fame of the brigand, creating discussions and brochures. The author of the *Histoire de la vie et du procès de Louis-Dominique Cartouche* had already invoked the "incredible avidity" of the public:

> The Public welcomed with incredible avidity anything that concerned Cartouche, and the name alone of this famous villain on the title of a book or a play was enough to sell the first and insure a prodigious success for the other. It was not only in France that there was interest in criminals. In Holland, in England, in Germany, there was the same enthusiasm as found in France: if a gazette said anything at all about Cartouche, other than that he continued to steal or they were looking for him in vain, etc., people willingly believed whatever was said because they always preferred a vague piece of news to nothing at all. Consequently, people hoped to one day have the pleasure of reading the History of this thief: even more so since it was based on individual memories of him, on details from his trial and on stories that all of Paris had heard from his own mouth, and with which he entertained anyone who came to see him.[97]

The irrepressible curiosity of the public, the superficiality of official information, the desire to know the real story of a famous contemporary: the rhetoric of celebrity already seemed to be established. In the case of criminals, public fascination was fed through a combination of repulsion and attraction, moral reprobation and secret envy, aroused by individuals who chose to live outside society, to transgress civil law and sometimes moral law. As one biographer wrote a few years later about another famous criminal, Henri-Augustin Trumeau, who could in no way be seen as a hero because he was nothing but a villainous poisoner: "All people have a natural desire to penetrate the heart of the guilty, to uncover their tricks, to see their audacity and to follow their dark path." Their death, in particular, seems to fascinate the reader, and here the author also uses the word "avidity": "One watches with a sort of avidity the effects on different organizations and on the various personalities of convicted criminals, regarding their fear of death and the certitude of dying."[98]

By progressively reducing the moral dimension in favor of "avid" curiosity about the singular life of an individual, by organizing documentary material around the thread of a biographical story, by loudly proclaiming the "true" nature of the story, these criminal lives created a transition between traditional chapbook literature and a new biographical genre, that of "private lives," which flourished especially in the second half of the eighteenth century in France, where it answered a public expectation and did not have its equivalent in the press. Generally studied as political calumny and clandestine literature, these "private lives" were, at the beginning, placed in the category of newly defined biographical writing.[99] Different from texts that were clearly pamphleteering and sometimes pornographic, like the *Gazetier cuirassé* de Théveneau de Morande, "private lives" offered an ambivalent form of reading, based much more on curiosity, sometimes even empathy, rather than exposé. Above all, they belonged explicitly to the category of biography: it was a matter not of gathering scabrous anecdotes about a group of courtesans, as in a libel case, but of recounting the life of a famous individual.

"Private lives" were different from the lives of illustrious individuals who had dominated secular biographical writing since the Renaissance, because they concerned contemporaries, either still living or just deceased, and they were not about great people from the past; they were based on anecdotes about domestic affairs and little details more than on memorable feats; they were aimed not at moral exemplarity, but rather at curiosity. As the name indicates, they were above all based on the contrast between public and private life and thus on the desire to unmask a hidden part of the lives of public men and women. The idea that certain individuals lived in the public spotlight helped organize the narrative and editorial logic behind such writings. The guiding principle was that women and men have private lives, which they hide from view, and this in some way explains their public actions or, at least, clarifies their personalities somewhat, so private lives must be revealed to a curious public.

The expansion of these "private lives" into a publishing genre corresponds precisely to a development in the idea of "public" and "private." In the seventeenth century, *public* designated the entire political body and, by extension, all actions by those who officially represented this political body, meaning the king and those magistrates who acted in his name. The king alone had the authority to "publish," to render public. From this perspective, that which was opposed to the public was not the private, but the "particular," that which concerned each person as an individual and not as a member of the political body. During the second half of the seventeenth century and especially in the eighteenth century,

80

a double evolution profoundly modified the meaning of this word. The word "public" started to refer to all the spectators together at a theater play, all the readers of a published work, all those who heard the widely circulated news.[100] Cultural historians, following the intuitions of Jürgen Habermas, strongly insisted on the fact that this development provided the public with the competency to make judgments, a legitimate right to evaluate the merits of a tragedy, to gauge the truth of a news piece, the guilt of a criminal suspect, the merits of a political decision. This evolution was the birth of the literary public, of public opinion, by way of a process that Habermas called the politicization of the literary public sphere.[101]

Another development came out of this new concept: the distinction, at the core of all human action, between the public dimension and the private dimension. Public was no longer the opposite of individual but rather private, that is to say, the domestic, the familial, the intimate. Now, the boundary was crossed between that which was known to everyone and that which was hidden, following along the line of secrecy. The word "public" designated the objects which were widely distributed, notably through the printed word and therefore available to everyone. The private, on the other hand, was not known, either because its contents did not interest anyone or because it was consciously hidden. Even more than with the recent definition of public, "private" as an aspect of human activity was a new category. A number of works at the end of the Ancien Régime tried to make it into a category of historical writing.[102] Between the two, there was a third category that dealt with "society" news known only by a few, circulated in certain circles but not accessible to everyone, not because it was willingly kept secret but because the information circuit it was based on was restricted.[103]

Given this new definition of public, which was no longer the opposite of individual but of private, all people, including the poorest, had a public life. All that mattered, for instance, was that one be involved in an event reported in the press. On the other hand, the king now insisted on having a private life, one free of constant images and public perusal. Even for an individual, the line between private and public was not written in stone, and it took the bourgeoisie a long time in the nineteenth century to stabilize and make the boundaries acceptable, and then to establish legally, in the twentieth century, the protection of private life.[104] Certainly, sexual or family life was obviously part of the private domain, contrasting with political acts or printed works, which seemed just as obviously to be part of the public domain. But because the distinction between public and private was less a matter of difference between spheres of activity than between a degree of disclosure, in other words *publicity*, in which information was the object, the definition was always susceptible to change, as we see today, in the endless debates about the legitimate limits concerning the right to information about the private life of politicians. The concept of "private life" is clearly based on the promise to make public that which is private. There are two arguments used to legitimate this proposition. The first states that private actions reveal the hidden motive behind public actions. The second suggests that the lives of celebrities are totally publishable because they are of interest to anyone who is curious. It is against this extended concept of celebrity that the rule of law later recognized the "right to a private life," as distinct from making defamation an offense.

Most of these "private lives" were full of criticism, even polemical, and targeted political figures. But it was not systematically the case. For example, in 1788, a few weeks after the death of Buffon, a *Vie privée du comte de Buffon* was published by Chevalier Aude, who had been his secretary for the last two years of his life and hurried to publish a series of intimate anecdotes about the great naturalist. Buffon at the end of his life enjoyed real celebrity. His *Histoire naturelle* had been one of the greatest book store successes of the century and the press regularly announced the sale of new portraits of the author.[105] Having retired to Montbard, he continued to write, receiving guests at the same time. In the early pages, Aude defined his subject: "It is only about his private life that I dare to take up your time: his lifestyle, his habits, his domestic behavior and routines."[106] The reader will not find any commentary on Buffon's work, no discussion of his magnum opus, but rather details of his intimate domestic, even sexual, life.

> As soon as he lifted his pen, I timidly withdrew; but I silently awaited the moment that he left his office, to watch what he would do and say with his friends, his relatives, his attorney, his priest, this man who had just been examining general theories about all human beings and calculating infinity. I will tell all, the hour he awoke, the way he dressed, his meals, his witticisms, his loves, or, if you prefer, his joys; because that was everything to him.

These anecdotes, Aude said, would charm "those who love to compare themselves to such a man when he has reached a degree of celebrity which focuses all the eyes of Europe on him."[107]

The result was curious. After a classic opening which offers a narrative biographical tone – "George Louis Le Clerk, the Comte de Buffon, Seigneur de Montbard, [...] born at Montbard, September 7, 1707" – the author strings together the most trivial anecdotes along with the most prestigious commentaries: the way Buffon got rid of rats which infested his chateau side-by-side with the marks of esteem the great man received from the Russian empress and from Prince Henry of Prussia. We also learn about how he got up in the morning and his taste for young prostitutes, as well as a correspondence between Joseph Aude and Mme Necker concerning him. This disparate collection, although it adds nothing to the glory of Buffon, claims to be an attestation in favor of the "immortal man that the European world of science has just lost," but who was also "the best and the most tender of husbands, a model for friends and fathers" whom the author had "the good luck to be close to."[108] Such a "private life" was not about the political or the scandalous. It had to do with the fact that Buffon, having acquired the status of celebrity, was *a priori* the focus of public curiosity and nothing concerning him escaped attention; the public expected revelations based on first-hand information.

Three years earlier, Marie Jean Hérault de Séchelles had published such an account based on his trip to Montbard and titled, with great gravity, *Visite à Buffon*. There is a detailed description of the famous scientist's daily life, his hourly schedule, the menu for each meal, the hour he took a nap, as well as his favorite subjects of conversation. Joseph Aude, moreover, drew heavily on it when he came to publish his *Vie privée de Buffon*. Hérault de Séchelles' work, which demonstrated a great admiration for Buffon, was nevertheless not an elegy but instead described precisely Buffon's work habits, the type of jokes he liked, and did not hesitate to highlight some of the writer's faults, notably his vanity, which humanized him.[109] Little by little the author created a personal bond with Buffon and that became the real focus of the book. When he had finished writing it and visited Buffon a few weeks later at Montbard, he was welcomed with open arms.

The book combined two descriptive currents: a description, firstly, of the intimate life of Buffon, and a discreet narrative describing the close relationship between the two men, as if that guaranteed the credibility of the text and was perhaps the real subject of the story. Buffon's celebrity, different from the future glory he would attain through his scientific writings, was as much a creation of his public as that bestowed on him by his writings. It was less about Buffon's ownership of something and more a relationship: the sum of innumerable bonds that Buffon's readers had created with him, either through their imaginations, or through a real encounter, for the audacious few.

At the end of the text, Hérault de Séchelles states that he wrote it only to have a memory of privileged moments. This was a manner of speaking, of course, because the work was published while Buffon was still alive. It was nevertheless published without the author's name, and in this way the narrator was special in the sense that he was both anonymous and very much individuated, since his direct contact with

Buffon validated his anecdotes about the private life of the famous man. By publishing the story of his visit, Hérault de Séchelles fed the curiosity of the public and created an observer, a curious friend, which gave each reader an ideal situation with which to identify, and the consequent admiration for Buffon's work aroused a desire to meet him, not in order to become a disciple and learn natural philosophy from him but in order to be part of his domestic life and also become his friend. The genre of "the visit" thus broke away from the tradition of the journey, undertaken for scholarly reasons, and acquired a new dimension associated with tourism: the famous man was now viewed as a curiosity, a "must-see."

Since visits were part of celebrity culture, they had to be shared in the form of stories which, as with "private lives" or newspaper anecdotes, bared the intimate life of the famous person through the observations of a privileged witness.

These various writings that detailed the private life of contemporaries did not just follow the celebrity; they contributed to the production of celebrity. This was notably the case when legal cases became real public affairs. From 1770 to 1780, memoirs published by lawyers became a successful publishing venture. Assuming a melodramatic tone, they expanded upon the life of private people made famous through their legal woes, often conjugal or financial, and then by the impact of the trial.[110] Unlike "private lives," these memoirs were directly linked to a judicial process and its effect, most often, on the lives of unknown individuals. But the dynamic of publicity at the heart of these cases, which transformed them into *causes célèbres*, engendered public controversies that were fed by a succession of memoirs that answered each other and finished by becoming an end in themselves, addressing public opinion directly. These prolific arguments made those who were the principal actors in these dramas famous people, at least for several weeks, public figures who aroused curiosity. That private morality was sheathed in a political dimension within the new cultural politics at the end of the Ancien Régime was undeniable. It was also obvious that the public's fascination with these memoirs rested not only on their political impact, but also on the soap opera aspect of private lives become public, on the mix of curiosity, empathy, or reprobation which seized readers as they read the scandalous and contradictory stories.

This mutation of private and public that characterized the second half of the eighteenth century and the transformation of the forms of notoriety that accompanied it were abundantly commented on by those who lived through it. The author of the private life of Cagliostro, an Italian adventurer who claimed to have the secret to eternal youth and who was implicated in the queen's necklace scandal, justified in this way the revelations he promised his readers: "Since the events of his life, the web of his impostures and the judicial proceedings which recently settled his fate forever, have for some time excited much curiosity, it can hardly be doubted that his private life would [not] be avidly received."[111] The short-term nature of the news, collective attention focused on a mysterious figure, general curiosity, avidity of the public for private lives: all the characteristic elements of a discourse about celebrity are collected here. Celebrity as a topic is beginning to take shape.

— 4 —

FROM GLORY TO CELEBRITY

The *Encyclopédie* does not contain an entry for "Celebrity." The term was too recent. One finds, however, a long entry consecrated to "Glory," written by Jean-François Marmontel, playwright, literary critic, journalist, academician, and iconic figure among men of letters during the Enlightenment. The entry opens with an attempt to distinguish glory from similar notions – esteem, admiration, and celebrity – all linked to the idea of a collective judgment about an individual:

> Glory is a brilliant reputation.
> Esteem is a peaceful, personal sentiment; admiration, a rapid and sometimes momentary reaction; celebrity, an extended reputation; glory, a brilliant reputation, the concerted unanimity & support of universal admiration.
> Esteem is founded on honesty; admiration, on exceptional greatness in moral and physical excellence; celebrity, on the reaction of the multitudes to the extraordinary and the amazing; glory, on the marvelous.[1]

By using this typology, which moves from the most to the least common element, from individual esteem to universal glory, Marmontel displays his rhetorical knowledge but is also boxed into a corner. His reader clearly sees the similarities between esteem and admiration: both of them resulting in an evaluation of an individual's merits, one a rather modest response, the other more enthusiastic. Marmontel shows how glory is different from these two, the recompense of a hero distinct from the average person. But the reader wonders how the idea of celebrity fits into this definition. How is "extended reputation" different from a "brilliant reputation"? Who are these multitudes whose astonishment defines celebrity? The reader will never know because the rest of the article focuses exclusively on glory, a much older theme, the criteria of which must necessarily be redefined in order to separate authentic glory from "false glory," that of conquerors and bad kings, whereas authentic glory is based on great virtues, major works, and, above all, a devotion to the "public good." Here one sees the social aesthetic of the Enlightenment; Marmontel adheres to it but tries to retain a certain aspect of the supernatural.[2] The essential aim of the article, from here forward, is to attribute the responsibility of dispensing glory to men of letters. Because a literary man combines the moral authority of a philosopher with the powerful sensibility of a poet, he is put in charge of the glory of great men: he is able to discern real grandeur and orchestrate the "unanimous chorus" of universal admiration. We understand that the man of letters is less at ease with celebrity, arising as it does from the astonished curiosity of the multitudes and for which the criteria are much more blurred. The word "celebrity," however, is finally launched. But how is it to be given substance? What value should be accorded it? What relationship does it have to glory?

Trumpeting Fame

The importance of "glory" in the *Encylopédie* might seem surprising. Historians have often said that Enlightenment philosophers deeply criticized the idea of glory and the hero. Resuming the criticisms of self-love (*amour-propre*) and the promotion of self-interest over passion, they developed an ethic based on social virtues, "*doux commerce*" (polite and civilized interactions), and usefulness, in contrast with the illusory prestige of heroism.[3] In the transformation from aristocratic ethics to bourgeois morality, the hero paid the price, quickly replaced by the great man. A text by Voltaire, often cited, testifies to just how this displacement played out in European culture:

> A hundred battles do nothing for the human race, but the great men I have spoken about have created pure and lasting pleasures for men who are not yet born. A canal lock that joins two seas, a Poussin painting, a beautiful tragedy, a discovered truth are things a thousand times more precious than any court chronicle, or any account of war. [...] For me, great men come first, heroes last. Great men are those who have excelled in usefulness or congeniality. Reavers of provinces are merely heroes.[4]

The issue seemed settled: the great man had replaced the hero; useful and pleasant, prosaic and reasonable values had taken the place of glory, which seemed to have a certain threatening enormity about it. In reality, it was nothing of the sort, as Marmontel's article shows. Even in the eyes of Voltaire, heroic exploits were far from having lost their prestige.

87

The vocabulary of glory, humanized of course, certainly belonged to the vocabulary of the Enlightenment.[5]

Moreover, one discerns in Voltaire's text a tension between the values he promotes, the useful and the congenial, where a ponderous idealism resonates, and Poussin, associated with the themes of excellence and the great artist. It is not the ordinary citizen whom Voltaire contrasts with the hero, nor a successful merchant or a good family man; he contrasts the hero with the great scientist, the great artist, the great writer, in a word, the "great man." It is a matter of defining a new form of excellence, a new category of individuals who, through their talents and their work, raise themselves above their peers and deserve to be remembered. At the same time, the modern figure of the genius was beginning to take shape, reaching a culmination in the Romantic era with the aesthetic of the sublime: he was an exceptional man, absolutely unique, capable of creating immortal works, of discovering the secrets of nature or changing the course of history.[6] Rather than directly confronting the theme of heroic glory, the figure of the great man was instead a redefinition, a reformulation, perhaps even a rehabilitation, following the "demolition of heroes"[7] whom the Augustinians and Jansenists attacked in the second half of the seventeenth century.

The great man idea retained several traits taken from the traditional hero. He was an exceptional being, not average, an incarnation of the supernatural secularized; he was an exemplary person because of the admiration he aroused, incarnating the values of a society, a model to be imitated; and, finally, he would be posthumously recompensed given the nature of the cult which grew up around him: Did anyone enter the Panthéon while he was alive? He was only great when he was dead, a characteristic of glory throughout the long history of Western culture, for both the hero and the saint. One already sees in the fate of Achilles, this founding figure of heroic glory, that glory was based on the idea of the *belle mort*, the good death of a warrior who preferred to die young in combat than to lead an ordinary life.[8] His glory is ineluctably joined to the poem that sings his praises: from the start, it memorializes him and unifies a community by commemorating the hero's great feats, incarnating to the highest degree, right up until his death, all the communal values. Dying young, but eternally celebrated, the hero is a luminary figure, that of an exceptional and exemplary man through his talents and his exploits. This heroic figure endurably marked Western culture through the epic genre, but also through the memory of conquering kings who were imbued with glory, notably Alexander and Ceasar.

As a humanized hero of the Enlightenment, the great man did not seek to emulate Achilles or Alexander, because warrior exploits were no longer the criteria for grandeur.[9] To strength and physical courage were added intellectual or artistic talent, devotion to the public good. Military grandeur was also valued on the condition that it was in service to the country: it was Epaminondas, the savior of Thebes against Spartan oppression, who was now set against Alexander, the conqueror of Asia.[10] But in every case, the principle by which true glory was measured, given the passage of time, when passions had calmed and bias was quieted, remained unchanged. The epic was succeeded by the eulogy, which triumphed throughout the eighteenth century and was always posthumous. Eulogies were written for dead academicians, but above all they were written for great men of the past. It was here that men of letters once again took up their edifying roles: promulgating new criteria for glory, establishing titles, assessing the achievement of great artists. Antoine-Léonard Thomas was the uncontested specialist in the genre and theorized about it.[11] Hazlitt, at the beginning of the nineteenth century, lyrically contrasted the glory of great dead poets with the simple and always dubious popularity of those still living: "Fame is the recompense not of the living, but of the dead. The temple of fame stands upon the grave: the flame that burns upon its altars is kindled from the ashes of great men."[12]

The contrast between posthumous glory, unanimous and legitimate, and the opinion of contemporaries, necessarily arbitrary and oscillating, is an old subject. Cicero already distinguished between posthumous glory (*gloria*), vast and enduring, the recompense of virtue, and reputation (*fama*), a factitious renown, ephemeral, based on an often questionable popularity.[13] This fundamental distinction was reprised tirelessly by the humanists, who tried hard to found a morality of virtuous emulation around figures of illustrious men, once again referencing the legacy of Cicero and Plutarch. Thus Petrarch, who restored honor to the genre of biography concerning illustrious men, and who never stopped wondering about the legitimacy of glory, drew a firm distinction between reputation (*fama*), a simple matter of collective opinion, susceptible to being falsified by jealousy or intrigue, and glory (*gloria*), which only recompenses great men after their death: "And you long for praise? Then you, too, must die. The favour of humanity begins with the author's decease; the end of life is the beginning of glory [*vite finis principium est glorie*]."[14] He affirms that not only were the greatest men of Antiquity not glorified while they were alive, but if they returned to life they would be the target of criticism and jealousy.

Seeking glory is thus justified because it encourages moral perfection, but only on condition that it is totally indifferent to contemporary opinion. If this theme became a commonplace of moral philosophy and if it resonated up until the eighteenth century, it was because it was a response to criticism from the Church which denounced "vainglory," a seeking after earthly honors at odds with the only glory of worth, that of God's, or, later, the criticism by modern philosophers like Hobbes who pushed even further the condemnation of glory and self-love (*amour-propre*), reducing them to the status of vain and narcissistic passions.[15] For all those who dreamed of finding a place in history, it was important to exonerate vanity by pointing out that ambition had nothing in common with the false status offered by popularity. Petrarch contrasted the "premature desire for praise" to that of the quest for real glory, a moral spur which aroused a desire for the esteem of posterity.[16] Diderot returned to an enthusiastic praise of posthumous glory in his passionate correspondence with the sculptor Falconet.

> Oh, how underrated is the value of glory! Not only is seeking after glory legitimate, but it is the only good that a great artist or even just the simple moral man should desire. It pushes one to demand the best of one's self, to turn toward posterity without being bothered by the judgment of one's contemporaries, this crowd of rabble that stands about noisily in the stalls hissing a masterpiece, stirring up controversy in the salon, and checking the reviews to see if something should be admired or criticized.

Diderot felt that as much as possible one should avoid public exposure while alive, and work only to merit the long-lasting glory that would be assured in the future. To those who saw simple vanity in this, he replied in his last writings: "What could be sweeter than to believe that one might enrich one's country with one more great name."[17]

In the same way, collections of work dedicated to illustrious men, from Paul Jove through the great iconographic series of the eighteenth century, highlighted the posthumous verdicts of glory, so very different from the simple rumors of *fama*. The collections varied greatly, depending on whether artists and writers were included, whether moderns were found alongside elders, but even in the *Hommes illustres* by Charles Perrault, which includes only men from his century, one never finds contemporaries in the strict sense. The cult of great men developed in eighteenth- and nineteenth-century Europe through the construction of funerary monuments, from the tomb of Newton in Westminster Abbey to the German Walhalla of Ludwig I of Bavaria, as well as the transformation of the Church of Saint Genevieve in the Panthéon during the French Revolution.[18] The great man became a national hero, but it took time.

In spite of everything that apparently seemed to humanize him, compared with warrior heroes of the past, the Enlightenment's great man did not correspond to the new mechanisms of celebrity. Of course a famous man, while still alive, might already be perceived by his admirers as a great man, in anticipation of his future glory. This was the case, as we have seen, with Voltaire, for instance, although it was a difficult operation. To the contrary, most famous people were not vocationally destined for the Panthéon or Westminster Abbey: actresses, brigands, singers, or fashionable writers, their notoriety was often ephemeral and their virtues arguable. The essential point was that the glory of a great man was, by nature, distinct from the celebrity of public figures, because it was based on temporal distance, which alone assured unanimous admiration. Not only did this not allow for the modern aspects of fame, short-term public curiosity, and current events, but, by definition, it kept such aspects at a distance because of the extreme distrust of oscillating and arbitrary public opinion. Celebrity, "extended reputation," according to Marmontel, had, it seems, more to do with what Cicero and Petrarch called in their time *fama* – that is, the social construction of reputation. Even so, it had taken on new and rather worrisome aspects.

In traditional societies, the value of individuals depended to a great extent on the judgments made about them by their peers, neighbors, acquaintances – that is, reputation. This was the basis of honor: individuals were judged on their capacity to conform to the moral codes and exigencies of their social position, and these factors exercised collective control over each member of the group. Honor was not only a value of the elite, even though it did play an important role in noble ideology. From the end of the Middle Ages up until the eighteenth century, honor was an essential element in the ruling of European societies, at court as well as in the tiniest village. Because honor depended on the judgment of others, it had to be defended whenever it was in doubt, through duels, compensation, or some sort of deed.[19]

Honor was the most dramatic aspect of reputation, but there were multiple forms. Ordinary conversations, rumors, gossip at the local community level, information and judgments about everyone and everything, about the quality of a husband or a wife, about a worker or a neighbor, about one's honesty or piety, all these solidified communal opinion. Starting in the twelfth century, under papal impetus, then in Italian communities, in France and in England, the clergy and learned men attributed to reputation a judiciary function. Honor could be the subject of an inquest aimed at determining the reputation of a suspect, what was known about him, about his actions and his morals, anything that could reveal his reputation. Arising from local forms of sociability, perhaps reinforced by inquisitorial practices, *fama* was the communal opinion that a community had about any one of its members, the result of an intense process of socializing individual judgments through rumors and gossip. But this process was, by definition, limited, linked essentially to relationships and oral communication, always oriented toward a moral evaluation.[20]

Sometimes the reputation of an individual while he was alive extended well beyond his original community or social group. This was not very frequent in places where there was little media, where information circulated slowly. It happened to a few great warriors, to successful clergymen, great Church reformers, sometimes a few learned men. Thus Bertrand du Guesclin, a minor noble from Brittany, managed to have an impressive career during the course of the fourteenth century which led to his appointment as High Constable of France, thanks to his military prowess and his reputation as the "best knight in the world," and to the fact that his feats were celebrated musically by minstrels and poets, his reputation spread everywhere through the *Chanson de Bertrand du Guesclin*, composed on his death by a clerk at the French court.[21] The term "renown" (*"renommée"*) was usually used in French texts of the period to designate his *fama*. This term was clearly distinct from glory, which could not be associated with the profane exploits of a man from modest lineage, but it did connote an extension of reputation which largely exceeded the local group and spread throughout the kingdom of France. In fact, a reputation as extensive as du Guesclin's or later that of Erasmus, widely known in the scientific world of Europe in the sixteenth century, foreshadowed, to an extent, the system of celebrity that we have seen develop in the eighteenth century. It appeared to escape the local, interpersonal logic of reputation and instead came closer to the figure of the illustrious man. *Renommée* was also the French word for "Pheme," the mythological personification of fame. In the sixteenth and seventeenth century, often linked to the theme of illustrious men and symbolized by a winged woman with a trumpet, *Renommée* drew closer to the idea of glory, which became a quasi-synonym for it, all the while avoiding the Christian interdiction, in particular when it was a matter of secular renown, that of soldiers and artists. It was the image of *Renommée*, for example, that decorated the frontispiece of Vasari's *Lives of the Artists*, an elegiac biography of great artists. But the disadvantage of renown was its ambiguity: it did not distinguish clearly between posthumous renown and that of contemporary reputations. In the eighteenth century the term was less used, having taken on an archaic sense, often synonymous with glory. Certainly this ambiguity is to be found in Marmontel's text, where renown serves as a generic notion defining both glory and celebrity, and obscuring that which distinguished them.

Conceptualizing Celebrity

Authors in the eighteenth century, confronted with new forms of notoriety that were developing on the spot and of which they themselves were sometimes the object, did not have the tools to deal with the change. Not only was there no convenient word, but even more troublesome was the fact that all the common notions, all the moral examples, all the arguments that had been passed on to them by a long intellectual tradition, had to do with a contrast, affirmed and elaborated over and over again, between reputation and glory. However, the choice between posthumous glory, unanimous and objective, and the local and arbitrary game of reputation was not sufficient. Reputation took on an unprecedented magnitude. Living people, sometimes without talent, were better known than great men from the past, opera dancers had their portraits sold on the bridges of Paris. Was this still a matter of reputation, or already a form of glory, or something else? Besides, was success not now something to be wished for and public opinion a positive value? Should its verdicts be scorned? Could posthumous renown really be preferred to the satisfaction of seeing oneself lauded by peers and by the public while still alive?

Charles Pinot Duclos was among the first to try to answer these questions, for example in his *Considérations sur les moeurs de ce siècle*, which had great success in 1751.[22] The book subscribes to the moralist tradition concerning the passions and behavior of human beings, but it is adapted to the exigencies of the period. For individual studies, which investigate typical characteristics, Duclos prefers groups and uses informal sociological categories: "literary men," "great minds," "business men." In place of long-standing maxims, he substitutes an analysis of the current evolution of practices and manners: this is the area of the essay, where a non-systematic method is used for observations and reflections. "*Moeurs*" (manners): this was the key word for the early social sciences of the Enlightenment, also in the field of anthropology (the *Moeurs des sauvages américains comparées aux moeurs des premiers temps* by Joseph François Lafitau), in history (the *Essai sur les moeurs* by Voltaire), and in moral philosophy (*Les Moeurs* by François Vincent Toussaint). A friend of Diderot and Rousseau, Duclos produced a text emblematic of the moral and social thought of the Enlightenment, a cross between moral philosophy and a prehistory of sociology. His goal was to establish through observation a "science of manners."[23] It is true that the text sometimes suffered from a conflict between this stated goal and its normative ambition, as well as from a sometimes troubling philosophical eclecticism. This no doubt explains why historians interested in the history of ideas have been so little drawn to Duclos; he possessed neither the rigor of Montesquieu nor the radicalism of Helvétius or Holbach. On the other hand, this theoretical fuzziness coupled with a sharp sense of observation makes the text extremely interesting if one wants to understand the problems raised in the eighteenth century concerning new forms of notoriety.

Duclos had an intuitive sense that society was not exclusively a matter of material relationships but also symbolic ones, the opinion that people had of each other: "People are destined to live together in society; they are obliged to live together because they need each other: there is a mutual dependence. But it is not simply material needs which link them: they have a moral existence which depends on their reciprocal opinion of each other."[24] In a society where social identity had become more unstable, where commoners were richer than nobles, where the manners "mixed and equalized social class even though the State separated and subordinated the various classes,"[25] esteem was no longer necessarily a question of social status, and individuals tried to control, often in vain, the image that others had of them. Or, to put it differently, in the middle of a changing society, where identities and social hierarchies were no longer as visible as before, especially in the big cities, the mechanisms of reputation took on an exaggerated importance. The game of reputations became decisive in two particular areas: the literary world, where success allowed authors to break through all social barriers, and in polite society, where one's reputation as a congenial man opened doors to the best salons and where ridicule was an indelible stigma.

Duclos knew what he was talking about in regard to the literary world and polite society. Born into the 1704 *petit bourgeois* world of shop-keepers in Brittany, he managed to become one of the principal figures of cultural life during the Enlightenment, a successful author, the king's historiographer, and a member of the Académie Française, gaining the post of its permanent secretary in 1755. This brilliant career path opened doors at court to him (in 1750 he was granted "access to the king" in his role as historiographer). Duclos owed his reputation as an historian to the success of his libertine novels and to the protection accorded him by the aristocratic circles he managed to penetrate. Having reached the pinnacle of honors, he was able to observe with acuity the mechanisms of reputation that allowed a young bourgeois from the provinces to be received informally by the king's mistress, the Marquise de Pompadour.

Duclos, classically, contrasted reputation and *renommée*. Reputation was limited to a circle of peers and neighbors: it was the result of moral judgment about an individual's virtue, his integrity, his respect for the law: Was he honest, useful to society, a good father, a good husband, a good merchant, a good doctor, and so forth? Duclos identified the reputation of an individual by the "esteem" afforded him by others who "knew him personally," but he was well aware that this esteem was socialized, that it rested on the circulation of information, rumors, and on the idea each person had of public opinion. This created the unstable and contradictory character of reputation, whose nature it was to be localized: "So and so has a certain reputation in one place, and another in a different place." On the other hand, renown spread, circulating in space and time, especially after death, and concerned only a few exceptional individuals, either by their status (princes, who were by default renowned), or by their talents (great writers, great artists). The vocabulary of renown was that not of virtue but of "brilliance." It was close to the glory of kings and great men. As much as reputation fluctuated, renown was consensual: "Renown is quite constant and uniform, reputation almost never is."[26]

Duclos was much less confident when it came to preferring one or the other of these forms of notoriety. Renown had the advantage of brilliance and universality. Thus the statesman had to sacrifice his reputation to renown, choosing grand actions that gained him the admiration of posterity to lesser actions that offered ephemeral popularity. As we have seen, this was the traditional stance of literary men. However, if renown was more showy, it was also less tangible. It could only be enjoyed through the imagination, and it was often about name recognition, not the real merits of a person: "Renown is only a homage rendered to the syllables of a name." Besides, it was less universal than one imagined: "In terms of numbers, how many men have never heard the name of Alexander?"

As for reputation, it was often arbitrary, based less on the direct evaluation of merit than on the phenomenon of collective opinion (imitation, fashion, rumors), which produced fads or unjustified rejections. "Nothing could make a person more indifferent to reputation than to see how it fluctuates, how it often creates and destroys, and who the authors of these changes are." Those who made the reputation of others, through their position or their influence, were not necessarily the most virtuous or best judges: "There you are! Just look at these judges of reputation! Those whose feelings one distrusts and who are looking for votes." And sometimes public opinion was manipulated on purpose. "They set out with a plan in mind to make a reputation and it works." The supreme ambiguity of these reputations did not mean they were always lies and fiction; they sometimes lived up to their merit. This was so to the extent that one could never decisively conclude one way or another when it came to a favorable reputation.[27]

Why should the reputation of an individual not be the synthesis of individual judgments made about him? The difficulty Duclos raises is that reputation is never the simple workings of personal esteem for another individual, the recognition of merit in someone else. Reputation is a collective judgment, dependent on mechanisms of socialized opinions, either spontaneous or manipulated. Although he starts with a definition of reputation as meaning esteem among those who are acquaintances, those one knows "personally," all the examples he uses to highlight judgments about others refer to more extended reputations, those for whom the judge is the public. But the public is an ambivalent figure that "creates reputations capriciously," that detests conspiracies wherever it sees them, but easily lets itself be fooled and deluded, caught in its own wild dreams: "The public is often astonished by certain reputations it has made; it searches for the reason why, and, not discovering the reason because it doesn't exist, has even more respect and admiration for the phantom it has created."[28] The public is not only the passive receptacle of conspiracies, it is also the new collective actor that creates reputations.

The problem raised by Duclos is as follows: when the original tenuous bonds of reputation are broken, bonds of respect and esteem proffered by people who know someone personally, when reputation becomes part of a larger social realm, through the play of sociability, as in polite society, and even more so with literary reputations governed by spread of the printed word, the role of critics, intermediaries, and cabals, how can one be assured that "public" judgments conform to the merits or the faults of an individual? Public opinion acting as a judge is doubly troublesome given its changeability. At the level of justice, how can a fair distribution of public esteem be assured?[29] At the individual level, what importance should a person accord to public reputation? At what moment does the desire to be known by one's contemporaries become dangerous?

Torn between the classic division of reputation and renown, Duclos found that the social transformations in his century had enormously enlarged the mechanisms of reputation, without for all that making reputation the equal of renown. Could one still speak of "reputation" when the facts and actions of an individual were widely known not only by those who "knew him personally," but also by those who read newspapers and constituted what had begun to be called public opinion? Perhaps it was better to find a more adequate term.

As early as the first edition of Duclos's book in 1751, a third word appeared several times to designate a sweeping reputation, or renown in its infancy, or even a sort of generic term to designate notoriety: this term, never fully defined, was that of "celebrity." The augmented edition of 1764 tried to distinguish more clearly the notion of celebrity, which could not be encompassed by either reputation or renown. Even the title of the chapter was changed. At first called "On Reputation and Renown," it became "On Reputation, Celebrity, Renown, and Consideration."[30] From the first sentences of the text, celebrity was introduced as a third term. Where the 1751 edition read: "The desire to be somebody in the eyes of the public has given birth to the idea of *reputation and renown*, two powerful aspects of society which both start from the same principle but whose means and effects are not totally the same," it now read: "The desire to be somebody in the eyes of the public has given birth to the idea of *reputation, celebrity and renown*, powerful aspects of society which start from the same principle but whose means and effects are not totally the same."[31] Even so, the body of the chapter is very little changed, as if Duclos understood that the term "celebrity" needed to account for the media aspect of reputations in the cities, a term he heard more and more frequently in the language of the period, without, in the end, being able to find a consistent meaning for it.

One of the rare passages in the chapter specifically concerning celebrity is of particular interest. Duclos imagines a man surrounded by men who "without knowing him personally praise him in his presence." This experience, implying a society where anonymity reigns as well as a wide circulation of proper names, was enjoyed, of course, by the man: "He took great pleasure in his celebrity."[32] Celebrity was characterized by an asymmetry between the celebrity, who knows that he is being talked about, and those who are talking about a man they do not know personally. Certainly in regard to our modern criteria, and even in some way to that of the eighteenth century, it is a matter of an incomplete celebrity, because the image of the famous man does not circulate at the same rate as his name, or not sufficiently enough to be recognized. However, one sees the kind of pleasure such celebrity can bring once it happens: that of being the spectator of one's own notoriety, the object of conversation and the only who is aware of it, the narcissistic focus of everyone's attention with none of the inconveniences.

Nonetheless, Duclos adds a strange remark:

> If the man is tempted to reveal himself, it is because he can, and because it is an open-ended game of self-love. But if it is absolutely impossible to reveal himself, his pleasure no longer a choice, his situation could perhaps become painful, as if he were listening to people talk about a third person, someone other than himself.

In this fictional scene, the pleasure felt by the celebrity is based entirely on his freedom, the fact that he is in control of the situation, that he is taking advantage of the asymmetry and he can at any moment turn his celebrity into admiration by publicly revealing himself as the person being discussed. In the opposite case, however, he loses control, is locked into the position of passive spectator, excluded from the performance, incapable of transforming the show, which is controlled by the public. This hypothesis, fictional and not very realistic, is at the core of the celebrity experience as soon as the chains of media exposure are too numerous to allow a famous person to "reveal himself" to those who are talking about him. Without saying so explicitly, it appears that Duclos targets, or rather confusedly focuses on, the situation of an individual celebrity confronted not by rumors in a café but by an anonymous reading public. "[It is] as if he were listening to people talk about a third person, someone other than himself." This conclusion is stunning, because the feeling of profound alienation, the impossibility of identifying oneself with the celebrated person that one is, will be one of the great critical themes of celebrity as a social experience.

At the same time, on the other side of the Channel, Samuel Johnson was throwing himself into the *Rambler* adventure. Having lived in London the past ten years, Johnson had yet to really break into the English literary world as he dreamed of doing, but his *Dictionary of the English Language* would soon make him a major figure in London intellectual life. From 1749 to 1752, he published a periodical two times a week, offering with each issue an essay with a moral theme. His essays, where a description of mores in the great, modern metropolis that London had become was illuminated by his immense repertoire of quotes and by his own, often snide, reflections, brought him critical esteem; they were picked up by other newspapers, then published in volumes. As befitting Johnson's popularity, there were a dozen editions of these essays published before his death. Like the *Considérations sur les moeurs* by Duclos, the *Rambler* articles were emblematic of the kinds of ideas suggested to provincial writers who had become observers of literary life in the capital. Inscribed in a moral tradition, they combined a description of social behavior, great psychological wisdom, and an attempt at detachment. On the other hand, where Duclos wrote first of all for a worldly public by making polite society the object of a privileged analysis, Johnson's essays were addressed to a less differentiated public, that of newspapers and cafés, describing an urban society where the consumer revolution and changes in the public space were more advanced.[33] Johnson did not try to develop a workable morality, but instead wanted to adapt current society to the wisdom of the Ancients who had mentored him, and he accomplished this with an inimitable and witty mélange of seriousness and satirical humor.

Several of the *Rambler* texts are dedicated to the uncertainties of literary celebrity, which subjected writers, as well as military and political figures, to the vagaries of luck. The wheel of fortune and the illusory happiness that the search for glory brought was a classic theme. But Johnson interpreted it in his unique way: the suspect character of celebrity, often ephemeral, was not a matter of earthly vainglory but rather the nature of public recognition in contemporary society. Literary notoriety was no longer a matter of judgment by one's peers, nor the result of a voluntary relationship between the writer and a prince, as it was during court patronage. It depended more often now on the "sudden caprice of the public" or an excessive taste for novelty.[34]

Not only was the public capricious and its criteria for judgment unstable, even the conditions of celebrity were fragile, given the great number of candidates and the limited attention of the public.[35] To illustrate this generality, Johnson wrote little scenarios about the search for celebrity in contemporary London society. He imagined an author, impatient to know what the public thought of his book, walking around town, devouring newspapers, listening in on café conversations, only to discover, with bitterness, that no one was talking about his work. Johnson had fun contrasting the excitement and impatience of the author, convinced of the importance of his book, and the variety of conversations going on around him: talk of a cricket match, a theft, a bankruptcy, a lost cat, a dancing dog.[36] The irony of this passage comes from giving equal value to the book's merits and the minor events which interested the public. Minor events, that is, in the mind of the author, outraged to find his book in competition with these subjects of discussion which he judges unworthy of him, although he feverishly seeks the attention of this public he secretly disdains.

Johnson dissects this contradiction with irony and perspicacity. He is careful not to denounce the desire for celebrity as a quest for vainglory. Throughout his career, he affirms that the quest for renown is perfectly legitimate. What interests him are the psychological constraints which weigh on the writer when he searches not only for the recognition of his peers but also that of the public, getting caught up in a vicious circle of competitive struggle for celebrity. This becomes a warning lesson which Johnson addresses to himself as well: "When once a man has made celebrity necessary to his happiness, he has put it in the power of the weakest and most timorous malignity, if not to take away his satisfaction, at least to withhold it."[37] In this last quote, Johnson uses the word "celebrity" rather than "fame," probably in order to insist even more strongly that celebrity was a matter of contemporary notoriety, fundamentally a result of public opinion.

This text reinterpreted the old theme of passion and glory through addressing the issue of public success, and it initiated another theme promising a great future: that of the public as more capricious and tyrannical than other patrons. Writers, at the moment they began to free themselves from the system of court patronage, found themselves even more constrained. Johnson knew that the new mechanisms of literary life imposed a frenetic search for success. He saw that the desire for celebrity was different from the desire for respect: it was first of all a need to be talked about, to be the center of public attention and to arouse curiosity. The writer seeking celebrity wanted to be knighted by a public made up of anonymous readers whose legitimacy he was far from recognizing, so much so that he sought less the judgment of the public than its interest, less its approbation than its curiosity.

Johnson went even further in the psychological and sociological description of celebrity by writing an essay in the form of a letter, obviously fictional, from a young writer who had just published a book and bitterly regretted it because the public revelation of his talent had caused him great unhappiness.[38] The long narrative about his misfortune is a small comic masterpiece concerning the perils of public recognition. The opening paragraphs describe the inaugural scene, crossing the Rubicon: the moment of publication. Although Johnson had praised freedom of the press in England in a previous article, the print shop in his essay is compared to hell, from where one never returns once a book is published in one's name. The anxiety and excitement that accompany the publication of a book are nothing compared with what the author will soon endure. Overwhelmed by enthusiastic visits, he is destroyed by the effects of dinners given to thank him and he has no time for himself. Then he discovers the jealousy of his contemporaries. In the cafés, his words are misinterpreted and he no longer takes pleasure in spontaneous conversation. Even his friends flee from him, because his superiority and his renown are so obvious. "I live in the town like a lion in his desert, or an eagle on his rock, too great for friendship or society, and condemned to solitude, by unhappy elevation, and dreaded ascendancy."[39] He cannot tolerate greatness or at least the image of greatness that others have of him. His celebrity becomes a burden. And what is worse: afraid he might be broken into by pirate publishers or see his portrait published without his consent, he lives like a hunted man. His psychological balance is threatened by his success.

You must have read in Pope and Swift how men of parts have had their closets rifled and their cabinets broke open at the instigation of piratical booksellers for the profit of their works and it is apparent that there are many prints now sold in the shops of men whom you cannot suspect of sitting for that purpose and whose likenesses must have been certainly stolen when their names made their faces vendible. These considerations at first put me on my guard and I have indeed found sufficient reason for my caution for I have discovered many people examining my countenance with a curiosity that shewed their intention to draw it. I immediately left the house but find the same behaviour in another. Others may be persecuted, but I am hunted. I have good reason to believe that eleven painters are now dogging me, for they know that he who can get my face first will make his fortune. I often change my wig, and wear my hat over my eyes, by which I hope somewhat to counfound them: for you know it is not fair to sell my face, without admitting me to share the profit.

Johnson was having fun but he was right. His description touched precisely on the new aspects of celebrity, in particular the sudden appearance of cheap engraved portraits, the unequaled multiplication of printed books as well as the role of new urban sociability found in taverns and cafés, where conversation made the public figure someone well known beyond the circle of his acquaintances. Johnson also emphasized the commercial aspects of celebrity: writers as a source of profit for booksellers who wanted to use their names, and portraitists who wanted to make engravings. The name, the face: these elements constituted the personal identity of an individual in the eyes of others, the interface between one's individuality and one's public identity were reduced to the status of commercial products, threatened by the venality of unscrupulous merchants. The success of a book, far from elevating its author, belittled him, transformed him into merchandise. Celebrity obliged the celebrated writer to flee, alone and hunted, constantly changing his address, taking his manuscripts with him, not daring to talk to people for fear of being recognized, no longer writing letters, afraid they might be published. He became absolutely suspicious of everything: he suspected his servants and his friends of stealing his manuscripts, the first for money, the second in the name of "the public."

Johnson completely reversed the classic condemnation of a desire for praise. It was no longer lack of success that made an author miserable, confronted as he was by the unfair treatment of contemporaries and by being pushed to seek illusory glory that he could never enjoy when alive; it was celebrity itself that was the burden, the malediction. Here one saw a reformulation of the Christian condemnation of vainglory, but *failed* vainglory, which made Johnson's theory original: his irony and his sense of observation rendered him particularly sensitive to the social conditions at work in public recognition, changes he observed in the English capital. He thus formulated, in an almost burlesque way, the disadvantages of fame. This portrait of the famous man as a paranoiac whose writing success leads to a rupture with his friends and then to a solitary, persecuted life, fleeing celebrity as if it were a curse after avidly having sought it, cut off from the world by his success, is even more remarkable in that it appears to announce with extraordinary prescience the figure of Jean-Jacques Rousseau.

In the middle of the eighteenth century, Johnson, like Duclos, was conscious of a new form of emerging notoriety linked to the mutations of the public sphere, which could not be reduced to either reputation or glory. The two men intuited that celebrity was a paradoxical form of greatness: a sign of success exercised on authors – and more generally on all those who produced work for the public – a powerful attraction, but it was at the same time unstable and not quite legitimate, because it rested on the judgment of a vast anonymous public whose criteria were changeable, inexplicit, or uncertain. It was above all dangerous and could turn out to be a formidable trap. This most unexpected intuition constituted one of the elements of celebrity, a topic that was starting to develop.

Celebrity

The word itself was not totally new in the mid-eighteenth century, but it was only just starting to take on the sense that it has now. During the previous century, it was rarely used and designated exclusively the solemn character of an official ceremony. Antoine Furetère offered this definition, "Pomp, magnificence, a ceremony which renders an event celebrated." And he proposed the following example: "The entrance of legislators makes a grand celebrity," and adds: "This is an old usage." La Bruyère gives the word this same sense of solemn ceremony when he writes: "He mocks the piety of those who send offerings to the temples on days of great celebrity." The irony in this formulation lies in the etymology of the word, which implies the idea of a place that is often frequented but where the piety is more ostentatious than sincere. In classical Latin, *celebritas* means both the presence of numerous people in a place and the solemn character of a celebration attended by a crowd of people, thus the idea of multitudes and great activity. On the other hand, the term rarely means an extended reputation, and then solely in the formulation *celebritas famae*. Only a few authors (Aulu-Gelle and then Boethius) tried, late and in vain, to give the word this sense. In the Middle Ages, it did not have this meaning, except for very rare exceptions. When the word appeared in French, it only meant the solemn character of a celebration. On the other hand, the adjective *celeber* in Latin already meant a place, an event, or a known individual. In French, "celebrity" took on this meaning rather early, in competition with "illustrious" and "famous."

The use of "celebrity" to mean the great notoriety of an individual appeared diffidently in the 1720s. There is one use of it in Montesquieu's *Persian Letters* with the word meaning an extended but unfounded reputation: "A few days ago I was a guest in a country house where I met two scholars who are widely celebrated here [*qui ont ici une grande célébrité*]."[40] The term appears in both Marivaux and de Crébillon, but it was still very recent when Duclos used it in 1751. On the other hand, it is used extensively in the following decades, proven by principal lexicon databases. The ARTFL-Frantext database, for example, shows that it was almost nonexistent before 1750. During the decade 1750–60, occurrences grew regularly and reached a peak in relative frequency from 1770 to 1790.[41] Ngram Viewer software, which relies on the digitized collection of Google Books, produces similar results: almost no frequency of use in 1730, a steady rise and a peak toward 1780, then a higher peak in 1812, followed by a long diminution. In terms of relative frequency, the period 1750–1850 clearly marks the high point for the use of the term "celebrity" in French publications.[42]

Graph 1: Use of the term "celebrity" in French publications.

The proliferation of the term accompanied an evolution in its meaning. In the years 1750 to 1760, it remained close to that of "reputation," implying a rapid, extended notoriety that was somewhat suspect. Adversaries of Enlightenment philosophers, for example, used the word to denounce a reputation in their rivals which they felt was excessive. In his *Lettres sur de grands philosophes*, Charles Palissot grumbled about the "refrain of fastidious praise that these men sent to each other, and the certifications of celebrity that they in turn distributed throughout their writings."[43] At the same time, François Antoine Chevrier denounced the women in houses where there was always an open invitation to dine: "It is there that authors who want a fleeting celebrity should go to read their ephemeral writings."[44] Celebrity with a negative connotation reflected a form of self-promotion, publicity orchestrated artificially by groups of fashionable intellectuals.

The word partly lost its negative connotation between 1760 and 1770, gaining in specificity. "Celebrity" was associated with the curiosity of the "public" and imposed a certain number of constraints on those who were the object of it. The *Mémoires secrets* regularly used the word in this sense. One also found it in letters. Julie de Lespinasse wrote to Guibert: "Your talents condemn you to celebrity. Therefore abandon yourself to your destiny and tell yourself that you are not made for this sweet, introverted life that tenderness and sentiment demand."[45] Celebrity does not here have the aspect of an ephemeral and suspect reputation but means, instead, as with Duclos, a notoriety so expansive that it becomes incompatible with a private life. Note the apparent paradox in this formula by Julie de Lespinasse: "condemn you to celebrity." Celebrity is not only an attribute, but a condition which modifies lifestyle, almost like the social status of a person. To become a public figure, to be the object of permanent public curiosity because of one's talent, is a trial that can be exultant but also painful and which can change the "destiny" of an individual. One formulation summarizes well this new consciousness of celebrity and the sometimes disagreeable consequences of success and talent: "the disadvantages of celebrity." This idea is found in Diderot's *Entretiens d'un père avec ses enfants*,[46] and it forms the subtitle of Mme Dufrénoy's 1812 book *La Femme auteur*.[47]

In England, the development was both similar and different. As in France, the word "celebrity," referring also to rites associated with ceremonies, progressively took on a new meaning, notably in the 1750s, to designate the notoriety of an actor or a writer. With a slight time lag, the same kind of peak in relative frequency of use happened at the turn of the nineteenth century.

Graph 2: Use of the term "celebrity" in English publications.

Nonetheless, the English had at their disposal another word, "fame," whose meaning was broader, because it included the French idea of "celebrity," but also simple reputation or, to the contrary, lasting glory, sometimes for the same author. In the seventeenth century, Francis Bacon, in his *Fragment of an Essay on Fame*, used the term in a way close to that of rumor, whereas in his *Advancement of Learning* he used it to mean the prestigious rewards given to a scholar.[48] The etymological reference for English during the eighteenth century was Samuel Johnson's *Dictionary*. It did not distinguish clearly between the two terms, sending the definition back and forth to the one, then the other. Johnson even suggested the word "celebriousness," next to the word "celebrity," as a synonym for "fame" and "renown." If the adjective "famous" won out in the end, in the long run "celebrious," and above all "celebrated," are often used to mean a celebrated person, which proves a certain linguistic effervescence in the language. An older usage, lending itself very well to various uses, "fame" slowed the development of the word "celebrity," for which it was often a synonym. It continued being used in this way until modern English usage, when it referred to designated forms of media celebrity as well the more legitimate reference to glory. The lexical game turned out to be more complex.

"Chastisement for Merit"

At mid-century, Duclos and Johnson tried to define celebrity as a specific condition suffered by someone who was subjugated to the insatiable curiosity of the public. Thirty years later, the word was common usage and the phenomenon had grown markedly, beginning with the transformation of literary life. For writers, always quick to study their own social situation, celebrity became a recurrent theme. Some were satisfied with denouncing the desire for celebrity as a form of vanity, which boiled down to simply being talked about. The playwright Vittorio Alfieri criticized the "*aura passeggiera de vana glorietta*" (which the French translator sympathetically rendered as "facile and ephemeral celebrity") and contrasted it with the classic posthumous glory of a great writer.[49]

Others, just as critical, tried to understand the novelty in terms of publicity. One was Nicolas Chamfort, a master of paradox, who was well placed to recognize the ambivalences of celebrity. He had written some well-known aphorisms about it: "Celebrity is the advantage of being known by those who do not know you," often misquoted as: "The advantage of being known by those whom you do not know," placing the emphasis on the asymmetry between the celebrated person and the public. Celebrity is thus identified as an extension of reputation beyond the interconnected circles of acquaintances. But the actual quote by Chamfort is more profound, creating a paradox by recognizing the gap between two forms of knowing someone: indirect knowledge through media hype, by which one identifies the individual because one knows his name, perhaps his face, as well as a series of stories about him, and personal knowledge, which implies a direct and reciprocal relationship. The aphorism immediately raises the question: What is known about the celebrity by those who know him without knowing him? A name, an image, rumors, rhetoric, a series of media projections circulating in the public sphere that have only a distant relationship to the person himself: this can be called the public face. The celebrity, known without being known, is only a name supported by stories, not to mention fantasies: he finds himself in the situation described by Duclos of the man who thinks the group is talking about "someone other than himself." The irony in the term "advantage" chosen by Chamfort makes it clear: celebrity, so greatly sought after, is simply a lure; it creates an artificial situation, expressed in the apparent contradictory formulation "to be known by people who do not know you." This condemnation of the fictive character of celebrity rests on a contrast between the authenticity of personal relationships and the artificiality of indirect media relationships. Chamfort begins his criticism of the society of spectacle at this point, inaugurating a long history, and anticipates the romantic criticism of alienation through publicity.

But Chamfort's relationship to celebrity is more personal, based on social and literary success. Like that of Duclos or Marmontel, Chamfort's beginnings seemed to be the start of a successful literary career. Arriving in Paris from Clermont-Ferrand, he did well in academic competitions, had the public support of Voltaire and powerful aristocratic protection, a resounding theatrical success, and even a chair in the Academy. And all of this imminent celebrity at just forty years old. He had an enviable position, an adequate income; as a fashionable young man beginning to have success as an author, he could calmly envision still greater notoriety, along the lines of his mentor Voltaire or his friend Beaumarchais. And then something happened; one will never know exactly in what way disgust or disillusionment undermined Chamfort's profound ambition, his taste for worldly pleasures and literary honors. He renounced the generous pension from the Prince de Condé, ceased visiting the salons, withdrew to the countryside, and stopped publishing, taking refuge in a long literary silence. Unlike Rousseau a few years later, this rupture was not spectacular, it was not accompanied by blustering justifications; it was silent, more a defection. It took nothing less than the French Revolution to bring Chamfort out of his mute state, rousing his revolutionary enthusiasm, which lasted until the tragic episode of his near suicide and then his death during the Terror.

There is much speculation about what pushed Chamfort to renounce publication, to be seized with "Bartleby's syndrome."[50] The main reason, to my mind, had to do with Chamfort's reflection about the public and about publicity, his bitter awareness about what it implied for an author to want public approval when public authority in matters of artistic taste was not even recognized. Chamfort's criticism was not so much about public judgments as it was about the dynamics of publicity, about the artificial character of success. In a series of wry and caustic maxims, he inverted the idea of celebrity as an indicator of merit and a desirable form of success, and saw it as a punishment: "Celebrity is chastisement for merit and the punishment of talent."[51] And again: "Given the tone that has reigned the last ten years in literature, M. said, literary celebrity seems to me to be a kind of defamation which does not yet have as many bad effects as a straitjacket, but that will come."[52] This second formulation anticipates with acuity the "economy of symbolic goods" that will arise during the nineteenth century, along with the empowerment of

106

the literary field and the development of mass literature, where public success appears to be contradictory to art for art's sake and the literary avant-garde.[53] Celebrity was becoming a mark of infamy.

In a letter to Abbé Roman, written in 1784, Chamfort again decided on solitude and tells his friend about the gap he had discovered between the dreams of glory that had driven him at the start of his career and the reality of celebrity. His experience of literary life, of the jealousy and hatred that success aroused, and also the way this "unfortunate mania for celebrity" perverted human relationships, were revelatory factors: "I had as much hatred for celebrity as I had love for glory."[54]

Louis Sébastien Mercier, a contemporary of Chamfort's whom he knew well and whom he frequented at the Association of Playwrights, was another close, attentive observer of the transformations taking place in cultural life. His *Tableau de Paris*, which began appearing in 1783, is not only an extraordinary description of the working-class city, it is also a reflection of the new conditions of cultural life in a large capital at the end of the century, and notably literary and theater life, to which Mercier was a privileged witness.[55] More than others, he emphasized the servitude attached to the condition of celebrity. The private life of a celebrity was always on view to the public. "The life of a pretty woman is less scrutinized than that of a celebrity," he wrote, not without irony, in *De la littérature et des littérateurs*.[56] It was meant to illustrate the prestige of writers, who, even without any specific social status, could arouse general interest, sought out by the elites as well as the public. But there was already a hint of criticism, the comparison not necessarily flattering. In the *Tableau de Paris*, he returned to the theme several times, openly criticizing the new culture of celebrity. One of the most revealing chapters is dedicated to the habit of the audience at the Comédie-Française, who clamored for the author at the end of the first performance. This new practice, initiated with Voltaire, should have pleased Mercier, who had been, along with his friend Beaumarchais, an ardent promoter of copyright protection for playwrights as opposed to the privileges of actors and the control exercised by a favored few.[57] Nonetheless, the chapter is extremely critical. This practice for Mercier illustrated an irritating displacement of the pleasure offered by seeing a play onto a desire to see the author, from the work itself to the writer of the work. This apparent recognition of the author, which others might perhaps see as the start of the consecration of the writer, appeared to Mercier to be a debasement. Far from recognizing in the author an authority, a creator, it made a spectacle of him.

> Often at the end of a play and as if to add a scene to what has just been performed, the crowd shouts out *Author*, with the most frantic

stubbornness; the shouts having a brutal character, dishonest, shamefully demanding that which rightfully could be refused; the clamor is redoubled until the victim is led out from backstage, and the public applause at that point nothing more than an outrage.

These scathing words were categorical. Public homage was like a humiliation. The author was caught in a psychologically damaging confusion between his social being, reduced to only a face and a body, subjected to gawking and applause, and his moral being.

> I do not know how Authors can respect themselves so little as to obey the imperative clamors of a delirious stall. How can the Public itself not feel that every Author has the right to refuse its madness, because there exists no relationship at all between the artist's work and his person? It is his verses or his prose that must be judged and not his physiognomy, his dress and his bearing.[58]

It is understandable that Mercier did not appreciate the ceremony in honor of Voltaire, at the performance of *Irène*, and that he saw it as a debasing farce.

Mercier clearly understood that this seeming public celebration of the author was in reality a double displacement, from the text to the author, but also from the author as artist to the author as person, whose exposure was only an addition to the pleasure of the performance. Not only did the public confuse the work and the author, but the author became an object of curiosity, an appendix to the spectacle. The author's liberty and dignity were rejected in this acclamation, which claimed to be a mark of collective admiration (the "applause"), but revealed an aggressive will to reduce the author to a persona. Mercier had very little use for this ceremony that under cover of rendering homage to the author showed, actually, the power of the public, its tyranny, its desire to transform everything into a spectacle for its own purposes. In this light, one can understand the virulent formulation so full of paradox: "applause [is] nothing more than an outrage."

— 5 —

LONELINESS OF THE CELEBRITY

Rousseau is a case both exemplary and exceptional. The author of *La Nouvelle Héloïse* was not only one of the best known writers in all of Europe during the Enlightenment, arousing curiosity and sometimes spectacular excitement, but he was also one of the first to comment on his own celebrity. Obsessed by the question of his public persona, Rousseau, in his correspondence and his autobiographical texts, engaged in a fascinating reflection, partly social philosophy and partly paranoid delirium, about the consequences of a celebrity that he judged "disastrous." His career trajectory is particularly well documented and offers a stunning plunge into the workings of celebrity: it allows us to follow the destiny of a writer who was not really ready to become, from one day to the next, among the most celebrated men of his time for the next twenty years. Far from enjoying it, Rousseau felt this notoriety as a burden, a curse that condemned him to live "more alone in the middle of Paris than Robinson on his island, and sequestered from intercourse with men by the crowd itself, eager to surround him in order to prevent him from allying with anyone."[1] How is such a paradox to be understood?

"The Celebrity of Misfortune"

Like many after him, Rousseau had the experience of being a sudden celebrity, an event that threw him brutally onto the public stage. Beginning in the 1750s, before the success of his *Discourse on the Arts and Sciences*, he was only one of a number of writers trying to break into the Parisian literary world. At nearly forty years old, ten years after his arrival in the capital, he had only one piece of writing to show, *Dissertation on Modern Music*, which had had almost no success, and an opera, *Les Muses galantes*, that had not yet been performed. His system of musical

109

notation, on which he had based all his hopes, was not accepted by the Academy of Sciences, while his talent for composition angered Rameau and raised suspicions, which closed the doors of the court and of patronage to him. Even his experience as embassy secretary in Venice, in 1743–4, ended with a stunning failure. He was lucky to obtain employment as secretary through Mme Dupin, the wife of a Farmer-General, and had gained the confidence of her son-in-law, Dupin de Francueil, the tax collector. Another glimmer of hope was his friend Diderot, who assigned him some articles about music for a vague encyclopedia project. All in all, his path resembled the banal one of a provincial autodidact who had come to Paris in the hope of succeeding but whose reputation had not made it beyond the narrow confines of the literary underground.

Everything changed in 1751 with the impact of the *Discourse on the Arts and Sciences*, which won the Académie de Dijon prize. Starting in December 1750, Abbé Raynal published the best sections in the *Mercure de France*, then the entire text in January 1751, which caused lively controversy. The text was an immediate sensation, far above the usual success of an academic dissertation.[2] Diderot wrote him that no "example of such a success" existed. Several attempts at a refutation, including that of the former king of Poland, Stanisław Leszczyński, fed general curiosity and gave Rousseau a chance to refine his positions. He soon became a noted writer. Mme de Graffigny, herself a successful novelist, was overjoyed to meet him: "Yesterday, I met this Rousseau who is becoming so very famous for his controversial opinions and his response to your king."[3] A few months later, the *Journal de Trévoux* invoked the "splash" that his dissertation had made, even across borders. Antoine Court, at that time a theology student in Geneva, attempted to follow "the crush of writings" that appeared in opposition to the *Discourse*.[4]

From that moment on, Rousseau would never stop making cultural news. The following year, he continued to publish responses to his critics, had a play, *Narcisse*, performed, then, in spite of its failure, published it with the addition of a very long preface – forty pages – in which he wrote a self-justification which had an unexpected benefit: again it set off the interest he had aroused earlier. His opera *Le Devin du village* was a triumph at its Fontainebleau performance a few months later. Rousseau fed this incipient celebrity through a series of polemics against French music, against the theater, and then against his old friends the *encyclopédistes*. Finally, at the start of the 1760s, with the unprecedented success of *La Nouvelle Héloïse*, a publishing phenomenon, and the scandal provoked by the publication of *Émile* and the *Social Contract*, along with his condemnation in 1762 by the Paris parliament, his notoriety reached a zenith.

Threatened with arrest, Rousseau had to flee France immediately. This began a period marked by successive exiles which earned him the "celebrity of misfortune,"[5] an expression he liked. He became both a successful writer and a public person, his life reported in detail in all the gazettes, his portrait reproduced in every form and avidly sought after by numerous admirers. In the mid-1760s, Rousseau was undoubtedly, along with Voltaire, the most renowned writer of his time. The European press reported the tiniest details of his life. In England, where his writings were translated and commented on, newspapers like the *Critical Review*, the *Monthly Review*, and also the *London Chronicle* or the *St James's Chronicle* often gave readers news of him.[6] In 1765, given that the situation in Geneva had made him not only a literary celebrity but also a political one, there were articles about Rousseau every week.[7] When young people threw stones at his house in Môtiers, the *London Chronicle* reported, with special emphasis, that the "celebrated John James Rousseau just missed being assassinated by three men."[8] A few months later, with his arrival on English soil, the author of *Émile* aroused a real media frenzy, even more because the English press saw him as a victim of the political and religious intolerance which held sway on the Continent. But it was above all the singularity of his rise to stardom and his personality which caused all the curiosity. "All the world are eager to see this man, who by his singularity, has drawn himself into much difficulty; he appears abroad but seldom, and dresses like an Armenian," announced the *Public Advertiser*.[9] As for David Hume who had persuaded him to come to London and who had not yet cut off ties with him, he did not know whether to be surprised or amazed by the spin that the British press give the tiniest details about Rousseau: "Every circumstance, the most minute that concerns him, is put in the newspapers."[10] When Rousseau lost his dog, Sultan, the news was announced the next day. When he found it, a new article appeared![11] When he arrived in London in January 1766, Rousseau went to the theater to see Garrick perform, but he was the one who was the veritable attraction that evening. All the newspapers recounted the event, describing the crowd that pushed to get a glimpse of him, emphasizing the curiosity aroused by his presence, and even more so because he was in his Armenian costume and sitting in the first row of the balcony, where he reacted in a very animated and dramatic way.

In February, the *London Chronicle* published a long biography of Rousseau that emphasized his immoderate taste for publicity. Rousseau, not surprisingly, was one of the most cited people in the *Mémoires secrets*, appearing more than one hundred and eighty-five times. Of course his writings were announced and commented on, but it was essentially the daily exploits of his life which fed the curiosity and interest of readers. The *Mémoires secrets*, and its readers, seemed fascinated by the persecutions which assailed Rousseau, by the quarrels which put him in opposition to authorities and his former friends, but above all the endless questions about his character.[12] When he took refuge on Île Saint-Pierre, the *Mémoires secrets* affirmed that "The persecutions he has experienced have darkened his imagination, and he has become wilder than ever."[13] When he returned to Paris in 1770, his appearances were regularly reported in the *Mémoires*; as soon as he first appeared in the Café de la Régence, they were surprised at the "publicity surrounding the author of *Émile*," in spite of the order for his arrest that in theory still threatened his liberty:

> J.-J. Rousseau, tired of his obscurity and no longer being in the public eye, came to the city a few days ago and went to the Café de la Régence, where he was soon surrounded by a considerable crowd. Our cynical *philosophe* accepted this little triumph with great modesty. He did not seem alarmed by all the spectators, and his conversation was amicable, unlike his usual behavior.[14]

Rousseau's return to Paris was quite an event.[15] His first appearances drew a crowd of gawkers eager to see the celebrated man. In the *Correspondance littéraire*, Grimm ironically described this fascination:

> He showed up several times at the Café de la Régence in the Palais-Royal, his presence drawing a prodigious crowd, and the populace even gathered around the Place in order to see him pass by. We asked half of the people what they were doing there; they answered that they had come to "to see Jean-Jacques." We asked them who Jean-Jacques was, and they answered that they had no idea, but he was passing by.[16]

"Jean-Jacques" had become an empty word, the rallying cry which announced an odd spectacle, a word the crowd repeated, a publicity slogan disconnected not only from the work of Rousseau, but even from his person. His celebrity was transformed into a pure tautological phenomenon, self-sustaining, where there only existed the excitement of the "populace," the least enlightened and the least critical, at the idea of seeing a famous man, no matter who it was. Mme du Deffand made ironic comments herself about the "spectacle" that Rousseau made, worthy of street theater, and used the same pejorative term of "populace" to expand the derision to include all those who admired the writer, many from polite society: "Jean-Jacques is here. [...] The show that this man puts on is at the level of Nicolet. It is really only the quick-witted among the populace who pay any attention."[17] Rousseau, however, soon ceased going to cafés at the request of the authorities, who reminded him that his presence in the capital was only just tolerated.[18]

In this last period, Rousseau played to the hilt the role of a famous man who hid from view, who sought anonymity in the heart of the capital. "The name of Rousseau is famous throughout Europe, but his life in Paris is murky," wrote Jean-Baptiste La Harpe to the Grand Duke of Russia.[19] The untold numbers of visitors who wanted to meet him had to outwit and foil his suspicions. The Duc de Croÿ expressed a desire to meet this Rousseau, a writer as difficult to see as he was famous: "For some time, I had wanted to see the famous Jean-Jacques Rousseau, whom I had never seen and who, three years ago, had come back to retire near Paris. We knew that Jean-Jacques frequented a certain café: we rushed there to see him, but he no longer went there and it was, it seemed, very difficult to approach him."[20] After hoping to be presented to Rousseau by the Prince de Ligne, he finally decided to go alone to the writer's home, in rue Plâtrière, where he was received without any trouble and spent two hours discussing botany with him.

The public figure of Rousseau was cemented the moment he refused celebrity. He was not only famous, he was famous for not wanting to be famous. He no longer published, claimed he no longer read books, and was satisfied to live frugally copying music. He systematically refused curious visitors or admirers. Many of his visitors competed with each other in finding ways to meet him, some bringing him music to copy, others, like the Prince de Ligne, pretending that they did not recognize him in order to better allay his suspicions. A visit to see Rousseau thus became a veritable literary genre, a necessary phase in narrative accounts of journeys to Paris. Later, in contemporaries' memoirs, all the same issues were almost always mentioned: the simple, austere life of Rousseau, his refusal to talk about books, his mix of friendliness and misanthropy, the quiet presence of Thérèse Levasseur, and, finally, his conviction that he was being persecuted. In most of these narratives, written down a few years later, many after the death of Rousseau and the publication of the *Confessions*, it is difficult to know what is true and what is fiction.

Thus, when Mme de Genlis describes in her memoirs a meeting with Rousseau in the autumn of 1770, she first of all paints a comic scene in which she mistakes him for an actor playing a role, then she describes the beginning of a friendship and edifying conversations, followed by a sudden rupture, Rousseau accusing her of taking him to the theater to show him off to the public, to be seen with him. This image of a sensitive, good man but one who was unjustly suspicious, who had an almost pathological relationship to his celebrity, corresponds perfectly to the collective portrait that numerous witnesses painted of Rousseau in the last years of his life and one which he himself accommodatingly maintained. The essential lesson of such stories was that a meeting with Rousseau had become a necessary encounter for anyone writing their memoirs. Even the glazier Jacques Louis Ménétra, though living in another social world than that of Mme de Genlis, recounted his lucky encounter with Jean-Jacques, their walks together, and the crowds that the presence of Rousseau excited in a café, with curious passersby climbing up on the marble tables to catch a glimpse of the author of *Émile*, much to the great distress of the owner of the establishment.[21] As for Alfieri, who did not wish to meet the "famous Rousseau" during his visit to Paris in 1771, he felt obliged to justify himself when he drafted his memoirs.[22]

In spite of the silence in which Rousseau enclosed himself, not publishing and going out little, his celebrity did not seem to diminish. In 1775, his comedy *Pygmalion* was performed at the Comédie-Française without his permission and with great success, due to the name of the author. The novelist Louis François Mettra was not fooled: "*Pygmalion* continues to be successful. I repeat, it is the name of *Jean-Jacques* that gives verve to this sketch, which is not very theatrical."[23] The least little incident concerning Rousseau was reported in the press, which is shown in one episode that he himself recounted at length in his *Reveries*, when he was knocked over by a dog running in front of a carriage in Ménilmontant. All the European newspapers reported the event as well as the worry that it caused. One read in the *Gazette de Berne*, for example:

> Paris, Nov. 8: J.J. Rousseau was returning from Ménil le montant a few days ago, near Paris, when a big Danish dog running very fast in front of a carriage with six horses, caused him to take a very bad fall. [...] This celebrated man was transported to his home and there is still doubt that he will survive it. Everyone in Paris is very concerned; people constantly go to his place or send someone to find out how he is doing.

The *Courrier d'Avignon* even announced his death by mistake, which gave Rousseau the doubtful privilege of reading his own obituary.[24] When he actually died the following year, the lively rumors concerning the possible publication of his *Confessions* showed that his celebrity had not dried up. The following years saw the apotheosis of Jean-Jacques, his transformation into a great man, as pilgrimages to Ermenonville show, then the publication of his complete works, and, finally, his induction into the Panthéon in 1794. This history goes beyond his celebrity. It became the history of his posthumous glory, his literary, intellectual, and political fortune. It was already part of the Rousseau mythology.[25]

Rousseau's celebrity became an aspect of his identity while he was alive. It was normal to associate him with celebrity, although a new concept, either to mock his taste for publicity or, to the contrary, to complain about his destiny. Starting in 1754, a visit by Rousseau to Geneva raised intense curiosity. The account of Jean-Baptiste Tollot, an apothecary and a Genovese man of letters, shows clearly that the interest of the observer was in the phenomenon of celebrity even more than in Rousseau himself, the way a celebrated man was capable of fascinating the public and focusing attention on himself.

> I will confine myself to telling the truth about a man of genius, indeed, whose works are famous but who likes obscurity and who, far from wanting to be renowned, would rather that such renown be silenced; in a word, I am talking about the celebrated Jean-Jacques Rousseau, who through his eccentric, paradoxical life, through his energetic style, through the audacity of his pen, has attracted the attention of the public, which sees him as a rare phenomenon meriting its curiosity. [...] All of Geneva has seen him, as I have, and from the highest to the lowest, everyone rushes to contemplate the man from Paris who has made a great many enemies, and the hate and jealousy coming from them have only made him more well known. [...] It is obvious, of course, that not *all the curious are in Paris*; everyone wants to see this star, who is sometimes eclipsed, sometimes covered by a cloud.[26]

If the star metaphor foreshadows the "stars" of the twentieth century, most of the elements that form the basis of Rousseau's celebrity in the following years are already present. The author focuses on the avid curiosity that this singular man aroused, his mania for paradox and his encouragement of controversy: the notoriety of his name induced a desire to see, to contemplate even, this celebrated man. However, this enthusiasm also engendered criticism, which had to do with the excesses of public curiosity, not with the writer himself. Far from being accused of willfully nourishing this fascination, Rousseau is credited with the contrary desire for anonymity.

Tollot was one of the first to describe in specific terms the celebrity of Rousseau, the crowds who pushed and shoved to see him when he walked by, admirers who wrote to him and came to visit while he tried in vain to preserve a quiet, obscure life. He was not the only one. Most of his friends and admirers talked endlessly about the troublesome nature of celebrity, which Rousseau himself fostered whenever it pleased him, as we shall see. So, when he complained to Mme de Chenonceaux about the annoying visits he received, she said: "It is the misfortune of celebrity and in my opinion it is not a small one."[27] During the same period, shocked by reading in the press about Rousseau's misfortunes, his friend Deleyre wrote to him: "When I think, my friend, of all the pain caused by your talent and your virtue, your celebrity makes me tremble. [...] How indignant I am to think of all the annoyances you have been subjected to these last six months and which I did not know about until I read of them in the newspaper!"[28] As for Bernois Niklaus Anton Kirchberger, he offered him asylum: "My dear and loving friend, come and take refuge in my house, where you can stay as long as you like, and I promise to protect you from your celebrity, at least from that which is tiresome."[29] The same idea appeared in the newspapers: "This famous man, tired of being talked about, seems to want to retire to the countryside and live there in obscurity."[30]

What is the basis of such a strong and long-lasting celebrity? At first, particularly in the 1750s, the notoriety of Rousseau rested on his capacity to excite scandal and controversy through the clever use of ambiguous opinions and a consummate sense of intellectual guerrilla warfare. The success of the first *Discourse* rested in large part on the fact that Rousseau turned the most well-established idea of his time on its head, shared both by Enlightenment philosophers and by most of their enemies, that of the link between progress in the arts and lifestyle. His discourse intrigued and invited refutation. "Isn't this simply a paradox with which he wanted to amuse the public?" asked Stanisław Leszczyński, one of Rousseau's first opponents. Intellectual polemics were followed by quarrels and noisy ruptures with his former friends, d'Alembert and Diderot, as well as a long-distance confrontation with Voltaire.

The romantic image of Rousseau as a solitary walker meditating on the meanness of his contemporaries has overshadowed his talent, although undeniable, as a polemicist. In 1752, he made up for the failure of *Narcisse* by publishing a provocative and rather arrogant preface in which he affirmed: "Here I am not writing about my play but about me. I must, in spite of my repugnance, speak about myself," and he took advantage of the occasion to respond to all his critics. Just when all the debates aroused by his *Discourse* seemed to be exhausted, he started them going again by reaffirming his positions and by attacking his adversaries with new energy, reproaching scholars for defending science as a way to assure their authority the same way ancient pagan priests defended religion.

The following year, his *Letter on French Music* provoked a scandal. Rousseau was not content to simply defend Italian opera; he unleashed an all-out attack on French music, the violence of which surprised people.[31] Thus it was hardly surprising to read in the *Correspondance littéraire* a few weeks later that he "had just set fire to the four corners of Paris." "Never," it added, "has one seen a quarrel louder or more intense."[32] The scandal was, indeed, so intense that musicians from the Opera decided to burn Rousseau in effigy. For a writer almost unknown two years before, this was already proof of his remarkable visibility.

Repercussions from the *Letter on French Music* did not only result from the aesthetic positions defended by Rousseau, but above all from the patriotic scandal aroused by his total rejection of French music. This episode reinforced the image of the paradoxical man which now accompanied him everywhere. How could an author who had just enjoyed such success with *Le Devin du village*, a French opera whose refrains were on everyone's lips, categorically condemn French music? This astonishment also came from the fact that Rousseau seemed to escape every possible category found in the intellectual field, an impression reinforced by the publication of the *Discourse on the Origin and Basis of Inequality* in 1755, then by his brutal rupture in 1757 with the *encyclopédistes*. Radical positions, a sense of provocation and polemic, even a taste for scandal, these elements constituted an explosive combination which could only incite the curiosity of the public. In the 1750s, Rousseau seemed in many ways to be a master of self-promotion.

In 1762, when *Émile* appeared, Rousseau was still this paradoxical author figure putting his eloquence to work writing provocative theses, which the *Mémoires secrets* invoked in order to explain the expectations raised by the book: "This work, announced & awaited, piques the curiosity of the public because the author combines great genius with a rare talent for writing with as much grace as energy. He is reproached for sustaining paradoxes; in part this has to do with the seductive art he uses and to which perhaps he owes his great celebrity; it is only since he took this path that he has been distinctively singled out."[33]

Ami Jean-Jacques

At this point, however, the celebrity of Rousseau was enriched by another dimension: to the curiosity aroused by the eloquent writer, never short of paradoxes, was added a sentimental aspect found in *La Nouvelle Héloïse*. The novel's success, published early in 1761, was prodigious. In spite of its often lukewarm, even disdainful, reception by writers and critics, the book was adored by the public. "Never has a work created such an astonishing sensation," noted Louis Sébastien Mercier, describing the public's fascination. The first editions were immediately sold out and bookstores loaned the book page by page to readers. Even those who did not read the book could not escape the collective enthusiasm. The young Princess Czartoryska, sixteen years old and visiting Paris, got caught up in the latest fashion and ordered miniatures inspired by the book: "I don't read anything and I have never read anything by Rousseau, but they talk endlessly about *La Nouvelle Héloïse* and every woman wants to be like Julie. I thought I had better join the ranks." Having managed to obtain a visit with Rousseau at his house, she showed up "with the eagerness one has to see something new, to see a show."[34]

Many people, however, had read the novel and received a real emotional shock. "From the first pages, I was delirious. [...] Days were not long enough, I read at night, and had one emotional upheaval after another. I reached the last letter from Saint-Preux, no longer crying but screaming, howling like an animal," General Thiébault remembered in his *Mémoires*.[35] The publication of *La Nouvelle Héloïse* marked a date in the history of reading, as many readers testified by writing to Rousseau and telling him about their emotions. From that time on, Rousseau seemed to be the master of feelings, a man who spoke the language of virtue and whose works had the power to make his readers better by pulling tears out of them. The young Charles Joseph Panckoucke, at that time a publisher in Rouen, did not hesitate to write Rousseau a passionate letter:

> Your divine writings, Monsieur, are a fire which devour, they have pierced my soul, strengthened my heart, enlightened my mind. Having for a long time been given over to the treacherous illusions of impetuous youth, my reason had gone astray in the search for truth. [...] A god was needed, a powerful god, to pull me back from the precipice and you are, Monsieur, the god who has worked this miracle. [...] Your tender and virtuous Héloïse will always be for me the code for moral sanity, the source of all my ecstasy, all my love and all my desires, and you, Monsieur, will have my most profound veneration and respect. I adore you and your sublime writings, all those lucky enough to read your work will find in you a trusted guide who will lead them to perfection and to love and to the practice of all those virtues that make up the essence of a good man.[36]

Behind the bombast, very characteristic of the sentimental style of the period, one can perceive the moral and spiritual experience that *La Nouvelle Héloïse* represented for many readers. Up until that moment, Rousseau had been a censor, denouncing the vices of modern society. He now became a guide, opening up for his readers a path to moral regeneration and happiness. The letter also revealed the transfer of feeling to the author, which authorized, even stimulated, the writing. The bond was no longer simply curiosity or admiration, it was primarily an outpouring of gratitude, of "eternal acknowledgment," which invited effusion and led the reader, when he began writing, to imitate the hyperbolic style of the novel, sentimental and moral, where tears and pity led to virtue.

It is likely that Panckoucke, a young publisher from the provinces, was not totally disinterested in showing his admiration for a successful writer. But such an effusion went beyond professional flattery and Rousseau received several hundred similar letters in the months following the novel's publication. These letters were so numerous, several hundred in just a few months, that Rousseau talked about a "multitude" and even thought about publishing them.[37] Sadly, not all the letters were saved, but those we have demonstrate this same sentimental enthusiasm for the work and for the author. Most notable of all are the large number of ordinary readers, sometimes anonymous. One of them thanked Rousseau for "the only good moments" he had had in the last six years. He found in the novel echoes of his own situation and his impossible love: "I was so carried away that if the immensity of the oceans did not separate me from you as from my Julie, I would not be able to stop myself from giving you a huge hug and thanking you a thousand times with the delicious tears that you pulled out of me. Perhaps one day I will be impelled to meet you, and I will certainly find a way."[38]

Some readers, it is true, kept a calmer tone, even a critical one. Thus, Pierre de La Roche, a man from Geneva who was living in London, wrote long letters in which he discussed the work point by point. But even this gesture, although without passionate feeling, was only possible because Rousseau was not simply an author, but a public figure one could talk to. Most of the time, readers wrote to thank him and above all to talk about the change the book had produced in their lives. Jean-Louis Le Cointe, a Protestant from Nîmes, owed Rousseau for his discovery of the "charms of virtue." When he wrote to Rousseau, he hesitated between the distance which separated him from a great writer and the affective proximity allowed by the novel: "I feel all my temerity and I condemn it; but the more you inspire me with respect, the less my heart can refuse the pleasure of telling you about the feelings you have caused to be born in me." Then he opened up even more to the person who had given him the means to understand his life differently. "Being sincerely attached to a young wife, you have made it known to the two of us that what seemed a simple attachment through the habit of living together is the most tender love. Father at age twenty-eight of four children, I will follow your lessons in order to make men of them."[39]

Not all readers wrote directly to Rousseau, certainly not when they discovered the novel several years after its publication. Manon Phlipon, who would play an important political role during the Revolution under the name of Mme Roland, was only seven years old when *La Nouvelle Héloïse* appeared, but, in the 1770s, she was enthusiastic about the author, whose books she devoured and whom she dreamed of meeting. "I'm angry that you do not like Rousseau, because I like him more than I can say," she wrote to her best friend. "Just talking about this excellent Jean-Jacques my soul is moved, animated, warmed: my taste for study is reborn, for the true and the beautiful of every kind." Openly proselytizing, she insisted on sharing her fascination: "I am so astounded that you are amazed by my enthusiasm for Rousseau: I regard him as a friend of humanity, its benefactor and mine"; and: "I know that I owe to his writings what is best in me. His genius has warmed my soul: I feel it wrapping me in flames, lifting me up and ennobling me."[40]

The enthusiasm created by the reading of Rousseau's books, *La Nouvelle Héloïse* and *Émile* above all, translated into an attachment to his person. This was reinforced by Rousseau's misfortunes, by the stories in the press of his bad luck and his successive exiles. It obviously opened up the theme of a persecuted Rousseau, constrained to live in retirement and in solitude:

> The persecutions, the injustices by men, almost gave Rousseau the right not to believe in their sincerity. Tormented in every country, betrayed by those he thought were friends in a manner even more painful because his sensitive soul saw their evil ways without being able to delicately unmask them; persecuted by his ungrateful country, which he had exemplified, enlightened, served; exposed to the traits of envy and meanness, is it any wonder that retirement seemed to him the only desirable asylum.

Rousseau's fans easily went from admiration for his writing to an unconditional defense of the man.

In a seminal essay, Robert Darnton highlighted one of Rousseau's readers, Jean Ranson, a merchant from La Rochelle who kept up a regular correspondence with the director of the typographical company in Neuchâtel. He ordered books, but also took the opportunity to ask after his "*Ami* Jean-Jacques." Although he had never met him, Ranson saw in Rousseau a familiar person, a friend of the family to whom he was bound by a long-distance intimacy, thanks to the reading of his books, but also thanks to the news about him found in journals and in his letters. Darnton clearly showed that this attitude was related to a new practice of reading adapted to the Rousseauistic language-of-the-heart rhetoric. Because readers found in the novel, or in other writings by Rousseau, elements that seemed to describe their own lives and clarified their subjectivity, they in turn went further than the text, which was only a pretext for directing their admiration and affection toward the author. "The impact of *Rousseauism* therefore owed a great deal to Rousseau. He spoke to the most intimate experiences of his readers and encouraged them to see through to the Jean-Jacques behind the texts."[41] This affective reading was so successful it logically led the reader to entertain a mesmerizing relationship with the person of the author. However, determined to create a history of reading based on an ethnographical approach to the culture of the Ancien Régime and a "mental world that is almost unthinkable today," Darnton depicted the affective link forged between Rousseau and his readers as the expression of a mysterious attitude, favorable to sentimental effusiveness, that would seem strange to us now: "The Rousseauistic readers of prerevolutionary France threw themselves into texts with a passion that we can barely imagine, that is as alien to us as the lust for plunder among the Norsemen or the fear of demons among the Balinese."[42] But is this enthusiastic attachment so completely strange to us today when crowds stood in line for hours at the appearance of a new volume of *Harry Potter*, or vast numbers of inconsolable fans grouped together to weep at the death of Princess Diana or Michael Jackson?

Reader reactions to Rousseau's work were not so "naïve," nor so exotic. Far from believing that Julie and Saint-Preux really existed, as one often thought, most had fun with the ambiguity upheld by Rousseau concerning the authenticity of the letters, according to a procedure which was already, at that time, a hackneyed commonplace. A number of readers enjoyed, as readers would do today, imagining keys to an auto-biographical reading, persuaded that Rousseau was inspired by his own amorous dalliances in order to imagine the fate of his characters and give them such eloquence. Consequently, interest in and pity for the charac-ters transferred to Rousseau, who had been capable of creating them and who could not have done so, they thought, unless he had himself lived through comparable ordeals. The main principle of the romance novel, to move readers emotionally and to give to virtue a romance form through a process of identification with the moral dilemmas of the characters, strongly encouraged such an affective transfer to the author.[43]

The enthusiasm expressed by Rousseau's correspondents, their desire to weave an intimate bond with him, both friendly and spiritual, in spite of distance, were not the traits of an old and irrational attitude, but rather the joint effects of a work that lauded romantic effusiveness and of new forms of literary communication. The religious vocabulary, very present in Panckoucke, that of moral and spiritual conversion employed by so many readers, should not be construed as an error. This was not a matter of a "cult" or a quasi-mystical surrender, but a new formulation of the bond that individuals who made up a public had with a contempo-rary celebrity, one with whom they identified or whom they had chosen as a guide and virtual friend. This relationship, a truly intense one, had strong affective or moral dimensions, especially when the famous person, as was the case with Rousseau, offered through his work or the example of his life means to a "recovery of oneself."[44]

The relationship that numerous readers wove with Rousseau, through his books, came from this friendly imagined intimacy. This is what clearly appears in the Jean Ranson correspondence. This was not a young reader, passionate and fanatical; he was a rational merchant but one who found in "*l'Ami* Jean-Jacques" sound moral principles. "Everything that *l'Ami* Jean-Jacques has written about the duties of husbands and wives, of mothers and fathers, has had a profound effect upon me, and I confess to you that it will serve me as a rule in any of those estates that I should occupy." This does not arise from an improbable identification, nor from a religion, nor from confusion between fiction and reality. Ranson forged a long-distance friendship with Rousseau, both real and imagined, which served him as a guide. It was under this form of amicable intimacy that he took a "lively interest" in the person of Jean-Jacques, demanding on several different occasions of Jean-Frédéric Ostervald news about "his friend Jean-Jacques's" health. When Rousseau died, Ranson cried out: "So, Monsieur, we have lost the sublime Jean-Jacques. How it pains me never to have seen nor heard him [...] Tell me, I pray, what you think of this famous man, whose fate hs always aroused the most tender feelings in me, while Voltaire often provoked my indignation."[45]

It is clearly this conjunction of Rousseau's celebrity, the emotional and moral power of his books, and the sympathy toward his misfortunes which pushed people to react: readers wrote to this celebrated man, without knowing him, to testify about their feelings and the desire they had to meet him. No one expressed this aspiration more strongly, perhaps, than a nobleman from the south of France who affirmed that his soul felt "the strongest passion" for Jean-Jacques and he would now write to him each week until Rousseau decided to respond to him. "If Rousseau did not exist, I would need nothing. He exists, and I feel that something is missing in me."[46] As for the clock-maker Jean Romilly, he ruminated for several months over his letter and admitted openly the place that Rousseau, as an imaginary friend, had in his daily life, to the point of becoming an obsession:

> I can no longer defer talking with you, it is almost two years now even three that I have wanted to tell you about all the idealized conversations I have with you because you should know that whether I'm sleeping or walking about, you are always present in my mind and I am only at ease in company when I can talk a little about you, either to those who love you or those who do not love you at all.[47]

The correspondence that Rousseau and Mme de La Tour maintained for ten years shows how the bond starts, sentimental and playful, asymmetric and fragile, between the author and one of his admirers. This admirer, a member of the gentry, separated from her husband and thirty years old when *La Nouvelle Héloïse* appeared, did not start a correspondence with Rousseau on her own initiative. It was her friend, Mme Bernardoni, who began a correspondence with him, half-flirtatious, half-serious, assuring him that she knew another Julie possessing all the merits of the book's heroine. Taking the role of Claire, she got Rousseau to answer the letters. Thus began a game among them where Mme Bernardoni, who would quickly disappear, played the role of mischievous go-between with her devoted friend Mme de La Tour as the obliging admirer, with both of whom Rousseau, at first, did not mind multiplying allusions to the novel and to the trio that they could, themselves, create. Then developed a long-standing correspondence between Rousseau and Mme de La Tour, which lasted until a rather sudden rupture was imposed by Rousseau ten years later. Mme de La Tour was demanding, endlessly restarting the correspondence over and over again, tirelessly asking news from Rousseau, showing her interest and her worry, reading and reading his works ("My friend, I must tell you about my enchantment: I am reading *La Nouvelle Héloïse* for the seventh or eighth time: it moves me more than the first time I read it!"),[48] always multiplying enthusiastic commentaries and indiscreet questions. Rousseau moved from an amicable tone, even tender ("Dear Marianne, you are hurt, and I am disarmed. I feel nothing but tenderness when I think of your beautiful eyes in tears"),[49] to much more distant phrases, even long suspicious silences; but all in all, he wrote more than sixty letters to her, turning these long, improvised gallantries into an epistolary friendship.[50]

It was not enough for Mme de La Tour to read and reread the works of Rousseau, dreaming about the loves of Julie and Saint-Preux, and writing to her "dear Jean-Jacques" long letters in which she deplored the fact that he did not answer more assiduously. Her zeal pushed her to take his side when he was attacked. Thus, at the highest point of the quarrel with David Hume, in 1766–7, she published a libelous, anonymous piece meant to justify Rousseau, and then she drafted a second one. When Rousseau died, she took up the pen again to defend his memory, with a series of letters addressed to Élie Fréron's *L'Année littéraire*, in the form of a volume entitled *Jean-Jacques Rousseau vangé [sic] par son amie (Jean-Jacques Rousseau Defended by His Friend)*.[51] Mme de La Tour was not the first to go from private admiration to public apology. Panckoucke, whose emotions we saw when *La Nouvelle Héloïse* appeared, took up the pen a few weeks later to reply in the *Journal encyclopédique* to jokes made by Voltaire.

What is revealed here is the complexity of the reactions aroused by the celebrity of Rousseau, not only a successful author whose paradoxes were intriguing, but also the "champion of sensitive souls," the author of a great romance novel that certain readers read over and over again, a persecuted writer, forced to flee France, then Geneva, then Switzerland, in search of refuge. Beyond the curiosity fed by the chronicle of his misfortunes and his eccentricities, causing crowds of curiosity seekers to gather wherever he went, there existed a more profound attachment between "Jean-Jacques" and his readers, woven from empathy and a desire for intimacy, from admiration and gratefulness. For readers like Ranson, Panckoucke, Manon Phlipon, or Mme de La Tour, just a few examples among many known and unknown, Rousseau was not only a fashionable person, he was an imaginary friend they were always ready to empathize with and defend. The characteristic paradox of celebrity, and more generally mass culture, was that Rousseau's readers lived their bond with "*l'Ami* Jean-Jacques" in a particularly personal and singular way, even though the bond was perceived identically by numerous other readers.

The public reaction to the heated quarrel between Rousseau and David Hume in 1766 demonstrates this attachment to the celebrated man. Hume had agreed to the demand of two of Rousseau's friends and protectors in polite Parisian society, Mme de Luxembourg and Mme de Boufflers, to find him asylum in England at the height of the persecution exercised against him in France and in Switzerland. Sadly, the relations between the two men worsened very quickly. Rousseau, convinced that Hume was in league with his enemies, refused the pension offered by George III that Hume had been able to obtain, writing Hume a shocking letter full of insane reproaches. Sickened and worried, Hume hurriedly wrote to Holbach and d'Alembert to show them the tenor of the letter and ask their advice. The move was maladroit and had dreadful consequences. The quarrel between the two men resounded everywhere, first in the closed circles of Parisian salons, where Rousseau's enemies were overjoyed, then in the press. A private dispute between two men became a literary event, a veritable public quarrel, the effects of which were felt by Rousseau for a very long time, alienating him from the support of his powerful protectors.

I have described elsewhere the mechanisms and the social stakes at issue in this quarrel.[52] But the public dynamic must be emphasized here, the reactions of anonymous readers who wrote in defense of Rousseau. Hume himself was stunned: "I little imagined, that a private story, told to a private gentleman, could run over a whole kingdom in a moment; if the King of England had declared war against the King of France, it could not have more suddenly been the subject of conversation."[53] Hume's strategy and that of his Parisian friends was to keep the grievances against Rousseau private, in order to avoid engaging in a public polemic that might have destroyed Hume's image, a most hazardous outcome. They hoped to keep the situation within the world of the salons and the closed circles of polite society, that area where reputations were made and lost. There, thanks to an intense campaign to denigrate Rousseau, emphasizing the spotless renown of the "good David," who had been,

124

during his visit to Paris, the darling of polite society, it was a matter of definitively destroying the reputation of Rousseau in the minds of Mme de Luxembourg, Mme de Boufflers, and his other patrons. Moreover, the mission appeared easy because Rousseau had opted to keep silent, not responding to those who asked him for explanations, unless he just told them to mind their own business.

Hume's friends made one mistake: they underestimated the celebrity of Rousseau. He was not only a player in the little literary world of the capital, he was also a public figure. In just a few days, extracts of the letter from Hume to Holbach were widely circulated, much beyond society circles, feeding "public rumors." Less than a month later, the newspapers seized on the affair, first with an article in *Le Courrier d'Avignon*, then in the English papers. The *St James's Chronicle*, for instance, published a series of articles about the quarrel over the course of the summer and into the autumn of 1766.[54] Confronted with the sudden publicity given his rupture with Rousseau, Hume was forced to change strategies. Convinced he was right and in order to put an end to the rumors, he asked his friends to publish articles, including the long accusing letter written by Rousseau, accompanied by Hume's own commentary. However, contrary to his intentions, far from ending the affair by proving the ingratitude and madness of Rousseau, this started the controversy all over again and engendered numerous reactions. Mme de La Tour, as we saw, took up her pen to defend Jean-Jacques. But her text only strengthened the *Justification de Jean-Jacques Rousseau*, the author of which was anonymous. In the form of pamphlets and letters from readers, there were numerous admirers of Rousseau who took up his defense.

Rousseau's letter to Hume, which the latter thought was a madness, was read conversely by many readers as proof of the author's innocence: unhappy, sincere, and persecuted. The effectiveness of this text was due to the fact that it was drafted in the romantic and hyperbolic style of *La Nouvelle Héloïse*, certain passages even using the same sentences employed by Saint-Preux.[55] The identification of Jean-Jacques with Saint-Preux, which had already been used successfully in the 1761 novel, worked again five years later. The conflation was almost total between the individual Jean-Jacques Rousseau, the author of *La Nouvelle Héloïse* and *Émile*, and the public figure "Jean-Jacques," constituting a series of collective representations, certain of which were driven by the press, others kept alive by his writings.

The relative isolation of Rousseau in the Paris literary world, and even his silence, his refusal to respond and to defend himself, worked in his favor because it seemed, for his public, to testify to his sincerity. In the eyes of his admirers, Rousseau was not an author like others, fighting for his reputation, but a reasonable man who was suffering. "I do not live in the world, I do not know what is going on there; I have no reference points, no associates, no intrigues," he wrote to Hume on July 10.[56] On the other hand, he had many readers for whom he was "*l'Ami* Jean-Jacques." The anonymous author of the *Justification de Jean-Jacques Rousseau dans la contestation qui lui est survenue avec M. Hume* claims to have seen in Rousseau's letters to Hume "only the traces of a beautiful soul, generous, delicate and too sensitive, just as Rousseau has shown us in his writings and even more by his behavior."[57] After having claimed that he did not know Rousseau personally, he concluded:

> Who would not admit that Rousseau was forced to conduct himself the way he did in regard to M. Hume, and that on this occasion he showed his soul to be beautiful, delicate, and sensitive, an intrepid soul above adversity? Ah! Who is the virtuous man who could be distanced from the society of Rousseau by this event? And who, to the contrary, would not desire to become the friend of a man so full of candor, so worthy of esteem.[58]

In the same vein, the similarly anonymous author of the *Observations sur l'exposé succinct de la contestation qui s'est élevée entre M. Hume et M. Rousseau,* in an eighty-eight-page brochure, dissects almost word for word reproaches addressed by Hume to Rousseau and makes a judgment about this quarrel between "two celebrated men" almost entirely in favor of the latter. The thesis he defends is that of a conspiracy plotted by Rousseau's enemies, in Geneva and in Paris, of which Hume was the more or less conscious agent. While claiming twice that he did not know Rousseau "except by his work," he claims to be among his "friends." These various pamphlets answer for Rousseau and are a comfort. The author of these observations comments:

> As I finish these observations, a pamphlet is being published [it is the *Justification de Jean-Jacques. Rousseau*] which brings honor to the heart of the person who wrote it: it is wrong in supposing that the friends of M. Rousseau have been beaten: the ones I know are tireless; certain of the probity and sincerity of their friend, they imitate his silence: my decision to break this silence rests on the notion that virtuous men will always recognize each other, and someone who is unknown cannot be accused of bias.

The defenders of Rousseau constituted a sort of elective community, not a claque like the one around Hume, accused of working together secretly to destroy Jean-Jacques, but a group of the writer's friends who often did not know him except through his work but were convinced of his innocence, his sincerity, and the persecutions that hounded him. They made of their anonymity an argument for impartiality and perceived their public commitment in his favor as an act of justice that they would tirelessly uphold.

Hume and his friends, and some historians after them, were surprised by the public support Rousseau received and the turn the quarrel took.[59] Although they had intended to discreetly destroy the reputation of Rousseau in literary and social circles, they found themselves instead mixed up in a public quarrel that left Hume with a bitter taste. Although there was no doubt in their minds that Rousseau was wrong on all counts regarding the norms of polite society – he had virulently attacked, without proof, a man who was his patron – a large part of the public judged the affair differently. Hume's strategy, along with Holbach and d'Alembert, was based on a series of social conventions (politesse, patronage, etc.) which guaranteed the control of reputations through conversation and within inner circles. The public was held in suspicion. Holbach, as prudent in the salons as he was radical in his writings, wrote to Hume that "the public thinks very badly of quarrels that demand a judgment from it," while d'Alembert warned him: "It is always disagreeable and often a nuisance to be tried by written word before this stupid animal called the public, which asks nothing better than to speak badly of those whose merit offends it."[60] What matters, Holbach resumes, is to retain "the esteem of enlightened and impartial persons, the only people a gallant man desires the approval of."[61] But this strategy ran up against another principle, a new one, that of celebrity, which immediately nullified their attempt to keep the affair quiet and provided Rousseau with anonymous, albeit widespread, support.

One of the aspects of the quarrel, from the outset, was the pension that Hume had obtained for Rousseau from George III. Rousseau had refused all pensions the previous fifteen years because he wanted above all to be independent, and thus the royal pension bothered him. The affair was complicated; it seems that at first Rousseau accepted the pension on condition that it be accorded in secret; then he changed his mind. Whatever happened, he ended by believing that Hume had only made the request in order to put him in an impossible position, forcing him to contradict himself and be discredited. In the eyes of Rousseau, this was a grave situation that put into question his whole way of life. For Hume and for most of his contemporaries in polite society, this was only a pretext. Turgot assured him: "No one in the world could imagine that you asked for a pension for Rousseau in order to dishonor him. Only he would think that a pension was dishonorable."[62] Rousseau's readers, on the other hand, had another opinion: "Rousseau ungrateful! It's been proven that he is nothing of the sort. Rousseau is proud, perhaps. But a pride that is above money, which leads us to live off the fruit of our labors, which protects us from all cowardly compromises, is an estimable pride, and, unfortunately, far too rare among men of Letters!"[63] the author of the *Justification de Jean-Jacques Rousseau* exclaimed again. What was at stake here was Rousseau's singular position in the literary world, his refusal of common norms, his wish to construct an atypical public persona. This attempt to create an exemplary public image was itself a powerful factor in his celebrity.

Eccentricity, Exemplarity, Celebrity

Detractors and flatterers of Rousseau were alike on one point: he did nothing the way others did. His public image was that of an absolutely unique and eccentric man. A mad man, said his enemies; a sensitive man without equal, responded his admirers. He, as we know, made of this singularity, at an existential level, the very heart of his *Confessions*: "I am not made like any of the [men] I have seen; I dare to believe that I am not made like any that exist. If I am worth no more, at least I am different."[64] But this originality is strongly projected into the public sphere through the persona of "Jean-Jacques." Rousseau, however, was not content just to be different; he wanted to let it be known.

The element that contributed most to the construction of an eccentric public persona was the famous "personal reform" that Rousseau undertook at the beginning of his notoriety, after the publication of the *Discourse on the Arts and Sciences*. It consisted in making his lifestyle conform to his principles, and breaking with traditional forms of patronage and the lifestyle of writers in the Ancien Régime. Rousseau gave up his position as secretary to Dupin de Francueil, renounced habits of dress customary in polite society, refused presents and pensions, and chose to earn his living by copying music. He thus manifested, both publicly and in his own eyes, his independence in regard to the elites.[65]

Before evaluating the consequences of this principle, one needs to take it seriously. The insistence on an exemplary life fulfills several functions. For one, it assures Rousseau of his own authenticity. This decision is part of a long intellectual and moral tradition which goes back to ancient philosophy and was revived in the Renaissance, during which philosophy was not simply a question of doctrine, but also an ethical question, a way of life, a self-exploration to find a more authentic, a truer way of existence.[66] Rousseau says it again in the *Reveries of the Solitary Walker*: "I have seen many who philosophized much more learnedly than I, but their philosophy was, so to speak, foreign to them."[67] Opposed to philosophy as simply knowledge about the world, an intellectual exercise, Rousseau defended a concept of thought which was much more personal, first of all an exercise in self-knowledge and a means to perfectionism. On the other hand, while publicizing this philosophical and moral exemplarity, Rousseau also meant to guarantee the credibility of his philosophical discourse, and in particular the biting criticism that he addressed to his contemporaries. As he always said, an authentic thinker is the one who is ready to sacrifice everything for the truth. According to a suggested formulation: "If Socrates had died in his bed, people today might suspect that he was nothing more than a clever Sophist."[68] Returning to the *Confessions* concerning this double conversion, at once theoretical and biographical, which marked his sensational entrance into the world of letters, Rousseau wrote: "Moreover, how could the severe principles I had just adopted be harmonized with a station which had so little relationship to them, and would not I, a Cashier of a Receiver General of finances, be preaching disinterestedness and poverty in good grace?"[69] This formulation draws attention because of its ambiguity: Is it meant to save the credibility of his principles by avoiding ridicule? This ambiguity is at the heart of Rousseau's choices, always worried about the public effect that would be produced, even as he openly fretted about the theoretical and ethical logic of an idea. One can opt for either a comprehensible or a critical reading of these choices. In the first case, one judges that the claims of exemplarity by Rousseau necessarily have two sides. In relationship to oneself, an ethical concern, it is fundamentally a private affair. In terms of a pedagogical argument, meant to balance his works by giving them extra weight, it is necessarily public. In the second case, a less charitable reading might be that this concern about exemplarity was, first of all, a concern about attracting public attention. The result is the same: the claim of authenticity and consistency is not only a personal and intimate experience, a solitary investigation of self; it is, from the beginning, loudly proclaimed by Rousseau through indiscreet acts such as refusing a royal patronage following the success of *Devin du village,* or adopting an incongruous but practical piece of clothing, a kind of Arab kaftan that he called his "Armenian robe" and which was meant to show his disdain for conventions and inner circles, his choice of a simple life, without luxuries, close to nature. These clothes became a recognizable sign of the "Jean-Jacques" public persona, feeding in his enemies a suspicion of histrionics.[70]

Rousseau's worry about exemplarity illustrates perfectly the public dynamic for him: it was matter of pride to publicly take responsibility for his ideas, to sign all his books with his own name rather than hide behind pseudonyms or a clever anonymous usage. While Holbach, for example, published treatises on atheism under pseudonyms and managed to stay anonymous all his life, and Voltaire endlessly played the game of pseudonyms, even when they were transparent and only served to save face, Rousseau, for his part, refused to play even the most minimal game by pretending not to recognize his writings when they were published without authorization.[71]

When Rousseau voluntarily published the *Social Contract* and *Émile*, only four years after the scandal provoked by Helvétius's *De l'Esprit* and condemnation of the *Encyclopédie*, everyone saw in this a real political provocation. His refusal of anonymity, even the façade of it, particularly irritated the authorities and increased their severity. The decree from the Archbishop of Paris explicitly reproached Rousseau, and the same went for the parliamentary injunction against *Émile* on June 9, 1762: "That the author of this book, who has not feared to give his own name, should be prosecuted swiftly; that it is important, since he has made himself known, for justice to make an example of him."[72] The choice that Rousseau made to sign his works, to publicize his name, appeared to be a major part of the scandal. Voltaire himself did not understand why Rousseau refused to take the most minimal precautions and reproached him for putting the entire philosophical movement in danger. He notes in the margins of his copy of the *Letter to Beaumont*: "And why did you use your name? poor beggar [*pauvre diable*],"[73] which, for Voltaire, meant a writer trying to live from his pen, "literary riff-raff," as he sometimes said, opposed to the figure of a gentleman writer who knew how to elegantly stage his public appearances.

For Rousseau, on the other hand, the choice to sign his texts was a fundamental element in taking political responsibility as a writer.[74] He explains this in his *Letter to Beaumont*, the Archbishop of Paris,[75] and especially, and at length, in his *Letters Written from the Mountain*, a polemical text written in response to the public prosecutor Tronchin, in the troubled context of political conflicts in Geneva and following the condemnation of the *Social Contract* by the Geneva Advisory Council.[76] Rousseau demanded to be judged in person and developed an argument in which a book signed could not be condemned in the same way an anonymous book could be. The condemnation of a book recognized by its author could not be made against a text alone; it had to necessarily include the intention of the author and implied a proper trial. The argumentation was laid out in two stages. Rousseau first of all delivered an ironic satire on the usual practice of anonymity, denouncing its hypocrisy:

> Several are even in the practice of avowing these Books in order to do themselves honor with them, and of disavowing them in order to put themselves under cover; the same man will be or will not be the Author,

130

in front of the same man depending whether they are at a hearing or at a supper. [...] In that manner safety costs vanity nothing.[77]

Then he demanded to defend himself. Because he had signed and taken responsibility for his text, he insisted it was not possible to dissociate his writing from his person. It was not the text itself which was condemned, but the act of announcing it and the intention of the author.

> But when a clumsy Author, that is to say, an Author who knows his duty, who wants to fulfill it, believes himself obliged to say nothing to the public without avowing it, without naming himself, without showing himself in order to respond, then equity, which ought not to punish the clumsiness of a man of honor as a crime, wants one to proceed with him in another manner. It wants one not to separate the trial of the Book from that of the man, since by putting his name on it he declares that he does not want them separated. It wants one not to judge the work, which cannot respond, until after having heard the Author who responds for it.[78]

This theory about the author's intellectual responsibility and criminal liability rested on the impossibility of distinguishing the book from the writer. But it is clear that a statement like this implies transforming the author into a public figure since, as soon as the book is published, he "is known and ready to answer for it."

Here again, claiming responsibility is accompanied by a desire for recognition. In *Letters Written from the Mountain*, the vocabulary of honor is omnipresent. Rousseau strongly reproached the Advisory Council for having "destroyed his honor," and for having "stigmatized [him] by the hand of the Hangman."[79] The entire text thematically works by contrasting the honorable man, who insists on signing the books he publishes (one could say he makes it a point of honor), and the infamy which touches him by the condemnation of his book: "When one burns a Book, what does the Hangman do? Does he dishonor the pages of the Book? Who ever heard it said that a Book had any honor?"[80] The honor associated with a work of literature sometimes expressed itself in the form of proud claims of authorship, as when Rousseau wrote to his printer Marc Michel Rey concerning the publication of the *Letter to d'Alembert*: "Not only can you name me; but my name will be there and it will even be in the title."[81] It is difficult not to see here a publicity strategy as well, one based on an acute awareness of the scandal that the book will provoke and the notoriety of its author.

This willingness to put his name on his books, when it was traditional to hide names, by prudence or out of respect for the values of the elite, was made clear by Rousseau in his preface to the second edition of *La Nouvelle Héloïse*:

131

R. Own it Monsieur? Does an honorable man hide when he addresses
    the Public? Does he dare to print what he would not dare acknowl-
    edge? I am the Editor of this book, and I shall name myself as Editor.
N. You will name yourself? You?
R. Myself.
N. What! You will put your name on it?
R. Yes, Monsieur.
N. Your real name? *Jean-Jacques Rousseau*, in full?
R. *Jean-Jacques Rousseau* in full.[82]

And indeed, the cover of the book carried the name of Rousseau
starting with its first edition, a rare practice with novels. Behind his justification of sincerity and transparency, Rousseau burst with pride, even
jubilation, at repeating and almost trumpeting his name; this authorial
gesture showed an ostentatious break with standards of literary seemliness, provocation being part of the challenge. This attitude was logical
given his refusal to imitate the aristocratic or fashionable figure of the
writer. Writing was neither a job nor a hobby, but a vocation, even
a mission, complete with social and public usefulness. This emphatic
affirmation, often repeated by Rousseau,[83] was here treated in a rather
ironic way. It contributed to associating the name of Rousseau with his
works. The attachment Rousseau had to his family name, his refusal
of pseudonyms, was not only a principled stance; it was inseparable
from an affirmation of self by way of a proud announcement of his
identity, social, personal, and authorial, where the name was the mark
of credibility. Even during those periods when he was threatened by
the authorities, Rousseau generally refused to travel under an assumed
name. He wrote to his friend Daniel Roguin, for example, who wanted to
invite him to Yverdon after the condemnation of *Émile*, that "in regard
to going incognito, I cannot bring myself to take someone's name, nor
to change it. [...] Therefore Rousseau I am, and Rousseau I want to
remain, whatever the risk."[84]

These different elements (the refusal of pensions and presents, avowed
suspicion of the manners of polite society, the choice of unusual clothing, the declaration of his name) all went together: they created the
Jean-Jacques persona, not only a talented polemicist or romance novelist, but also an eccentric person who did not seem to conform to any of
the ways of the literary world at the time. This individuality nourished
Rousseau's discourse in an obsessive way: Was he sincere and authentic,
or was it only a pose, a way to attract public attention – a publicity
gimmick, in other words? On this point, Grimm for once outdid Fréron.
The latter denounced Rousseau, as early as 1754, for "his frantic need to
be talked about in society"; the former described Rousseau, a few years
later, as "this writer famous for his eloquence and his singularity," and

sarcastically added: "The role of eccentric always succeeds for those who have the courage and the patience to carry it off."[85]

Others went even further, denouncing in Rousseau a pathological desire for celebrity, even more obvious because all such desire was ostentatiously denied. The Duchesse de Choiseul wrote to Mme du Deffand: "He is mad, and I would not be surprised if he expressly committed crimes which did not simply debase him but led to the gallows, if he thought it would augment his celebrity."[86] Even Rousseau's refusal in the last years of his life to appear in public could excite this kind of reader. The Prince de Ligne accordingly said of his interview with Rousseau when he visited him in rue Plâtière: "I will allow myself a few truths here, a bit severe, about the way he understands celebrity. I remember telling him: M. Rousseau, the more you hide, the more you are seen: the more untamed you are, the more public you become."[87] In contrast with the earlier quotes, these words were written a few years before, probably during the Revolution, and Ligne attributes to himself a certain retrospective lucidity. Nevertheless, this text, along with others, reveals the point to which celebrity had become the subject of study at the end of the eighteenth century. It also shows that the phenomenon which for us seems linked to contemporary excesses in the media sphere was already noticeable at that time: at a certain level of celebrity, manifestly refusing all publicity could become an excellent way to stir up public interest.

The Burden of Celebrity

Rousseau did not leave it to his contemporaries to reflect on his celebrity. He made it one of the themes of his autobiographical writings. This is hardly surprising in a writer obsessed by the theme of social recognition and given to introspection about his own destiny. However, though he was one of the first authors to meditate so explicitly on the changes in public recognition implied by celebrity, this aspect of his work has not greatly interested critics, probably because it was not immediately apparent, hidden behind themes of conspiracy and persecution. Nevertheless, as we shall see, when he opened himself to the public as a whole and when he aimed, above all, to project a public figure, that of "Jean-Jacques," totally different from the real Rousseau, conspiracy became the inverse twin of his celebrity. Using the hallucinatory aspect of nightmare, he described the mechanism of alienation experienced by the famous man: the dispossession of his own being.

Rousseau had aspired to celebrity for a long time, something which seemed to him highly desirable. When he wrote the *Confessions*, and when it now seemed to him to be a burden, he admitted this aspiration of his youth and realized that when he arrived in Paris he used every means possible to become a celebrity. Above all he was looking for a way to achieve social success and prosperity, hoping that his system of musical notation would help him attain this success: "I persisted in wanting to make a revolution in that art with it, and in that way to arrive at a celebrity which in the fine arts is always joined with fortune in Paris."[88] When he finally became a celebrity, ten years later, the public success of his *Discourse* at first seemed to him like a happy confirmation of his personal worth:

> This favor of the public, in no way courted and for an unknown Author, gave me the first genuine assurance of my talent which I had always doubted until then in spite of the internal feeling. I understood all the advantage I could take from it for the decision I was ready to reach, and I judged that a copyist of some celebrity in letters would not be likely to lack work.[89]

One sees the apparent paradox in this formulation: Rousseau decided to become a music copyist to live from manual labor, abandoning the literary life but hoping that his literary celebrity would draw customers to him. The contradiction is even more striking when he once again takes up his work as a copyist during the 1770s, at the moment he officially renounced all literary activity and spurned the mechanisms of celebrity. Most of his customers followed him in the hopes of getting close to the wild and famous man.

The contradiction only appears to be so. When he decided to break with the accepted salon model of the man of letters, the one that powerful aristocrats supported, Rousseau built on his celebrity in order to escape the constraints of society life. In contrast with these social constraints, which built reputations and assured the careers of authors, he counted on the support of the public. As we saw from the quarrel with Hume, it was not an inconsequential choice. Rousseau very rarely explicitly admitted his desire for celebrity. However, in an unpublished text, evidently written at the beginning of the 1760s, he wrote: "I prefer for less good to be said about me and that I be spoken about more."[90] What Rousseau designated as "another turn of self-love" (*amour-propre*) testified above all to a remarkable lucidity in terms of strategic publicity. What difference did it make what they said about him; he just had to be talked about and talked about a lot. Whether they said good or bad things, the essential thing was that his singularity be emphasized: "I would prefer to be forgotten by the whole human race than regarded as an ordinary man."[91] Self-love entails here less a demand for esteem than a desire to be distinguished, to be the center of all public discussions, which is exactly the definition of celebrity. And this, Rousseau adds in a burst of lucidity, needs to be nourished. "Now if I let the public, which has spoken so much about me, act, it would be much to be feared that soon it would no longer speak about me."[92] Soon, however, he became aware of the dangers of celebrity, capable of perverting the most innocent human relations, making every authentic relationship impossible, and he continued: "But as soon as I had a name I no longer had any friends."[93] Celebrity separated him from his friends, brought on jealousies and persecutions. It imposed false human relations because the public persona he had become came fatally between him and others. Therefore, the visits his admirers made to see him became a recurrent motif among Rousseau's complaints. He complained while in Môtiers of receiving too many visits:

> Those who had come to see me up to then were people who, since they had some talents, tastes, maxims in common with me, alleged them as the cause of their visits, and immediately introduced matters about which I could converse with them. At Môtiers that was no longer true, above all with regard to France. It was officers or other people who had no taste for literature, who even for the most part had never read my writings, and who did not fail, according to what they said, to have traveled thirty, forty, sixty, a hundred leagues to come to see and admire the famous, celebrated, very celebrated man, the great man etc.[94]

Empty talk, hypocritical flattery, these visits, which might have been a comfort, were odious. What made them importunate was that they were not based on elective affinities nor on true esteem linked to real interest in his work, but on an unhealthy curiosity which, in the eyes of Rousseau, seemed more or less like spying: "One feels that this did not make for very interesting conversations for me, although they might have been so for them, depending on what they wanted to know: for since I was not mistrustful I expressed myself without reserve about all the questions they judged it appropriate to ask me."[95]

While Voltaire, a few kilometers away, welcomed visitors from all over Europe with jubilation, knowing they would recount in their letters and over dinner their visit to the great writer, Rousseau was suspicious of it all, seeing such visitors at worst as perfidious spies, at best as curious people come to see a show. He created an inextricable knot between the consequences of his celebrity and the feeling of persecution that was beginning to consume him, even more painful because in those years he was forced to flee from one refuge to another. Interpreting every show of interest as a menace or a debasement, he rudely spurned visitors. To the Comtesse de La Rodde de Saint-Haon, who ardently wished to visit him, he replied: "I am sorry not to please Madame countess, but I cannot do the honor of the man she is curious to see and she has never stayed with me." When she insisted, he reproached her concerning the "hyperbolic and outrageous praise with which your letters are filled," which "seem to be the hallmark of my most ardent persecutors." Then, refusing to be turned into the showman: "Those who only want to see the Rhinoceros should go to the fair and not to my home. And all the banter with which this insulting curiosity is peppered is but one more outrage which requires no greater deference on my part."[96]

The end of this refusal, expressed with such brutal and almost insulting frankness, which he readily adopted when he felt threatened, showed the two themes used by Rousseau to interpret his admirers' desire to see him: that of conspiracy and that of unjustified curiosity. If the first came from a Rousseauistic idiosyncrasy, often called paranoia, the second touched the heart of celebrity mechanisms, which tended to reify the famous person by transforming him or her into a circus act. The rhinoceros comparison, which foreshadows in a striking way the nineteenth-century development of spectacles where all sorts of human monsters and exotic specimens were exposed to public curiosity, thus becoming, as it were, "freak shows," was less comic than it seemed. This was a reference to the famous Clara the Rhinoceros, who came from Rotterdam in 1741 and was exhibited for almost twenty years throughout Europe from Berlin to Vienna, from Paris to Naples, from Kraców to London, becoming a true international star, the object of books, of paintings and engravings, making her owner enormous sums of money. The memory of Clara, who was shown at the Saint-Germain fair in 1749 and which Rousseau perhaps visited briefly at that time, was no doubt brought to mind again by the arrival in Versailles in 1770 of a new rhinoceros in the king's circus, which also caused a sensation. This obsessive fear of visitors who came to see him as they would to see a circus act – if not to spy on him, then to trick him or make fun of him – became a leitmotif in Rousseau's texts for the last ten years of his life. The testimony of Bernardin de Saint-Pierre, who was very close to him, merits quotation:

> Men came from everywhere to visit him, and more than once I witnessed the brisk way in which he dismissed some of them. I told him: Without knowing it, am I not as importunate as these people are? "There is a great difference between them and you! These people come out of curiosity, to say they have seen me, to find out how I live, and to make fun of me." I told him they came because of his celebrity. He repeated, greatly irritated: Celebrity! Celebrity! The word infuriated him: the celebrated man had made the sensitive man very unhappy.[97]

It is difficult to know if the anecdote is authentic, but it is, at least, perfectly credible, since it corresponds to the avowed reactions of

Rousseau in those years. It is striking that Bernardin insisted on the word "celebrity," which, as we have seen, was a rather recent usage and one Rousseau himself used at different times. The expression "the celebrated man had made the sensitive man very unhappy" subtly suggests that the person who experiences celebrity has a certain capacity to laugh at the human comedy, to agree to play a role while at the same time keeping a distance from others. Rousseau was completely devoid of this aptitude. The sensitive man, to the contrary, lives each human relationship intensely, expects from every contact that he be recognized in his singularity and his authenticity, that he fully invests himself in an affective exchange.

Rousseau's experience of celebrity corresponded to the painful discovery of a public sphere that had become entirely controlled by the media, where one could never be known directly. In contrast with romantic interpretations which only saw in his work a desire for solitude, a condemnation of vanity and happiness found in self-love, it must be remembered that Rousseau was always driven by a powerful desire to be recognized. One can find psychological or sociological causes for this, but there is little doubt that this need was a great motivational force in his life and one of the great themes of his philosophical work.[98] One important part of his moral and political philosophy can be read as a search for forms of recognition allowing for harmonious and just social relationships, far from the narcissistic competition found in self-love and the endless struggle for prestige.

The desire for recognition which motivated Rousseau took two forms, closely linked, that one must separate. The first manifested as a demand for social recognition, pushing him, for instance, as the son of a self-taught watch-maker, to avidly seek the esteem and friendship of Parisian aristocrats, to convince them that he would be absolutely dishonored to eat in the same room as the servants. Sure of his intellectual worth, Rousseau recounted in the *Confessions*, with a certain delight, several scenes of little social triumphs where he stood out by reason of his mind and his talent among those more powerful than himself.[99] This aspiration fed a suspicion of hypocrisy: How could this sworn opponent of aristocratic privilege and the pretentious life of polite society appreciate the friendship of the Maréchal de Luxembourg, the Prince de Conti, and the Comtesse de Boufflers, before ending his life on the property of the Marquis de Girardin? Was Rousseau secretly a snob? In reality, this demand for recognition was very different from that of the classic social climber who aspired to be known as an actual member of the dominant class, and of whom the bourgeois gentleman was the perfect archetype. Rousseau was not seeking status; he did not demand to be admitted to a social group, whether it be the nobility, polite society, or that of "men of letters." His aspirations were effectively linked to a second form of recognition, intimate and personal, which concerned less his intellectual, artistic, or social worth than his goodness and his innocence. It was less social than moral. And it resulted not so much in a desire for admiration and esteem than in a need to be loved and pitied.

This two-sided desire for recognition that motivated Rousseau explains the apparent contradictions in his character and his attitude, a particular mix of pride and sentimentality, a way of narrowly linking the language of honor and emotion, a taste for scandal, and a desire to be loved. Out of this also came the modern desire for recognition that he expressed. From social elites who always held a monopoly on prestige and social esteem, he demanded to be recognized not as one of them, but as different. Whereas most of the writers of his time aspired to be accepted by polite society through showing their perfect understanding of the social codes, by behaving as perfect gentlemen according to the Voltaire principle – "one must be a man of the world before being a man of letters" – Rousseau wanted to force the esteem of this same society by demonstrating his difference and his singularity, even his contempt for this way of life. Most of the scenes of social triumph in the *Confessions* are based on this dynamic: Rousseau imposed his own rules and gained recognition both for his talent and for his indomitable singularity, a recognition as much affective and sentimental as social. Take the most striking case, that of the performance of *Devin du village* in Fontainebleau. The story in the *Confessions* links the two elements: the opera was a success and garnered admiration and applause for him, while he himself refused to bow to the usual courtly dress code, appearing in casual dress, with "a big beard and a badly combed wig." So his success was not a simple artistic or social success, and it did not rest solely on his talent as a composer but on his authenticity as well, which allowed him to both move the audience by his music and at the same time remain faithful to himself in every way. "To be always myself wherever I am I must not blush at being dressed in accordance with the station I have chosen."[100]

One can see the difficulty that such a desire for recognition posed when it was associated with traditional forms of social recognition in an unequal society where esteem came essentially from the position one occupied, and then mixing it with a new form based on the affirmation of an eccentric self, a unique subjectivity. The first level was collective, rising out of a form of co-option in which members of the elite recognized the new arrival as one of themselves, receiving him into their salons, treating him with consideration, according him exterior marks of social respect. These were the mechanisms which permitted tacit ennoblement by lifestyle in the sixteenth century, or integration into polite society in the eighteenth century. The second level, intimate recognition, was almost, by necessity, personal, and ideally played out between two individuals, if possible in direct interaction. The ideal model for this was the love relationship and, even better, tender friendship, love and compassion fused. *La Nouvelle Héloïse* can be read as a series of variations on this theme, from close friendship, almost like that of twins, which links the cousins Julie and Claire, through a combination of esteem, love, and tenderness, which characterizes the bond between Julie and Saint-Preux, once they have given up one another. This is why the happy scenes of recognition in the *Confessions* are always described as moments when the habitual social mechanisms are suspended and give way to emotional effusions in which women play an essential role. Mme Beauzenwal's guests who wanted Rousseau to eat in the servant quarters could not hold back tears when Rousseau read them a poem, and the daughter, Mme de Broglie, imagined seeing in him a "man of good fortune."[101] The female spectators of *Devin du village* let themselves be carried away by a sweet and touching "drunkenness" while the author, moved to tears, burned with "the desire to collect with my lips the delicious tears which I was causing to flow."[102] But these are fictitious scenes, moments of imagined happiness, or at least excessively rare and fleeting, because the rules of the social world made this fusion of the collective and the sentimental highly improbable.

The place for this ideal recognition, both social and intimate, collective and individual, is literature, which places the author in the gaze of an infinity of readers, each in their individuality. Rousseau developed a theory about reading which could be qualified as sentimental and moral.[103] For him, reading permitted an honest and immediate access by the reader to the sensibility of the author, and thanks to which the author was both recognized as a talented writer and loved as a sensitive human being. What allowed for this passage from reading to recognition was the moral transformation that reading induced in the reader. By observing his or her own emotions, the reader could judge the author's soul. This created a tautological circle: because Rousseau's books made his readers good and sensitive, touching them through the spectacle of virtue, they prove his authentic goodness, but, inversely, it is because he is sincere that his books produce these effects. It is a point that he will never cease making, in particular in *Rousseau Judge of Jean-Jacques*: one must not read his books looking for problems or logical contradictions, but as a way to judge by one's own emotions the sensibility and the morality of the author. This concept of reading is not entirely Rousseau's own. As we have seen, it is part of the context of the romance novel. But Rousseau gives it a particular twist by going from the epistolary novel to autobiographical writing. To the sentimental concept of reading, which up until then concerned only fiction, he added the authenticity of self.[104] Because this kind of reading put the author and the reader in direct contact, Rousseau thought it allowed an escape from all traditional societal forms, in which the relationship with others was founded on the socialization of esteem: the game of reputation. Reading was the ideal way to get intimate recognition. In a salon, one judged others on appearances, on their mastery of certain worldly accomplishments, on the art of repartee, witticism, elegant compliments, or even what others said about them. One's value depended on the image one offered and what others thought. Because Rousseau had a doubly sensitive nature, or he was late to be socialized, he never mastered the codes of worldly interaction, he lacked quickness and flexibility. "I would love society as much as anyone else if I was not sure of showing myself, not only to my disadvantage there, but completely different from the way I am."[105] In society life, where everyone watched oneself being watched and in turn watched others, there was an immense distance between awareness of self and the image projected. Let us just say that Rousseau made a bad impression. But he immediately added: "The decision I have made to write and hide myself is precisely the one that suits me. If I had been present, no one would ever have known what I am worth, they would not even have suspected it."[106] To be recognized, he had to hide. But how was one to prove one's worth, the person one was, without showing it? He had to write. He had to trust in books to reveal the real Jean-Jacques.

It is understandable then that the ideal situation for this kind of social and intimate recognition, for the sentimental fusion between Rousseau and his readers, would be when a woman of high standing read one of his books. For example, the episode in *Confessions* when the Princesse de Talmont declines to go to the ball because she has begun to read *La Nouvelle Héloïse*; she prefers to stay in bed and spend the night reading. Rousseau, to whom this is reported, is moved because "I have always believed that one could not take so lively an interest in the *Héloïse*, without having that sixth sense, that moral sense with which so few hearts are endowed, and without which no one can understand my own."[107] And it is better still when he reads his own writings out loud because he does not have to hide from himself: reading has the capacity to suspend the weight of social constraints. Although the wife of the Maréchal de Luxembourg, the indisputable authority in polite society, intimidates him to such a degree that he feels incapable of speaking in her presence, he manages every morning to read to her, face-to-face, *La Nouvelle Héloïse*, with unhoped-for success:

> Mme de Luxembourg was crazy about Julie and its Author; she talked about nothing but me, was interested in nothing but me, said sweet things to me all day long, kissed me ten times a day. She always wanted me to

140

have my place at table beside her, and when some Lords wanted to take that place, she told them it was mine and had them put elsewhere.[108]

It is difficult not to see in this passage an ideal scenario of the effects of reading: Rousseau obtains pre-eminence over the nobility by literally seducing the wife of the Maréchal de Luxembourg, by arousing an affective fascination which goes directly from the book to the author and allows him, for a moment, to reign at the table of honor, in spite of his clumsiness and conversational ineptitude. Social recognition and sentimental recognition are joined thanks to the charm of reading.

This reading model underlies the project of the *Confessions*, where it is not so much a matter of Rousseau justifying himself, convincing readers that he is right to act as he does, but rather of arousing an emotional recognition, in the present, woven of compassion and empathy. It is very much in this sense that one should read the famous opening, with its inimitable mix of pride and humility. Rousseau's project was to have "unveiled his interior," to tell us not only what he had done but above all what he had thought and felt ("I feel my heart"), and thus this statement:

> Eternal Being, assemble around me the countless host of my fellows: let them listen to my confessions, let them shudder at my unworthiness, let them blush at my woes. Let each of them in his turn uncover his heart at the foot of Thy throne with the same sincerity; and let a single one say to Thee, if he dares: "*I was better than that man.*"[109]

Rousseau did not claim to be better than others. He thought instead that if each person made an effort to be sincere, to open him- or herself, the question of comparison would lose all pertinence. No one would dare say: "I am the best," because that would have no sense. There would be only individuals, equal and unique, adamantly incomparable, capable of being mutually moved emotionally. Competition for esteem would be replaced by empathy ("they blush") and compassion ("they groan").

It is not the time to critique this idea, which rests not only on the myth of an authentic "self" (*moi*), accessible through introspection and intimate feelings, but also on the idea that it is possible to share this self with others, if they agree to overlook social appearances and abdicate their obsession with judging. Rousseau was the first to explicitly secularize the Christian theme of the transparency of souls in the eyes of God, in order to elaborate the romantic theme of the transparency of hearts in the eyes of men and women. But one must first of all focus on the immediate relationship that reading was meant to allow. What threatened the permanence of such a relationship, to the contrary, were all sorts of intermediary elements (writers, journalists, the curious, the gossips, society people) that came between Rousseau and those from

whom he was seeking recognition. As soon as the intermediaries multiplied, it was no longer a situation of recognition; the gaze no longer
carried an attestation of authenticity, but transformed the object of the
gaze into a spectacle. "Appearances" overwhelmed the "feeling of intimacy."[110] It is understandable that the drama of celebrity, for Rousseau,
was based on the multiplication of images and talk that proliferated in
the public sphere, that which made up his public persona and created
a barrier between him and others. The public could no longer see him
because they looked at him through this persona that they took him
to be, but in which he could not recognize himself. How could one
know if the admiration, the affection, the compassion, expressed were
being addressed really to him, or if these feelings were aroused by this
imaginary figure made up of all the images that were being circulated,
benevolent or malevolent, written or figurative, oral or visual (rumors,
press articles, engravings)? Everybody talked about him and nobody
listened to him. Everyone looked at him and nobody saw him. Everyone
knew him and nobody knew him. And this is exactly the definition that
Chamfort proposed for celebrity, one may recall.

In 1764, Rousseau had already written a draft for the preamble that
would become the *Confessions*: "Among my contemporaries, there are
few men whose names are more known in Europe and whose person is
more unknown. [...] Each drew me according to his whim, without fear
that the original might come to give him the lie. There was a Rousseau
in high society, and another in retirement who bore no resemblance to
him."[111] This fundamental text describes perfectly the inevitable tension
between the mechanisms of celebrity based on name notoriety, on the
proliferation of images, and on the romantic myth of the individual completely conscious of who he is. The success of the first *Discourse* seemed
like a confirmation to Rousseau of his ability for expressing his feelings,
based on public delight in his talent. In these first moments of celebrity,
there seemed to be a match between his public persona and his awareness of self. But very soon, he discovered that the proliferation of images
and discourse allowed each person to have his own Rousseau "fantasy
figure," and there was no longer a correspondence between persona and
self-image but instead a growing gap, until there was a total disjunction between himself and the public image: "another [...] who bore no
resemblance to him." One could certainly read in this text an expression
of pride which manifested itself in two forms at once, contradictory and
complementary: a celebrated person throughout an entire continent, but
with a uniqueness so great it escaped the observation of many people. This
is a penetrating description, although largely intuitive, of effects directly
linked to a media-based society, Rousseau being one of the first to experience it. Not only could one be both known and unknown, but it was

probable that celebrity could, to the contrary, reinforce the feeling of not being understood.[112] This impression that famous people had of not being recognized for who they were, as though a multitude of "figures" came between them and the world and condemned them to solitude, would later become a commonplace aspect of celebrity in the twentieth century: "I'm a rich man and my name is everywhere but all I want is love," as Johnny Halliday, the French rock star, used to sing in the 1960s.[113]

Rousseau rarely chose his words haphazardly. When he wrote: "Each drew me according to his whim, without fear that the original might come to give him the lie," the term "original" was especially important.[114] Of course he was contrasting the source (the original) with the copies that were circulating, according to his ideas of authentic and false. But he emphasized the uniqueness of the true Rousseau (this "original" being), who was irreducible to the images of himself that others had formed. He also contrasted the word "retirement" with "high society," as distinct from the public. The imaginary and false images still remained implicitly attached to the construction of reputation in society, in the heart of the elite. Later, in *Reveries of the Solitary Walker*, he would refer to the same opposition, in a more radical form: "If my face and my features were as perfectly unknown to men as my character and natural temperament are, I would still live in the midst of them without difficulty."[115] It was celebrity which condemned him to solitude, because it did not allow him to aspire to any authentic human relationship. It was no longer polite society which was targeted here; it was all men and women. In the meantime, Rousseau had to give up the struggle, through his writings, against the effects of celebrity. *Confessions* was a failure, a cruel deception. The readings that Rousseau gave in small select circles did not produce the desired effect. "I completed my reading this way and everyone was silent. Mme d'Egmont was the only one who appeared moved; she visibly trembled; but she very quickly recovered and kept silent as did the whole company."[116] No tears, no ostensible manifestation of compassion for the misfortunes of Jean-Jacques. Rousseau drew the conclusion that his project was illusory. He would never write the rest of it.

Rousseau Judge of Jean-Jacques

At the beginning of 1770, Rousseau renounced any further work on the *Confessions*. But he did not abandon the idea of fighting against the persecution and calumny of which he believed he was a victim. He dedicated considerable energy to drafting a complex and fascinating text that was ignored for many years by the critics: *Rousseau Judge of Jean-Jacques: Dialogues*. Published after his death, between 1780

143

and 1782, the text disconcerted even his admirers and was considered by others as evidence of his madness.[117] Certainly, the text has dark, strange, sometimes offputting aspects in which Rousseau's deliriums of persecution seem to be unleashed. The form, however, is quite astonishing, made up of three dialogues between a person named "Rousseau," who is the speaker for the author but who is not his double, and "the Frenchman," an individual who shows none of the normal characteristics of psychological or biographical depth. Their exchanges are about a third person, "J.J.," identified as the author of La Nouvelle Héloïse, of Émile, the Discourse, and so forth. The Frenchman, persuaded like all his compatriots that this J.J. is a mean, depraved man, candidly exposes the plot that has been hatched to ruin his reputation, never explaining it to him: everything happens as if J.J. has been declared guilty, without specifying his faults or allowing him to defend himself. The conspiracy is presented as a given, known by everyone, and a legitimate undertaking by a salubrious public. It is an aberrant situation, constructed as such, but presented by the Frenchman as perfectly normal. Rousseau then defends Jean-Jacques, whom he goes to meet. This leads the Frenchman to doubt the basis of the conspiracy and convinces him he must read Jean-Jacques's works, which he evidently had never read, not even one line. This is the decisive element, which successfully persuades him of Jean-Jacques's innocence. "I feel and assert just as you do: the moment he is the Author of the writings that bear his name, he can only have the heart of a good man."[118] But this revelation – and it is a surprise – does not lead to a campaign to rehabilitate his public image. The two men decide to keep the secret of Jean-Jacques's innocence to themselves, aware that it will do no good to oppose unanimous hostility. They settle for going to live with Jean-Jacques in order to comfort him.

This brief resumé does not do justice to such a complex text, to its rich sinuosity, which rests both on a very rigorous architecture and on a series of repetitions, digressions, and developments that are sometimes tedious, intercut with moments of great eloquence. The most unbelievable hypotheses are laid out with such logic and precision that the reader is sometimes stunned before this seemingly "reasonable madness." The system of dialogues allows the author increased scope to make comments, even in the notes, not counting the two texts framing the work, and to comment in the first person. This system also allows the Frenchman to describe the conspiracy and the numerous maneuvers put into place to isolate and destroy Jean-Jacques, without ever telling him what he is reproached with. In this way, the general persecution is presented not as a supposition, nor as an hypothesis, nor even in the form of an accusation, but simply as a fact. The question is to find out whether or not the persecution is justified. The aim of the text is to discover logical reasons for that which has no credibility, the "unanimous agreement" of "a whole generation" aimed at outlawing Jean-Jacques.[119]

Given all this, the text is dominated by themes of imprisonment, obscurity, surveillance, and trickery. This persecution plunges Jean-Jacques into a universal silence and deprives him of any means of action. In this way, *Rousseau Judge of Jean-Jacques* describes at length, almost endlessly, the solitude of a Jean-Jacques who has become the play-thing of his enemies and the victim of a universal conspiracy manipulated by the "Gentlemen." One finds in the text the author's most sinister obsessions, the impenetrable shadows, the labyrinth in which he is lost, the distortion of every sign: "They have discovered the art of making a solitude for him in Paris more awful than caverns or the woods, so that in the midst of men he finds neither communication, consolation, nor counsel, nor enlightenment."[120] It was a darkness that always seemed to stem from a universal plot, referring not only to his enemies but now to people in general. In the Afterword, entitled "History of the Preceding Writing," Rousseau used his own name and reinforced the paranoia surrounding the work by recounting the impossibility of distributing the text. He had tried to give the manuscript to a few people he still trusted, but they all betrayed him: "Could I be unaware that for a long time no one approached me who wasn't sent expressly, and that putting my trust in the people around me is throwing myself to my enemies?"[121] Desperate, he resolved to place the writing on the altar at Notre Dame, but the gate was locked; with his head spinning, he abandoned all hope of having the work recognized, but not without muttering a murmur of indignation: "I was seeing Heaven itself collaborate in the iniquitous work of men."[122] There could be no better symbol for this persecution delirium – God as part of the plot! – and the absolute impossibility of breaking out of such a psychological trap.[123]

The *Dialogues* again pick up the apologetic thread found in the *Confessions*, but they do so in a totally different way, to the point that Michel Foucault, the first to have seized on the importance of the text, talked about them as "anti-*Confessions*."[124] The first-person narration allows for a dialogue and facilitates a burst of enunciations. Rousseau no longer tries to say what he is feeling inside but, to the contrary, attempts to see himself from the outside, imagining the motivations of his enemies, unbelievable as they appear to him, and creating an image of himself that a totally impartial observer or a benevolent reader might have. "I had necessarily to say how, if I were someone else, how I would view a man such as myself."[125] An obviously illusory project, but for Rousseau it was no longer a question of intimate feelings, nor of justifying himself by affirming the lucidity of a clear conscience, but to understand the way the judgment of others was constructed. The complex and perverse mechanisms of public opinion were invested with extremely negative meaning. It seemed to be the result of a general manipulation orchestrated by those in power, intermediaries, opinion makers. As usual, Rousseau criticized the role of social mechanisms in creating reputation, but it went much further: it was no longer the judgment of polite society that was at fault, but the unanimous opinion of the public: "Public opinion" was not an impartial tribunal that men of letters could set against the arbitrary and the despotic, as some contemporary authors thought, but rather a sort of hegemonic device which allowed small organized groups to universally impose false judgments and persecute the innocent. The conspiracy against Jean-Jacques also included "Nobles, Authors, doctors (that wasn't hard), all the powerful men, all the courtesans, all the official bodies, all those who control the administration, all those who govern public opinions."[126]

A list of the powerful counted less than the effect of the whole. The Frenchman tried in vain to remind Rousseau that the majority was against him: "Don't you give any weight to the tally of voices when you are the only one to see things differently from everyone?" To which he replied by criticizing the effects of imitation and intimidation which easily allowed the public to be tricked: "To what extent could the public be deceived if all those who lead it, either by force, or authority, or opinion, made an agreement to delude it by hidden dealings whose secret it would be incapable of finding out?"[127] Public opinion here is not a directly political idea – it is, moreover, never political with Rousseau, because it is a question of mores – it refers not to the result of a critical deliberation about public affairs, but to a state of unanimity concerning the reputation of an individual.[128] Rousseau used the term in way that was very close to the way Duclos used it – one of the rare authors with whom he stayed friends and admired for a long time, up until the beginning of the 1770s – when he reflected on the uncontrollable reach of reputation under the new mechanisms of celebrity. "Public opinion" meant precisely the image the public had of him – this undifferentiated mass of individuals who did not know Rousseau directly, but had an opinion about him, about what could be called his persona. This persona, in his eyes, was so totally perverted that it radically reversed all values and portrayed an innocent person as a guilty person. "One could see Socrates, Aristides, one could see an angel, one could see God himself with eyes thus fascinated and still believe one were seeing an infernal monster," Rousseau did not hesitate to write, in a proudly sublime comparison.[129]

The eyes of the public were "fascinated," that is, mesmerized, as if under a magic spell. The term, based in magic, means, first of all, trickery, an illusion, and it is in this sense that it is usually employed in the eighteenth century. Nonetheless, the modern sense, the one which refers more to seduction than to magic, already existed, and its connotations implied that the public was not only tricked by the false image that was presented, it was seduced and subjugated; it could not break the spell and took a certain confused pleasure in contemplating it. This ambiguity (was the public tricked or was it complicit in mocking the imitations that were offered? was it wrong in good faith or out of meanness?) was one of the mainsprings of the *Dialogues* and something new in Rousseau's thinking. Up until then, and notably in the *Confessions*, he had denounced the conspiracy of his enemies, but he counted on the public, on readers of good faith. The success of his books at least had the advantage of assuring him that he was talented and convincing him that a large part of his readership had direct access to his thoughts. In *Letters Written from the Mountain*, he affirmed optimistically that "the public uses reason" and he accepted its verdicts.[130] At the beginning of 1761, in fragments which announced *Confessions* but which he did not publish, he wrote this rather astounding sentence in regard to the rest of his work: "From the manner in which I am known in the world I have less to gain than to lose in showing myself as I am."[131] How could the future author of the *Confessions* and the *Dialogues* write this? In fact, he was convinced that as a celebrity he projected a flattering figure and that public opinion of him was favorable: "I pass for so singular a man that, since everyone takes pleasure in amplifying, I have only to rest myself upon the public voice; it will serve me better than my own praises. Thus, consulting nothing but my own interest, it would be more clever to let others speak about me than to speak about me myself."[132] When he wrote these words, Rousseau detected in the "public voice" a tendency to amplify every positive aspect about the eccentric persona that had been created.

By contrast, in the *Dialogues*, the public image is entirely reversed. Not only is the public no longer favorable to Jean-Jacques, but it has become the driving force behind a universal plot. To understand the unbelievable unanimity of hatred that surrounded him, Rousseau introduced the hypothesis of bad faith readers, those who read the books of Jean-Jacques with the sole aim of finding contradictions and faulting him for them. This hypothesis had disastrous consequences. As long as the conspiracy was an action created by little groups of identifiable enemies (philosophers, those in power, society people), it was still possible to call on readers to break with these inner circles, demanding justice be brought against high society's verdicts. This was the very project of *Confessions*. But by throwing suspicion on the readers, Rousseau denied himself all hope, all exteriority, as seen in the Notre Dame episode. The text deepened criticism of public opinion, which was not only manipulated but also wanted to be. Added to the denunciation of the

147

mechanisms of opinion was this cynical statement by the Frenchman: "The public is deceived; I see it, I know it. But it likes being deceived, and would not want to be disabused."[133]

This theme of the public's gullibility, spellbound and happy to be so, finding a strange and perverse satisfaction in the profusion of fake personas, becomes central for Rousseau, and it is hard not to see in it a description of the mechanisms of celebrity. When it is a matter of celebrities, the public, "which asks nothing other than to believe everything,"[134] happily welcomes the most unbelievable rumors. The publicity which surrounds famous people is the non-critical face of the public. Rousseau here foresees in a remarkable way the criticism of media-manipulated public opinion, which would become a recurrent theme of social criticism in the second half of the twentieth century, but he did it, obviously, in his own fashion, by making the description unique and personalizing it to the extreme:

> As soon as it is a question of J.J., there is no need to put either good sense or plausibility in the things that are uttered about him, the more absurd and ridiculous they are, the more eager people are not to doubt them. If d'Alembert and Diderot took it upon themselves today to affirm that he has two heads, everyone who saw him pass in the street tomorrow would see his two heads very distinctly, and everyone would be very surprised that they hadn't perceived this monstrosity sooner.[135]

This apparent comedy should be taken seriously for its image of a credulous and malleable public opinion lost to all critical sense when it came to celebrities. What is clearly apparent through this image of a universal conspiracy denounced by Rousseau is celebrity itself, the growing distance between the man he knew himself to be and the various representations of himself that the public delighted in believing were true. In several different places, the *Dialogues* explicitly associate the "celebrity" of Jean-Jacques and the persecutions that hound him. "He believes, for example, that all the disasters of his destiny since his fatal fame are the fruits of a long-standing plot."[136] He lamented the fate of J.J., who, instead of advantages, found only insults, misery, contempt, and defamation attached to celebrity.[137]

Of course, by describing celebrity as a form of persecution, Rousseau outrageously blackened his public image. Every form of curiosity and admiration was transformed into hostility. "Admiration is above all a word which signals a traitor. It is like the politeness of tigers who seem to be smiling at you the moment they are coming to tear you apart," he wrote to the Comte de Saint-Germain, in a letter laying out all aspects of the conspiracy.[138] It is the nature of delirium to push an admired and popular writer to think that he is unanimously detested. But once the

148

core problem has been identified, the proliferation of public representations, discourse, texts, and images associated with his name, which he does not control and in which he does not recognize himself, it matters very little, in the end, whether or not these images are favorable or unfavorable. They are painful because they imply that "Jean-Jacques" has become an autonomous public person, creating a kind of shield between Rousseau and his contemporaries. Paranoid delirium makes the description of celebrity particularly sinister, because it transforms curiosity, even admiration, into hate and contempt. But above all, there is a striking contradiction between the prestige associated with the public proliferation of a name and the impossibility of private recognition. Being too well known makes one unknown and blocks every authentic affective relationship. Bernardin was not wrong: "the celebrated man had made the sensitive man very unhappy."

The *Dialogues* are preceded by a Foreword, "On the Subject and Form of this Writing," that leaves no doubt what is at issue in the book, the hostile entity to which Rousseau attributes his misfortunes: "the public." In just a few pages, the term appears six times, always in an operative position, as the main cause of defamation, not simply the passive recipient of calumnies. Immediately, in the first lines of the text, Rousseau invokes "the public, [...] perfectly sure" of its rights, a pretension he later contrasts with "the incredible blindness of the public." Jean-Jacques is "the person the public delights in disfiguring and slandering." The objective in the *Dialogues* is to closely "examine the conduct of the public in relation to [him]." Later, other terms take the place of the word "public," to show that Rousseau, from this point on, is denouncing less the conspiracy of a small number of adversaries and focusing more on the hostile unanimity of "all Paris, all France, all Europe," of "a whole generation" or even his "contemporaries." This last expression, present from the first sentence onward, shows the temporality of celebrity, acquired while a writer is still living. Rousseau was never really interested in the question of posterity, even if this did appear to be a recourse when confronted with the injustice of his peers. Faced with reports of a public in bad faith, fascinated by false images and rumors, lost to reason, he only weakly called for a future rehabilitation. Instead, he turned in on himself: "Did I know the vanity of opinion only to place myself under its yoke at the expense of my peace of soul and my heart's repose? What does it matter to me if men want to see me other than as I am? Is the essence of my being in their looks?"[139] This demand for an unalterable authenticity, for an autonomous self, insensitive to others looking at him, will be examined in the *Reveries*, the basis for a philosophy of the soul.[140] But this comes after a reaction to the increase in media outlets which characterize new forms of publicity. It rests on an untenable distinction between the individual who knows himself through self-awareness, and the images that others forge of him, a distinction between Rousseau and Jean-Jacques: "They make a J.J. that suits them in vain; Rousseau will remain the same always despite them."[141]

The Disfiguration

In the Foreword to the *Dialogues*, Rousseau justified his choice of "Rousseau" and "Jean-Jacques" in this way: "In these conversations I took the liberty of resuming my family name, which the public judged it appropriate to take from me, and following its example, I refer to myself in the third person, using my Christian name to which the public chose to reduce me."[142] The fault of the public then was to have "reduced" Rousseau to nothing more than a first name, almost a nickname, which he himself reduced to a double initial, "J.J.," designating an imaginary person. To counter this reduction, which is a reification, Rousseau meant to take back his family name, both a social identity and the authorial name he had always claimed. It was obviously significant that his first name became the "public" name of Rousseau, associated with his media figure, and even though it was the most personal, that of an irreplaceable individual, not the member of a lineage. This use of the first name to designate a celebrity with which the public had an empathetic, affective relationship was to have a promising future (Marilyn, Elvis...). It underlined, of course, the publicizing of that which was private, the very heart, as we have seen, of the celebrity culture. "Jean-Jacques," in fact, was the preferred name used by friends and admirers of Rousseau, not by his enemies, and used also by literary historians who wanted to show their attachment not only to the author but also to the man. Jean Ranson, the merchant from La Rochelle, asked warmly for news about "*Ami* Jean-Jacques." This way of designating a contemporary whom one had never met by his first name came from a desire for long-distance intimacy, from the familiarity which established itself between a celebrity and his fans.

Once again, it was Rousseau's own editorial and publicity strategies which turned against him the moment he had reached a certain degree of celebrity. If the first name "Jean-Jacques" became progressively the rule in the press and with his readers, it was in large part because he himself had promoted it to distinguish himself from the other Rousseaus. Several people testified that he was preoccupied, after his initial success, with not being confused with other Rousseaus, and in particular with the poet Jean-Baptiste Rousseau, "a famous man with the same name as you," he noted in the *Confessions*.[143] And elsewhere he wrote with bravado: "During my life some authors wore themselves out calling the

150

Poet Rousseau the great Rousseau. When I am dead the great Rousseau will be a great Poet. But he will no longer be the great Rousseau."[144] It is true that at the moment Rousseau became famous, beginning in the 1750s, the memory of Jean-Baptiste, who died in 1741, was still very strong: not only was he considered to be one of the greatest French poets, but his tumultuous life, a good part of it lived in exile, aroused great interest. When the *Mémoires pour server à l'histoire du célèbre Rousseau* appeared in 1753 in Liège, it was about Jean-Baptiste. Other Rousseaus added to the confusion. In 1750, when he was awarded the Academy of Dijon prize and became famous, and Raynal, editor of the *Mercure*, wrote to him asking if he would "open his portfolio," Rousseau complained that he mistook him for a poet, confusing him with someone of the same name (Pierre Rousseau, probably):

> It is strange that having published one work only and certainly not Poetry, today I am considered a Poet in spite of myself. Every day they compliment me on the Comedies and other pieces of verse that I never wrote and that I would not be capable of writing. It is a mix-up in the Author's name which brings me all these honors.[145]

A little later, by using his first name, he was able to refuse the title of "Monsieur," which he detested, markedly contrasting himself with his adversaries, who were identified by their titles and functions, while he added nothing to his first name, all the better to show his simplicity, his independence, and his uniqueness. Think, for example, of the title page of the *Letter to d'Alembert*, which we have already mentioned: "Letter by J.-J. Rousseau to M. d'Alembert of the Académie Française." Later, in the *Confessions*, he sometimes referred to himself in the third person as "Jean-Jacques." Thus, the fact that Rousseau was the first writer uniquely designated by his first name, far from being a desire by the public to deprive him of his name, was a result of his own editorial practices, even publicity strategies, and the mechanisms of affective attachment on which his celebrity was based.

To be dispossessed of his surname, in Rousseau's eyes, did not simply mean being reduced to the public persona of "Jean-Jacques." It was the entire authorial image he had patiently constructed that was threatened. One form that persecution takes in the *Dialogues* is the publication without his consent of pirated and falsified editions of his work and even works bearing his name that he had never written a word of. His own books became unrecognizable: "But do you know how much they can be disfigured[?] [...] Unable to annihilate them, and their most malicious interpretations not yet sufficing to discredit them at their whim, they began the process of falsifying them, and this enterprise, which seemed almost impossible at first, has become extremely easy to carry out through the connivance of the public."[146] It is easy to see behind these horrified descriptions the current practice of eighteenth-century booksellers, who readily published illegal editions of popular works and did not hesitate to use the name of a successful author to sell mediocre works. It was celebrity blackmail, as Rousseau ironically wrote to Madame de Chenonceaux, telling her that they had published in Paris a letter from him to the Archbishop of Auch, which he deemed wrong: "It is an honor granted to celebrities – an honor that you have not yet had."[147] Rousseau was a victim of his success, but, in the *Dialogues*, these mechanisms are interpreted in the guise of a conspiracy: they falsify his texts, render them unrecognizable (they are "disfigured"), they attempt to destroy him by adding scandalous statements. So he will not write anymore. His enemies, Rousseau states, "make him scribble books endlessly and take great care to have these books – very worthy of the pens that write them – dishonor the name they make them carry."[148] Rousseau's authorial strategy, aimed at making his name prominent, linking forever his person and his writings, turned against him. His responsibility and his honor were trampled on by such usages of his name.

The contradictions of celebrity closed around him like a trap. A person's last name is what makes an individual unique; it is his or her personal identity, but also that which is the most public, the basis for notoriety, in terms of one's renown. Rousseau's willingness to link his authorial name and his person, as if the texts he published came directly out of his subjectivity, contradicted the existence of numerous intermediaries, editors, copyeditors, booksellers, critics, the whole world of books where business strategies mixed with intellectual issues. Confronted with this growing number of intermediaries between him and his readers, Rousseau found an extreme solution, the disavowal of all texts bearing his name. In 1774 he went as far as to circulate a handwritten letter in which he "declared all books, old and new, now printed under his name, no matter where, either false or altered, mutilated or falsified with the most cruel malignity, disavowed, some for no longer being his work, others for being falsely attributed to him."[149] The handwritten signature which guaranteed the author's name, in place of the name on the cover of the book, had become suspect. One sees the difficulty Rousseau was up against, looking for an impossible authenticity.[150] This statement itself was printed without his authorization[151] and doubtless he feared that it had been falsified. Every piece of writing was disfigured, "and no matter how positively something presented itself to his mind, something to do or to say, he had to realize that the minute he was allowed to execute it, aspects of the work would be turned against him, rendering it a disaster." Out of this fear came the permanent idea of being caught in nets which grew ever tighter around the author when he tried to defend himself, an apt metaphor for the condition of the famous man losing control over the way his words and his actions were talked about and interpreted. To justify oneself, to refute what was said about him, played into the hands of the opinion makers. The only thing left for him was to be silent and not move, "not to act at all; to agree to nothing that is proposed to him under any pretext whatsoever."[152]

When he talked about the falsification of his books, the language of disfiguration came spontaneously to Rousseau. What was at stake, in fact, was the control of his "figure" in the larger sense we have discussed, all the representations which circulated under his name. Obviously, figure in the narrower sense, the physical appearance of his face, was a touchy subject. Rousseau did not escape this development of the visual culture of celebrity. From the start of his notoriety, a few months after the success of the first *Discourse*, his portrait in pastel, drawn by Maurice Quentin de La Tour, was exhibited at the 1753 Salon. But although he liked the portrait very much, Rousseau for a long time refused to allow prints made of the engraved copies. It was not until 1762 that he agreed, pressured by his editor and his friends. From then on, numerous engraved portraits of Rousseau were reproduced and put up for sale. He tried to keep control of his public image, suggesting to Duchesne, for example, publisher of *La Nouvelle Héloïse*, to have a portrait made of him in his Armenian outfit. But soon, he noticed that it did not make any difference, and he began to worry about the proliferation of portraits, the sales of which were announced in newspapers, including very large print runs. People he did not know wrote asking him for copied images, like a certain Lalliaud, from Nimes, who sent him three engravings asking which was the best likeness because he wanted to have a marble bust of Rousseau made for his library. He was at first seduced because he thought Lalliaud's "soul was in the same key as mine," but he rapidly reneged and reproached Lalliaud for having "a hideous portrait engraved, which did not fail to circulate under my name, as if it bore some resemblance to me."[153]

This concern about the multiplication of his image did not cease and reached a peak in *Rousseau Judge of Jean-Jacques* when he focused on the portrait painted by Allan Ramsay in 1766 and on the engravings copied from it. The portrait was made during Rousseau's visit to England, at Hume's request and before their rupture. Ramsay, one of the best portraitists of his time, made a diptych, composed of the portraits of Hume and Rousseau. Most admirers of Rousseau sincerely liked the painting because it showed him as they imagined him, dressed in his Armenian outfit, a fur cap on his head, with a serious and worried look. It offered a striking contrast with the portrait of Hume, painted in all the beatific splendor of a successful man of the world.[154] One can speculate about Ramsay's real intent and any possible irony, but there is little doubt that the painting caught certain characteristic traits of Rousseau and that this painting corresponded to the image that many of his contemporaries had of the author of *Émile*, a sensitive man but one who was worried and suspicious, having renounced the rituals of polite society.[155] The success of the numerous engravings made from this painting attest to its mastery and the desire of the public to own pictures of Rousseau. One large engraving, made in England and then widely distributed on the continent, which included the motto *vitam impendere vero* (devote life to truth), was acclaimed by Rousseau's admirers, who found it a good likeness.[156]

Figure 15: Allan Ramsay, *Jean-Jacques Rousseau – Vitam impendere vero. From an original Picture by Mr. Ramsay, in the Possession of David Hume*, engraving, 1766.

This was not the opinion of the principal person involved, who profoundly detested this portrait, and even more the engraving, which accentuated the somber, worried aspect. In 1770 he had a visit from M. and Mme Bret. He learned that Mme Bret owned an engraving of him in his Armenian outfit. "'Get out of here,' Rousseau said furiously. I never want to see a woman who can look at this portrait and like it, who can keep this monument to my shame, a portrait made to dishonor me, to vilify me; I would rather die than have dinner with her."[157] A few months later, his friend Mme de La Tour wrote to him that she had hung his engraved portrait done by Ramsay above her writing table, "just like a place of devotion above a shrine, an image of the saint to whom she was most fervently devoted."[158] Furious, he did not answer her for a year. The misunderstanding was obvious. On the one hand, sincere admirers of Rousseau were thrilled to have his portrait and preciously conserved an image which nourished their feelings of intimacy with him, even if they knew how to keep an amused distance concerning how they used the image. (In order to show that the image of the devoted was both sincere and ironic, Mme de La Tour added: "Alas, I do not receive more inspiration because of it.") On the other hand, Rousseau himself only saw in the portrait a way to dishonor him and he reacted either by erupting in violence or taking refuge in silence. The *Dialogues* spend a lot of time on this portrait, from the pose itself, described as almost a torture scene, up to its success. For Rousseau, it was surely the fruit of a machination aimed at spreading an image which showed him having the traits of "a dreadful Cyclops."

> By dint of importunities, he extracts J.J.'s consent. J.J. is made to wear a very black hat, a very brown coat, and he is positioned in a very somber place; and there, in order to paint him seated, he is kept standing, bent over, leaning with one hand on a very low table, in a posture where his tightly tensed muscles modify his facial features. The result of all these precautions had to be a most unflattering portrait if even it were faithful. You saw this terrible portrait. You will judge the resemblance if you ever see the original. During J.J.'s sojourn in England, this portrait was engraved, published, sold everywhere without it being possible for him to see the engraving. He returns to France and learns there that his portrait from England is announced, famous, touted as a masterpiece of painting, of engraving, and above all of likeness. He is finally able, not without difficulty, to see it. He trembles, and says what he thinks of it. Everyone ridicules him.[159]

No one, in fact, wanted to believe that this portrait was the result of a conspiracy, for good reason: his interlocutors liked the work very much. This for Rousseau was the real puzzle, almost incomprehensible:

How could his contemporaries so appreciate a portrait which he thought disfigured and dishonored him? The very idea of these portraits he had no control over and that circulated unbeknownst to him was obviously an ordeal for Rousseau: it was the objectification of his public figure not only on the level of physical resemblance, but also the whole series of psychological traits that were associated with it. Although he perceived himself to be a sensitive being, soft-hearted, and quick to show tenderness, the portrait by Ramsay projected the image of an austere man with a tormented psyche. Other writers found it difficult to recognize themselves in their portraits. Diderot reproached Jean-Baptiste Van Loo for having made him the look like an "old coquette," and not a philosopher.[160] For Rousseau this ordeal was even more brutal because copies of his image were widely circulated and he had developed an exacerbated and acute sensitivity to the question of public representations of himself. Above all, since this portrait was linked to his quarrel with Hume, he saw it as part of the conspiracy and detected behind the mechanisms of celebrity a conscious desire to "disfigure" him, to replace his true physical traits with false images that did not resemble him at all. The connection between celebrity and conspiracy is then explicitly invoked:

> *The Frenchman*
> But aren't you attributing too much importance to trivia? That a portrait is deformed or bears little resemblance is the least extraordinary thing in the world. Famous men are engraved, distorted, disfigured every day, without anyone concluding from these vulgar engravings anything like that you conclude.
> *Rousseau*
> I agree. But these disfigured copies are the work of bad workmen who are greedy, and not the products of distinguished Artists, nor the fruits of zeal and friendship. They are not loudly extolled all over Europe, they are not announced in public papers, they are not displayed in residences, adorned with glass and frames. They are left to rot on the quays, or to decorate the rooms in cabarets and the shops of barbers.[161]

In this passage, Rousseau outlines a description of the social uses of engraved portraits, sold on the quays for pennies, hung in barbershops. He was not ignorant of the emerging market for celebrity images. Nevertheless, he excluded himself in a way that was not very convincing, confusing his celebrity with the alleged conspiracy. One of his arguments rested on the publicity that was created in the press for his portraits, announced very pompously in newspapers and in magazines, which is true, but for reasons that had to do with the advertising demands of the market and with the interest of specialized dealers. For Rousseau, what mattered was the loss of his image, the transformation of his face – this visible translation from a unique personality offered to the gaze of close friends – into a public image, open to the regard of everyone and over which he had no control. The mask was not the mask one wore to hide one's face, the composed impassive face, as in society rituals, but the mask that others forced you to wear so they did not have to look at you. Once again, through this commodification, the media image contrasted with the ideal portrait which only Rousseau himself was able to draw, thanks to an intimate knowledge of the model: "Here is the only portrait of a man, painted exactly according to nature and in all its truth, that exists and that will probably ever exist," he wrote as he began his *Confessions*.[162]

It is significant that the portrait of Rousseau painted by Ramsay, where he is shown with a somber air and in his Armenian costume, was the focus for so much of his resentment. What he discovered was that taking a critical stand against the portrait, like the one he held and defended, was full of traps laid out by the mechanisms of celebrity. His entire criticism, as we have seen, was linked to the exigencies of authenticity. The imperative of exemplarity meant a discourse was not simply a discourse, as strident as it might be, but rather a matter of "devoting one's life to the truth" (*vitam impendere vero*), according to the motto that Rousseau had chosen. This concept of critical engagement echoed the tradition of *parrhēsia*, the courage of truth, of speaking the truth, the issues that Michel Foucault investigated.[163] One of the most spectacular forms of *parrhēsia* in Antiquity was that of the Cynics, most notably Diogenes, the philosopher whose doctrine was entirely contained in his acts, a direct and brutal way to explode scandalous truths by denouncing the superficial character of social conventions. A whole series of well-known anecdotes, recounted notably by Diogenes Laertius, made of Diogenes, living in his barrel, masturbating in public and responding insolently to Alexander the Great, an eccentric philosophical figure, living on the edge of madness, where even the philosopher's life took on the form of activism and critical discourse. By displaying an ethical dissidence in the heart of the city, Diogenes sought to condemn the excesses of civility.

It is not surprising that Rousseau was so often compared to Diogenes by his peers, either by his enemies or by his admirers.[164] Without ever explicitly identifying himself with the Cynic, Rousseau did not hesitate to refer to him implicitly, most notably by using his famous formula "I'm looking for a man," which Diogenes pronounced while carrying a lantern to show that his contemporaries, as he saw it, had lost all dignity.[165] But the level of celebrity reached by Rousseau opened some doubt about his sincerity, and when he was compared to Diogenes, it was often to suspect him of being an imitator, a false Diogenes: "Diogenes' monkey, how you do condemn yourself!" Voltaire raged in the margin of his edition of *Discourse on the Origin and Basis of Inequality*, facing the passage where the author criticized the "ardor to be talked about" and the "furor to distinguish oneself."[166]

Confronted with this criticism, often repeated by those who suspected him of being cynical, of playing a role, Rousseau found himself obliged to exculpate himself. He protested that his decision to copy music was not "an affectation of simplicity or poverty to copy an Epictetus or Diogenes as your Gentlemen claim."[167] But he was well aware of the ambiguity of his position. He discovered that *parrhēsia*, a public exhibition of his authenticity and his sincerity, was ambivalent in the already media-hyped world of the eighteenth century. His eccentricity fed the curiosity and even the fascination of the public, but it seemed like a threat, because it transformed Jean-Jacques into a person he did not recognize. No matter what he did, the logic of his celebrity was too powerful: "I felt then that it is not always as easy as one imagines to be poor and independent. I wanted to live from my profession; the public did not want me to do so."[168] Rousseau could not escape being a toy for adults or the showpiece of a public hungry for entertainment. If public exhibition of an exemplary life was no longer a weapon used for social criticism, but a publicity stunt, an object of curiosity, how could an authentic philosopher revolted by injustices be distinguished from an opportunist looking for fame? We can then understand the strange paradox of an admired writer, beloved, even passionately so, who would continually lock himself away convinced that he was universally hated. The odd nature of Rousseauism was not so much in the emotional community that formed between readers and the author, but in the fact that Rousseau, who so much desired such a community, ultimately rejected it. More than a psychological pathology, we can read in his behavior the angst of becoming a curiosity, a spectacle. Rousseau constantly reaffirming his authenticity, multiplying conflictual gestures.

Not every celebrity becomes paranoid, certainly. In fact, *Rousseau Judge of Jean-Jacques* or similar pages in his correspondence and the *Reveries* would not have been seen as representative of anything if it had not been for the excessive nature of Rousseau, which bordered on delirium, or his way of pushing to the extreme the distance between intimate recognition and public recognition. In the first case, we would read his texts as many did, in order to document the pathological psyche of Rousseau, his "paranoia"; in the second instance, we would read them as philosophical fiction. In both cases, we would find an exteme singularity, either that of a man with a deep persecution complex leading him to see his most sincere admirers as fearful spies, or that of a brilliant writer, the precursor of both Kafka and Debord.

Is any of this useful to the historian? I hope I have shown to what extent the writings and the life of Rousseau reflect, though much more radically, the experience of celebrity that his contemporaries were beginning to describe and analyze. Think back to Duclos, who imagined how painful it must have been for a man who heard himself discussed without being able to reveal his identity, "as if he were listening to people talk about a third person, someone other than himself." Think of Sarah Siddons, trapped by curious and importunate admirers who shamelessly gawked at her and kept her from returning home. Think of Chamfort, who saw in celebrity a "punishment" and decided to withdraw from the literary world. And above all think of the text by Samuel Johnson in which success and celebrity drove a young writer to paranoia. Seen in this context, Rousseau's obsessions no longer seem strange. Of course, in order to better show the violence which celebrity represented for those who were the object of it, he transformed it into persecution and defamation. He made it both unrecognizable, since it is not easy to identify admirers of Rousseau in this "entire generation [that] would, by a unanimous agreement, find delight in burying [him] alive,"[169] and perfectly recognizable, because the mechanisms were so minutely described. This wild description, crazed even, is not crazy: it is like an extreme stylization that reveals the essential substance, celebrity experienced as a burden, an alienation, a disfigurement. What difference did it make what was said about him, good or bad, whether he was loved or detested, if everything said about him was felt as a violation? The nightmare that Rousseau describes happened because an individual, losing control of the image others had of him, became the disempowered spectator of the show that he had become.

At the time of Rousseau's death, rumors of suicide were everywhere, as if this were the obvious consequence of his chaos and solitude. The hypothesis, probably false, was not absurd. Numerous stars in the twentieth century committed suicide, testifying in this way that celebrity, which in our day appears to be an enviable condition, even a criterion for social success, sometimes brings with it great psychological and existential suffering. Rousseau, no doubt thanks to his capacity for transforming his suffering into writing, escaped the tragic destiny of so many stars after him, from Marilyn Monroe to Kurt Cobain. He is like them, however, even at a distance of two centuries, in his solitude amidst a noisy crowd of admirers, fighting, as if robbed of himself, against self-dissolution in a maelstrom of innumerable representations of Jean-Jacques.

— 6 —

THE POWER OF CELEBRITY

The night of November 9, 1799, 18 Brumaire, while young General Bonaparte, wearing the virtual halo of his budding prestige, rose to power thanks to the maneuvers of Sieyès, the clever rhetoric of his brother Lucien, and the brutal efficiency of Murat's men, Mme de Staël, on her way to Paris, heard the political news at a coach house. She reported the surprise she felt on hearing the name of Bonaparte ceaselessly invoked:

> It was the first time since the Revolution that the name of an individual was heard in every mouth. Till then it was said, the Constituent Assembly has done so and so, or the people, or the Convention; now there was no mention of any but this man, who was to be substituted for all and leave the human race anonymous; who was to monopolize fame for himself, and to exclude every existing creature from the possibility of acquiring a share of it.[1]

In writing these lines ten years later, at the height of the Empire, Mme de Staël was focused on the immense prestige of the emperor.[2] She projected onto the author of the *coup d'état* the victorious aura of Austerlitz and she already saw Napoleon peeking through the persona of Bonaparte. The tyranny that loomed, even more terrible than political tyranny, was that of "celebrity": an unearthly monopoly exercised by a single man, relegating everyone else to obscurity. Even more significant, Mme de Staël chose the word "celebrity" to designate the universal renown of Bonaparte, rather than the term "glory," usually associated with an emperor and his military and political triumphs. From Bonaparte propaganda to the literature of the nineteenth century, it was the theme of heroic glory that was evoked continually to convey the incredible impact of the Napoleonic period. Hegel saw Napoleon as a great man,

160

one who incarnated the totality of an era, the "world spirit," and who gave, through his actions, a sense to modern history.[3] Heroes, great men – Napoleon's glory seemed to be a fusion of the traditional models of military glory that ran through Western history, from the time of the ancient heroes up to sovereigns and modern monarchs, and the new model of great men.[4] However, Mme de Staël did not choose this term, nor even the term "renown." By insisting on the "celebrity" of Bonaparte, she stressed the proliferation of his name among her contemporaries. What she also referred to was less the admiration aroused by the exploits of the victor of the Battle of Arcole than his ability to capture public attention by introducing a strictly singular, individual principle at the heart of collective action. Mme de Staël did not inscribe Bonaparte, as did Stendhal, Hegel, and many others, in the historic line of great conquerors, following Alexander and Ceasar. She referred to something new: an individual capable of attracting to himself, during his lifetime, the attention of all his contemporaries.

The advent of Napoleon was the marriage of power and celebrity. In the monarchies of the Ancien Régime, the celebrity of the sovereign was not an issue: the king was known because he was the king, but this notoriety was not a condition of his authority; it was based on fundamental laws of the monarchy and on the divine right of kings, transmitted through sacred ceremonies. The king was more or less loved by his people, but this collective and diffuse feeling, so difficult to measure, neither added to nor took away from his authority. His renown could be nourished by praise from men of letters or by allegorical paintings, but the king's celebrity was of an entirely different nature from theirs. Between a royal patron and artists, the exchange was much more rich than it was unequal.

The revolutionary era profoundly changed the autonomous nature of political power because of the phenomenon of public opinion. From the middle of the eighteenth century, monarchs were subjected to a new sort of criticism based on the recent principle of public opinion. Even the status of royal family members had profoundly changed, with the new culture of celebrity progressively contaminating the traditional concept of monarchical representation. In England, at the same time, the existence of an autonomous political space, centered in Parliament, but also nourished by the press, made possible a career like that of John Wilkes. This forerunner of personal liberties, the idol of Londoners who demanded "Wilkes and liberty" was also a known libertine whose scandalous episodes aroused curiosity and intrigued his contemporaries. His celebrity, used by the radical and noisy opposition to the government, resulted in prison and votes, honors, and criticism, spreading like a trail of gunpowder across the Continent, notably during the two years he spent exiled in France.[5] In this persona of a lone libertine activist, trying his best to transform the English political scene into a circus, responding to liberal, even democratic, demands, Wilkes invented a new political figure. He drew his power from popular support and public curiosity, but this was only possible in the context of English society in the second half of the eighteenth century, where scandals at the heart of polite society accompanied the progressive and difficult emergence of a public political scene. An expanding daily press lying in wait for political and diplomatic scandals during these same years, 1760–70, allowed a person as controversial as the Chevalier d'Éon to obtain considerable celebrity, first of all by tying his attacks against the French ambassador to the demands of Wilkes' followers, by tirelessly threatening to reveal state secrets, and then by inventing for himself a new sexual identity, causing interminable speculation all over Europe.[6] The *fin-de-siècle* revolutions, from one side of the Atlantic to the other, accelerated the accession of this new political figure, the celebrated man, by offering him new possibilities. This embodiment of power, once the people were recognized as sovereign, became one of the stakes in the laboratory of modern democracy. The mechanisms of celebrity were to play a great role in this development.

It took a *coup d'état* for Bonaparte to seize power, but this was only possible because the heroes of the Italian wars knew how to brilliantly orchestrate the impact of his victories and then use his prodigious celebrity. His military exploits earned him great prestige, but they could just as well have run up against republican suspicion toward this lucky man and his military might. Representatives of the Directorate worried about his pronounced taste for celebrity. One of them warned: "It is understandable that a young man of twenty-five or thirty have a love of celebrity, someone who at the head of fifty thousand republicans has, in two months, conquered or subjugated almost all of Italy. But I would hope that this passion, laudable in itself, does not became a disaster for public affairs."[7] Bonaparte was cunning in maintaining his celebrity, most notably by creating newspapers aimed at reporting the story of his exploits, like the *Courrier de l'armée d'Italie*, and especially the *Journal de Bonaparte et des hommes vertueux*, and through giving his celebrity a more intellectual aspect, by regularly attending the meetings of the Institute the minute he returned to Paris. In response to his greatest Italian victories, Paris theaters produced plays about his glory, cheap engravings showed him crowned with laurels, poets sang his praises. This massive propaganda effort, which made Bonaparte the first media general, had good results: police reports recorded the popularity of the young general among the Parisian population.[8] His permanent presence

162

in public opinion, even during his far-flung Egyptian adventure, made him a good match for men who wanted to pull down the Directorate. It was this new celebrity that frightened Mme de Staël.

There were other noted people before Napoleon, such as Washington or Mirabeau, and in a lesser way Lafayette and Robespierre, who focused on the personal dimension of power, the capacity of individuals to arouse admiration and obedience, to unite popular feeling around their name. *Celebrity* from then on became *popularity*: a type of collective anointing, arising partly from political adhesion, partly from affective attachment to a public person. Popularity was not a synonym for celebrity, nor its identical political aspect, because it implied a favorable judgment. Nonetheless, it shared many aspects: focus on a unique individual, the impact of publicity, the instant judgment of contemporaries, a mix of curiosity and attachment. Popularity was the introduction of media mechanisms into the political sphere of celebrity: the "people" referred to were neither a body of subjects to be governed, nor an abstract principle of sovereignty, but rather a politicized group, individuals subjected to an influx of information, of texts and images, and who brought to bear on actors in political life mercurial judgments, a sense of curiosity, interest, and affection. Like celebrities in the cultural domain, popularity maintained an ambivalent relationship, often judged to be impure, with specific political expectations. Certain individuals knew very early how to play the game; others simply denounced the principle itself. Often obscured by more theoretical debates about the nature of sovereignty or about forms of representation, the emergence of the popularity principle was a major aspect of democratic revolutions at the end of the eighteenth century. It changed the way people thought about power. To follow this half-century of change in political celebrity, we will follow four emblematic trajectories: Marie-Antoinette, the queen of France who became the queen of fashion, the unfortunate symbol of the crises in monarchical representation; Mirabeau, the most popular man of the Revolution, a true political actor, as much impugned as admired; Washington, founding father of American democracy, a reticent celebrity; and, finally, Napoleon himself, who, at the end of his reign, was exiled to Saint Helena, a deposed emperor but with his celebrity intact. Four exceptional destinies, doubtless, but above all four observatories for understanding political transformations induced by celebrity, at the very moment that the public/people rose up as a new principle of legitimacy. Although all four were faced with this new reality, their different ways of adapting to it or resisting it make clear, better than theoretical considerations, the shock produced by the entrance into politics of the media era.

A Fashion Victim?

Marie-Antoinette was hardly lucky where her contemporaries were concerned, and not much luckier with later generations. She was either politically condemned, or she aroused sympathetic feelings that painted her as a sacrificial victim, unjustly persecuted. Neither betrayal nor martyrdom explains the destiny of this young, frivolous woman who had a decisive historical role but one she did not know how to analyze, living through profound transformations in public life at the end of the eighteenth century without really understanding them. However, over the last twenty years, she has once again attracted the attention of historians, less for her actions than for the abundant literary pamphleteering of which she was the target throughout her reign. These works show the intensity of the hatred aroused by the "villainous queen,"[9] attacks that grew ever more virulent, culminating during the Revolution in a veritable political and pornographic delirium. Infidel, lesbian, and incestuous, the queen was the embodiment of every fantasy. In search of imaginary revolutionary politics, historians have attributed this clandestine lampooning to popular dislike of the queen and, more importantly, to the desecration of the monarchy. The pamphleteers allegedly destroyed the people's attachment to their sovereign by discrediting the queen. Then the historians emphasized the symbolic and political meaning of the sexual attacks. When the lascivious queen justified the exclusion of women from the regenerated political body, pornography was rightly considered a political weapon. These investigations, which had the merit of extracting texts from library "hell," imposed an essential political interpretation.[10] Pamphlets that one could hardly take seriously supposedly sapped the legitimacy of the monarchy and showed the fundamental misogyny of Jacobin republicanism. Isn't this going a bit too far?

Let us return to just before 1789. At that time, the pamphlets against Marie-Antoinette were not numerous, hardly destructive, and, above all, not well distributed. It is important therefore, in retrospect, not to project onto the first part of her reign a situation which developed during the Revolution, when political radicalism, ill-considered choices by the queen, and liberty of the press combined to unleash the pamphleteers. Before the Revolution, most licentious books attacked the memory of Louis XV and his mistresses.[11] As soon as the queen and her reputation were involved, the police were watching: she bought up or ordered the suppression of any scandalous texts and succeeded fairly well, apparently, in limiting their distribution. Most of the pamphlets before the Revolution only really started to circulate in 1789, after the Bastille fell and a secret warehouse was discovered by the police.[12] This

164

happened, for instance, with the *Essai historique sur la vie privée de Marie-Antoinette*, no doubt reissued at the beginning of the 1780s, and had a great success in 1789, immediately inspiring an augmented edition.

This also happened with *Les Amours de Charlot et Toinette*, published in England in 1779, which was not distributed until the start of the Revolution. In the beginning, if this poem that described the clandestine loves of the queen and her brother-in-law, the Count of Artois, was unacceptable in the eyes of the royal police, its offensive nature rested more on the eroticization of the queen than the denunciation of her political role. The pamphlet put the reader in the role of an excited voyeur, not in that of a scandalized citizen. Marie-Antoinette, abandoned by her royal spouse, gave herself over to the pleasures of masturbation until she discovered more torrid ecstasies, thanks to the Count of Artois. In the same vein as the best libertine literature, the poem awakened desire in the reader by shamelessly and empathetically describing erotic scenes. In this, the text is very different from revolutionary pamphlets, many of them more violent and explicitly political, which had recourse to a sometimes abject pornography as a way to dehumanize the queen. A text like *Les Amours de Charlot et Toinette* implies an audience highly curious about the queen's intimate and even erotic life, including a certain fascination with or a desire for a disreputable lifestyle. But this does not solve the mystery completely. How could the queen of France, this person so traditionally solemn and distant, protected by imposing customs, become the object of erotic desire, a public figure whose sexual life aroused curiosity and provided entertainment?

These texts, which belong to the scandalous chronicles of erotic literature, should be read not as foreshadowing the fall of the monarchy and the death of Marie-Antoinette, but rather as a continuity of the rhetoric which allegedly revealed the private life of artists, of courtiers and royal mistresses. Here lies the true transformation of the queen's status: she was now considered to be on the same level as actresses or Mme du Barry. The *Essai historique sur la vie privée de Marie-Antoinette*, which presented itself as a history book but instead revealed the dark side of decorum thanks to veracious anecdotes, began with a comparison between Mme du Barry and Marie-Antoinette, two "celebrated women" who had debased a weak king through intrigue and debauchery. The spice in the comparison came from associating a courtier and a French queen. Both had in common the "publicity" given to their excesses.

The former [du Barry] astounded the world, the back alleys and crossroads of Paris, by her villainous and disgusting debauchery: according to her, nothing was off limits. The same thing with Marie-Antoinette, the same passionate spirit: men, women, she liked everything, tried everything, and her thoughtless blundering gained publicity for her behavior in the same way the former sought it by condition.[13]

Publicity, whether consciously sought or obtained by chance, is the very principle which drives the *Essai historique*. The queen became a public woman, similar to courtiers and actors, whose sexual life was the object of every indiscretion, and this was even more justification for the revelations from which the queen claimed to be hiding. The public/private rhetoric was already recognized; the unmasking of private life was rendered legitimate through the public exposure of celebrated persons that had been the basis for newspaper discourse since the middle of the century. The novelty now was that the queen herself had become part of this universe and added to an interest in scandal sheets was the political denunciation of royal vices.

The publicizing of private life was not specific to Marie-Antoinette nor to the situation in France. At the same time in England, the malady of George III was talked about in the press and readers were not spared any of the humiliating and intimate details surrounding the sovereign, as well as the youthful indiscretions of the Prince of Wales, heir to the throne; these were the delight of pamphleteers and satirists, and they did not stop the English monarch from gaining in patriotic popularity.[14] In the first two decades of the nineteenth century, Queen Caroline, treated badly by her husband, was accused of adultery and forced into exile. She became astonishingly popular because her cause served as a rallying point for all opposition, as much for the moral discontent of the middle class confronted with the lifestyle at court as for the more radical protests of artisans and workers. At the same time, popular enthusiasm for the personality of Caroline, through a mix of royal prestige and a familiarity which came from her unconventional attitudes, did not have political outcomes. Both partisans and adversaries of the queen collided in the press and in the street. The quarrel become a national melodrama causing chaos among the most radical reformers and popular militants, sometimes veering toward a media hullabaloo, which ultimately reinforced propagation of the monarchical model and adhesion to traditional values. The flood of pamphlets, articles, and caricatures which rained down on England and reached a peak in 1820 when Caroline returned from exile did not destroy the monarchy. It showed that an intense public curiosity surrounding the youthful indiscretions of the royal family, the emergence of a veritable scandal culture, did not contradict a deep attachment to the royal institution itself.[15]

For the French, where the prestige of the court was culturally better established and politically more crucial, the rising tide was also a matter of change that the queen brought to the royal ceremonies. Marie-Antoinette never succeeded in bowing to French court protocol; she judged it stuffy and outmoded, in spite of the exhortations of her mother, the Empress Maria Theresa, who continually reminded her about the political importance of ceremonies and ritual. It was useless. For the Dauphine, then a young queen, the rules were simply senseless constraints. She hated to be bothered, she balked at the constraints imposed by royal representation. Her mother saw in this her capricious nature, a mixture of frivolity and indolence. "The minute it had to do with something serious, and she thought she would be bothered by it, she no longer wanted to think about it and acted accordingly."[16] But beyond her eccentricities of character, Marie-Antoinette was in step with the times. A taste for private life, for the pleasures of friendship and intimacy, an almost sickening sentimentality, were shared with her entourage of young nobles, who applauded the changes she imposed on court life once she was queen and free to affirm her choices. The Trianon perfectly incarnated her desire to possess a place where she could escape the watchful eye of the court and "enjoy the sweetness of private life," as reported by Mme Campan, her first chambermaid, whose *Mémoires* furnished a detailed account of Marie-Antoinette's efforts to construct an anti-Versailles in the middle of Versailles, a space run by the rules of fashionable society, and not by royal protocol.[17] With her small circle of friends, Marie-Antoinette enjoyed leading the life that young women of nobility enjoyed in their Parisian townhouses and their country homes: dinners, games, social theater and little concerts, laughter and flirting. The life of the queen and her close friends was "free from all representation."[18] It was a great success, in fact. The young nobles who had deserted Versailles during the long reign of Louis XV came back and changed the habits of the old court. Marie-Antoinette was not a useless and unconscious monster, but a young, modern aristocrat, more driven to enjoy the conveniences of private life than to submit to the constraints of the court.

Deserting the classic terrain of sovereign representation and royal protocol for the pleasures of private life has often been criticized as a major political error. Gabriel Sénac de Meilhan, a royal attendant close to the court, astutely analyzed the situation as early as 1790. He wrote that at the end of the eighteenth century "the face of the court had changed." Formal and imposing protocol was replaced by a freer, more informal way of life, modeled on that of Parisian salons.

> The queen was persuaded to shake off the yoke of bothersome formalities which condemned her to perpetual ceremonies. The charms of society were described to her, where freedom and trust reigned, where she would find great delights, where her approval would procure her much more flattering success than homage demanded by custom. [...] Without seeing

167

the consequences, the queen, driven by a desire to please, by a feeling of generosity which she wanted to share, got off her throne, so to speak, in order to live intimately with courtiers, to eat at the king's table with people of the court. It is easy to sense how this way of life was dangerous in a nation where it was so easy to become familiar with others. Slowly, profound respect for the monarchy diminished, a respect created by the monarch's great distance from his subjects and even greater in the case of the queen, which assured that people did not mingle with royalty, where even the slightest familiarity could easily be misinterpreted.[19]

This remarkable text makes very clear the political consequences of these new practices. By substituting a form of familiarity based on intimacy for "perpetual ceremonies" based on distance, the queen provoked nothing less than a crisis in monarchical representation. The model court was that of Louis XIV, an ideal – and idealized – figure who used political ceremony to the profit of the monarchy. Sénac de Neilhan implicitly contrasts the court of Louis XIV with that of the 1780s. The life of the king had earlier been entirely public, in the sense that it was always on show and never ceased to embody sovereignty. In the words of La Bruyère: "The only thing kings lack is the sweetness of a private life." Louis XIV had refused the projects of Pellisson, meant ostensibly to encourage stories of the king's reign by staging scenes of his domestic life. Even the idea of mentioning the private life of Louis XIV was a political aberration. A king was not supposed to have a private life.

Representing majestic royalty in a kingly spectacle had a double function. It exhibited the sovereign, in the eyes of courtiers and subjects, as a being apart, one who represented the absolute power of the monarchy, the center of an entire curial system, distinct from other men by the costumes he wore, emblematic symbols of power. This very specific position permitted him to embody power, but it also served as a balancing point between different groups which struggled for supremacy in the hearts of the elite. Because the king was a being apart, exhibited and kept at a distance by protocol, he could not be identified with any one group. Louis XIV was perfectly conscious of the grave political importance of spectacle. He wrote in his *Mémoires pour l'instruction du dauphin*:

Those people are gravely mistaken who imagine that all this is mere ceremony. The people over whom we rule, unable to see to the bottom of things, usually judge by what they see from the outside, and most often it is by precedence and rank that they measure their respect and obedience. As it is important to the public to be governed by one person alone, it also matters to it that the person performing this function should be so elevated above the others, that no one can be confused or compared with him; and

168

one cannot, without doing harm to the whole body of the state, deprive its head of the least mark of superiority distinguishing it from the limbs.[20]

In a masterful chapter of *The Court Society*, Norbert Elias has proposed a theory about the king's position.[21] He shows that the protocol of the court was a powerful instrument of domination in the hands of the sovereign, as long as the ruler agreed to submit himself entirely to the role. The power of Louis XIV contrasted in every way with that of a charismatic ruler whose authority rested in risky audacious undertakings crowned with success, which permitted him to gather a clan of enthusiastic followers who owed him their social positions. An absolute king, to the contrary, could in no way rely on personal charisma, nor on any specific talent, unless it was the capacity to scrupulously maintain his role. This explains why he could be essentially passive and silent, letting the court move restlessly around him, contrasting his majesty and his distance to the worried activity of courtiers. The king was not a leader; he was the master: he aroused admiration and deference, not curiosity and empathy. There would be little sense for a courtier to want to imitate Louis XIV.

By submitting entirely to ceremony, Louis XIV assured a balance between the different elites and projected an integral public image of himself, in the sense that the man disappeared behind the sovereign. Marie-Antoinette modeled the reverse attitude, almost point for point. Her refusal of protocol led her to break the balance of political and social tensions, appearing to be the head of a group led by the Polignacs and their close friends. The queen disappeared to the profit of the woman, with her friendships and her enmities, her whims and her desires. By withdrawing from ceremonial imperatives, she ceased to publicly embody the monarchy; by advertising her familiarity with certain courtiers, she risked reducing the distance which separated her from her subjects.

Of course, Marie-Antoinette was not the king, but in the ceremonial plan of the monarchy the role of the queen was essential.[22] Besides, she was not the first or the last to react against the constraints of protocol. Louis XV cleverly worked around the ceremonials of his great grandfather, preserving in "little apartments" an area of relative freedom. Marie Leszczyńska opened the way for a queen's more intimate life by not submitting gracefully to the constraints of the court, as was the wont of Maria Theresa before her. A few decades later, Louis XVI and even more so his brothers, Artois and Provence, were in unison with the queen. Marie-Antoinette was in no sense a court revolutionary, nor even a brash reformer. She was simply the most visible and the most exposed of all the royal family, in contrast with the discretion and the prudence of the king. She was above all the most affected by a desire for intimacy and the new culture of celebrity, to which she was not indifferent. Court society would not survive it.

Marie-Antoinette's taste for disguise was a sign of the flagrant contradiction of her refusal of ceremonial obligations, even a taste for privacy, and the reality of the public person that she was. From time to time she decided to attend shows in Paris, at the Comédie-Française and the Opera. Her incognito disguise was of course just a token gesture; she was immediately recognized, but the effort spared her weighty obligations and allowed her to innocently enjoy her popularity, which, at the beginning of her reign, was enormous. This is how the *Mémoires secrets* reported one of these soirées in 1775:

> Yesterday, the queen went to the Opera, as announced. S.M. [Her Majesty] was wearing a kind of incognito outfit because nothing about her appearance seemed to demand her presence in a box seat. She sat down in the second balcony, across from the stage. People, however, showed her indispensable honors, that is, Monsieur le Maréchal-duc de Brissac, as well as the governor of Paris, and Monsieur le Maréchal-duc de Biron, as commander of the guard for the show, stood at the carriage door with S.M., as well as the directors, who had torches, and they walked in front of the queen lighting her way to her balcony. S.M. was accompanied by Madame, by Monsieur and by Monsieur le Comte d'Artois. When she arrived, S.M. was received with the warmest, most sincere acclamations of joy on the part of the public. S.M. responded with three curtsies. Madame imitated her; the two princesses were presented; then Monsieur joined their circle, accompanying the three women, and Monsieur le Comte d'Artois, having taken his place, repeated the same ceremony. No one could imagine the beauty of such a moment.

A troublesome phrase – "a kind of incognito" – strongly indicating it was simply a fiction aimed at upholding the idea of the private presence of the queen, even though "indispensable honors" were nevertheless proffered. The queen, in a way, played both sides of the coin. She benefited from her popularity as a young queen, a known patron of Gluck, a fashionable composer of the moment whose *Iphigénie* was playing at the Opera that day. But her presence in the second balcony and not in the grand royal box seat gave the idea that she was a simple individual whom the public happened to like. At whom were the spectators' "sincere acclamations" aimed? At the queen or at Marie-Antoinette, this young elegant woman who modestly refused to occupy the royal box seat? The theater was an ideal place for such ambiguity, because the public which gathered there was both representative of the political body, assembled subjects of the queen, and a group of spectators, a public which observed, judged, and showed its pleasure or its displeasure. The written account, which implicitly contrasts the "indispensable honors" proffered by the authorities (the governor of Paris and the commander of the guard) and the "sincere acclamations" of the spectators, suggests a blurring of the homage awarded a sovereign and the enthusiasm shown a young woman. The spectacle that Marie-Antoinette, her brothers-in-law, and her sister-in-law offered from their balcony had nothing to do with the ceremony of Versailles, where obviously no one thought of applauding the appearances of the royal family. The queen was not fulfilling a role prescribed by protocol; she was inventing herself as a public figure, celebrated as a fashionable author would be celebrated, or an actor. Applauded by the audience at the Opera, Marie-Antoinette was the center of attention, which moved from the stage up to where she was sitting, in the same way Voltaire, three years later, would be applauded at the Comédie-Française when he was coronated. It would be tempting to draw a parallel, or rather a divide, between these two polar opposite destinies: an author celebrated as a sovereign, whose bust was crowned on stage, and the queen of France applauded as a private person. But maybe that's too easy an interpretation. At this point what was important behind the fictional incognito was, above all, a certain ambivalence in regard to the status of the queen, about which her contemporaries were probably not clearly conscious.

Perhaps troubled by these developments, the editor of the *Mémoires* used the word "ceremonial" to designate the bows made by the royal family, as if it were difficult to qualify or be precise about such a gesture, when the queen and the princes by blood saluted the public at the Opera. The situation became more complex still when, in the second act, the actor playing the role of Achilles had the presence of mind to change a verse. "Sing, celebrate your queen" became "Let us sing, let us celebrate our queen." There was an immediate reaction: "All eyes instantly fixed on S.M. as soon as the chorus finished, and they repeated it. The queen, emotionally moved at the sign of such transports, which Monsieur and M. le Comte d'Artois continued to excite by their applause, could not contain her gratitude and they saw tears of joy run down her cheeks." Emphasis on the political identification of the queen, on the singers and the public, did not restore solemnity and distance, but instead emotionally fed the young woman, who burst into tears, revealing a sensitivity perfectly adapted to the circumstances, given that Gluck's *Iphigénie* aroused in the public just such an outpouring of emotion. Marie-Antoinette in this instance inaugurated the model of a sovereign who did not primarily arouse deference or distant admiration, but, instead, affection and sentimental closeness.

In other circumstances, Marie-Antoinette pushed her worries about escaping from the constraints of ceremonials even further, in order to fully feel the emotions of a young aristocrat who was, with impunity, having fun. She showed up several times at the Opera balls, and counted on her disguise to create a real camouflage. The news obviously got around and created scandalous rumors, contributing to the blurring of the queen's public image. "She thought she was never recognized, but she was, by the entire group right from the moment she entered the room: by pretending they did not recognize her, they always created a kind of intrigue at the ball and this made her disguise enjoyable."[23] It is important to study the queen's desire not to be recognized, a desire which is inherent in the culture of celebrity insofar as it allows one to escape from one's personal image, to break the asymmetry that implies that one is immediately recognized by those one does not know. A vain desire, obviously. The face of the queen was too recognizable, even behind a mask, and the people with her, although not in formal dress, were always noticed. Marie-Antoinette was experiencing the fate of contemporary celebrities, whose efforts not to be noticed lead inevitably to their discovery. Disguise, even in this case, is a fiction based on the indulgence of the dancers.

This kind of playing at secrecy had its risks. These secret visits of Marie-Antoinette aroused more or less harmless gossip. Young men at a ball talked to the queen with a familiarity authorized by the fiction of disguise and bragged of having seduced her; others, like the likable libertine the Duc de Lauzun, imagined that they were loved. "I saw these pretensions begin simply because the queen asked one of the men to find out if the second play would be late in starting," Madame Campan remembered.[24] From then on malicious rumors began to tarnish the reputation of the queen. By opening herself up as a private person, Marie-Antoinette modified her public position: she slid from monarchical representation into public media hype. What is important here is not the supposed youthful indiscretions nor the political burden brought on by ongoing scandal, but the fact that the queen of France, generally a discreet person, superior, reserved, should become the stuff of fantasies, an object of desire, like an actress or a singer, but with the immense prestige of her royal standing. This mixture of guarded distance (because the queen was the queen, after all) and seductive familiarity made Marie-Antoinette, to her great peril, the first glamour queen.

This parallel between the image of Marie-Antoinette and that of celebrity figures in the theatrical and literary worlds also came from her fascination with fashion. Before representing the rogue queen, she was a fashion icon, passionate about clothes and wigs, encouraging extravagant hairdos, which irritated the Empress Maria Theresa.[25] For the first time, the queen of France did not use a court hairdresser but had the talented Léonard come from Paris, bringing a large team with him to Versailles and becoming a personality known by all of polite society. Rose Bertin, a fashion designer, succeeded in gaining the confidence of the queen, and by advertising this relationship her Palais-Royal business had a stunning success.[26] All polite society women, the rich bourgeoisie, wanted to dress like the queen. Bertin herself enjoyed a certain celebrity, which arose in part from the traditional registry of royal favor, but also from a new factor, that of virtuosity. Like some artists, particularly gifted artisans succeeded in mixing creative talent and self-promotion, constructing a public image in the service of a commercial business. At the same time, unlike a comparable case, that of Jean Thomas, called the "Great Thomas," a popular and spectacular, though truculent, dentist, who became a celebrity in the first half of the century, or like the innkeeper Ramponneau, Rose Bertin knew how to associate her merit and her notoriety with that of the queen.[27] Her image was joined to the court and polite society. This associative alliance between the queen of France and a fashion designer recently moved to Paris was mutually beneficial, but was also immensely transgressive.

The queen's taste for finery was not simply an anecdotal and picturesque trait, nor even just an irritation, confirmation of her legendary frivolity. In reality, the emergence of a fashion system at the end of the eighteenth century testified to a profound evolution in the culture of appearances.[28] In cities won over by the first consumer revolution, ways of dressing were dictated not by social position and submission to tradition, but by imitation and the cult of constant change. By becoming an integral part of this fashion culture, by making a Paris dress designer her official fashion consultant, by accepting all innovation, Marie-Antoinette attracted attention from everyone and became the center of imitation.[29] Here again, there was an enormous gap between this lifestyle and the traditional regime of monarchical representation. Sovereigns, the king and the queen, were distinguished by their clothes. Marie-Antoinette was imitated.

This taste for fashion, including its most exuberant and ostentatious forms, dangerously linked the image of the sovereign with that of actresses. Marie-Antoinette's interest in the world of spectacle encouraged this association. Thus, her constant public support for Mlle Raucourt, even when the tragedian was the object of great criticism having to do with her alleged dissolute morals, contributed to a blurring of the queen's image through her association with the world of actresses, singers, and courtesans. In pamphlets, on the eve of the Revolution, one more step was taken: "It is impossible that the most elegant prostitute in Paris could be better outfitted than the queen."[30] Conscious no doubt of the danger, Marie-Antoinette made the choice, starting in the 1780s, of a less cluttered clothes style, even rejecting the emblematic royal dresses as too fastidious, favoring instead a simpler, more natural look. But this evolution was only one more step in the fashion spiral because these clothes were now easily imitated not only by a few aristocratic women, but by all women who wanted to be fashionable.

Abandonment of the traditional principles of monarchical representation in favor of an image of simplicity and accessibility is visible even in the portraits of the queen. Unhappy with the initial portraits painted of her when she first arrived in Paris, which represented her in court costume, even in a great ceremonial cloak covered with *fleurs de lys*, Marie-Antoinette, sought a painter capable of rejecting this type of formalism in favor of a more natural look. She found this painter in the person of Élisabeth Vigée-Lebrun, who painted several portraits of the queen starting in 1779, and succeeded in capturing her vivacity and her facial features. If the first painting, given to the empress, was still a portrait in court dress, including numerous attributes of royalty and notably the crown carefully poised on a cushion, as well as a bust of Louis XV, the next paintings focused on the person of the queen, emphasizing her beauty and her individuality. But this simplicity was not without risk, because it always threatened to endanger the prestige of the monarchy and its habits of monarchical representation. In fact, it was a long way from the great iconographic style in honor of Marie de Médicis who had planned out the allegorical representation of the queen's sovereignty two centuries earlier. When Vigée-Lebrun exhibited a portrait of the queen in 1783 at the Academy Salon wearing a simple blouse of white muslin like that which Rose Bertin was starting to make fashionable and which Marie-Antoinette liked to wear in the Trianon, there was a terrible scandal (Fig. 14).[31] The Salon critics were offended to see the queen shown publicly in such a simple outfit, something domestic, part of her private life. The light muslin dress was mistaken for a simple blouse, and part of the public thought the queen had been painted in her underclothes. An added irritation, the portrait made no mention of the king or the royal family. This left the queen to be regarded as a private person, autonomous, free to wear whatever she wanted, and not like the queen of France. Ironically, while the Trianon was meant to keep the queen from the eyes of the court by giving her a private space, the portrait painted by Mme Vigée-Lebrun displayed an image of the queen in her private space, which caused many of the Salon visitors to look twice. Vigée-Lebrun had to withdraw the painting and substitute it with a more conventional portrait in which the queen, dressed in a classic silk dress, was arranging a bouquet of roses.

174

The muslin dress, nonetheless, was going to be copied. The portrait, in spite of the critics' dislike of it, was a success with the public.[32] Named the "Queen's Dress," it was widely imitated, starting in the 1780s by European aristocracy, then even more widely by upper-class city women at the end of the century. The political scandal created by the portrait was not incompatible with the status of fashion icon that Marie-Antoinette had agreed to accept, to the contrary. Fashion was not only a matter of clothes; it was a lifestyle, a concept of freedom and simplicity; feelings took priority over social constraints, all of which was affirmed by the painting. Marie-Antoinette had become a public figure not only in the classic sense of monarchical representation, but also in a new sense, defined by the culture of celebrity: a person whose individuality was looked at and commented upon by the public.

It is even possible that for the queen this transformation seemed to be a great success at the beginning of the 1780s. While Louis XVI was content to live in the shadow of his ancestors, trying his best to seriously, and a bit fearfully, carry out a job for which he had no taste, the queen was congratulating herself on having escaped a destiny apparently intended for her and which frightened her a great deal, that of a closely watched sovereign, imprisoned by an abstruse ceremonial, reduced to giving birth to princes, forever bored or else taking refuge in the Church. However, the criticism created by the 1783 portrait marked a reversal in public opinion. By publicly exhibiting herself, Marie-Antoinette took the risk of stirring up all sorts of criticism, and, in fact, what followed were attacks on her outlandish spending, her attachment to Austrian interests, her imagined lovers. These criticisms were not new, but they were strongest just at the moment when fascination with this modern princess, a model of elegance and independence, was beginning to fade. She was vulnerable because she had made a spectacle of herself. Malicious rumors were soon circulating about the nature of her secret life.

The following year, 1784, the "necklace affair" precipitated the queen's public disgrace. The story has been told many times. One only has to remember that a female schemer, Mme de La Motte, managed to convince the Cardinal de Rohan that the queen wanted a very valuable necklace, formerly bought by Louis XV for Mme du Barry, and it would be worth it to him to serve as an intermediary. In order to convince the cardinal, there was even a midnight meeting organized with a substitute Marie-Antoinette, in the gardens of Versailles. Once the affair was known, the scandal, already considerable, grew once the queen insisted on taking Rohan to court. At this period, when court cases were becoming part of public opinion, thanks to the universally popular memoirs of lawyers, there was a risk of great public notoriety. Passionate emotions were unleashed by the trial. The effect was even more devastating because the affair brought up all the usual reproaches concerning the queen: her taste for finery and lavish spending, her rejection of monarchical ceremonials. (How could the Cardinal de Rohan believe that the queen would be out walking alone at midnight?) It put a spotlight on the young woman who had impersonated the queen, Nicole Le Gay. Marie-Antoinette was the first queen to come with a lookalike!

The public image of the queen was irredeemably damaged, but it was with the Revolution that attacks grew immeasurably. Marie-Antoinette, who was in no way prepared to understand the events, did nothing to gauge their force and never sought to adapt to them. And yet it was perhaps not an impossible mission. At least so thought Antoine Barnave, who hoped to convince her to help the moderate revolutionaries stabilize the new regime. After the disastrous flight and arrest in Varennes in June 1791, he wrote several letters in which he exhorted her to accept the Constitution and become a smiling, consensual figure in the constitutional monarchy. After all the jolts and violence of the Revolution, he wrote, the people were going to need celebrations, diversions, emotional release. "Who could be better equipped than the queen to carry out these arrangements? Had she not known brilliant popularity? Even if opinion had changed, at least people were never indifferent to her, and when the heart is not cold, it is always possible to get it going again."[33] The "popularity" to which Barnave referred, hoping the queen would commit to gaining it back again, was a political concept which promised to have a great future. It renewed royal legitimacy, based on an affective link with the new sovereign, the people. This political mechanism, because it was based on feeling, a form of affective attachment, should, it seemed to Barnave, be activated by a woman, on condition that she showed her attachment to the Revolution. Everything else was a matter of politics, or rather publicity: "We will do everything to lead hearts back to her," he promised.[34]

As is known, the queen did not want to listen to this kind of counsel, or she was incapable of reviving such popularity. But it was this very principle of monarchical legitimacy which had been tossed about since the end of the Ancien Régime, the Revolution only precipitating and sanctioning an evolution that had already begun. Louis XVI was both witness and victim of the passage from "king-principle" to "king-person," a legitimacy founded on the eternal seniority of the sacred monarchy through the paternal and debonair figure of a king attached to the happiness of his people.[35] The consequence of this evolution was to base the legitimacy of royal power on the personal virtues of the king and thus to encourage praise or criticism about the human, private person who held power. "Popularity" now became the new criterion for political success within a democratic regime. But the king and the queen were not the only ones claiming popularity.

Revolutionary Popularity

Marie-Antoinette had another correspondent who understood perfectly the importance of popularity. Mirabeau, a great political figure of the first years of the Revolution, "voice of the Revolution," according to Michelet, has not been much appreciated by modern historians. Revolutionary memory retains his famous response to Dreux-Brézé. By proudly contrasting the will of the people to the force of the bayonet, Mirabeau formulated the principle of national sovereignty and left no doubt about the resolve of the deputies. But historians have not focused attention on his remarkable destiny. Ideologically dubious, too corrupt, too moderate, Mirabeau seemed suspect, and he has often been reduced merely to this single proud response, a clichéd image of the Revolution, as if his role was limited to one inaugural speech.

He was, however, for nearly two years, the most popular orator in the National Assembly, symbolizing the Revolution in the eyes of the public, and his death was experienced as a real drama. But Mirabeau was even more than this: he was the first great star of political democracy. His rise shows his transformation from a scandalous celebrity, a noble *déclassé*, a libertine writer and a paid pamphleteer, into a new political star, based on an indisputable aptitude for embodying the new principle of popular sovereignty. The two halves of his astonishing life are often contrasted, that of the failed publicist for the Ancien Régime and that of the politician who found his calling because of the Revolution.[36] But beyond the obvious caesura represented by the Revolution, Mirabeau's whole career displayed an inexhaustible energy for and an innate sense of publicity. The Revolution gave his talent a forum and a destiny.

When the Estates-General met in May 1789, Mirabeau was already a public figure. He was forty, son of a provincial aristocrat, and already a man of letters and an economist, author of a successful book, *L'ami des hommes*, which won him his nickname. Mirabeau's father, who had just died, as if to free his son, was not only an ambitious writer and self-proclaimed philanthropist, he was also a domestic tyrant who hounded his son. It is true that Mirabeau was willful and very early led a dissolute and adventurous life. His recklessness and the strong hatred his father had for him led him to prison several times, thanks to *lettres de cachet* (sealed letters) that he would soon make the symbol of despotic justice. Moving from irrational impulses to spectacular deeds, he broke away from the role of prominent citizen he was destined to be and became a colorful *déclassé* aristocratic figure. He gained celebrity in 1782 with the spectacular and scandalous trial that set him against his wife, a rich heiress from the Aix parliamentary nobility. He seduced her with his audacity and temerity, surprising everyone, and then married her, stealing her right out from under the nose of official suitors. Meanwhile, he was imprisoned in the Fortress of Roux, escaped with the young wife of an old parliamentarian from Besançon, took refuge in the Basque Country, and was arrested and imprisoned for three years in the dungeon of Vincennes. Then he was released and attempted to save whatever could be saved. The trial pitted him against all provincial polite society. Mirabeau defended himself in defiance of twenty-three lawyers in his wife's family, demonstrating for the first time the power of his oratory. He lost the case, which left him ruined and nearly banished, but it was a public success. Mirabeau had made his mark. The trial was sensational. It captured the imagination of everyone in Provence for six months, and it was even talked about in Paris. Mirabeau's legal arguments drew an immense crowd, including the Archduke Ferdinand, brother of the queen. One eye-witness invoked the "enthusiasm" of the public in favor of Mirabeau, the crowd pushing forward to catch a glimpse of, or at least hear, the man.[37] His father, naturally, complained about Mirabeau's taste for scandal, which only seemed to increase his son's energy tenfold: "Rumors here, rumors in Pontarlier, that's all he needs."[38]

Ruined and banished from his family, crowned with a suspect celebrity, Mirabeau became one of the many literary adventurers at the end of the eighteenth century, continuing to maintain talk about himself through various publications: erotic writings, commissioned books, political pamphlets, more or less digested compilations, he wrote anything. His denunciation of the *lettres de cachet* made him an editorial success. *Ma conversion, ou le Libertin de qualité*, a pornographic novel published anonymously in 1783, was quickly attributed to him by the *Mémoires secrets*: "What increases interest is that everyone has guessed the identity of the prisoner at the Château d Vincennes: it is the Comte de Mirabeau."[39] Lacking money or position, he made a name for himself.

If Mirabeau, like most of his contemporaries, was fascinated by literary celebrity, politics monopolized more and more of his time. All the while writing against despotism, he dreamed of a diplomatic career and survived thanks to pamphlets he edited at the request of those in power. Calonne hired him to argue against his rivals, then sent him on a mission to Germany. But if Mirabeau was a versatile writer, celebrated and inflammatory, he was not greatly respected. Many more talked about him than respected him; polite society avoided him.[40] His celebrity had the whiff of scandal; it was neither honorable nor flattering and it made him a mongrel, half-way between a libertine whose indiscretions sold

178

newspapers, like Sade, whom he met at Vincennes, and professional polemicists like Linguet. In 1788, he used his energy to combat Necker, when in fact Necker, returning to power, seemed to be at the peak of his popularity. Mirabeau's friend Chamfort urged moderation. "To get yourself talked about is not an admirable trait under the circumstances; you have another talent whose force must be disciplined and readied for the moment of battle."[41]

It is true that the political situation had changed. Mirabeau was one of the first to understand the importance of this change and to adapt to it. In 1787, he turned on Calonne and published a pamphlet against financial speculation. It earned him a resounding success and forced him to take refuge for several months in Liège. He then refused a proposition from Minister Montmorin to argue against parliament. At the time, May 1788, he gauged the crisis and made his choice: he wanted to be a man of the nation. The convening of the Estates-General convinced him that a new career was opening up for him: "It is the step of a century that the nation has taken in twenty-four hours. Oh, my friend, you will see what a nation this will be the day when talent is also power."[42]

The electoral campaign in Provence was going to offer a first glimpse of his political acumen, a mixture of audacity, energy, and a taste for publicity. His arrival in Aix in January 1789 caused an uproar, according to his own estimation.[43] Having obtained a seat in the provincial government, in the Assembly of the Nobility, he immediately took positions favorable to the demands of the third estate, the people, giving two long speeches hostile to privilege for the nobility, which he promptly published, and then edited an address to the provincial nation as well as a long text in which he presented himself as a forum for the people, comparing himself to Marius and the Gracques. He thus ensured his popularity with the third estate and then returned to Paris, letting the situation simmer. When he returned in mid-March, an insurrection was on the point of erupting.[44] The peasant and urban revolts increased, while the political situation seemed blocked. Mirabeau then gathered the fruits of his thus far equivocal celebrity. He was triumphantly welcomed as soon as he arrived on the outskirts of Aix, where they shouted his name, and then with great fervor in Marseille. He himself complacently recounted, with a bit of exaggeration perhaps, to the Comte de Caraman, commander-in-chief of the province:

Imagine, M. le Comte, 120,000 people in the streets of Marseille, an entire industrious and commercial city giving up the whole day: windows rented at one and two *louis*: just as many horses: communal carriages covered with palm and olive fronds: people kissing the wheels, women offering up their children: 120,000 voices, from babies to millionaires, shouting out acclamations and crying "Long Live the King!" 400 or 500 of the most distinguished young people of the city walking in front, 300 carriages following: this will give you an idea of my exit from Marseille.

Other eye-witnesses confirmed this success, but Mirabeau well understood the virtue of self-promotion. Impressed, Caraman called on him a few days later to calm the rioters. Mirabeau drafted an *Avis de Mirabeau au peuple marseillais*, which he then had plastered around the city, reestablishing peace, and showing the political power of his name. A few weeks later, he was elected deputy for the third estate, in Aix as well as in Marseille.

Thus, on the eve of the Revolution, the scandalous celebrity of Mirabeau metamorphosed into political popularity. For this noble *déclassé*, a libertine in constant revolt, but convinced of the necessity for profound political change, the Revolution came at just the right time. Mirabeau's prestige in the eyes of the provincials was due to the fact that he was both a noble *and* hostile to the nobles; he benefited from the traditional aura of the elite while at the same time arousing sympathy by his rejection of absolutism and privilege. Both the son of a genteel family and a misfit, he combined the old aristocratic precepts and the new democratic principles, allowing him to convert his equivocal celebrity into political popularity. Make no mistake: such a transmutation is rare. It would take the personal equivalent of a Mirabeau, noble and rebel, aristocrat and plebian, his incomparable talent for publicity, and, finally, exceptional circumstances in order to make this alchemy work. And, in fact, Mirabeau's transformation was incomplete. If his sense of self-promotion and his political acumen gained him numerous votes, he could not quiet the prejudices that his person aroused, notably among Parisian nobles. At the opening of the National Assembly, his name was received with as many boos as applause: "Insults and contempt showed him the nature of his celebrity."[45]

The National Assembly gave Mirabeau more than a forum. Right from the moment of his first speech, he was a success, and the jeers changed to applause. Very quickly he was in the ascendancy among his colleagues, one of the most listened to voices, and among the few capable of changing opinions in the Assembly. They came to see him and hear him. By the time of his death in 1791, he had given 439 speeches in the Assembly, making him the most prolific orator of the period. He was also the most influential, even if many deputies were suspicious of him just *because* of his talent for oratory.[46]

Mirabeau's power rested on a belief in the establishment of a constitutional monarchy and an extraordinary eloquence. But the orator was also a performance artist, playing on his corpulence, his smallpox-scarred features, his lion-like mane of hair, and his booming voice. His ugliness was an advantage, because it signaled power and energy, an indomitable determination, the irrepressible will of the people. "When I shake my terrible head, there is no one who dares interrupt me," he said proudly.[47] Mirabeau clearly understood the inherent theatrical nature of a revolutionary politician. From the very first weeks of the National Assembly, meeting in an immense room in the Palace of Versailles, the third estate agreed to allow spectators. They were often numerous and noisy, which helped excite the deputies and radicalized the debates, but which also changed the very form of the parliamentary exchanges. The orators addressed themselves as much to the spectators as to their colleagues. After moving to Paris in October 1789, the National Assembly met in the *Manège* (Carousel) room in the Tuileries gardens, an enormous room that was used to keep racehorses before the Revolution and which had two balconies for spectators. It was not enough to have good arguments; a speaker had to make himself heard in this immense and tumultuous arena. And Mirabeau knew like nobody else how to put on a show. After his great speech about bankruptcy, which definitively assured the supremacy of his oratory, the actor Molé congratulated him and added, jokingly, that he had missed his vocation; he could have had great career as a dramatic actor. He was not the only one to make the comparison between Mirabeau's political talent in the Assembly and that of a stage actor. The comparison became a commonplace among his friends and his enemies. Mirabeau, conscious of his theatrical potential, enjoyed drawing attention to himself. He did not hesitate to rehearse his speeches in front of a mirror: "He had this tic of vain men who got pleasure from simply hearing their name and liked to repeat it to themselves: he imagined dialogues where he named himself as the speaker: the Comte de Mirabeau will address you, etc."[48]

The theatrical nature of Mirabeau's political eloquence should not be surprising. It is true that the revolutionary meetings were usually thought to have been rather solemn, as if politics, *a fortiori* revolutionary politics at the heart of a modern democracy, were something too serious to be combined with the dramatic effects of amateur actors. In reality, as the American historian Paul Friedland has remarked, the political debates were invested with a great deal of theatricality; they took the form of a spectacle acted out in front of listeners in the balconies and in front of the entire French nation. The spectators applauded and whistled, as in a theater; sometimes they interrupted the speakers and became emotional. Even during the most serious sessions, such as the trial of the king during the Convention, women in the audience ate ice cream and applauded the debates.[49]

This theatricality can be interpreted at a theoretical level as political representation paralleling theatrical representation. But it can also be seen more simply as the porosity between two extremely public spectacles that captured the attention of the people. Theaters, which multiplied at the beginning of the Revolution, were considered more and more an important aspect of politics, serving the cultural regeneration of the nation and the political projects of the Revolution. As for the Assembly meetings, they were new ways to deliberate, where the collective future of the nation was at stake, very moving spectacles, whose principal protagonists were real stars. To insist on this association does not necessarily reduce the greatness of the Revolution, in the way that Burke ironically wrote about revolutionary histrionics; it shows that the spectacle of politics is not a modern invention, but a key element of public representation and democratic debate. Democratic public space replaced the ritual monarchical spectacle not with abstract committee meetings, but with another kind of spectacle, where citizens were both actors and spectators. Politics also needed an audience.

In this new context, celebrity took on a prestigious hybrid form, based both on the entertainment world and on the world of politics. Mirabeau was both an embodiment of the Revolution in action and an actor of genius. Many witnesses emphasized the curiosity aroused by his talent and his notoriety: "He was the one that strangers looked for in the middle of all his colleagues; they were happy if they heard him talking, his most familiar expressions became aphorisms."[50] But this celebrity also had an advantage that was directly political, beyond what the public thought of Mirabeau. His name was inevitably invoked by Parisians in the first days of the Revolution as they tried to rally more citizens. They shouted for Mirabeau when they wanted to go to Versailles to oppose the right to veto. It was the end of summer 1789. "The name Mirabeau was the rallying cry. They thought his life was in danger because he wanted to reverse this odious veto, the royal veto," joked Brissot, editor of *Le Patriote français*. He knew very well that Mirabeau was, in fact, favorable to the veto. The episode showed that his celebrity was already based on his name, which symbolized the ongoing Revolution and the national interest.[51] A few months later, the name Mirabeau was even more famous, and Étienne Dumont was surprised to learn that the stagecoach drivers in Picardy gave the name "Mirabeau" to their packhorses, those animals that did the hardest work.[52] It would be wrong to treat this anecdote as simply an amusing curiosity when, in fact, the celebrity of Mirabeau covered a wide range of heterogeneous phenomena: an admired and influential politician, an orator whom everyone wanted to see and applaud, a public figure who aroused curiosity and confidence among the masses, an excessive and contested personality, a name synonymous with power.

Mirabeau, in 1790, was at the height of his political celebrity. Joseph Boze, a Provencal painter who had already painted him the year before, made another enormous full-length portrait, the engraving of which was immediately advertised in *La Gazette Nationale*, declaring that the painting could be seen at any time in the painter's studio.[53] Certainly, Mirabeau remained a controversial figure with his outlandish lifestyle, making numerous enemies. But in the eyes of the people, he was in all respects the most famous political man of his time. He was ceaselessly sought after, his house always full of visitors, and every day a crowd of strangers waited at his door "for the great pleasure of seeing him in person." In spite of the abolition of noble titles, he was known to everyone as the Comte de Mirabeau, "not only to his friends and to his visitors, but also to the masses, who liked to decorate their idols," remarked his friend Dumont, not without irony.[54] Moreover, Mirabeau scathingly chastised a journalist once for using his family name Riqueti, saying he had "thrown all of Europe into confusion."

With the arrival of Mirabeau, the mechanisms of celebrity that had developed in the literary and theatrical worlds invaded politics. A man who was fascinating because of his individuality and his talent acquired political power based on the curiosity that he aroused, the attachment the people had to him, and his capacity to embody a new collective sensibility. It was difficult to name this new form of power based on renown and popular affection. The word that rapidly imposed itself and remained endurably in the political vocabulary was "popularity." In the eighteenth century, the word designated the popularist nature of an individual or taste. In 1788, Féraud's dictionary defined the word as the fact of affecting the language of the people, and he gave an example: "This word has an active sense, meaning the love of a man for the people, and not the love for a man by the people." But Féraud raised the possibility of a passive use in French, one he denounced as an Anglicism.[55] This usage, which is now ours, was just beginning to germinate. It became standard during the Revolution. The popularity of Mirabeau and Lafayette was talked about. Mme de Staël, the daughter of Necker, even reproached Mirabeau for having doggedly "depopularized" his own father.

People at the time were conscious of this new importance of popularity among revolutionary leaders and that it had become part of the political game, but the notion was still a bit mysterious. In 1791, *L'Ami des patriotes*, a revolutionary newspaper edited by a moderate patriot lawyer, a deputy to the National Assembly, dedicated a long article to this difficult question: "What Is Popularity?"[56] The article first of all defined popularity as "being in public favor," a term that was then more usual and that was inscribed in classical political vocabulary. A popular man was one favored by the people, whereas in the past there had been favorites of the king. The people's taste thus had a negative connotation, using this comparison. Then, the article tried to contrast popularity with public opinion. The first rested on excessive passions, even on the manipulation of opinion. It referred to collective fads, as sudden as they were ephemeral. Public opinion, also called "public esteem," was, to the contrary, based on rational and solid judgment. "Public opinion is always more or less well thought out, popularity never is. Time confirms public opinion: it almost always becomes historical opinion; time destroys popularity; there is no example of a man who has maintained his popularity throughout his whole life."

In a political context, the contrast was between celebrity and glory. Celebrity had to do with matters of opinion based on collective infatuation by the majority, passion and arbitrariness being naturally part of the equation. Glory was based on calm reflection by "wise men." These men "almost always judge their contemporaries as posterity would judge them, because they keep a great distance from the movement and the intrigue; they do not let themselves be dazzled by splendor; they judge for themselves." In this, one again finds the same criticism, in the same terms, of the deceptive effects of sudden and fleeting celebrity, as well as praise for true merit, which justifies public esteem and posthumous glory. But it is nonetheless confusing. On the one hand, how is one to distinguish these two publics, one which frivolously accords its favor to celebrated men and the other that calmly judges their merits? How is one to reconcile the sovereignty of the people, *a fortiori* the elective principle, and the suspicion that popular favor is arbitrary and misleading, as capricious as the favor of princes? The article proposes a solution found in the classic perspective of Enlightenment optimism: development of a real public sphere that would allow people to form better judgments. Freedom of the press, "by enlightening the people," would transform it into a real public: "Make no mistake, popularity will be changed: the influence of bought applause and the influence of the marketplace will continue to diminish." Great optimism, but illusory because development of the press is as much in the service of the mechanisms of celebrity as are more reasoned judgments: newspaper readers are rarely immunized against collective infatuation. A second mystery raised by the article remained unsolved. If popularity was "nothing, absolutely nothing," neither true love of country nor the esteem of good people, if one could obtain it by any means, even the least honorable, if "one could be famous while at the same time being universally despised," why was it so desirable? How could it be the most powerful resource of democratic governments? The author, it seems, confused the moral

FIGURE 1: Jean Huber, *Le lever de Voltaire*, oil on canvas, 1772. The many engraved copies of this painting and the enthusiasm of the public irritated the Ferney patriarch.

FIGURE 2: George Romney, *Emma Hamilton as Circe*, 1782, one of the numerous paintings of Emma Hamilton, whose face was among the most celebrated of her time.

FIGURE 3 (following page): James Gillray, *Dido in Despair*, engraving, 1802, turns the celebrity of Emma Hamilton into caricature.

Ah wher & ah wher is my gallant Sailor gone? ─ He's gone to figh the Frenchmen he loose to ther Arm & Eye.
He's gone to Fight the Frenchmen for George upon y throne. **DIDO in Despair** And left me here on the old Antique to lay me down & cry.

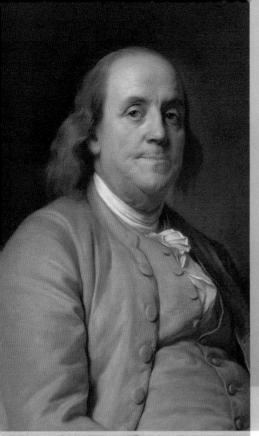

FIGURE 4 (top left): Joseph Siffred Duplessis, *Portrait of Benjamin Franklin*, 1783. An often reproduced semi-official portrait that became the one fixed in the public mind.

FIGURE 5 (top right): Jean-Baptiste Houdon, *Bust of Benjamin Franklin*, 1778. There were many plaster copies made of this sculpture.

FIGURE 6: (left) Pierre Adrien Le Beau, *Benjamin Franklin*, engraving, 1777. A cheap engraving, sold by Esnault and Rapilly.

FIGURE 7: Jean-Baptiste Nini, a medal in terracotta representing Franklin, 1777. Numerous variations of this medal exist.

FIGURE 8: A candy box, with a miniature by François Dumont, 1779.

FIGURE 9: A porcelain cup by Sèvres which testifies to the celebrity of Franklin in the 1780s.

FIGURE 10: One of the first ceramic medals of Franklin created by Josiah Wedgwood around 1774.

FIGURE 11 (below): A ceramic bowl ornamented with a portrait of Franklin, copying an engraving by Cochin. On the other side is a portrait of Washington.

FIGURE 12 (following page, l): Thomas Gainsborough, *David Garrick*, 1770, one of the numerous portraits of the greatest English star of the eighteenth century, who knew how to manage his public image.

FIGURE 13 (following page, r): Gilbert Stuart, *George Washington*, 1796, the great official portrait of the first president, austere and distant.

FIGURE 14: After Élisabeth Vigée-Lebrun, *Marie-Antoinette*, 1783, an English-style portrait considered too informal, created a scandal when it was exhibited in the Academy salon.

order and the political order, public esteem and political popularity, the merits of a statesman and the power of a popular man. To be fair, though, the tension between an ideal democratic sovereignty and the reality of popular favor has never stopped causing confusion in political thinkers over the last two centuries. It corresponds to the ambivalence in the idea of "people" found in classical political thinking, between the *plebs* and the *populus*, the common people and the people in general, a tension that Mirabeau himself clearly underlined when he tried to find a name for the assembly that came out of the Estates-General, but the tension stems even more from an insoluble tension that haunted all political thinking in the nineteenth century between "the masses and the nation": "On the one hand, the vile common people given over to their passions, the uncultured masses, vast threatening numbers of people; on the other hand, the wisdom of sovereignty, the peaceful form of the general will."[57] This contrast was not strictly social; it did not simply contrast the people and the elite, rather it was a sociological reality, that of fiercely avid individuals, steeped in prejudice and passion, and a political ideal, the rational aspect of democratic sovereignty. The difficulty of conceptualizing the people and the notion of popularity in the context of theories about democracy was, and is even today, at the heart of reflections about what is called populism.

However, "popularity" was not created as part of political theory. It became a tool for the media practice of taking polls, where it served to measure the fluctuations of collective attachment to a personality (the "popularity edge"), but seemed, for this reason perhaps, to be held in suspicion. Studies of both philosophy and political science prefer the idea of "public opinion," in spite of known problems with the term, no doubt because from the start public opinion was constructed as a legitimate democratic value and because it did not simply concern judgments made about political actors but rather had to do with all the opinions and judgments made by a population. When it concerns the capacity of a politician to arouse feelings of infatuation and fascination, political scientists call it "charisma." Max Weber imported the word into the vocabulary of social science to describe a type of authority that did not rest on either tradition or legal and administrative rules. From its theological origins, the word "charisma" retained a supernatural dimension, an unexplained magical and spiritual power by which individuals could ensure obedience. Applied first of all to the power of dictators or revolutionary prophets, charisma is not unknown in a democracy, because the embodiment of power implies the existence of leaders whose authority goes beyond the simple anointing by votes or by the prestige of a position.[58] But it was not without consequence that charisma supplanted popularity in political thought: charisma came from power, from authority, once again recalling the idea of great men, those who made history, who were obeyed by the masses, and it was recognized from the start as an eminently serious political component. Popularity was more ambiguous, defining not an authority, but a notoriety; it did not describe enthralled fascination, but rather a frivolous, even ephemeral, attachment. It was a contested value and above all a fragile power, half-way between the political sphere and the cultural world, including the world of entertainment. It could sustain a pretension to power, but it did not guarantee obeisance in any form. How many popular men were unable to transform celebrity into durable political action?

The essence of popularity at the beginning of celebrity entailed the fact of being ephemeral. Necker, so popular in the summer of 1789, was the subject of absolute indifference when he left France barely a year later without having made any difference at all to the outcome of the Revolution. Lafayette had the same experience. Extremely popular at the beginning of the Revolution, he wasted political capital by making unlucky choices, incapable of choosing between the king and the National Assembly, until he found himself almost unanimously detested in the summer of 1792, and obliged to flee to Austria, where he was imprisoned for several years. He had to wait four decades to find public favor again, with his voyage to America in 1824–5 and during the July revolution of 1830.[59]

Mirabeau, having died early in April 1791, a victim of his celebrity, did not have time to live through the ups and downs of political popularity. His death was a major event, offering a precious glimpse into the ambiguities of political celebrity and unmistakably evoking more recent examples. From the very first announcement of Mirabeau's illness at the end of March 1791, a mix of curiosity and worry seized the Parisian populace. "An enormous crowd gathered every day all day long in front of his door," Mme de Staël recounted, with, however, no hint of sympathy.[60] Cabanis and two other doctors drafted signed bulletins several times a day about the health of the patient, which were printed, distributed, and then published in newspapers.

From the first day, Mirabeau's illness was of interest to the public. Tuesday night, they were already rushing from every corner to get news of him.... Wednesday, several newspapers talked about the loss they were threatened with.... Day and night people from every walk of life, every party, every opinion, waited in front of his door. The street was full of people; and in public places groups talked only about this illness that they thought, with reason, was an enormous event. Health reports were given out several times daily, but they were not enough to quell the universal worry.[61]

Mirabeau himself, although prey to atrocious attacks of peritonitis, was not indifferent to his popularity. He asked that his window be opened so he could hear the "public hubbub" which rose up from the street. During periods of calm between convulsions, he amicably received visitors and delivered a few witticisms destined to be repeated. "He saw himself as the object of attention from everyone," Dumont reported, "and he never ceased to speak and to conduct himself as a great and noble actor on the national stage."[62] There was always the theatrical dimension, the spectacle, of which Talleyrand, a close friend of Mirabeau and a careful observer, was very conscious: "He dramatized his death," Talleyrand declared. Even events as intimate as sickness and death were, for a celebrated man like Mirabeau, the object of spectacle. Everything that concerned him had become public, everything was dramatized. Of course, the last moments of a dying person's life are often, more or less, material for drama; Mirabeau was not the first to strike a pose at the moment of death. What was new was that his public was not made up simply of family members come to listen to his last words, but comprised a whole nation that followed the daily newspaper accounts of his unexceptional agony (there were no historical formulas, no spectacular conversions), which became a real serialized media event. Le Patriote français dedicated long articles every day to Mirabeau's dying and then to his funeral, conscious that "the public took a great interest in everything that concerned him."[63]

When Mirabeau died on April 1, emotions were at an all-time high. The Paris Department decreed eight days of mourning and closed the theaters. The National Assembly decided to transform the Saint Genevieve church into a "French Panthéon" for illustrious men. Spontaneous ceremonies were organized in popular quarters of the capital. In the Saint Marcel quarter, a committee for the Saint Victor battalion decided as early as April 3 to declare eight days of mourning. Then workers in the Gobelins area organized a wake. In turn, workers in Saint Genevieve organized a ceremony in the basement of the church in order to show, as they said, that "those of the poorest class" wanted to render homage to "their benefactor."[64] The provinces were not idle either.[65] In Paris, Boze immediately commissioned a new full-length engraving of Mirabeau to be sold by subscription, in order to "increase the number of images of the Great Man who has just been taken from France."

Everyone was very impressed by the spectacle of the funeral ceremonies, especially since no procession orders had been given in advance. The crowd hesitated, different groups forming here and there, before uniting spontaneously. The Journal de Paris described the collective emotion: "On the boulevards, in the road, as far as Saint Eustache, the enormous Paris population seemed to press forward together, walking, standing in the windows of houses, on the roofs, in trees: never has death attracted so many spectators to such a magnificent and lugubrious spectacle."[66] Here again it is significant that the vocabulary of spectacle comes so spontaneously to the journalist. The life of Mirabeau was a permanent spectacle, always excessive and exuberant. His death was every bit as theatrical. But the funeral procession also had a political significance; it represented one of the great revolutionary days: the public, through the death of its first great man, by sharing the same moment together and the same feelings, by witnessing as one this tragic and macabre spectacle, demonstrated its political tenor.[67] The death of Mirabeau recalled the short and fragile life of a human being, aroused worry about the future of the Revolution, which could have appeared threatened, and reinforced the feeling of living a unique moment in history together.

One can, of course, wonder about the real sentiments experienced by Parisians at the announcement of Mirabeau's death and their feelings when they saw the ceremony. Would we agree with Michelet, who said the "pain was immense, universal"[68] and the "funeral rites were the biggest, the most popular there had ever been in the world before those of Napoleon?" What sources exist for this evaluation? The testimony of witnesses, journalists or contemporaries, who described the demonstrations, and we do know, thanks to current examples of media-hyped political deaths, that what is described in the heat of breaking news, the feelings aroused by an event, should not always be taken literally but rather be understood for what is meant: discourse itself aimed at creating an event, at giving such an event historical credence, even inventing the event that is being reported.[69] The media capacity to create an event by describing it before it is actually an event, the popular response echoed by this, is perceived today as a characteristic trait of the society of spectacle. How much more striking to discover this awareness with the death of Mirabeau.

The interpretation of events given by witnesses should not, however, be overlooked. Instead, everything indicates that two types of reactions coexisted. One view, mostly spontaneous, was offered by a population both curious and emotional, conscious of living a memorable new day of history-in-the-making, rich with events, and the other view, that of numerous journalists and publicists using the death of the most popular political man of his time to advance their own interests, selling books and newspapers, affirming their role as privileged interpreters of the Revolution. Both views came together in a mutual feeling of making news, of being part of a public that was assisting at an extraordinary event which concerned it directly, in which it was both actor and spectator. In the end, looking closely at numerous accounts, it is not so much the emotional vocabulary or the popular communion which dominated, but rather curiosity and the spectacle. In the spring of 1791, even though the French were split as to their judgment about the political actions of Mirabeau, all of them at least believed that his destiny was extremely interesting. Parisians who followed the funeral procession were not the only ones to be preoccupied by the death of a celebrated man, as shown in an article in *La Feuille villageoise*, a cheap newspaper distributed in the countryside and often read collectively: "Country dwellers have heard M. Mirabeau talked about so often they are no doubt curious to know the details regarding his last days; we are going to satisfy such a justified curiosity."[70] The press, by affirming this curiosity and feeding it, played the role assigned to it since the explosion of newspapers during the summer of 1789: it produced continual commentary about events, offering readers the feeling of everyone sharing, in real time, revolutionary political news-in-the-making, even for those who could not participate directly in what was happening daily in Paris.[71]

Writings about political death have rested, for over a half-century now, on the theory of the king's two bodies, first proposed by Ernst Kantorowicz and then developed by Ralph Giesey, which states that medieval jurists put together the fiction of a sovereign's immortal body, distinct from his physical body.[72] But Mirabeau was not a sovereign; no one thought of endowing him with an immortal body. His death was not the object of political ritual wherein one could read a constitutional ideology, as one could in the ritual of royal funerals. Mirabeau's death instead opened a period of uncertainty and improvisation, where the Assembly seemed to swing between popular expectations and its own interest. Nor was it marked by demonstrations exacerbated by collective passion. In contrast with the death of Marat two years later, the death of Mirabeau aroused not fear or desire for vengeance, but rather a mixture of emotion and curiosity produced by the improvised spectacle the crowd put on for itself.[73] Michelet was conscious of this, although he did excessively dramatize the stories of these funerals. Next to striking expressions about "sinister premonitions" that fired imaginations in "the light of trembling torches," he also wrote about: " Streets, boulevards, windows, roofs, trees full of spectators." Mirabeau's funeral was the last act of the public spectacle that was his life, and for whom the people were both the audience and, now, the main actor.

The funeral procession was also echoed in other kinds of performances, confirming the thin line between politics and theater. Olympe de Gouges had *Mirabeau aux Champs-Élysées* performed, starting April 11, at the Théâtre des Italiens, Then the same theater performed *L'Ombre de Mirabeau*, and at a theater in the rue Feydau spectators came to applaud *Mirabeau à son lit de mort*.[74] The death of the orator caused a flood of publications which confirmed that in spite of his popularity, feelings about him were far from unanimous. His enemies did not give up. Marat accused him of having betrayed the Revolution and he published a violently hostile article in *L'Ami du peuple* that invited everyone to rejoice over the death of "his most formidable enemy."[75] A pamphlet entitled *Orgie et testament de Mirabeau* published the rumor that it was Mirabeau's libertinage that was the cause of his death, owing to venereal disease. One printer, sensing a good deal, put together a series of texts relative to the death of Mirabeau, articles, speeches, pamphlets, poems in his honor. The originality of this brochure, which sold for thirty *sous*, was that it made clear the contested aspects of Mirabeau's reputation by also including articles by his enemies.[76]

Among the numerous publications that immediately followed his death, two merit our attention in particular; they show that Mirabeau's political popularity included numerous elements issuing from the culture of celebrity. The first is directly linked to the death of Mirabeau, because it had to do with the account of his illness, published by his own doctor, Cabanis. The doctor was only thirty-four at the time, and showed promise of a brilliant career in the medical and philosophical areas of the Consulat and the Empire. Cabanis met Mirabeau through his friends at the salon of Mme Helvétius. They became friends and Cabanis doctored him devotedly during his illness. A few weeks after his death, Cabanis published the *Journal de la maladie et de la mort de Mirabeau*, a detailed account of the fatal weeks. From what we know, Cabanis wanted first of all to justify himself, given that some were reproaching him for not knowing how to care for the great man and others suspected him of poisoning Mirabeau, so that finally an impressive ceremonious public autopsy was necessary.[77] But this apologetic aspect was not explicit. What seemed most important was a desire to respond to public curiosity, to offer in some way a deep and logical sense to the reports that Cabanis himself had written during the crisis. The result was an astonishingly precise account that spared readers no detail of the colic that afflicted Mirabeau, and at the same time gave a day-by-day, almost hour-by-hour, description of the care that he was given. The tone was essentially medical, sometimes technical, but without hiding the effusive affection that Cabanis admitted he had for Mirabeau, a "passionate admiration," along with the emotions that overwhelmed him once again when he started to write a "too cruel account," his "soul still moved by the sublime scenes which accompanied this great catastrophe." And so the last moments of this political man, the very intimacy of his agony, were delivered to the public through the perspective of a privileged witness, both a doctor and a friend, and now a biographer. He used the witness device, of great importance in new forms of biographical writings about celebrated men. What might appear in another context

190

as an indiscretion is here seen as a homage rendered through friendship, justified by Mirabeau's public character and a life lived "in the theater of opinion,"[78] the agony of which was almost entirely public and whose death could in no way be a private event.

A few months later, another work unleashed a veritable scandal. Pierre Manuel, public prosecutor for the District of Paris, already famous for publishing the archives of police findings at the Bastille, published letters that Mirabeau had written to Sophie de Monnier during his imprisonment in the dungeon at Vincennes.[79] These passionate letters offered a glimpse of the love life of the orator, previous to his political actions. Manuel counted on the curiosity of the public in regard to the private life of Mirabeau, and he drafted a particularly categorical "introduction." Claiming to defend the "reputation of Mirabeau," he quickly turned to considerations of his romantic and sexual life, referring to him by first name to better mark the intimacy that the reader had a right to expect from such a text. "Who told me these secrets? Reader, I am sorry for you if you have not guessed as I have who the person in the *Gabriel* letters is." The publication's interest lay entirely in revealing the most intimate secrets of the person whom the author designated as the "Messiah of the Revolution." To give the reader an even greater illusion of having access to well-hidden secrets, Manuel published the code that the two lovers used to encrypt their letters.[80]

The Mirabeau family tried in vain to stop the publication by having a confiscation order carried out at night, seizing the manuscripts and the proofs from the printer and the bookseller. The bookseller took it to court, but also announced in the press that he was justified in possessing and making public the "*Gabriel* letters," which were meant to "honor the person who was supposed to open the French Panthéon." Then in a speech at the Bishop's Club, Manuel demanded the ideal of transparency ("the common house must be made of glass"), not hesitating to use the revolutionary principle of *publicity* in the service of a commercial enterprise which sought to exploit the curiosity of the public concerning the intimate life of a celebrated man: "People, publicity and mistrust! These will save your freedom."[81] In January 1792, without awaiting a court judgment, he published the collection of letters, which were a commercial success, but for which he was criticized by the press. The *Affiches*, for instance, reproached him for wanting to profit from the famous name of Mirabeau in order to accede himself to a "celebrity often imaginary and always fragile."[82]

Between the spectacular funeral rites of a great orator and the revelations, more or less lurid, about his love life, the gap seemed immense. The traditional divisions of historiography reinforced this impression. On the one hand, there was political history, dealing with the great revolutionary days; on the other, cultural history, with its interest for lesser works, pamphlets without literary or political value. But the powers that weave together the framework of societies, even in moments as serious as revolutions, are never unequivocal. Mirabeau's popularity was nourished both by his political pre-eminence in the National Assembly and by the captivating curiosity that his contested personality and romantic life aroused. Mirabeau was a star as much as a political hero.

Obviously, this is why his pantheonization, decided in a crisis, was a failure. It arose out of the extreme popularity of Mirabeau, the emotion elicited by his death, and the need for the Revolution to celebrate itself in a moment when troubles were accumulating. It flowed almost logically from the idea of the great man, this renewed form of the hero, which asserted itself in the second half of the eighteenth century. Voltaire followed Mirabeau into the Panthéon. But caught up in the emotion of his death, the decision to glorify the deputy from Aix did not allow for the passage of time necessary to make an impartial and dispassionate judgment. Contemporaries appropriated the role of posterity without taking into consideration the rapidity of political time during a revolution. A year and a half after the death of Mirabeau, the discovery of his secret correspondence with the king was devastating. The hero was a traitor! The bust of Mirabeau was strung up in the Place de Grève (now Place de la Concorde) by the *sans-culottes*, while at the Convention it was Manuel himself who proclaimed on December 24 that an indictment against his memory had been drawn up. Nearly a year later, the Convention decided that because "no one can be a great man without virtue," they would remove the body of Mirabeau from the Panthéon, where it was to be replaced by Marat, dead some weeks earlier.[83] The short time of political and popular celebrity was not the long period of time necessary for the renown of great men.

Even when he was alive, Mirabeau's rise irritated other deputies, who did everything to stop him from occupying a pre-eminent place, and in particular from becoming minister. The revelations which followed his death caused revolutionaries to distrust, even more, excessive forms of personal popularity. Suspicion in regard to openly displayed ambition, associated with the haunting memory of Caesar and even the dangers of "idolizing individuals," was a dominant trait of the culture of revolutionary politics, renewed during Thermidor (July 19–August 18) with the denunciation of the Robespierrist "dictatorship."[84] The cult of revolutionary heroes leaned by preference toward collective heroes, such as the conquerors of the Bastille or the Swiss at Chateauvieux, or toward martyrs for freedom (Le Peletier, Marat, Chalier), those already dead and, if possible, unknown, like the child martyrs of the Year II (1793/4), Bara and Viala, for whom the Committee for Public Salvation actively orchestrated posthumous heroism. The revolutionary leaders themselves distrusted celebrity. Robespierre, who had no taste whatsoever for dramatizing himself and even less taste for his nonexistent private life, rose politically without all the accompanying aspects of celebrity, and without, perhaps, enjoying real popularity, even if that remains difficult to measure. He was proud of continually denouncing the pursuit of "popularity" as a dangerous tool in the service of personal ambition. The true revolutionary, of which he thought he was the embodiment, renounced popularity, because he refused to flatter people and lie to them.

Only Marat benefited, perhaps, by real popularity, thanks to his work in journalism and his image as an aggressive defender of the oppressed, a popularity more ambivalent than that of Mirabeau. His omnipresence in the public revolutionary space, thanks to *L'Ami du peuple*, his canny sense of political one-upmanship, his physical appearance, all of it made him an immediately identifiable public person, easy to love or hate. His death was the occasion for a striking case of celebrity transfer. If he was the object of a hero cult orchestrated by David, which ended finally in semi-failure, Charlotte Corday, absolutely unknown, became a celebrity overnight. Her act was immediately described and commented on in the press, her portrait distributed widely. She quickly went from the political pages to the entertainment pages. Her trial in September 1793 was reported in detail, fascinating the public by the accused's assurance, her poise and her beauty. Portraits of Corday multiplied, even engravers who had drawn Marat now concentrated on his murderer. Absolutely unknown a few weeks earlier, Corday rose to real celebrity, a curious synthesis of a celebrated criminal from the Ancien Régime and a revolutionary hero.[85]

The President is a Great Man

French revolutionaries distrusted the effects of political celebrity and manifested a reluctance toward any sort of personalization of power. On the other side of the Atlantic, to the contrary, the young American republic encouraged a real cult around the person of George Washington. Today, one readily talks about the "founding fathers," combining Washington, Jefferson, and Franklin, even Adams and Hamilton, men collectively admired, but as historians have often pointed out, the prestige of the first, at the end of the eighteenth century, was completely different from that of the other participants in the War of Independence. It seems natural to think that the hero of the war should become the most celebrated man in the United States. In reality, the way in which Washington managed to embody the battle for independence and then the survival of the United States remains rather mysterious. Nothing destined him to play such a role: only moderately cultivated, of normal intelligence but nothing special, he was not a great military strategist. His achievements during the Seven Years' War against the French and their Native American allies did not allow him to be employed by the regular British Army, as he wanted to be. Even during the War of Independence, the principal victories could not be credited to him, beyond the successful but limited Princeton operations at the beginning of the conflict. However, this respectable person, though lacking in charisma and genius, was, in his lifetime, the object of an impressive hero-making process.[86] The career path of a Virginia farmer, a former soldier in the colonial army who became, when he was over forty, an American icon and finally a figure known worldwide, provides another configuration of political popularity. Washington was not a political agitator and had nothing of the theatrical orator in him as Mirabeau had. His extraordinary renown came from his military glory, from his clever, disinterested political attitude, and above all from his ability to embody the heroic and emblematic figure that the new nation needed. However, even if Washington's political prestige always had a somewhat traditional dimension, maintaining, for example, a firm distinction between public and private life, he could not totally escape from certain new aspects of political publicity. His renown was a hybrid form, relating to both glory and celebrity, and he always tried to fit within the limits of *fame* one particular virtue that was extremely important to his contemporaries. This virtue was associated with honor, reputation, and public esteem, as well as posthumous glory – in other words, the praise accorded great men.

From the moment Washington was nominated to be commander-in-chief of the Continental Army in 1775, leaders of the patriotic movement orchestrated an intense publicity campaign around his name and his image, in order to give the insurgent cause an emblematic and consensual representative. Cities and counties were named after him, his portrait was widely distributed through every media channel, newspapers enthusiastically reported his smallest movement as though reporting incredible exploits. Celebrations were organized in honor of "His Excellency," and public parades celebrated his birthday every year. In a sign of the times, images became part of the campaign. John Hancock, president of the Intercontinental Congress, commissioned a painting by Charles Willson Peale in 1776, which was subsequently reproduced many times during the war, to the point of becoming one of the most famous images of the American Revolution. Hancock and other patriotic leaders were aware from the start that there had to be a substitute figure for that of the king, in order that the fight for independence could be inscribed in the traditional framework of political allegiance, marked by a stalwart embodiment of power. From George III to George Washington, the passage from the monarchy to the republic was incarnated in a form that was ready-at-hand, that of the protective father figure, "father of the country," as the commander-in-chief was beginning to be called.

After the December 1776 battles of Trenton and Princeton, during which Washington gave evidence of his physical courage, the idealization knew almost no bounds. If historians are generally skeptical about his actual military merits, contemporaries saw in him a true hero, "one of the greatest generals the world has ever known," as the *Virginia Gazette* proudly wrote in 1777, a date when his military exploits were especially modest.[87] More than his deeds, and even more than the final victory, it was the way he kept the army on its feet in the middle of the sad winter of 1778 which forever assured great esteem for Washington in the hearts of those living in the colonies. Although the military situation seemed hopeless, the army no more than a pathetic group of badly trained survivors, poorly dressed, worn down by sickness, having, for better or worse, managed a retreat back to Valley Forge in southern Pennsylvania, Washington embodied the spirit of resistance and organization, a dogged refusal to give up. He never doubted they would win at the very moment it seemed most unlikely.[88] A few years later, when the Battle of Chesapeake clinched the American victory, no one ever forgot those first disastrous years. At the head of an army of non-professional soldiers, ill equipped and badly outfitted, Washington was the general who challenged the leading world power and in the end inflicted a defeat as resounding as it was unexpected.

More than his military aura, it was his return to civilian life once peace was signed which struck his contemporaries. For men in the eighteenth century, nourished on classical culture, but also on the memory of the English Revolution, the danger that threatened republics was the personal power of a military leader. By refusing the destiny of a Caesar or a Cromwell, and once again renewing the Cincinnatus myth, Washington won a double victory in the eyes of the world, over human nature and over history. His decision was perfectly logical given his attitude during the war, always faithful to Congress. Nonetheless, the decision was cleverly dramatized, notably during his resignation ceremonial in December 1783. This renunciation of power amazed his contemporaries and allowed Washington to acquire a new dimension, that of a selfless hero. He became the embodiment of patriotic virtue, the perfect combination of courage and restraint.[89]

Washington's start in politics, beginning when he agreed to participate in the Convention of 1787, and then when he was elected the first president of the United States, simply reinforced the image of a man as quick to sacrifice his private life to the common good as he was to return to his home in Mount Vernon once his military role was ended. If Washington at this point embodied the figure of a national hero, it was because he represented the perfect equilibrium between two important values in American culture at the end of the eighteenth century: one, a strong dedication to the public good, nourished by references to traditional republicanism; the other, a distrust of power, to which the puritan culture, part of an aristocratic ethos, contrasted the peaceful life of a farmer on his land. Political action was perceived as superior action on the condition that it never be associated with ambition but always with sacrifice. Washington, the "reluctant hero," knew how to cleverly stage-manage his aspirations for a peaceful life, and he identified himself with this particular political virtue.

Seen from Europe and notably from France, the American general appeared to be the ideal great man as defined by writers of the Enlightenment. From the start of the war, Washington excited admiration, even if his celebrity in France was eclipsed by that of Franklin. In 1778, a medal was forged in Paris to honor him, apparently commissioned by Voltaire.[90] However, since no portrait of Washington existed at that time in Europe, an imaginary figure was engraved on the medal. His name and his exploits had traveled faster than his image, given the transatlantic circulation of his celebrity. After the war, Washington's renown spread well beyond the intellectual milieu. In December 1781, two months after the Battle of Yorktown, Mr Duval, a candy maker in the Palais-Royal, sold bonbons "à la Washington."[91] Published articles from French witnesses of the American Revolution contributed to popularizing the figure of Washington.[92] Abbé Robin, chaplain for the Rochambeau army, published his *Campagne de l'armée de M. le Comte de Rochambeau* in 1782, consisting of a long enthusiastic description of Washington, gifted, he said, with every fine quality, both military and personal. Robin's slightly naïve admiration rested on the impression he had from direct contact with the general: "I saw Washington, this soulful man, supporter of one of the greatest revolutions which has ever happened. I stared at him with the attention that the sight of great men always inspires."[93] But Robin also described the enthusiasm, the almost idolatrous public cult that surrounded the hero of the New World:

> He was seen in all these countries as a beneficent God; old men, women, children, everyone together ran out to see him when he went by, congratulating themselves on seeing him: they followed him into the cities with torches; they celebrated his arrival with public light shows: Americans, a phlegmatic people, who up until the middle of the troubles had never followed any impulse other than that of methodical reason, came alive, were

passionate about him, and the first songs that feelings dictated to them were in celebration of Washington.[94]

The laudatory testimonials continued to multiply. A visit to see the great man from the New World now became a major stop for Europeans who undertook a trip to America. Brissot spent three days at Mount Vernon in 1788 and described with admiration the conversation with the "celebrated general," a "good farmer," modest and selfless.[95] During the Revolution, he often used this patriotic political myth to give force to the theme of the citizen-soldier. In 1797, Fontanes published a discourse in which he proposed Washington as the model for leaders of the French Republic.

Washington benefited from this kind of aura in the United States and in Europe because he had succeeded in offering an image of himself as a modest hero who had accepted against his will to sacrifice his private life for public office. Thus, when the publishers of his correspondence discovered in the twentieth century the almost maniacal importance he attached to his public image, to the point of weighing the effects of each decision on his reputation, they were, to say the least, disconcerted. Such vanity did not correspond to the myth of a modern Cincinnatus. This is all it took in the eyes of certain biographers dedicated to pushing the great man off his pedestal: Washington now appeared to them to be an ambitious person ravenous for recognition and glory. He seemed "mad for glory," according to John Ferling, who saw in him a cunning politician, playing the selfless role in order to better get what he wanted: power.[96]

If this interpretation had the merit of highlighting the ambiguities of a figure who was too unequivocal, it was based on an anachronistic concept of ambition. It attributed to Washington an idea of political popularity that he could not share. For him, what was important above all was his reputation, the way he was perceived and considered by his peers. In this, he was a worthy representative of the Virginia colonial elite, rich planters who had adopted the way of life and the values of the English nobility. Very soon, Washington incorporated into his life the rules of seemliness that distinguished a gentleman, and he firmly respected them his entire life. His sometimes haughty, and always distant, tone was a mixture of reserve and courtesy which very much struck his contemporaries, the result of self-control that was even more powerful because Washington had had to struggle to acquire his social position.[97] He very early understood the need for the social esteem of his peers among the elite in the Virginia colony, and he also knew the vagaries of a military reputation. This had been contested during the Seven Years' War when he was accused of having the French officer Jumonville executed. Ever after, he never ceased to jealously guard his reputation.

With the War of Independence, under the impact of his immense celebrity, this obsession with his reputation took on new and slightly frightening dimensions. Having become a public figure, Washington not only had to defend his local status against rumors, but also had to carefully monitor the image others had of him, those who only knew him by name. It does not seem that he sought, or even appreciated, the adulatory demonstrations that he had begun to arouse. In return, he was deeply worried about preserving his public stature and about the mark he would leave in history. This is exactly what the word "fame" meant, public esteem spread far and wide, so unanimous that it seemed to anticipate the posthumous glory promised a great man, but which was extremely fragile because it was at the mercy of bad decisions, rumors and scandals, a lost battle or an unlucky word. From this came, obviously, one of Washington's most characteristic traits: caution, reserve, calm, and self-control. Where some historical figures drew part of their charisma from a rage to expatiate, from their eloquence, from the enthusiasm which animated them, Washington seemed willingly "taciturn," responding evasively when it was impossible to keep silent.[98] And it explains his hesitation before every important decision: what would be the consequences for his reputation, he worriedly asked his friends. Even though he had become the hero of the New World, Washington was still tied to the traditions of the elite, where the social value of each individual was measured by the esteem that his contemporaries accorded him.

Put another way, Washington was a man of honor. In his eyes, nothing was more important than being perceived as honorable, which implied conformity with the values of his social group. In this, he was anything except a revolutionary, and his relationship to public opinion was diametrically opposed to that of a Mirabeau or Wilkes. Scandal horrified him. Like all men raised in a society where honor plays an eminent role, he knew perfectly well that social esteem was not a spontaneous phenomenon, that it was the duty of a gentleman to act honorably, but also to monitor as much as possible the image others had of him. For Washington, this implied defending his military reputation and promoting his historical role as commander-in-chief. Six months before the end of the war, when the outcome was uncertain and in spite of financial difficulties for the American commanders, Washington had Congress hire a team of secretaries to copy all his military correspondence. Twenty-eight volumes were sent to Mount Vernon.[99] Some months after his return to civilian life, his former *aide-de-camp*, David Humphreys, suggested that Washington write his memoirs, which he refused to do, claiming that he did not have the talent and, above all, he did not want to be accused of being immodest.[100] The following year, Humphreys tried again, proposing that he write them himself. In the meantime, he had gone to Paris for a long visit, wrote a poem to the glory of Washington, and visited numerous admirers who pressed him to write a biography of the great man. "Be assured the advocates of your fame are very numerous in Europe," he wrote to Washington to convince him.[101] He accepted, no doubt delighted to promote his reputation in Europe, where his name was now so celebrated, but where the confused memory of his role during the Seven Years' War was still an issue.

But, even so, still worried about giving Humphreys free rein, Washington offered to lodge him at Mount Vernon and to put his archives at his disposition, as well as all his reminiscences.[102] Both had an interest in accepting the arrangement. Humphreys would have rich documentation at his disposal and would be treated as a "member of the family"; Washington could monitor the advancement of the work. In fact, he consciously annotated the manuscript bit by bit as it moved along. However, the projected biography was never completed.[103] Humphreys probably was not up to the job, lacking the energy and the talent. And it is also probable that the difference was too great between the expectations of the European public, growing more familiar with the new form of biographical writing that demanded anecdotes about the character and private life of General Washington, and the anecdotes which Washington wanted to give the public, accounts of his military comportment during the War of Independence and above all during the Seven Years' War, without venturing into the more dubious domain of his emotional and family life. For Washington, his "fame" had little to do with celebrity culture as it was developing in Europe, fed by publicity and even scandal. Nothing was more horrifying to him than being put on the same level as a successful actor or a fashionable author. Nor was it driven by political ambition in the modern sense of the term: at this point in his life, he was not seeking popularity. It was his military reputation and his honor as a gentleman that were essential. His fame was based on the enlightened opinion of people of merit, as well as on posterity from which he awaited a dispassionate judgment.

It is possible, too, that Humphreys' work was interrupted by Washington's accession to the presidency. Washington was to discover, especially during his second mandate, that his celebrity did not shelter him from new forms of political partisanship, such as those which were developing in the young republic. Re-elected president in 1783, he remained extremely popular, but the political context had changed. The gap between federalists, favorable to industrialization and the re-enforcement of federal power, and republican-democrats, openly Francophile and more attached to the ideal of rural America, deepened and became confrontational. The peace treaty with England, negotiated by John Jay, caused an explosion. The federalists considered it a useful compromise which allowed the United States to stay out of revolutionary European wars. For the democrats, abandoning the alliance with France for submission to an old colonial power appeared to be an abnegation. The campaign for ratification brought with it new forms of political mobilization, marking the sensational entrance of public opinion as a new force in the political game: mass demonstrations, partisan press, petitions. Washington, who had agreed to sign the treaty, was violently attacked by the democratic press, in particular by the *Aurora*, a newspaper owned by Franklin Bache, the son of Benjamin Franklin.[104]

Washington's position regarding the rise in power of public opinion and the new techniques used in partisan politics turned out to be more complex than expected. Numerous attacks, sometimes very violent, had undeniably hurt him and tarnished his accepted image. It was a wounded man who left the presidency in 1797, shocked by the new tone in political debate. Nonetheless, in spite of the noisy attacks, which came from the most militant fringe of opposition to the treaty, Washington remained popular. It was in fact his public intervention in favor of the treaty which reversed the situation. While opponents seemed largely in the majority, in terms of opinion and in Congress, his intervention gave the treaty all the authority acquired by Washington since the War of Independence. At least that is what Thomas Jefferson thought, greatly irritated by the ratification *in extremis* of the treaty by Congress in May 1796.[105]

Washington's public image did not emerge intact from its immersion in the troubled waters of partisan politics. His popularity, however, proved to be a formidable weapon, not on the level of oratory competence or radical mobilization, like Mirabeau or Marat, but as a power for legitimacy. But popularity also revealed his fragility. As soon as Washington found himself associated with federalist positions, he was no longer sheltered from criticism and took the risk of seeing the aura attached to his name progressively disappear. His decision to leave office after two terms no doubt had something to do with his weakened popularity. Leaving office would restore his reputation as a self-effacing man. Retired to Mount Vernon for a second time, Washington once again became the modern Cincinnatus. Two years later, his death was acknowledged with national mourning, public ceremonies, and sermons preached in churches: a veritable "apotheosis," the stamp of religiosity.[106]

The return of consensual feeling for Washington irritated certain principal actors of the period, including some of his political allies. John Adams, his vice-president and then his successor, observed it with a certain bitterness. Adams very early distrusted the excesses of collective admiration, even the "superstitious veneration" which surrounded Washington. In early February 1777, he warned Congress about the political dangers. Later, he was reassured by the General's legalism and his great loyalty to Congress, but he never ceased to observe his public success with a mixture of jealousy and clarity. Much later, after his own presidency and the death of his predecessor, he continued to be irritated by the cult surrounding the great man, which was due, he thought, to displaced idolatry, the adoration of the "Divus Washington."[107] The abundant correspondence at this period between Adams and his friend Benjamin Rush reveals the ambivalent opinion the two of them had of the former president, whose merits they never ceased discussing.

When he launched into an enumeration of the real talents of the first president, Adams mentioned above all a "handsome figure" and added with irony that beauty was the first talent, a saying he attributed to...Mme du Barry. Here the worth of a modern Cincinnatus was reduced to the level of a vulgar royal mistress. Adams continued in the same ironic vein: the talents he recognized in the hero of freedom were an imposing presence, richness, the gift of silence, and even the very fact of being originally from Virginia. In this, we are far from the heroic figure of a great man. But if the virtues of Washington were so banal, his exploits so thin, how could his renown be explained? This, if Adams is to be believed, was essentially the phenomenon of public opinion, orchestrated, what is more, by those who privately did not hide their distrust.[108]

The frequency with which Adams and Rush returned to the merits of Washington and his public image proves their need to understand a collective phenomenon which never ceased to astonish them. These men who had directly participated with him in the War of Independence and in the governing of the young republic, who saw him up close, were stupefied by the effects of notoriety that created a halo of unreality around the figure of Washington and behind which his real qualities were unrecognizable. Faced with something that to them seemed mystifying, they hesitated between exasperation and a wry acceptance, realizing that this symbolic pre-eminence was obviously necessary, as excessive as it was, to the comfort and the unity of a young nation unsure of its viability and its future. In spite of the feeling of injustice that Washington's extreme celebrity and his monopoly on prestige inspired in them, it was better not to risk weakening a symbol that was the best assurance of their communal work.

Adams was sometimes overcome with irritation and moodiness when he foresaw, with reason, that history would be blinded by the celebrity of Washington, as by that of Franklin, and would not fairly judge the roles that various political figures played.[109] More often, however, he seemed to be resigned to the situation, and not without a certain admiration. To understand the issues involved, though, he did not employ the topic of celebrity as it was beginning to develop in Europe, but rather the idea of "fame." The term kept appearing. In a revealing passage, he reported the words of William Cobbett: "There never was a greater difference between two men than between Washington and Adams in one point, the desire of fame. Washington had an enormous, and insatiable thirst for it; but Adams was excessively careless of it."[110] Make no mistake: this comment was in no way a criticism of Washington. As for Adams, he had no illusion that these words were not to his advantage, and he himself recognized that his indifference was one of his gravest faults. Of course, a certain vanity and pride were part of this comment, but it does allow us to realize to what extent desire for "fame" was then considered a legitimate motive for action, a wish to advertise oneself by glorious and virtuous feats, and to gain the respect and admiration of one's peers.[111]

Strongly centered on a neo-Ciceronian morality and a culture of honor, the topic of "fame" which structured the social and political imagination of the generation of Adams and Washington rested on an almost perfect continuity between social reputation, public image, and posthumous glory. For these men, brought up as provincial gentry under the aegis of the British Empire, the republican culture was grafted onto the honor code of the English gentleman with no allowance for the new potentialities of celebrity. This implied for Washington that he had to maintain a strong distinction between his public deeds, about which he tried to control perceptions, and his private life, supposedly protected from every sort of curiosity. Some years later, Nathaniel Hawthorne wrote: "Did anybody ever see Washington nude? It is inconceivable. He had no nakedness, but imagine that he was born with his clothes on, and his hair powdered, and made a stately bow on his first appearance in the world."[112] This not only testified to the transformation of a war hero into a historic monument, intimidating and distant; it also pointed out a fundamental aspect of Washington's public figure about which his contemporaries already were strongly aware. His notoriety was immense throughout the whole of the Atlantic, but with regard to the classic style of hero, unanimously admired for military and political virtues, he was not a celebrated man who aroused curiosity and empathy.

Washington carefully constructed a public persona that was always distant and in control. This was also the case with his portraits, which remained hieratic and formal. When he posed for Gilbert Stuart, the painter hoped to capture a less formal aspect of his illustrious model and asked him to forget for a moment that he was George Washington posing for a portrait. He got only an angry response. The final result, if it was dignified, hardly invited a sense of intimacy with the first American president (Fig. 13). A far cry from this austere and serious portrait was the debonair image of a smiling Quaker which Franklin knew how to play so easily during his Parisian sojourn. That is to say, it is hard to imagine an American Jean Huber painting Washington pulling on his pants in the morning, or simply having breakfast. However, there was a real demand from the American public to see Washington in person, attested to by the abundant mail that he received from every corner of the United States, as well as the numerous visitors, sometimes unknown, who showed up at Mount Vernon, so much so that Washington often complained that he had not dined alone with his wife in several weeks. But far from being a Rousseau who played the solitary role and fled when visitors arrived for fear his camaraderie would be disappointed, Washington unstintingly offered his hospitality to all visitors, according to the codes of civility among the Virginia elite and incorporating a perfectly rehearsed ritual which gave the impression that the guests had seen the hero of the War of Independence in his domestic environment, without, in fact, being intimate with him in any way.

On the other hand, Washington firmly refused all requests to talk about his private life.[113] To his mind, this only concerned him and his family. His wish to strictly separate the public man – the commander-in-chief and then the president – from the private man was almost always respected. However, certain of his admirers did not spare their efforts to humanize him. From the minute he died, several biographers circulated personal anecdotes. The most well known was Mason Weems, an Anglican pastor who published the initial biography about the first president. Originally from Maryland, Weems became in the 1790s a rather prolific author, but he also had a career as a traveling salesman, to the profit of Mathew Carey, an Irish bookseller in Philadelphia. As early as 1797, Weems proposed that he publish a cheap collection about the lives of great generals of the American Revolution, aimed at exploiting public curiosity and generating large profits. At the death of the former president, Weems offered to Carey a *Life of Washington* that he had worked on the previous six months: he hoped to sell the book for twenty-five or thirty-seven cents by being the first in the field.[114] In the end, not having convinced Carey, the book came out through another printer and was re-issued four times in the course of 1800. There was a new edition in 1806 and this time with Carey, who finally understood the commercial potential of the book, and then a greatly augmented edition that appeared in 1808. The book had grown; it now had two hundred pages against eighty-five in the original. There would be twenty-nine editions between 1800 and 1825 (the year Weems died), and a hundred by the end of the century.[115] It was one of the largest bestsellers in the history of American politics.

Weems never intended to do the work of an historian. He wanted to create a publishing coup, playing on the curiosity of the public, and although the greater part of the book consisted of an epic account, heroic and well known, of the War of Independence and the presidency of Washington, the book's main attraction resided in the chapters dedicated to his childhood and the character of the great man. Several anecdotes were included, some of which would become classics of popular American culture, such as the one about the cherry tree that young George admitted cutting down at the risk of unleashing his father's anger, demonstrating his inherent honesty: "I cannot tell a lie, Pa." The book, overall, remained classical in form. Far from aligning itself with the new formats developing around the culture of celebrity and now having success in Europe, it used the proven model of biographies written about illustrious men. Even the childhood anecdotes were drafted as exemplary stories that foreshadowed Washington's heroic qualities, his courage, his loyalty, his honesty. Easily interpreted, the stories aimed not at revealing an intimate Washington, but rather at illustrating his value. Weems even included the account of a dream, allegorical and premonitory, that Washington's mother had about the future president when he was five years old. In the dream, the boy succeeds in putting out a roof-top fire, thanks to his composure and quick thinking; afterwards, he proposes to build a new and more satisfactory house! This edifying aspect of Washington fit perfectly into the political, religious context at the beginning of the nineteenth century that saw the publication of numerous writings aimed at the working-class public and at forging a Christian, republican nationalism based on the renewal of evangelicalism. The figure of Washington, a national hero, was a major piece in this patriotic discourse. Weems openly sought to construct a pious vision of Washington, to transform this enlightened God-fearing man into an evangelical Christian.[116]

The introduction to Weems' book testified to the transformations taking place in ethical culture. Weems focused on the contrast between the public man and his private life. If Washington's glory was already well known around the world, popularized by his deeds and by gifted speakers, the private man was still unknown. The grandeur of a man had to be judged by his private life, where he was loyal to his true nature, and not by his public greatness, when he was on show before all his contemporaries. "Private life is always real life," Weems wrote. However, this concession to private life remained stunningly classic: Washington's private life revealed no secrets, revealed no hidden weaknesses, aroused no empathy; it was a moral and edifying confirmation of his virtue. The greatness of Washington was total: he was the true American hero, because his private virtue conformed to his public virtue. He aroused not affective attachment but rather moral emulation. Explicitly written for children, *The Life of Washington* only appeared to take on the monumental Washington. It made a show of humanizing him in order

204

to better politicize the man and make him an edifying hero for the American nation.[117]

The opening lines of the book can be interpreted in this way: they begin with General Bonaparte, ready to leave for Egypt, asking young Americans about Washington, about his health, then saying that his name will go down in history much more than his own. Bonaparte's curiosity is first of all of a political nature, curiosity about "the founder of a great empire." The immense notoriety of Washington, through circulation of his name and his image, from the banks of the Potomac to the shores of the Mediterranean, was made possible by new media, but it remained a classic story about the glory of a great man. Popularized by Weems, the figure of Washington was that of a national hero who embodied the virtuous and conservative values of the United States. His symbolic function was to embody the unity of a nascent nation. His prestige was constructed from the beginning around a kind of transcendence, which explains the religious vocabulary that accompanied it and which irritated Adams so much. As a pastor, also an author of sermons, Weems was particularly well placed to popularize this edifying image of the founding father of the United States.

It is not surprising that the evocation of Bonaparte began to show up in the writing of Weems. Contemporary writers often made a parallel between the two men. Bonaparte himself bandied about the reference during the Consulate and then distanced himself from it. He returned to it again in the *Mémorial de Sainte-Hélène*.[118] Chateaubriand also used the parallel in a chapter of *Mémoires d'outre-tombe* which immediately followed his visit with Washington in 1791. Chateaubriand was not at all surprised by the man. He did not, as he said, belong to "the race of people that surpass human stature. There was nothing astonishing about his person."[119] He was a silent man, who acted slowly, because he did not act for himself but for his country and for freedom. That was the source of his prudence, but also the endurable nature of his work. In contrast, Bonaparte was an extraordinary being who immediately struck the imagination, but he thought only of his own glory. "Bonaparte had none of the traits of the serious American: he crashed about fighting on old land. He was interested simply in creating his own renown. He was only interested in himself." Conscious that his role in history would be short, he was always active in the political game, and let himself be overcome by the euphoria of success: "He was in a hurry to enjoy his glory and take advantage of it, like a fugitive youth." The parallel, in the form of a systematic contrast, was pushed as far as possible: on the one hand, a serious man, faithful to liberty, who created a new people and died a respected magistrate; on the other, a passionate hero who betrayed liberty and died in exile, his work destroyed. The conclusion was almost entirely to the detriment of Bonaparte. He was a man of the past, who compared himself to Greek heroes and was devoured by ambition that was completely personal. His grandeur was anachronistic. Washington's, on the contrary, was profoundly modern, conforming to the new values of democratic societies that needed ordinary men through which people could act collectively.

The contrast was seductive, but Chateaubriand passed over in silence what Bonaparte's renown introduced into political culture, what Washington in fact did not have: an affective and sentimental aspect. He pretends in his chapter written "just after Bonaparte died" that news of his death was received with indifference. But soon, in the following year, affection and nostalgia in regard to Napoleon would be deployed with a power never known before; Chateaubriand himself would not be totally insensitive to it.

Sunset Island

The modulation of Napoleon's image in the years immediately following his death, when the black legend of an ogre was erased, leaving in its place the glorious legend of the Saint Helena martyr, led to the Napoleonic myth, rising to its apogee under the July monarchy. Aiding in this reversal, the *Mémorial de Sainte-Hélène*, published by Emmanuel de Las Cases in 1822, was both a tool and an incomparable source of documentation, given that its influence was so great.[120] It allows us to hear behind the great organs of the Napoleonic legend the little music of celebrity, because Bonapartism was more than nostalgia for greatness or a political program.

This enormous and long-lasting bestseller (more than eight hundred thousand copies of the Las Casas book sold in the course of a century) was most often presented negatively, reduced to an instrument of propaganda, a brainwashing program for a reinvented Bonapartism.[121] This political reading of the *Mémorial* almost erases the figure of Emmanuel de Las Cases completely, as if he had simply been the emperor's pen. This is what those thought who had not read the *Mémorial*: a sort of political testament by Napoleon, dictated from Saint Helena to an obscure but loyal follower, a way to change the English assessment of him in the present, and that of posterity in the long run. But going deeper into the book, something else is discovered: not so much the voice of a self-assured Napoleon but the omnipresence of Las Cases, his immoderate use of the first person, his insertion of himself into the picture as he observed the daily life of the fallen emperor, his gathering of intimate information, and his defense of Napoleon's reputation. This presence of

Las Cases, both as actor and as author, is at the heart of the narrative structure which constitutes the originality of the *Mémorial* and that, doubtless, contributed to the fascination felt by those who read it.

The modern reader on opening the *Mémorial* is struck by the polyphonic style of this complex text. Personal conversations between Las Cases and the emperor are interspersed throughout the narrative, dictated by Napoleon himself, of his greatest victories.[122] The *Mémorial* is evocative because of a combination of two tones: the classic epic tone of triumphal and victorious military glory; and a new tone, that of everyday heroism, which culminates in the fallen emperor's determined, almost laughable, resistance to the bullying and humiliations of the English authorities. On the one hand there is the epic tone that consolidates the glorious image of the leader so spectacularly constructed by reports coming from the Great Army; on the other there is Las Cases' account of the fallen man's struggle for recognition – minute, pathetic, but not without a certain grandeur in the face of Governor Hudson Lowe's refusal to grant Napoleon any legitimacy.[123] In this dual tonality we can hear the registers of heroic glory and that of celebrity. The first is found in the discourse of praise, the second in the personal account of day-to-day existence.

It is not insignificant that Las Cases was a newcomer in Napoleon's entourage. He was a late convert who almost did not participate in the imperial era at all. He was first of all an aristocrat from the Ancien Régime who became a man of letters under the Empire, and only joined the most important levels of power at the last minute. He understood perfectly that to follow Napoleon into exile, once he abdicated, was the chance of a lifetime. It offered Las Cases a way to fulfill his writer/courtier fantasy: to live in close permanent contact with a great man who would otherwise remain out of his reach. And it was just because Napoleon was a hero of the new era, a hero who aroused a desire for intimacy, that Las Cases pushed so hard to follow him, surprising even the emperor himself. This experience of being close to a sovereign who no longer exercised power was what Las Cases undertook to communicate in the *Mémorial*.

He had therefore to show his personal relationship to Napoleon. Of course his plan had political significance: Las Cases was hostile to the French Revolution to the point of fighting in the princes' army, and he did not rally around the new regime until the Consulate, after the Amiens peace accords. Thus, he embodied the politics of national reconciliation, for which Napoleon wanted to be the guarantor. And it was Napoleon's military glory as a vehicle for national glory that Las Cases invoked to explain his attachment to the emperor: "After Ulm and the flash of Austerlitz, I was vanquished by glory: I admired, I recognized, I loved

Napoleon, and from this moment on I became fanatically French."[124] There was, nonetheless, a subtle displacement which led to this admiration, a tone typical of glory, of gratitude, a matter of both political legitimacy and personal choice, and, finally, love ("I loved Napoleon"), the assertion of a sentimental bond between affection and passion that did not accord with the traditional themes of heroism.

And in fact, the account of daily life at Saint Helena was far from the account of an heroic emperor. Las Cases transformed the private man, Napoleon, into an intimate spectacle: he showed the emperor from the perspective of a friend in exile who was close to him and who not only admired but loved him. The 1822 preface written for the first edition of the *Mémorial* emphasizes the transfer from admiration to love, from glory to intimacy:

> Admiration made me follow him without knowing him; love put me forever near him as soon as I knew him. The universe is full of his glory, his deeds, his monuments; but no one knows the real nuances of his character, his secret qualities, the landscape of his soul: it is this great void that I will undertake to fill, and from a perspective perhaps unique in history. I have collected, archived, day after day, all my observations of Napoleon, everything I have heard him say, during the eighteen months I have been close to him.[125]

Unlike the epic poet who sings the exploits of a hero, or the panegyrist who addresses an elegy to a great man, both of whom disappear as narrators in recounting the subjects' feats, Las Cases asserts his presence, the subjectivity of his observation and his narrative. Celebrity is a spectacle, both public and intimate, and it therefore implies a spectator. Las Cases acts as the representative of a captivated public, the delegate closest to Napoleon, capable of observing the most ordinary details, somewhere between curiosity and sentimentality, almost voyeurism. Las Cases embodies, therefore, neither the traditional figure of the courtier, seeking by proximity to a sovereign a token of social and curial distinction, nor the author of elegies such as those that Thomas brilliantly composed in the second half of the eighteenth century.[126] Rather, he seems to be the modern figure of a fan, devoted to a celebrity, guided by both admiration and love, and by a desire to witness the private and day-to-day aspects of a man whose every word, every gesture, was of interest. In this way, he is in the same line as Boswell, who profoundly transformed the art of biography by writing *The Life of Samuel Johnson*. This work by Paoli's friend was no doubt known to Las Cases.[127]

In his chronicle of daily life on Saint Helena, Las Cases alternates between two perspectives. The first is that of a curious spectator noting every anecdote, even the least important, for example when Napoleon scalds himself while taking a bath that is too hot, scrupulously noting details of his health, his slow deterioration, transcribing conversations. The second perspective is that of a sentimental and devoted friend, always ready to be concerned and sympathize. In April 1816, Napoleon told Las Cases about some "domestic 'trouble.' His words, his gestures, his accent, pierced my soul; I would have gone on my knees to him, I would have kissed them if I could have."[128] These bursts of emotion, which were not inconsequential in the success of the *Mémorial* with the romantic generation, kept the text from falling into voyeurism, since the intimacy which is revealed is perceived through the prism of an omnipresent sentimentality, one with which the reader identifies, being present at domestic events as though an authorized witness. The identification game was played to the hilt, identifying not so much with Napoleon – who would think to identify with him apart from the madmen who in the 1830s filled the Parisian hospitals with their monomaniacal delirium?[129] – as with Las Cases himself, who was impelled to share the life of a deposed emperor, to gain his confidence, and to feel a mixture of admiration and compassion for him.

From that time on, the personal relationship between Las Cases and Napoleon became a recurrent theme. Bits of imperial protocol (it was always Napoleon who started the conversation) gave way progressively to personal confidences founded on the common experience of exile. However, this staging of an intimate and personal relationship with the emperor took on a dynamic form, as if the sentiments of Las Cases had become the real subject of the book. After a walk with Napoleon on the first day he arrives on Saint Helena, October 17, 1815, Las Cases comments: "I am thus alone, *tête-à-tête* in the desert, almost intimate with the man who governed the entire world! With Napoleon at last!!!! All this is happening to me! All this experienced by me … !"[130] By revealing his emotions in this instance, combining familiarity and grandeur, Las Cases made the narrator the ideal intermediary between the celebrated man and the reader. Unlike glory, celebrity aroused intimate curiosity, and even an affective and subjective attachment. The paradox, particularly evident in the case of Napoleon, was that each reader imagined a unique relationship with him, familiar, intimate, although the reader would never meet him and would share with thousands of other people images and stories which constituted Napoleon's public persona.

Las Cases perfectly embodied the realization of the habitual and illusory desire to share the private life of a celebrated person. He both maintained and abolished the distance between himself and Napoleon, in this way allowing for affective attachment. The tension between observer and confidant, between closeness and distance, gave official legitimacy to Las Cases' work, giving him access to the private man who was Napoleon, all the while maintaining the distance from him which made the emperor the object of universal public curiosity.

> Who living today could flatter themselves that they know the private man behind the emperor better than I? Who spent two months of solitude in the Briars desert with him? Who else enjoyed long walks in the moonlight, spent numerous hours with him? Who has known as I have known the time, the place and the subject of the conversations? Who has listened to the memories of his charming childhood, of his youthful pleasures, the bitterness of modern pain? I also know the depth of his character, and I can also explain many of the circumstances which seemed at the time difficult to understand.[131]

A major character trait emphasized by the author was Napoleon's ability to attach himself sentimentally to others; for this reason he could never separate himself from old friends.

Later, Las Cases was even more explicit about his undertaking: "My aim in this journal is to expose the man, to understand the nature behind the exploits."[132] To truthfully show the nature of a celebrated man was a project that could not help being marked by a Rousseau-like tone, the tone of the *Confessions*, but Rousseau had discovered its limits. If writing in the first person was a tool for knowing oneself, it was at the same time the wrong instrument for self-justification: the author was always suspected of being insincere, and the process ultimately did not lend itself well to compassion, so much so that the reader was often stopped in his desire to empathize because he perceived the whole project as too obviously an apologetic undertaking. This is why, as we know, Rousseau invented another device, which was *Rousseau Judge of Jean-Jacques*, which describes the day-to-day life of Jean-Jacques, man of nature, written by Rousseau. This is a perfectly illusory division because the imaginary witness is simply the fictional double of the author. Nonetheless, Rousseau understood the limits of intimate self-justification in the first person and, to the contrary, the efficacy of a device implying a third party, a sensitive and empathetic witness, one capable of relaying the justifications as well as testifying to his natural goodness.

This parallel between the *Mémorial* and the Rousseau-like moral aesthetic was not arbitrary. Bonaparte was powerfully influenced by reading Rousseau. If he became extremely critical of Rousseau's political thought and the uses to which it was put during the Revolution, Bonaparte nonetheless visited Ermenonville once he became First Consul. Most importantly, in the *Mémorial*, Rousseau is mentioned several different times in conversation. Napoleon reads and rereads *La Nouvelle Héloïse* and discusses "Jean-Jacques," his works and his life.[133] Las Cases, himself, admits being very sensitive to the novel: "This book produced a great impression on me, a deep melancholy mixed with sweetness and pain. I have always been strongly attached to this work; it brings back happy memories, and creates sad regrets."[134] During one of their conversations, Napoleon admitted he would not be able to "write the *Confessions* in the way Jean-Jacques" did, because it would be instantly contradicted point by point. Las Cases and Napoleon had both learned Rousseau's lesson: if celebrity aroused in the public a desire for intimacy with the celebrated person, it was not an autobiography that was wanted but a testimonial. It required the observation of a third person, in the position of a curious and admiring spectator.

The "celebrity" of Napoleon was not only the mainspring of a textual device in the *Mémorial*; it was also a recurrent theme proposed by Las Cases in a subtly depoliticized version of it, or at least disconnected from political adherence to the emperor. Celebrity is presented in the text as the dizzying effect of universal notoriety. Napoleon was known the world over, and people, no matter what their political opinions of him, wanted to know what he was doing, what had become of him, how he was getting along. One surprising passage reported a conversation the exiled emperor had with those closest to him in March 1816 having to do, as it were, with the "universal celebrity" of Napoleon.[135] The conversation began with a provocative remark made by Napoleon: "In spite of everything, Paris is so big, and includes so many people of all sorts, and some of them very bizarre, I suppose there are some who have never seen me, and perhaps some who have never heard my name." His interlocutors cry out and assure him that "there was no town in Europe, perhaps even in the world, where his name had not been spoken."[136] Then they multiplied the examples, describing unexpected situations further and further away where the name of Napoleon had been spoken. The first guest reported that during the Consulate, while he was taking refuge in the hills "totally wild and very high" in Wales, where thatched cottages seemed "to belong to another universe," preserved from "the sound of revolutions," one person inquired immediately "what the First Consul Bonaparte was doing." And another person in the room told of a discussion with Chinese officers where "the name of [the] emperor was celebrated and associated with great ideas about conquests and revolution." In successive editions of the *Mémorial*, Las Cases prolongs the discussion, adding other witnesses mentioned by the first readers of the book concerning the universal celebrity of Napoleon. One woman reported that after the fall of the Empire, looking for work in Persia and having been granted an audience with the sovereign, she was astounded to see "the portrait of Napoleon on his throne above the head of the Shah," while another woman told him that "the idea of Napoleon's power was so popular throughout all of Asia" that after his fall French authorities continued to mention his name in order to obtain "kindness and generosity along the roads they traveled."

It seems incongruous that a hypothetical Parisian who did not know the name of the emperor would be answered with a sort of bidding war about Bonaparte's renown reaching from the wilderness of Wales to Persia and China. This of course has to do with the idea of power and conquest, but it is virtual power, symbolic power, because Bonaparte never exercised real authority in any of these places. His celebrity was based on his political domination, shown by the surprising presence of the fallen emperor's portrait "above the head of the Shah" – a talisman of power, yes, but also a pure sign, an icon of power. This evolution of sovereignty into celebrity was particularly evident in the last example cited by Las Cases:

> A third person wrote to me that Captain R. of *Le Bordelais*, during the course of his voyage to the northwest coast of America, stopped in the Sandwich Islands and was presented to the king. During the audience, the king asked about King George III and Emperor Alexander. At the foot of the throne sat a woman, a favorite of the prince. As he mentioned each European name she turned to him with a disdainful smile and a marked impatience; when she could hold back no longer, she interrupted the king and cried out: "*And Napoleon, how is he doing?*"

This anecdote, rewritten in part as a put-down,[137] has a double function. On the one hand, it extends even further the spectacular nature of Napoleon's celebrity. The borders of civilization have been crossed, right up to the islands in the Pacific discovered by Cook barely forty years earlier, and moreover in the zone of English influence. On the other hand, there is a significant gap between the leader, who wants to know about the two most powerful sovereigns of the time, and his female favorite, who wants news of Napoleon. The celebrity of Napoleon is no longer directly or primarily political; it is not part of a sovereign space nor in line with political action; it arises out of curiosity about and perhaps fascination with an exceptional and unique man who has not been replaced by reigning monarchs. The figure of the woman connotes an almost erotic dimension to this celebrity. The interest that Bonaparte arouses comes from a form of desire (note the "marked impatience" and "she could hold back no longer," which are the inventions of Las Cases). Although improbable, one can see in this woman an implicit and obviously extreme representation of the readership of the *Mémorial*, a public universally curious to know "how Napoleon is doing." Moreover, did Las Cases not make the reverse journey of the one made by Captain R., crossing the ocean, arriving on an isolated island, and bringing news of a fallen emperor to an avid public? Like the anonymous woman, the public postulated in the *Mémorial* is driven by an impatient, almost uncontrollable, curiosity for everything that concerns Napoleon. Moreover, the scene is one that impressed readers; later editions carried an exotic illustration reinforcing once again this myth of renown without borders; it comes less from the glory of a great man, or the charisma of a leader, than from a celebrity without precedence: the name of a contemporary circulated globally and the passionate curiosity that the name aroused.

At the end of the *Mémorial*, one finds an almost comic echo of this "universal celebrity" extending to the ends of the inhabited world, when Las Cases, expelled from Saint Helena by the English, temporarily finds refuge on the Cape of Good Hope, and then in the desert of Tygerberg, "almost at the edge of the world with the wandering hordes."[138] In these deserted places, purposely presented as "extremes of the civilized world," as exotic as the Sandwich Islands, Napoleon is so familiar that animals are given his name. "The most famous cock in the land, the one most often victorious, was called Napoleon! The most renowned horse, Napoleon! The most unbeatable bull, Napoleon, Always Napoleon!!!" Las Cases was torn between laughter and amazement. This endless proliferation of the emperor's name would be funny if it weren't first of all the sign of celebrity: it was not about charisma or glory properly speaking, because it was hardly glorious to have one's name given to a cock or a bull; it was rather the diffusion of the name, a pure phenomenon of notoriety. Even if the name was associated metonymically with the idea of victory and prowess, it was in part detached from its referent, disconnected from an immediate political relationship. Napoleon had just become the most celebrated name in the world.

Everything had come full circle. From the outset of the *Mémorial*, the celebrity of Napoleon, the fascination that he exercised in the opinion of his contemporaries, was presented as relatively separate from the issues of political legitimacy. When Napoleon learned that he was going to be deported to Saint Helena, in spite of the shock, he walked out on the *Bellerophon*'s bridge "as was customary, with the same face and in the same manner, to look out at the crowd starved for a glimpse of him."[139] As described by Las Cases, the scene was no longer the farewell of a sovereign; it had nothing to do, for example, with the rallying scenes which marked the eagle's flight a few months earlier. On the bridge of the *Bellerophon*, Napoleon looked out at the crowd that was looking at him: he let himself be looked at like a spectacle presented to a public avid to contemplate him, though nothing was said concerning the politics of the crowd "starved for a glimpse of him," other than the desire to see the face of Napoleon.

Insisting on the mechanisms of celebrity relative to Napoleon in no way denies the political dimension, more classically military and heroic.

It goes without saying that the prestige of the emperor, while alive as well as after his death, owed a great deal to battles won and order restored, to the efficiency of his propaganda and his police, to his capacity to end the Revolution without totally betraying it. Nevertheless, Napoleon's renown was based on another form of notoriety and on collective bonding, which was not the renown of glory and power but that of modern celebrity. Far from being limited to France, his renown extended throughout the entire continent, including countries which had struggled against his imperialism, but who defended themselves less well against the fascination that his personality exerted, even over his enemies.

Investigating the celebrity of Napoleon allows the recounting of another story, one different from the classic account with its difficult amalgam of revolutionary legitimacy and military glory, democratic principle and heroic prestige; instead, the new story is a metamorphosis of political legitimacy, when the mechanisms of celebrity, having spread through the cultural world during the eighteenth century, began to penetrate the political game. This penetration started with the Revolution, transforming the public status of sovereigns and offering new political figures the capacity to act, on the English front above all. Incapable of controlling the effects of political celebrity, Marie-Antoinette was the victim of it. "Popularity" became an important part of the political process during revolutions. In the United States, Washington's celebrity, at one moment threatened by new forms of political partisanship, was quickly re-established through consensual acceptance that allowed the young nation to establish a founding hero. In France, the principle of popularity was slandered, distrusted by everyone. Even Mirabeau was unable to build uncontested authority on it.

Bonaparte was both Mirabeau and Washington together. He possessed the energy and taste for risk that Mirabeau had and the feeling for statesmanship exhibited by Washington. For him, glory was not only a matter of dynastic legitimacy or the divine grace of the sovereign. It did not get absorbed in the rituals of political representation and acclamation. It was the power of opinion which allowed a little corporal from Corsica to become the master of Europe. Certainly, celebrity was not worthwhile if it was not transmuted into power, into action, by the coup of 18 Brumaire (November 9, 1799) or by victories on the battlefield. We are still a long way yet, with Bonaparte, from the contemporary "democracy of opinion," assuming that this is more than a slogan. But on the other hand, to reduce the phenomena of public opinion to a sort of liturgical acclamation unique to all power, as Giorgio Agamben does, for example, is to risk missing the modern specificity of power.[140] It was not only tied to the glorification of the sovereign, based on a theological principle, but it was also combined with an inherent principle of choice by the governed about who governed them. This created a theoretical gap, or at least a difficult tension, between the democratic principles of the general will and the reality of political competition. This tension defined the basic ambivalence of representative government, the modern aspect of democracy, theorized about and applied at the end of the eighteenth century in the United States, in France, and in England.[141] Elections, whose principles were both democratic and elitist, implied a popular choice, but they also implied the irreducible distance between the representatives, often chosen for their notoriety, and the represented. It was in the midst of this tension that the mechanisms of popularity, the adherence of the greatest number to a single individual, were introduced, profoundly transforming the exercise of power.

To understand this, one simply has to acknowledge that the collective mechanisms of opinion cannot be reduced to the political principle of popular sovereignty or to the tribunal of reason invoked by Enlightenment philosophers; that the mechanisms also include the less well-known phenomenon whereby a public, made up of those who read the same newspapers, the same books, developed an interest in the life of celebrated men, sometimes a simple curiosity, sometimes a passionate one. These mechanisms of celebrity were not necessarily political, but they did not ignore the political field either. They progressively transformed the exercise of power and even the form of its embodiment, well before what one calls today, usually to denounce it, "celebrity politics." Far from being a regrettable aberration, the pernicious influence of the "society of the spectacle" on public affairs reveals that the democratic public sphere and the mediated public sphere are indissolubly linked.

Now to return to the quote by Mme de Staël at the opening of this chapter about the celebrity of Bonaparte. The fear she expressed was less a fear of political tyranny than of his monopoly on celebrity: the saturation of public curiosity by the figure of Napoleon, who was not content to exercise power but wanted to extend his influence over every form of notoriety. Mme de Staël herself was not insensitive to the call of celebrity. Napoleon, who did not like her and feared her, mocked her from Saint Helena, chiding her "excessive celebrity."[142] By placing celebrity on this terrain, up until then the bastion of writers, artists, and actors, political power changed its face, and also its relationship to the culture. One hardly imagines Racine being jealous of the celebrity of Louis XIV. In contrast, neither Mme de Staël nor Chateaubriand hesitated to use her or his literary notoriety in the service of political ambition, and to see in the celebrity of Napoleon a model, as if there were no difference in nature between the glory of an emperor and the celebrity of a writer. And maybe they were right, because the nature of celebrity, in fact, is to create an equivalency between notoriety that arises in different spheres. Do not newspapers today publish popularity awards by placing politicians, singers, and artists side-by-side, all participating in the same television programs and sharing pages of the same weekly magazines?

The reaction of writers to this new reality was anxiety about the over-riding influence of celebrity mechanisms that would "make every human species anonymous," would leave the celebrated person, the person at the center of the media spotlight, face-to-face with everybody else, admirers, adversaries, or the curious, all equally anonymous. No one expressed it better than Chateaubriand. After struggling against the emperor with virulent pamphlets, he, in turn, let himself be caught up in the protean form of Napoleon's renown and never struck a better great-man pose than when he stood facing the portrait of the emperor. The tyranny that Napoleon exercised was no longer for him a political tyranny, founded on the usurpation of the Bourbon throne, but a tyranny that reduced all his contemporaries, even after his death, to mediocrity and obscurity. Thus begins book twenty-five of *Mémoires d'outre-tombe*:

> Hasn't everything ended with Napoleon? Should I really be talking about something else? Who could be of interest outside of him? Of what or whom could it be a question, after such a man? [...] I blush to think that I must rut around at this point with that crowd of tiny creatures I am part of, dingy and nocturnal, as if we were on a stage from which the enormous sun had disappeared.[143]

— 7 —

ROMANTICISM AND CELEBRITY

In 1808, Napoleon met his new ally Tsar Alexander I in Erfurt, in the presence of many European princes. At the emperor's request, Talma also made the trip, along with other actors from the Comédie-Française who gave an air of splendor to the French theater. Napoleon did not stop there: he also requested to meet Goethe. The homage he rendered to the great German writer was seen as an important gesture. The emperor admiringly talked with him about *The Sorrows of Young Werther*, the work that had made Goethe famous when he was twenty-five, and which Napoleon had read several times. Talma and Goethe built a friendship and saw each other again in Weimar, the actor encouraging the writer to move to Paris, where he promised that his books would be on every table.

Talma, Napoleon, Goethe: the meeting in Europe of these three celebrated men, an actor, a statesman, and a poet, is a powerful symbol of the effects of celebrity at the beginning of the nineteenth century. The pre-eminence of the emperor in this context is unchallenged. But the bond established between these great figures of intellectual, political, and cultural life was not the usual relationship created by patronage. "You are a man," the emperor supposedly said to Goethe when he met him. Years later, the writer was still wondering how to interpret the somewhat mysterious sentence, although it well described the personal aura which surrounded him. Napoleon, by receiving Goethe, was a sovereign honoring a poet and also a reader satisfying his desire to meet a celebrated writer.

Over the space of ten years, Napoleon, Goethe, and Talma would all die, all three gone between 1821 and 1832. Besides having in common their immense celebrity, they embodied the transition toward the romantic myth of the demiurge hero, the creative genius, and the virtuoso actor. Today, the term "Romanticism" has become a cliché in literary history, hackneyed through overuse. Nonetheless, it is still useful for designating, in broad strokes, the cultural context of the first half of the nineteenth century. It was first of all marked by an acceleration in the development of printing and by the birth of the culture industry. Contrary to what traditional periodizations assume, there was no real rupture during this period but rather a deepening change that had already begun in the preceding century. Newspaper editions grew immensely, encouraged by the steam presses capable of printing many millions of pages an hour, and books became a more common consumer product for the new middle class. The entertainment economy continued to break the mold and in Europe aligned itself with the British style: freedom from royal patronage, multiplication of public concerts and commercial enterprises, and a growth in publicity that transformed cultural life in the cities. Romanticism as a literary, artistic, or musical movement was largely dependent on the accrued media development of cultural life.[1]

A second aspect of Romanticism was the importance given to the expression of feeling, to the acceptance of subjectivity as a construct of personal identity, and the search for authentic personal relationships. It included the idealization of love, the sublime, and strong emotions, but also a generalized culture of introspection, all of which were rightly associated with the movement. This new sensibility was especially evident in the omnipresence of the artist, the poet, in his work. Lyrical poetry lent itself well to the publication of intimate feelings, unthinkable one or two generations earlier. Obviously, the question was not whether these feelings were sincere or real, but realizing that they transformed both the concept of "the self" and the official forms of literary and musical communication. Even though he did not really reveal himself, the writer appeared to be a sensitive and misunderstood genius, a powerful being or a melancholy hero.[2] This new visibility of the artist was accompanied by an acceptance of the subjectivity of the reader or listener. The new aesthetic was not evaluated according to classical rules or to the social hierarchy of the Ancien Régime, but rather by public pleasure. Stendhal understood this very early: "Romanticism is the art of presenting the people with literary works that give them, in light of the actual state of their habits and beliefs, the most pleasure possible."[3]

In spite of the apparent contradiction between these two traits of Romanticism – the mediated aspect of cultural life, the ideal of an immediate meeting between the creator and the public – they are complementary. Clever booksellers and impresarios who specialized in new publicity techniques encouraged the meeting between artists eager to put their "self" on show, suffering or triumphal, and readers ready to be enthusiastic and to identify with them. Often, the romantic artist was both a master of self-promotion and highly sentimental. The public, however, was not entirely fooled. The culture industry, having supported the birth and then the triumph of Romanticism, was also the object of its distrust, shown by the recurrent denunciation of industrial literature, bad music, or street theater. Celebrity was caught in these contradictions. It progressively imposed itself as a characteristic of literary, artistic, and musical life, but it suffered from the duality of an affective one-to-one between an artist and his public and the management of the more prosaic realities of mass culture. It was not just the political forms of this phenomenon that were affected by the changes: sovereign or revolutionary leader, everyone now had to deal with the constraints of publicity.

Byromania

A few years after Erfurt, the momentous irruption of Lord Byron onto the public stage was, undeniably, an important step in celebrity culture. Byron's exceptional European notoriety was intensely described, analyzed, and decried. The Byron moment was Rousseau all over again, with an even greater impact.

George Gordon was the heir of Scottish lords and an old English aristocratic family. After publishing several unremarkable satirical works and traveling to Spain and Greece, he hesitated between a political career in the House of Lords, in line with his social status, and the more uncertain career of a poet. In 1812, he published *Childe Harold*, a long poem with an archaic tonality that described the adventures of a melancholy knight along the banks of the Mediterranean. It was a great success. "This poem appears on every table," the Duchess of Devonshire noted, and Byron "is really the only topic of almost every conversation." Byron became a fashionable poet, an artist everyone talked about and everyone wanted to see. Anne Isabella Milbanke, who met him at this point and married him three years later, was struck by the excitement that surrounded the young man. To describe the effects that seemed to her derived from collective hysteria, she invented the term "Byromania."[4] Over the following months, the triumph continued. Byron's new poems again dealt with the theme of a romantic and blasé hero and, as before, they had great success. *The Corsair* ran to ten thousand copies the day it came out in February 1814, a prodigious number for the period.

But already it was clear that Byron's success was not just a literary phenomenon. All the interest centered on his personality, arousing adulation or disapproval. His agitated love life and much disparaged morals created scandal. His affairs were the object of all kinds of speculation. His marriage was disastrous, his wife obtaining a separation after a year. Caught in a maelstrom of lurid rumors, Byron left England in 1816 and never returned. What happened next is as much a part of romantic legend as it is of history: the melancholy lord continued his sexual conquests and his poetry along the banks of Lake Geneva, then in Venice and Pisa, before joining with the Greeks in their struggle for independence and at thirty-nine dying in Missolonghi. This unexpected death created shock waves throughout Europe. In England, the press that had so vilified him was now full of praise; teenagers who had not known him were in despair. On the Continent, young fashionable men ostentatiously wore mourning dress. Even though the poet died of high fever without having really seen combat, he became an heroic figure for European youth, a liberator who combined the talents of a poet and the courage of a soldier, often associated with Napoleon as part of the romantic hero cult. Byronism left the realm of celebrity and entered the universe of myth.[5]

While alive, Byron's celebrity went beyond the normal literary recognition of his poetic talent. It grew between 1820 and 1830 and he became the most successful of all romantic poets for an entire generation in France, Germany, and England. But his first success, during his English years, brought together literary triumph and celebrity scandal. This type of celebrity, fed by rumors and court trials, was characteristic of provocative people in polite English society.[6] The success of *Childe Harold* was fanned by unhealthy curiosity kept alive through rumors published in the press. Byron was suspected of having numerous mistresses; his homosexuality was denounced, as well as his incestuous affair with his half-sister. The failure of his marriage led to an electrifying trial. As early as 1821, the *London Magazine* claimed that interest in Byron was more "personal" than "poetic."[7]

This interweaving of literary and celebrity scandal was effective because Byron purposely never ceased to combine his life with his work. His heroes all seemed related (Harold, the Corsair, Giaour, Manfred, Don Juan): they were adventurers, potentially very erotic, profoundly melancholic and disenchanted, sometimes hopeless, all of them living in exotic places. But the Byronic hero was also embodied by Byron himself, with his combination of great beauty and a physical handicap (he was born with a club foot), his taste for far-away places and a secret melancholy that consumed him, his open revolt against social conventions and his ambiguous morality – all of which he ostentatiously cultivated. At the same time, he invented and incarnated the idealistic and disillusioned rebel, refusing to bend to ordinary moral conventions, showing himself to be sardonic, seductive, and unhappy. At the very least, besides his immense impact on the European romantic culture of the nineteenth century, Byron also profoundly affected popular culture. Numerous stars in the twentieth century would again adopt these same romantic characteristics.

220

Byron skillfully maintained the autobiographical dimension of his poems. The first version of *Childe Harold*, to all appearances, was a transposed narrative of his Mediterranean travels. The medieval fiction was only thinly developed, and in the two songs he added in 1816, he cleverly multiplied allusions to his love affairs. In *Manfred*, he inserts a very veiled allusion to his half-sister. Numerous readers read Byron's poems in the hope of better understanding his secrets and his mysteries, his flaws and his prominence, as a way to satisfy their curiosity about such a celebrated and fascinating figure.

Byron's celebrity was not a biographical episode apart from his poetic work and his place in literary history; it was an essential element. As a legacy, Byron left not only the image of a romantic hero, melancholy and in revolt, or a body of poems that would be admired by a generation of readers, but also a form of almost voyeuristic poetic exchange between the curious reader and a shameless author who risked being accused of exhibitionism. The poetic fiction turned out to be a good way to feed the system of celebrity because of Byron's clever ability to carefully handle one aspect of the ambiguity. There is no doubt that Childe Harold, the Corsair, Manfred, or Don Juan were all doubles for Byron; but what exactly is autobiography and what is fiction? Byron made a game of this ambiguity, moving the curiosity of the readers from biographical revelations – the press took care of that – toward personal avowals of feeling and various states of mind, and thus toward a more empathetic relationship, a more sentimental one, with the author and his characters. This ambiguity maintained a mysterious, secret aspect that stimulated the interpretive effort of readers. It encouraged a "hermeneutics of intimacy," readings that attempted to gain intimate knowledge of the author through an interpretation of his work.[8] Ambiguity was a powerful resource for Byromania, weaving together the success of the poems, public curiosity about the writer, and the desire of many readers to gain intimate access to this sensitive and tormented soul.

This complex cultural phenomenon of celebrity was not solely based on an immediate encounter, sudden and passionate, between an author and his public, which seems to be indicated by Byron's famous sentence, often cited: "I awoke one morning, and found myself famous."[9] Actually, this sentence was only reported by Thomas Moore in 1830 and is perhaps apocryphal; at any rate, it was reported after the fact. It does, though, maintain the myth of immediacy that contemporaries as well as historians complacently upheld. If celebrity for Byron was precipitous, it was neither sudden nor spontaneous.

John Murray, Byron's editor, played a very important role in his success, employing subtle methods of marketing. Along with the first edition of *Childe Harold*, he inserted numerous ads in newspapers, but also sold a relatively luxurious and expensive edition aimed at a small number of the elite.[10] Moreover, the success of his first book was advertised by Byron's peers, members of polite society who knew him by name, if not by reputation, who shared with him a taste for archaic poetry, for the Grand Tour and the Mediterranean countryside, those who were likely to meet him in person in London social circles. That Byron found his first unconditional admirers among members of polite London society was obviously not inconsequential: it is there that the mix of literary success and the celebrity of scandal took root, giving a certain specificity to the early Byromania. It is where Byron first met the capricious Caroline Lamb, who professed an uncontrollable passion for him. Later, Byron's celebrity grew among the urban bourgeoisie. From that time forward, his work sparked a considerable number of imitations and parodies, while the Byronic hero became a standard reference for the new educated classes.

Byron was also a face made familiar by the circulation of a large number of portraits, so widely distributed that John Murray told Byron: "Your portrait is engraved and painted and sold in every town throughout the kingdom."[11] Preoccupied by his physical appearance to the point of following a diet to scrupulously control his weight,[12] Byron wanted to control his image by having engravings made from paintings he himself commissioned from reputed artists, but these artists generally portrayed him as serious and melancholic. Very quickly, he had to admit that his image had escaped him and that numerous portraits, more or less resembling him, had multiplied to satisfy the public demand, creating an icon that was instantly recognizable: the silhouette of a young man, generally seen in profile or a three-quarter pose, as in the first portraits, with wild black hair and wearing a long white scarf.

The celebrity of Byron was known throughout Europe, well before his death. Writers played an important role in this. Goethe admired the English poet and never ceased to quote him in his conversations with Eckermann: "I was filled with timidity and tenderness; if I had dared, I would have burst into tears and kissed Lord Byron's hand."[13] After 1818, infatuation with the disenchanted and desperate poet grew and included a larger and larger public, even before the translation of his poems; French newspapers repeated anecdotes written up in the English press, often focusing on Byron's debauchery. The English presented him as a poet of genius, evil but desirable. Mme Rémusat, reading *Manfred*, wrote to her son:

> I am reading Lord Byron; he charms me. I would like to be young and beautiful, without any restraints: I think I would go find this man and tempt him back to happiness and virtue. In truth, I think that this would

be at the expense of my own. His soul must cause him a great deal of suffering, and you know that suffering always attracts me.[14]

Attempting to describe the power of Byron over his public, metaphors increased: opium, alcohol, madness. Such excitement seemed to defy explanation.

Byron no doubt enjoyed the prestige his success and celebrity afforded him. But he also felt the constraints. His decision to leave England in 1816 was motivated by a desire to find some peace and to escape the devouring publicity. His celebrity, however, preceded him. Visiting near Lake Leman, he was invited by Mme de Staël to a "family dinner"; there he found a room full of guests who were patiently waiting his arrival and who shamelessly stared at him as though he were "some outlandish beast in a raree-show." One woman, overtaken by fear and emotion, fainted.[15] This story, part of the conversations published by Thomas Medwin when Byron died, testified both to the curiosity aroused by the exiled poet, and to the various narrative themes that illustrated the servility toward celebrity seen earlier with Rousseau and Siddons: the celebrity trapped by an invitation and surrounded by a crush of curious people, the comparison with circus animals, the confusion involved with being the center of attention. These themes progressively became commonplace, repeated and analyzed over and over again.

Prestige and Obligations

Like Rousseau before him, Byron became the archetype of a celebrated writer, one whose renown, for better or worse, rose above the level of his literary reputation to that of a person half-real, half-fictional, on which the collective imagination focused at will, a public figure confronted with the mechanisms of celebrity. Writers in the first half of the century were obsessed with Byron's destiny, a career they sought to imitate or distance themselves from. Chateaubriand, obsessed by his own public image, never ceased to measure himself against this famous contemporary, following him to Venice, criticizing his tastes, or enjoying a letter the young Byron wrote him when *Atala* was published. Chateaubriand also experienced his own *Childe Harolde*, an inaugural moment when success arrived for the unknown writer and threw him without warning into the headlights of the press.

He had been an unknown, and the discreet publication of the *Essai sur les révolutions* in 1797 did not bring him renown. But the publication of *Atala* in 1801, with a clever press campaign orchestrated by his friend Fontanes, brought him enormous success. Fierce criticism by the most established literary men such as the Abbé Morellet added to the book's attraction. Chateaubriand took off.[16] He embodied an aesthetic rupture as well as an ideological one: the lyrical evocation of beauteous landscape, a sonorous language, and a desire for a return to spirituality and its mysteries which caused virulent debates on the importance of religion and the legacy of the Enlightenment and the Revolution. But he also knew how to cleverly manage a notoriety that had suddenly quenched his thirst for recognition after years of exile. Several weeks after the publication of *Atala*, he hosted a grand dinner party in a restaurant and invited editors from all the Parisian newspapers. "No one is aware of how hard he worked for his renown," Mathieu Molé remarked of the dinner.[17] A few years later, during the Hundred Days of Napoleon, Jaucourt excitedly wrote to Talleyrand: "M. de Chateaubriand is obsessed by the publicity demon."[18] This taste for celebrity, this excessive attachment to his public image, would soon become one of the proverbial aspects of his personality. Rewriting his *Mémoires* almost forty years later, when the system of celebrity had become even more visible, he returned to that inaugural moment and devoted a lucid, funny, and melancholy chapter to it.[19]

After recalling the importance of the press, a necessity in preparing the reader and introducing the author before publication of the book, Chateaubriand insisted on the effect of novelty and surprise, on the "strange aspect of the work" that aroused controversy and debate. Celebrity was not the result of unanimous admiration, but rather a success due to scandal that caused debates and quarrels, apologies and sarcasm, endlessly creating a buzz around the book and the author. The applicable vocabulary included words like "noise," "clatter," and "fashion." Far from being the result of a calculated climb toward the heights of literary prestige, celebrity appeared to be an "emergence," as violent as it was sudden.

Chateaubriand's sudden celebrity, like that of Byron, already seemed commonplace, a formula. It had the sense of a revelation, an immediate anointing, far from the slow, constructed careers of professional literary men. In this, it was perfectly suited to the romantic myth of the impetuous hero, similar to his military counterpart: the one like the other demanding swift triumphs. But success could also be a flash in the pan, as ephemeral as it was sudden. Nothing guaranteed it would be different from other spectacular successes that went nowhere and seemed incomprehensible a few years later. In a text dated 1819, Chateaubriand is already suspicious:

> An author does not rejoice in this renown, the object of all his desires, which seems to be as empty as is happiness in life. Can it console him

for the calm which has been stolen from him? Will he ever know if this renown is a matter of partisanship, to particular circumstances, or if it is truly glory based on real merit? So many miserable books have had such a prodigious popularity! What is celebrity worth that is so often shared with a crowd of mediocre and dishonorable men?[20]

For romantic writers confronted with the success of their writings, this distinction between celebrity and glory was a recurrent theme. When Byron died, John Clare published an essay on the "popularity" of writers based on the conviction that this was not due to real glory, that "the trumpeting clamour of public praise" did not always mean eternal renown.[21] This was a classic theme, the legacy of Cicero and Petrarch, but it had taken on a new form. It was no longer possible in 1824 to totally disdain popular taste and public judgment. What Clare had in mind in writing his text was the prodigious celebrity of Byron, a poet he profoundly admired and whom he considered to be the equal of Shakespeare. Was he an exception to the general rule? Only the future would tell if Byron's celebrity, rapid and brutal as a storm, would acquire the calm and serenity of long-lasting and eternal glory. In fact, the traditional contrast between fictive and ephemeral reputations and posthumous glory was troubled by a new element: the common people, who loved simple, natural poetry. Thus, the popularity of contemporary authors was profoundly ambivalent: it could be related to the effects of fashion, to the role of literary critics, to the excessive enthusiasm of the public, but also a matter of *common fame*, something the romantic poet could not despise, although it was not as desirable as unanimous praise from posterity.

For anyone having experienced it, celebrity was both heady and worrying; it was a recognition and a constraint, a first step toward glory, but also a trap that threatened to close in on any author who was too vain. When he did a rewrite of the third volume of his memoirs in 1814, Goethe recalled the "prodigious effect" of his *The Sorrows of Young Werther*, the success which had made him a European celebrity at twenty-five. He had felt great pleasure at being admired as "a literary meteor," but he also experienced the importunate curiosity of the public, without being able to separate out the part that was pleasure from the part that was disagreeable.

> The greatest happiness or the greatest unhappiness was that everyone wanted to know who this unique young author was who had produced such an unexpectedly good book. They wanted to see him, talk to him, even from afar, to learn something about him, and in this way he experienced an excessive eagerness, sometimes agreeable, sometimes uncomfortable, but always meant to entertain him.[22]

All his efforts afterward were aimed at refining his celebrity, retaining only its advantages. When he was on a trip to Italy, he went incognito, then he consciously transformed his literary celebrity, vaguely scandalous, into a more classic renown, that of a courtesan author, a court counselor in Weimar, already glorified while alive by national admiration, not public curiosity. He never totally succeeded, of course, and his last work, like the conversations with Eckermann, showed some bitter-sweet opinions about the torments of celebrity, "almost as harmful as disrepute."[23] It was, in spite of all the satisfaction of self-love, an enormous challenge for the writer, who was obliged to play a public persona, to keep his opinions to himself about others and above all to sacrifice his poetic work to his social life: "If I had stayed more away from public life and business, if I had been more able to live in solitude, I would have been happier and I would also have been able to do more as a poet. [...] When you have done something that pleases people, it prevents you from doing it again."[24]

Chateaubriand said very much the same thing about the heady nature of celebrity and its false pretenses. Once *Atala* was published, he ceased to be his own man: "I stopped living for myself and my public career began." But there was another side to it: if success brought joy to the celebrated man, it also imposed constraints.

> My head was spinning: this was not the joy of self-esteem; I was drunk. I loved glory the way one loves a woman the first time. However, coward that I was, my fear equaled my passion: like a conscript, I walked into the fire. My primitive nature, the doubt I had always had about my talent, made me humble in the midst of my success. I escaped from my brilliance: I stood apart, trying to reject the halo that crowned me.

Nobody has to believe this story told retrospectively by Chateaubriand about his timidity. Nonetheless, the text in general is striking because it is careful not to separate these two aspects: the "stupid infatuation with vanity" that drives a celebrated man to delight in the public uproar he arouses, and the worry which this sudden notoriety engenders, the impression of no longer recognizing oneself, the desire to escape the stares of others in order to find oneself again. Chateaubriand said he sometimes felt the need to lunch in a café where the owner knew him by sight without knowing who he was, a place he could eat protected from the gaze of curious people. He would be recognized there as a regular and not as a literary celebrity. Even here, he never forgot that he had written a successful book and he looked for literary critiques in the press, but at least felt at peace thanks to the caged nightingales, whose songs relaxed him. The presence of these nightingales, in a scene where

Chateaubriand is looking for a way to escape the hold that celebrity has over him, reminds one unmistakably of a scene in the *Confessions*, when Jean-Jacques is sleeping under the stars and listening to nightingales. In case the reference is not clear enough, Chateaubriand carefully notes that the owner of the café is called ... Mme Rousseau!

A few lines later, reference to the author of the *Confessions* is made even more explicit when Chateaubriand casually remarks on the success he has with women, to whom he owes his celebrity, "young women who cry over novels" along with a "group of Christian females" who were eager to seduce him.

> J.-J. Rousseau talked about the declarations he received when his book *La Nouvelle Héloïse* was published and about the conquests he was offered: I do not know if anyone would have given me empires, but I know that I was drowning in a flood of perfumed love letters; if these letters were not today those of grandmothers, I would not know how to recount with proper modesty how they fought over every word I wrote, how they swooped up any envelope of mine, and how, blushing, they hid it, lowering their head beneath the veil that covered their long hair.

Celebrity was now eroticized. Chateaubriand wrote about the reciprocal seduction that was established between the celebrated writer and his admirers, men and women, written in a melancholy humor that was understandable given the years that had passed, but not without vanity. He focuses with false modesty on the dangers represented by the "beautiful young girls of thirteen and fourteen," "the most dangerous; because not knowing what they want nor what they want of you, they seductively mix your image into a world of fairy tales, ribbons and flowers." Real or imagined perils? This world of fairy tales expressed what was essential: for the author, as well as for his young admirers, celebrity was based on a mirage. It created a crack in the rational nature of social relationships.

The question of celebrity, the pleasures it procured and the worry it stirred up, was no longer the new and almost incomprehensible phenomenon it still was in the middle of the eighteenth century. It was a reality now, well rooted in cultural life, for which Rousseau appeared to be the tutelary figure, the first to have described it in detail.[25] Moreover, the shift was obvious. Where Rousseau had experienced the curiosity of the public as a form of alienation, the impossibility of being authentically oneself, Chateaubriand took up the theme with more distance and detachment. His own error, Chateaubriand wrote, was not in wanting to be a celebrity, but in claiming that he was not changed by it. In that resided the vanity of the author, the obviously illusory hope that success would leave him untouched, would let him live simply, without transforming him into a public person.

I thought I would be able to savor in my heart, *in petto*, the satisfaction of being a sublime genius, not wearing, as I must today, a beard and outrageous clothes, but I could remain dressed like ordinary people, distinguished only by my superiority: useless hope! My pride should be punished; I learned this lesson from politicians I was forced to know: celebrity is an advantage with moral obligations [*un bénéfice à charge d'âme*].

"Un bénéfice à charge d'âme": In French, it is a stunning expression and profoundly ambiguous, since it refers to the work of a priest taking care of souls. Irony can be read in it, since the obligations of celebrity that Chateaubriand lists are social and worldly constraints, like dinners in the country house of Lucien Bonaparte which he could not avoid. A priest taking care of souls might well have been, for a romantic writer, the ironic inversion of spiritual magisterium, especially for the author of the *Génie du christianisme*. This phrase also evokes the special bond between a celebrated man and his public. The shadow of Rousseau hovering over this text prepares one for such an interpretation. More subtly, Chateaubriand follows the sentence with an account of his meeting with Pauline de Baumont, already sick at the time, who would become his great love up until her death two years later. "I only knew this afflicted woman at the end of her life; she was even then marked for death, and I dedicated myself to her suffering." Dreamy adolescents had given way to another admirer, a dying woman.

Celebrity, for those who are the object of it, is not simply an attribute, the projection of a public image on the world; it profoundly transforms the celebrated person because it modifies the way others look at him or her, forever changing the person's perception of self and the nature of relationships with contemporaries. Chateaubriand's force, in this text, is to combine the magical memory of his public epiphany and the critique of an old man who had very often been reproached for his obsession with renown. Ironically, at the moment he finished his *Mémoires*, he found himself once again constrained by celebrity; he learned that the editor to whom he had sold the rights had, in turn, granted the rights to Émile de Girardin so he could publish them in serialized form in *La Presse*. Scandalized, Chateaubriand protested without effect that "his ashes belonged to him." In fact, the story of his life no longer did belong to him; harried by financial worries, he had sold the rights for a fortune and his life's work was now in the hands of advertising marketers.

Women Seduced and Public Women

When Chateaubriand referred to visits from enamored women admirers, he encouraged a platitude, the power of seduction associated with celebrity. Byron was obviously the great embodiment of this eroticization of celebrities. Specialists have focused on letters he received from readers where an imaginary acting out of sexual fantasies is imprinted like a watermark. The letters from Isabelle Harvey, for example, shot through with trembling desire, seem to illustrate the hold that Byron had over the feminine imagination: "You tell me I am deluded in my imagination with regard to the sentiments I bear you. Not matter if it be illusion, how much more delightful it is than reality. I abjure reality for ever."[26] Byron saved these letters, which were published and analyzed. Some are identifiable, others anonymous.

Might not the idea of a seductive woman, dreaming of meeting a celebrated poet or virtuoso musician and offering herself to him, be a masculine fantasy that very soon became commonplace? In the 1820s, at the height of Byron's success, English critics developed the theory of an hysterical female audience, women who were actually ill, possessed by an epidemic of enthusiasm that was vaguely literary and erotic. This collective pathology, according to these critics, was the sign of a grave social and moral disorder, and the denunciation was picked up by Victorian authors in the second half of the century, as much as by university critics, careful to distinguish Byron's legitimate work from the superficial effects, incomprehensible and grotesque, of his celebrity.[27] True, Byron, like Chateaubriand, and like Rousseau before him, did receive numerous letters from readers. The archives are, however, slanted because Byron carefully kept only the most admiring letters, the most flattering ones: "Don't we all write to please [women]?" he asked.[28] As for women readers, their letters often showed them to be more playful than passionate. They claimed a familiarity with the author, identified readily with his characters, but they kept an amused distance from their own epistolary adventures. Some anonymously constructed a symmetrical game, revealing aspects of their private life to Byron, then later implying a doubt about their authenticity, as Byron did in his books.[29] The result was that when these readers claimed that they wanted to cure Byron of his melancholy, they were partly playing a game, wanting to use the characteristics of fiction as their model and having fun with the ambivalences, as was also the case with Rousseau's readers.

A female reader seduced by a celebrated writer to the point of entering into an epistolary relationship with him became herself a romantic figure. In 1844, while Chateaubriand was revising his *Mémoires*, Balzac published a novel, *Modeste Mignon*, in the *Journal des débats*, in which a young provincial girl starts a correspondence with a celebrated Parisian poet, Canalis. The novel was in step with the times, an ironic reflection on literary prestige and the effects of celebrity. The previous year, the letters of Bettina von Arnim to Goethe had been translated into French;

Balzac, who wrote a review of the correspondence, gave his heroine a name borrowed from *Wilhelm Meister*, Bettina; the allusion could not be clearer. Publication of the Bettina letters drew attention to the practice of writing letters to celebrated authors, which had not abated since Rousseau.[30] Balzac knew perfectly well about this practice not only because he himself had received letters from men and women readers, but also because his own relationship with Mme Hanska, to whom the novel was dedicated, started out by correspondence.

In the novel, Modeste Mignon's interest in Canalis develops on two levels. The young woman's passion for contemporary literature and in particular the great authors, from Rousseau to Byron and Goethe, leads her to an "absolute admiration for genius." In her sad provincial life, literature offered her a refuge through an imaginary world which she filled with romantic heroes and where she could be the heroine. References to Byron are emphasized, and when Modeste takes a walk around the port of Le Havre to see the English disembark, she regrets not seeing a "lost Childe Harold."[31] The spark that ignited this romantic desire was, to the contrary, "a futile and silly piece of luck": the discovery of a portrait of the poet.

> Modeste happened to see in a bookseller's window a lithographic portrait of one of her favorites, Canalis. We all know what lies such pictures tell, – given that they are the result of shameless speculation, seizing upon the personality of celebrated individuals as if their faces were public property. In this instance Canalis, sketched in a Byronic pose, was offering to public admiration his dark locks floating in the breeze, a bare throat, and the unfathomable brow which every bard ought to possess. Victor Hugo's forehead made more persons shave their heads than the glory of Napoleon killed budding marshals.[32]

With somewhat forced irony, Balzac introduced into the heart of his story the base commercial motives that were the source of the increase in mediocre images, a certain ambiguity residing in the fact that the images were both vulgar, in terms of publicity artifacts, and grandiose, because they reproduced the recognizable traits of real genius; Byron and Hugo were not quoted by chance, nor, of course, was Napoleon. Such was the force of celebrity: images without quality, a cynical and commercial exploitation of the notoriety of great men, aroused sincere enthusiasm. Modeste is seduced by this "face made sublime through a marketing necessity," and undertakes to write Canalis. But it is his male secretary who responds in place of the poet, and he becomes involved in a correspondence with her that quickly turns amorous. This framework allows for reflections on celebrity, notably when the real Canalis, who is interested in the sudden and unexpected fortune of Modeste, goes to

230

Le Havre and squanders the aura of his celebrity in just a few days. He discovers that if "public curiosity is wildly excited by Celebrity," the interest does not last; it is fleeting and cannot survive a meeting with the actual person: "Glory, like the sun that is hot and luminous at a distance, is cold at the summit of an Alp when you approach it."[33] Genius in itself is not at all seductive; it is ruminations about celebrity that give rise to an illusory glamour.

The end of the novel sees Modeste, enriched by the unexpected and triumphal return of her father, choosing between three suitors: an aristocrat, representing the traditional elite; the celebrated poet; and the wise secretary, Ernest de la Brière, who has neither riches nor genius to offer but wins out finally because of the sincerity of his feelings. A bourgeois epilogue? Doubtless, but the subtlety of Balzac consists in suggesting that Modeste's attraction to Canalis did not concern crazy passion aroused by some verses and a portrait. Modeste, less naïve than she appears, was careful to find out about the poet's conjugal state. She used the mediated celebrity as a resource for dreaming, to pull herself out of the disappointing and uninteresting world that surrounded her, to become more than a passive reader, to participate in a romantic game and take control of what was happening to her. Her final decision was in no way thoughtless and impetuous. Dreaming about an idyll with a poet whose portrait adorned bookstore windows, she found a place in a media-hyped universe that was not hers, but when it came to choosing a husband she took her time deciding, enjoying the competition between suitors and opting for the most suitable one.

Nonetheless, the theme of celebrated men seducing young women who might anachronistically be called groupies revealed that access to celebrity was uneven. With Chateaubriand, as with Byron, the celebrated man seduced his female public and then had to protect himself from the excessive reactions. On the other hand, a celebrated woman was disgraced, illegitimate. Her potential for seduction was seen as inherently immoral, putting her on the same level as prostitutes and courtesans. It is no coincidence that the term "public woman" was used for a long time to mean prostitute. For literary women, public exposure was a threat to virtue and modesty. In 1852, Harriet Beecher-Stowe had immense success with *Uncle Tom's Cabin*, an abolitionist bestseller; in the first year three hundred thousand copies were sold throughout the United States and one and a half million in Britain. During a promotional tour in England arranged by her editor, she often sat in the area reserved for women, protected from public stares, letting her father and brother go to the podium and speak for her.[34] At the same time, however, signs of an evolution were felt. After the success of *Jane Eyre* in 1848 and after sowing seeds of doubt about her identity and her sex, Charlotte Brontë became extremely popular. When she died in 1855, Elizabeth Gaskell published a biography, partly fictionalized, which strongly affirmed the legitimate image of female writers.

In France, the case of George Sand is emblematic. Celebrated for her novels, but also for her public life, her political activities and her tumultuous affairs, George Sand suffered a flood of attacks. However, she had always been careful to publish under a pseudonym, starting with her first novel in 1832; she chose the male first name George, which in turn inspired another woman author, George Eliot.[35] Like many women authors, she actually wanted to publish anonymously but her editor pushed her to find a pseudonym for commercial reasons. In fact, despite the success of *Indiana*, she at first managed to maintain a certain anonymity. She even succeeded in sustaining for a while a certain question about her gender, at least for those who only knew her name. In *Histoire de ma vie*, published twenty years later, at the height of her celebrity, she re-affirmed this desire for anonymity, although it is not easy to distinguish between compulsory modesty and sincerity:

> I would have chosen to live obscurely, and as I had succeeded in remaining incognito during the interval between the publication of *Indiana* and *Valentine* – so that the newspapers always referred to me as monsieur – I flattered myself that this little success would not affect my sedentary habits or my small circle of intimates, composed of people as unknown as myself.

But she added that she was quickly disillusioned in this hope. She had visits from the curious, from beggars, from kindly as well as malicious persons. "Alas! soon I was to long for peace, in that as in everything else, and to seek solitude in vain, as did Jean-Jacques Rousseau."[36]

In *Les Célébrités du jour*, a collection of biographies published in 1960, Louis Jourdain and Taxile Delord included a preamble on female celebrity before presenting the portrait of George Sand, the only woman artist in the collection. What could be said about a celebrated woman whose life was surrounded by scandal and rumors? In this case, the usual argument used to justify publicity for a celebrity ran up against the more classical issue of feminine modesty, which rendered indiscreet any investigation into her private life:

> What right does a biography have to penetrate the private life of a woman, conversing with the public about her love life or her antipathies, her struggles and her weaknesses? But let us suppose that this woman has exceptional talent; she is an artist or poet, she sings, she writes, she paints, she sculpts, and the public has a very legitimate desire to know who she is, how she lives, who she loves, how she suffers. That the public feels this way is possible, but that the public has the right to satisfy that desire and,

232

in so doing, to scrutinize the intimate existence of a woman, to analyze each of her actions or words, to pore over her affections in order to taunt or pervert them, we do not agree.[37]

This gender structure for celebrity, the constraints of which weighed the most heavily on women authors, lasted a long time. At the end of the century and even during the Belle Époque, women writers would always be torn between the desire for success and celebrity, on the one hand, and the values of modesty and devotion to female domestic duties, on the other. Was it possible to become a public figure without running headlong in opposition to social norms? It became so difficult that any too obvious sign of authorial modesty was eventually perceived by the critics to be a secret desire for celebrity. More than one female author found herself trapped by this frightening contradiction.[38]

Virtuosos

As in the preceding century, theater remained a privileged vehicle, really the only legitimate one, for female celebrities, since the international tours of the Malibran, a Spanish opera singer, who sang in opera houses all over Europe, up until the success of Mlle Mars and Rachel on the stage at the Comédie-Française. After her success in *Phèdre*, Rachel successfully negotiated extremely favorable financial conditions at the Comédie-Française, to the great annoyance of other cast members, who had to bow before the celebrity of the tragedian.[39] Her death in 1858 elicited a deluge of praise, anecdotes, and biographies, and a race for autographs and intimate stories. The director of the *Figaro* had, several weeks earlier, prepared an article about her and he profited from her death to publish a special issue "composed of anecdotes, and an autograph by the illustrious tragedian, along with fifty new letters, the spiciest ones and the most varied."[40]

In cities, the theater continued to occupy a central role in cultural life, as it had since the start of the eighteenth century, providing the public with stars. In Paris, while Rachel triumphed in tragic roles, Frédérick Lemaître played opposite Marie Dorval in comedies and popular dramas, and in street theater, transforming the bandit Robert Macaire into a comic character. The term "star," imported from English, began to designate actors with top billing. In London, Edmund Kean, the unchallenged star of Drury Lane, did not attract attention uniquely because of his theater performances, but also because of the scandalous public persona he had created. Born into the theater, Kean came from an entirely different social stratum than Byron, but, like him, he owed his celebrity to the conjunction of a rapidly recognized talent and a turbulent private life well known to the public. A few years after Byron's impressive divorce, Kean was convicted of adultery in the wake of a trial that occupied the British press for several months. The comparison ends there. Kean did not embody a romantic, melancholy character, but rather an histrionic and capricious figure always eager to transform his life into a spectacle, casually feeding the craziest rumors by his extravagant comportment: the newspapers recounted his drunken sexual brawls, claimed that he fed a tame lion on live animals, and that he participated in boxing matches barefisted.[41] A Shakespearian actor and fractious star, Kean made an impact on his contemporaries in England, where the whiff of scandal permanently accompanied him, but also in the United States, which he visited on two occasions, and in France. Alexandre Dumas devoted a play to him three years after his death.

Ultimately, there was nothing very new in this. The real romantic revolution in the realm of celebrity was less a matter of the theater than it was of music. There were already stars in the eighteenth century, composers like Handel, Gréstry and Gluck, and the castrati singers Farinelli and Tenducci. But music was marked by its religious origins and by the courtly or aristocratic context in which it was most often played, so much so that it remained the privilege of a cultural elite. In spite of their success, neither Gluck nor Haydn was celebrated beyond the narrow confines of music lovers and patrons. Young Mozart, of course, amazed London and Paris audiences during his first European tour at age six. His celebrity, however, was based on being a child prodigy who seemed to embody new theories about the innate character of creative genius,[42] and the surprise and astonishment faded as he got older. If his musical reputation remained high among music lovers, in spite of his setbacks at Salzburg and up until his late success in Vienna, he had to resign himself to creating less enthusiasm than before. He was bitterly disappointed by the Paris welcome he received in 1778 and complained that audiences, often busy socialites, were relatively indifferent, showing only polite interest.[43] In contrast, the first half of the nineteenth century saw the triumph of great musical stars. The increase in public concerts, more or less freed from aristocratic patronage, and the invention of individual recitals changed the social conditions of performances.[44] Music no longer had the same status: it had become a pure art form, an ideal means for expressing feeling. Beginning with Gluck, this new relationship reached its apogee in the years 1830–50 with Liszt's great success. From Vienna to Berlin, from Pest to Paris, and from Naples to London, concerts attracted large audiences enthusiastic about the new music, the composers, and their performances. "Paris is drowning in a flood of music, there is hardly a house where one can be saved as on Noah's Ark from this sonorous deluge; at last, noble music has inundated our life entirely," noted Heinrich Heine with amusement in his Parisian chronicles.[45]

This was the moment when Beethoven became the incarnation of romantic genius. But in spite of his notoriety, he did not have the same celebrity as Byron. It is true that Beethoven had immense prestige attached to his name after the middle of the century, but this renown could not have been guessed at given his early career. Certainly, he had nothing of the cursed artist about him. His career in Vienna was dotted with brilliant successes. He was soon recognized as one of the great composers of his time, if not the greatest, and benefited from the support of important figures in the imperial court, who had a profound admiration for him and assured his financial security. But his growing reputation remained within the circle of musical patrons. His talent was challenged by a part of the Viennese public who found his works too difficult, too arduous, too far from those forms capable of pleasing a larger audience. Beethoven himself made very few concessions: "I do not write for the crowd," he exclaimed, dismayed and furious after the failure of his opera *Fidelio*. He could allow himself this kind of intransigence because of the loyal support of his patrons. Contrary to the legend, Beethoven's career unfolded for the most part in the traditional context of the imperial court and Viennese salons.[46]

It was not until 1814 that Beethoven acquired both international celebrity and real popularity in Austria, having composed works to celebrate the military losses of Napoleon. The November 1814 concert on the occasion of the Vienna Congress assured his reputation as a great patriotic composer. This celebrity, however, was not as long-lasting as one might imagine. A replay of the concert a few days later ended in a commercial failure. During the years that followed, Beethoven lost part of his court support, isolating himself more and more because of his deafness, but also because of his creative evolution. Beethoven kept his enthusiastic admirers and received commissions from England, Germany, and even the United States, but these came from groups of musicians and music lovers. It was above all in Vienna, and in some German cities, that his death in 1827 was an event. In Paris, at that time, he was seldom heard.

The case of Beethoven makes it possible to distinguish between the system of celebrity and the effects of reputation, even when exceptional, on an artist. There is no doubt that Beethoven obtained the unconditional support of the Viennese elite and European music lovers, who profoundly admired him early on, beginning in the mid-1790s, and even more clearly during his great creative period in the 1800s. With his triumphs in 1814, his reputation was better established but rested on an heroic and patriotic style that had made him successful but from which he tried to move away. Essentially, it was after his death that a real fascination with his work developed.[47]

While alive, Beethoven remained on the edge of celebrity, less popular, for example, than Rossini. Stendhal wrote in 1824, the same year as the creation of the *Ninth Symphony*: "Napoleon is dead; but a new conqueror has already shown himself to the world; and from Moscow to Naples, from London to Vienna, from Paris to Calcutta, his name is constantly on every tongue." He was talking about Rossini, then just thirty-two, whose success in Naples and Vienna and his triumphal tours of Paris and London occupied the attention of the public, as well as the press, and to whom Stendhal had already devoted a biography.[48] However, posthumous excitement about Beethoven's genius among romantic musicians continued to grow. This helped create a new relationship to musicians and to music, on which the extraordinary popularity of Franz Liszt would be based.

Liszt, of whom it was said that his face, when he died, was the most well known in Europe,[49] greatly contributed to the cult of Beethoven. Having benefited from a precocious celebrity starting with his first concerts as a child prodigy in Paris in 1823–4, ten years later he was the darling of the Parisian public, which was fascinated by his virtuosity, by the anecdotes of his affair with Marie d'Agoult, and by his provocative writings, borrowed from Saint-Simonism, in which he demanded the social elevation of the musician and pleaded for a form of spiritual music. As the adored pianist of polite society, he was welcomed into the best salons in the Saint-Germain quarter, where he had no fear of denouncing the "subaltern" role occupied by musicians ("Is the artist anything more than a salon entertainer?" he asked), of mocking the lack of musical culture in his admirers, or of appealing for a new kind of popular music, inspired, fraternal, and universal. "Vienna, oh, Vienna the hour is near for deliverance, when the poet and the musician will no longer say 'the public,' but 'the PEOPLE and GOD.' "[50] Liszt intelligently and successfully occupied a unique and very visible position in Parisian cultural life, half-way between the traditional figure of the salon pianist and that of the romantic artist, foreshadowing a new era.[51]

The summit of celebrity for Liszt came with his vast European tour beginning in 1838, which took the pianist from Vienna to Berlin and then to London and Paris, sometimes arousing extreme reactions in the public.[52] Such reactions also provoked criticism and mockery. In Berlin in 1842, the fervor surrounding his concerts reached an unprecedented intensity that fascinated critics and journalists. Liszt's performances created a new level of collective excitement. Vocabulary used to describe madness was commonplace as everyone tried to understand this recent form of pathology.[53] Cartoons showed Liszt's audiences being taken directly to the madhouse after a recital. Liberals saw in the musician's popularity the consequences of insufficient political freedom, as though public passions in Berlin were focused on this objective. Conservatives deplored such unrestrained behavior, which seemed excessive and inappropriate. They were alarmed by the reactions of women as though infatuation with the virtuoso came from sexual excitement. Overall, what predominated was a mixture of surprise, worry, and amusement. There were multiple repercussions from Liszt's success. Not only did spectators turn themselves into a spectacle, but commentaries provoked by these new reactions focused on the public's interest in Liszt's celebrity. Although the price of tickets meant that only the Berlin bourgeoisie and polite society could attend the concerts, curiosity aroused by Liszt's presence in cities, through newspaper stories, café conversations, and a profusion of cartoons, attracted the interest of a much larger population: Liszt was "talked about with delight in the palaces of the great as well as the cottages of poverty," wrote Gustav Nicolaï in a local newspaper.[54]

How could such celebrity be accounted for? First of all, Liszt's career path can be explained by the new conditions surrounding musical life. While he did remain dependent on aristocratic patronage in the first decades of his career, he benefited from the explosion of public concerts and revolutionary piano techniques. Whether he was performing his own compositions or those of others, from 1835 onward, Liszt created a model for the individual recital, where the musician was alone on stage facing his public. Even Paganini, the great virtuoso whose concerts so impressed Liszt early on, played with an orchestra. It was Liszt who invented the solo recital. At the same time, the bourgeoisie privileged the piano and imposed piano education on all young girls from good families, creating an even greater interest in the instrument and an increased curiosity in virtuosos like Liszt, but also Sigismund Thalberg or Henri Herz.[55]

Instrument virtuosity from this point on surpassed that of an aesthetic experience and became a performance resembling a sporting event. This aspect ended in duels, like that between Liszt and Thalberg, a rivalry fed by a series of successive challenges and provocative statements. The comparison with boxers, their rivalries and their matches, might seem grossly anachronistic, but it came spontaneously to mind at the time, in particular in England, where, since the end of the eighteenth century, boxing matches had become a popular spectacle assuring the celebrity of men like Daniel Mendoza, a vertitable entrepreneur when it came to his own sporting fame.[56] Even when music emancipated itself from this type of rivalry and the artist came face-to-face with his public, virtuosity remained a performance worth as much by the surprise it caused as by the emotion it provoked. People came to see a man perform seemingly impossible physical and technical feats. Comparisons of Liszt to Bonaparte were often made, Liszt appearing to be an audacious and conquering personality, readily adopting a martial posture and displaying his taste for astounding feats.[57] He threw out challenges such as playing the finale of Berlioz's *Symphonie fantastique* on the piano, causing an "indescribable delirium" in the public when confronted with this unlikely utilization of the instrument.[58] In March 1837, he surprised everyone by announcing a solo piano recital at the Opera, on a Sunday. The press could not get over it: "Playing piano at the Opera! Transporting the thin, sickly sounds of a solo instrument into this immense hall where the echoes of the *Huguenots* still resounded, a hall accustomed to every dramatic emotion ... and this, on a Sunday, in front of a mixed, uncultivated crowd! What a spirited undertaking!"[59]

Reference to the audience as "mixed" and "uncultivated" was decisive. In order to seduce his new public, Liszt did not propose original or difficult compositions; instead, he played improvised and whimsical airs from well-known operas. Adding to the public fascination with these performances was familiarity with popular melodies. Word about this new kind of music spread through the use of publicity, or rather, as one said in the nineteenth century, advertisements. Liszt was one of the first musicians, after Paganini, to use the services of an impresario, Gaetano Belloni, who was in charge of organizing his tours, inserting publicity announcements and laudatory reviews in newspapers, but also watching over the publication of engraved portraits of the composer.[60] Liszt himself possessed a cunning sense of self-promotion: he wrote short autobiographies in German and French, which piqued the interest of the public, never hesitating to be provocative in press articles, and published letters in newspapers that he wrote to friends and in which he recounted the welcome he was given at concerts. He especially liked to show off his charitable temperament, organizing concerts for humanitarian causes, for example after the floods in Pest, and taking care to make his selfless nature known.

The result of this intense music and marketing enterprise was the existence of a strange new public figure, a sentimental musician nurturing a dream of spiritual music; a showman capable of attracting crowds; and an ordinary man with a fondness for genteel and aristocratic poses. It was Liszt, better than any other musician of his time, who knew how to maintain this perfect ambiguity, that of the "subversive virtuoso," both hostile to elites and fascinated by their model of gentility, cultivating with his public a sentimental closeness and a rather haughty distance. And since Rousseau and Byron, two men dear to Liszt, had this type of ambiguity not become one of the powerful resources of celebrity?

This figure of the sentimental and virtuoso musician, pulling all the publicity strings, found an acerbic observer in the person of Henrich Heine, a German writer living in Paris, passionate about music, lucid and readily sarcastic. When Liszt returned triumphant to Paris in 1844, Heine, in a lengthy column that was both funny and cruel, wrote about the success of the "great agitator," "our Franz Liszt," "doctor in philosophy and sixteenth notes," "a modern Homer that Germany, Hungary, and France each claim as their own, while only seven little provincial towns" claimed to be the birthplace of *The Illiad*'s cantor, or the "new Attila, God's scourge on all the Érard pianos." After this succession of comic comparisons, he invokes the "incredible furor" that had electrified Parisian society, the "hysterical crowds" of women spectators and their "frenetic acclamations." He then pretends to be astonished that the Parisian public, which he thought was more blasé than the German, should be caught up in such passion for a pianist:

> What a crazy thing! I said to myself, these Parisians who had seen Napoleon, the great Napoleon, who had to engage in battle after battle in order to keep them focused on him and to get their approval, these same Parisians shower our Franz Liszt with acclamations! And what acclamations! A real frenzy, like there has never been before in the annals of madness.

He continues in a medical vein, suggesting that such collective enthusiasm was due to "a pathology rather than an aesthetic." He then abandons this convenient criticism and falls back on a more prosaic explanation: the real genius of Liszt lay in his ability to "organize his success, or rather to produce it."

Heine then gives free rein to a thorough critique of the publicity system of celebrity. He spared nothing, including the philanthropic reputation that Liszt so willingly put to good use. If Heine was to be believed, Liszt's success, it seems, was a fiction, supported by new commercial strategies: it was the role of Belloni, "the general intendant of his celebrity," to buy the laurels, the bouquets of flowers, "laudatory poems and other ovation expenses." It is clear that celebrity at this point entered a period of mistrust. It was a matter not only of criticizing the excessive enthusiasm of the public, but even of doubting the reality of the triumphal shows. And if it was all just a pretense, smoke and mirrors?[61] At this point, Heine, who detested the society of the spectacle and the "star-system," as moralists nowadays do, went even further, proposing a general criticism of celebrity earned by virtuosos meant less to denounce this celebrity than to bring it into balance: "Let us not look too closely at the homage that is earned by celebrity virtuosos. After all, their vain celebrity does not last long." And he wrote the same thing in a more unexpected and imagistic way: "The ephemeral renown of the virtuoso fades to nothing, without leaving a trace or any resonance, like the whinnying of a camel crossing desert sands."[62]

Liszt himself was not unaware of the limits of "sterile celebrity" and "egoistical joys," which he spoke about in an article published on the death of Paganini, contrasting him with real art.[63] Perhaps he wanted to avoid the sad fate that Heine promised him, that of an old virtuoso becoming anonymous once more, dwelling on the memory of a vanished celebrity. Certainly he had been torn for a long time between the headiness of success and the desire to produce authentic work. In 1847, at the height of his notoriety, he decided to end his career as a concert virtuoso and accepted a position in Weimar, dedicating himself to composing. This choice, accompanied by a return to the Catholic faith, leads one to think that his declarations of his mistrust of celebrity were more sincere than one might have believed. He had written almost ten years earlier, at the time of a triumphal tour in Italy:

> So, I confess I have often pitied the petty triumphs of satisfied vanity while bitterly protesting against the excitement with which I have seen works without conscience or portent welcomed; just so, I have wept over what others called my success, when it was clear to me that the crowd rushes to an artist to ask him for some passing amusement and not instruction about noble feelings. I felt as wounded by the praise as by the critics, refusing to recognize such frivolous judges.[64]

Instead of finding these words suspect, seeing in them only the coquettishness of a star, why not allow Liszt some credit and admit that he, like Rousseau, Byron, or Siddons, had a complex and ambivalent relationship to his own celebrity? Celebrity was not an entirely legitimate form of recognition, because immediate public enthusiasm broke the balance of recognition by one's peers. It was impure; it owed too much to commercialization, to the expedients of advertising and to the subterfuges of what was not yet called the marketing culture. The virtuoso was the embodiment of all this. Appearing first in the eighteenth century, he belonged as much to the world of spectacle as to that of art; he seduced through his performances more than through his art; he abdicated his artistic destiny, which implied slow maturation, choosing instead immediate satisfaction from a public which expected to be both astonished by his musical mastery and comforted in its taste. The virtuoso put himself on stage and became the center of a spectacle, making himself the entrepreneur of his own public persona.[65] He rejoiced in seeing his vanity flattered, but could remain conscious of the vanity of his success, because he knew, better than anyone, the artificiality of acclamation, that celebrity was only a selling point. In his most ironic mode, Liszt made fun of mediocre concerts given by "average, dull musicians who, in spite of two hundred posters, green, yellow, red, or blue, tirelessly advertising this celebrity to the two hundred corners of Paris, were condemned, nonetheless to remain anonymous forever."[66] Very early in his career, he felt a distrust of public success, although he would benefit from it in the following years. His relationship to music came from a sensibility torn by desire for immediate recognition that sustained his taste for success and a feeling of artistic independence where real recognition implied keeping a distance from the demands of the public.

Celebrity in America

Liszt's European career showed that the geography of celebrity had changed. His success, far from being limited to Paris or Vienna, took him to Zagreb and Pest, to Berlin and London. Other virtuosos traveled across the Atlantic, like the French pianist Henri Herz, the Austrian dancer Fanny Elssler, whose American tour was a great success from 1840 to 1842, or the Norwegian violinist Ole Bull, whom Heine called "the Lafayette of the puff," because "in terms of advertisements [he] was the hero of two worlds."[67] In fact, between 1830 and 1840, the celebrity system began to show a definite growth in the United States, becoming a prominent force in popular American culture of the twentieth century and later. As in Europe, it was first of all in the literary domain that the rapid urban growth occurred; an increase in print shops and new commercial techniques made their effects felt. The writer Nathaniel Parker Willis very much embodied this development. Somewhat forgotten today, he was a major figure in American cultural life in the middle of the century. He made himself known early by his recounting of a trip to Europe, and by vivid and funny stories about figures of New York high society. Both writer and journalist, he became the most celebrated and best-paid author of his time, managing several newspapers and, in particular, founding the *Home Journal* in 1846, in which he set the trend for cultural life on the East Coast. Both a celebrated author, an editor – he unfailingly supported the career of Edgar Allan Poe – and an arbiter of fashion, he illustrated social and cultural changes that accompanied urban growth in New York, the population going from 240,000 inhabitants to 1.2 million in thirty years (1830–60). Willis became a well-known public figure, but an extremely controversial one, often ridiculed for his effeminate and affected character. As one journalist wrote about him, "No man has lived more constantly in the public eye for the last twenty years than Willis, and no American writer has received more applause from his friends and more censure from his enemies."[68]

Willis had also been witness to the most profound transformation in public spectacles, especially in Europe, where their commercial development had been much faster. In contrast with the Old World, the United States did not have a tradition of court spectacle and aristocratic patronage, so the modern show-business economy could expand almost unfettered, driven by risk-taking entrepreneurs, and in particular the impressive Phineas Taylor Barnum. He has remained famous for his gigantic traveling circus, modestly called *The Greatest Show on Earth*, for his exhibition of monstrous humans, and for his collection of objects in the Barnum American Museum, making him a major figure in popular American culture, symbol of the wily and seductive entrepreneur, producer of ambitious spectacles. He began his career with less brilliant shows, notably exhibiting Joice Heth, an old black woman who claimed to be a hundred and sixty years old and the former wet nurse of George Washington. Then it was the turn of Tom Thumb, a child dwarf whom he made into a veritable star at the beginning of the 1840s.

Spectacles made up of human curiosities, notably racial, were not completely new. In 1796, citizens of Philadelphia had already seen a "great curiosity," a black man who had become almost completely white, exhibited daily in a tavern for half a shilling. The man, Henry Moss, was for a while a celebrity with a very ambivalent status, attracting crowds of curious people as well as scientists and philosophers.[69] Barnum, however, gave his productions a new dimension, adapting them to the latest spectacular forms of media, and starting a period of "Freak Shows."[70] But he wanted respectability. Once he was an impresario, he organized American tours for European celebrities, giving an almost business-like dimension to the art of the puff piece, which consisted of publishing ecstatic press notices about artistes in order to arouse public curiosity.[71]

His greatest accomplishment was to bring the Swedish opera singer Jenny Lind to the United States, who was already very popular in England and throughout northern Europe. At twenty-nine, she decided to renounce the opera and tour America doing recitals, a period that lasted two years and ended in triumph. Her arrival in New York and then in Boston in September 1850 was welcomed with enthusiasm by the press. On September 2, 1850, the *New York Tribune* reported that between thirty and forty thousand New Yorkers rushed onto the quays to see the boat that carried the singer, resulting in several injuries.[72] The crowds hurried to the concerts, and newspapers kept publishing articles about the singer and about the frenzy that overtook the public, what the Boston *Independent* described as "Lindomania" during the singer's visit to the city.

This triumphal tour by the "Swedish nightingale" marked the entrance of celebrity culture into the United States. Barnum was the great director;

first he tried out publicity methods like bidding sales for concert seats, which encouraged cheating and a rise in prices, at the same time assuring the anticipated publicity for the show (Fig. 16). Lind was not only a singer; she had become a product. Barnum, needing to amortize the considerable sums he had invested in the tour, did not hesitate to showcase the public person of Jenny Lind as the ideal young woman, virtuous and meritorious, poor, puritan, and philanthropic, her success owing everything to hard work – a veritable incarnation, in short, of American values. Several biographies of Lind were published the year she arrived in America, one of them written by Willis himself, and all the newspapers picked up on her most remarkable traits, even those that had been invented for the articles. Curiosity about the person of Lind was such that her vocal talent sometime seemed of secondary interest.[73] Barnum went so far as to claim, much later, that her success owed nothing at all to her voice and everything to the publicity that he had orchestrated. These statements, written after the rupture of their agreement, are no doubt exaggerated, but they show a strong awareness of the autonomous system of celebrity.

Vente à l'encan des billets pour les représentations de Jenny Lind en Amérique.

nov. 1850

Figure 16: Auction sale of tickets for
Jenny Lind performances in America, engraving, 1850.

The most striking aspect of Lind's success, one that historians have now clearly demonstrated, was the creation of a public persona, an incarnation of the natural, the authentic, and the selfless. However, Lind was not an innocent whose image supposedly was manipulated by Barnum. She was a smart woman who did not hesitate to question her contract with the entrepreneur when she found it profitable to do so. The construction of her public persona, that of the "Swedish Nightingale," built around simplicity and modesty, was a collective work in which she very much took part, along with Barnum and a large number of journalists who enthusiastically intoned hymns of glory to her. Some journalists, it is true, sensed something odd in the flagrant contrast between, on the one hand, the enormous promotional machinery, the outlay of press articles accompanying Lind's every change of venue, the profusion of products bearing her name and, on the other, the constant praise of her simplicity and naturalness, which led certain admirers to claim that she sang purely by instinct, out of pleasure, paying no attention to the audience. "A lot of artifice is necessary to appear so artless," one critic ironically remarked, but the discreet voice of skeptics was drowned out by the collective enthusiasm.

In the end, Lind gave almost a hundred concerts in two years, crossing the United States, north to south, from Boston to New Orleans, even giving a recital in Cuba, before returning to New York, where she once again had great success. The success of this tour was measured first of all in commercial terms, Lind and Barnum each taking home nearly two hundred thousand dollars.[74] But it was much more than that: it signaled a cultural change. Everywhere, the streets, public squares, and theaters were named after her, all the way to San Francisco, where the Jenny Lind Theater opened in 1850 above a saloon.[75] Numerous articles in the press accompanied this long tour and testified to the impact Lind made during her stay, but there was also the desire by the American public to be seen as equal to the displays of enthusiasm by European crowds. For Willis, as for so many others, Lind's success indicated the cultural level that the United States had attained with the emergence of a middle class, one capable of appreciating European culture. Once again, the rapid and spectacular effects of celebrity brought with it a flood of commentaries speculating about the nature of the phenomenon and its significance.

Who was Lind's public? First of all, contemporaries such as Barnum emphasized the varied and egalitarian nature of her audiences, where the common people supposedly mingled with the elite. Actually, the price of tickets separated the elite from tradesmen and rural laborers, and it seemed that some of the well-heeled elites from polite society in New York or Philadelphia kept their distance from a phenomenon which appeared to them lacking in dignity. On the other hand, the urban middle class, then in full expansion, was wildly enthusiastic. Whereas opera music was becoming an entertainment reserved for the elite, Lind offered them the great operatic airs from Bellini to Rossini, ending her tours by singing popular American songs such as "Home Sweet Home." Given the way the press presented her, she incarnated the bourgeois ideal of femininity:

modest, unaffected, and a philanthropist. Her celebrity, however, grew far beyond merely the public who attended her concerts, through the publicity sent out about her. In the Bowery, one of the working-class areas of New York, one could find cheap products sold with the name of Lind on them, in the same way luxury products associated with the singer were found in expensive boutiques. Lind's celebrity rose above the division in American social classes. While not being as universal as Barnum claimed, she paralleled the emergence of a commercial culture, aimed not at the distinguished elites nor at the traditional working class but created principally for the middle class, although capable of reaching a much larger market given the media reverberations of the stars who made up the celebrity culture.

The success of Lindomania also allowed Barnum to gain a greater cultural respectability. He pulled away from dubious entertainments to become a culturally important person, to the point that *Putnam's Magazine* proposed that he be named director of the New York Opera.[76] Five years later he wrote his autobiography, producing seven different versions up until 1889, as his success and his notoriety grew.[77]

Democratic Popularity and Popular Sovereignty

In the United States, as in Europe, the second third of the nineteenth century was marked by the blossoming of a new relationship to publicity. New strategies of advertising and "puffing," not yet called marketing, cleverly played with the ideal of sincerity and authenticity to which the new urban educated classes adhered. The encounter of these new audiences with the fanciful romantic created by writers and musicians led to a reinforcement of the celebrity system. It produced three figures: the tormented poet, the successful actor, and the virtuoso musician. In this context, political changes that we saw outlined at the revolutionary end of the eighteenth century could only accelerate. Democratic electoral campaigns as well as the more traditional exercise of sovereignty now had to deal with the effects of popularity. Even revolutionary struggles did not escape it, as in the case of the emblematic Garibaldi.

Various revolutions forced the question of popularity, the political variant of celebrity. In France, in 1848, republicans had a doubly bitter experience of this in the presidential election. The pitiful failure of Lamartine proved that literary celebrity did not spontaneously translate into political celebrity. One of the most famous romantic poets and a hero of the February revolution, he did not succeed in transforming his celebrity into popularity, convincing his compatriots that he had the soul of a leader. On the other hand, the triumph of Louis Napoleon Bonaparte made clear to republicans that the celebrity of a name, though inherited, was a powerful vector for popular votes. Of course, the actual political circumstances that ruined the earlier hopes played an important role after the June repression, as well as the particular nature of the rural vote. Nonetheless, the triumph of the emperor's nephew owed much to the power of a "known name," against which Jules Grévy had warned his colleagues at the time of the fall constitutional debates.[78] The former Ham Fortress detainee built his program not so much around a program, which was totally hazy at the beginning, as around his personal, even ambivalent, notoriety, and on the prestige attached to his name. His celebrity grew through the circulation of images and popular songs in outlets used for the distribution of the Napoleon legend.[79] Popularity, this essential resource for vote getting, rested on a strange alchemy between the voters and a politician. It was different from the celebrity of writers and virtuosos, given the political desire from which it developed – for a leader, capable of governing – all the while borrowing from its principal resource: a mixture of curiosity and empathy, directed at a public person. This collective espousal of a unique individual rather than coherent political content led to a personalization of the political struggle for which republicans were not prepared.

The success of Louis Napoleon has often been read from a strictly French perspective, that of Bonapartism, the idiosyncratic aspect of French politics. But this personalization of political life around a celebrated person, popular and authoritarian, found resonance elsewhere, notably across the Atlantic. In the United States, the election of Andrew Jackson twenty years earlier had changed the contours of politics in this sense. A former general during the war against the English in 1812 and during the Indian wars, Jackson was adulated by his troops, who affectionately called him "Old Hickory," a nickname that stuck well beyond the circle of old soldiers. His victory in New Orleans in 1815 made him the new military hero in America. His election to the presidency in 1828 became very personalized. Admirers defended him with enthusiasm when his adversaries readily attacked his authoritarian personality, his temper, his superficial education, his dueling matches a quarter of a century earlier, and even his wife's past. At the same time that he protested against this attack on his privacy, Jackson did not hesitate to expose his family life, breaking with the tradition of discretion so dear to the founding fathers.

Jackson's popularity had to do with his military success, but also with the democratic demands he was making for a greater opening into political life, for a stronger affirmation of popular sovereignty. If he was the new American military hero, he was also the spokesman for the South and the West against the political elites of New England, embodied by John Quincy Adams, the retiring president, son of John Adams. Historians have, today, cast doubt upon the idea that his presidency was the starting point for "Jacksonian democracy"; they insist on his authoritarian practices, his constant support of the slave system, and his politics of plunder concerning Native Americans.[80] Still, Jackson, as controversial as he is, embodied for his contemporaries the model of a powerful personality, having a direct and powerful, almost affective, link with those he called the people and for whom he fought. After the failure of 1824, when he obtained the majority of the popular vote but not that of the electoral college, and was sidelined in favor of Adams by a congressional vote, the election of 1828 was very much disputed, sometimes virulently. For the first time, all the states voted for universal suffrage. Public reunions were held throughout the territory, accompanied by the raising of money. The press played an important role, with the most widely distributed newspapers, like the *United States Telegraph*, giving Jackson decisive support. Numerous portraits of Jackson were published, but also violent caricatures, one of which showed the by then well-known face of the general composed of all the cadavers of the men he was accused of killing.

These attacks did not damage his popularity, however. The investiture ceremony of March 4, 1829 was open to the public, whereas it had previously been reserved only for Congress. Tens of thousands of people rushed to Washington, coming from all over the United States, to see General Jackson be sworn in. After the ceremony, the White House was overrun by a crowd of enthusiastic admirers, who almost smothered the new president and caused damage that consternated the political elite.[81] One could not imagine a better symbol than this intrusion by the people into the heart of power. But it was not "the people" who overran the White House buffet. It was admiring voters or curiosity seekers, who wanted to be part of the ceremony, to be present at the public event, to catch a glimpse of the new president.

It would be absurd to reduce Jackson's success to his celebrity. He was supported by a strong political machine. But the seeds were already sown during Washington's second term: American politics had become more partisan, more split, and also more popularist. John Adams, it will be remembered, remarked on Washington' s popularity with a mix of spite, admiration, and irony, noting that the victorious general had managed to embody the young republic. Twenty years later, his vast knowledge and competence, acknowledged by his own son, a scholar and renowned diplomat, did not help him when faced with the popularity of Andrew Jackson, the conqueror of New Orleans. When Jackson left the White House in 1837, the face of American politics had changed, marked by a conjunction of the presidency, bipartisanship, and popular sovereignty.

At the same time, on the other side of the Atlantic, the former colonial power achieved its evolution toward a constitutional monarchy where the sovereign had only minor power, but embodied national unity. Victoria, acceding to the throne, knew perfectly well how to adapt to her symbolic political role by mobilizing all the modern forms of political publicity. Mostly, she is remembered for her image as an austere and hieratic widow who had become the empress of India in 1876, the perfect incarnation of British imperial society at the summit of its economic power and its moral conservatism. But in 1837, the young sovereign was only eighteen and the first half of her reign was that of a seductive, approachable queen, worried about her place in the public sphere. The historian John Plunkett called her the first "media monarch."[82]

Victoria's power lay in enlarging popular support for the constitutional monarchy, thanks to her visibility. While parliamentary representation remained based on a rather strict census principle, in spite of progress in the Reform Act of 1832, the queen symbolized another form of political representation for the nation. Early on, she increased her visits, her charitable works, and her military reviews. These public manifestations, with their strong media focus, gave her real popularity. The queen was always visible, putting herself on show, and the newspapers commented on her activities. In 1843, the *Times* rejoiced that Victoria's visits helped to "cement the union between the Crown and the people by a reciprocity of confidence," while new, cheap weeklies, like the *News of the World*, described in length each of her visits, pointing out the maternal graciousness of the queen.[83] The enthusiastic London welcome of the queen during the World's Fair in 1851, conveniently written up in all the papers, contrasted sharply with the less glorious fate of the French monarchy overturned three years earlier.

As soon as Victoria acceded to the throne, her face was reproduced everywhere. There were dozens of official portraits in existence, but very quickly the demand was such that every print shop had the portraits engraved to more or less resemble the queen in order to satisfy public demand. In the early 1840s, images of the queen represented 70 percent of print sales.[84] They were found in every price range and every size, most of them unlike the ceremonial portraits, focusing, instead, on the queen's beauty. The "beauty books," a collection of fashion publications in the 1830s, seized on the figure of the queen to make her a symbol of femininity and seduction. These images, of very good quality but expensive, were destined for the elites, who gave them as presents. Cheaper and less refined images were made from these, which accentuated, sometimes to the point of vulgarity, the implicit eroticism of the queen.

Beyond these engravings, distribution of the royal image was greatly hastened by the illustrated press, which precisely coincided with the first years of Victoria's reign. At the beginning of the 1840s, illustrated newspapers increased rapidly, along the lines of the *Illustrated London News* and *Punch*, founded in 1841 and 1842, respectively. Whether dedicated to the classic treatment of information, as was the first, or satire, like the second, they included engraved illustrations. The queen occupied a considerable amount of space, sometimes taking up the whole illustrated section. Her public life was described at length, but also her personal and familial life. Her face was no longer a kind of royal portrait, but a media image, distributed throughout the country. Even if the monarchy continued to produce official portraits of the queen, her image was freed from political control. It was no longer a projection of sovereignty, like the royal portraits in the Ancien Régime; it was now formed by a myriad group of figurative representations, ranging from fashion images to caricatures, from press report images to cheap engravings. Each of the various media seized on the images according to their own conventions and the public used them any way it wanted. Each of the queen's subjects could create a personal representation of her starting with the different images available. Even the nature of political visibility had been transformed. In contrast with sovereigns of the Ancien Régime, only visible in the framework of the court, or at the time of monarchical rituals, and even then the carefully controlled effigies circulated only in a very closed circle, Victoria inaugurated an era in which images of leaders were widely distributed, thanks to numerous kinds of media, aimed at the governed.[85] Therefore, the image of incarnated power became both more banal, because it was an object of cheap consummation, and more powerful, capable of profoundly affecting feelings of loyalty or repudiation.

This enormous presence of the young queen in the public sphere, notably through media visibility, provoked numerous reactions from the public. Attachment to Victoria was not only a sign of monarchical or patriotic loyalty. This same attachment could be provoked by the beauty of the queen, having become the incarnation of feminine seduction, or even by the simple effect of fashion and imitation. It sometimes took the form of a desire for intimacy, even romantic fantasy. Before her marriage, many of the "queen's lovers," as the press called them, believed they were in line to win her hand. Among these were Ned Hayward, who flooded Buckingham Palace with demands of marriage and managed to stop the royal carriage in order to ask her himself; Tom Flowers, who had the audacity to enter the queen's *loge* at the opera; and Edward Jones, who slipped into Buckingham Palace and lived there for several weeks. These lovers of the queen, and numerous others, were arrested, but once freed they began all over again. Their youthful indiscretions aroused the sarcasm of satirists, but also worry among certain observers, perplexed by the irrational turn of events taken by popular affection for the queen.[86] The collective fascination that Victoria exercised, not only as a sovereign but also as an individual, found a fictional translation in one of the great popular successes of the moment, *The Mysteries of London*, an English adaption of *Les Mystères de Paris*, published in serial form in the press. Criticism of the luxurious life of high society was paralleled with an idealized and melodramatic representation of the private life of Victoria and Prince Albert, spied on by one of the novel's protagonists, Henry Holford. The extremely public visibility of Victoria had a political function. It brought a populist and affective touch to the representation of politics, in contrast with the more classic and elitist life of parliamentarians. But it also had a reverse side: it associated the queen's notoriety with that of actresses. Satirists did not hesitate to represent the life of Victoria as permanent theater and herself as a marionette dancing before the eyes of a bewitched but satisfied public. Once again, journalistic discourse, fictional and satirical, tried to describe and qualify a new phenomenon, one difficult to interpret, but which everyone felt was transforming the exercise of monarchical sovereignty beyond any and all institutional changes.

Among the commentaries aroused by this uncontrolled and devoted affection by the public to Victoria, that of the poet Elizabeth Barrett-Browning is the most interesting because the most spontaneous. She explicitly qualified the queen's situation as the "inconvenience of celebrity." The demands of the public, sometimes excessive, were only a "love-tax" in her eyes, the price to be paid by every public personality, celebrated writers as well as the queen. In the same way that writers should not complain about the fact that interest aroused by their works was displaced onto their private life, the queen had to take responsibility for her popularity and pay the love tax by bowing to the demands of the public and to the expectations of her admirers.[87] Barrett-Browning denoted the celebrity of the queen by calling it "vulgar sovereignty." Appearing as a turn of phrase in a private letter, the sentence has great acuity. It perfectly appreciates the transformation of monarchical legitimacy affected through changes in democratic ideals and visibility worked by the media. The people who applauded Victoria, who read the story of her visits in the press, who were passionate about her family life, or who bought images representing the queen's beauty were not idealized representations of popular sovereignty. They were the public, with all that implies about sometimes excessive, sometimes naïve reactions, those that might seem displaced in regard to the traditional dignity associated with the monarchy, but which were signs of attachment aroused by the new forms of political celebrity. A public figure, both a queen and a celebrated woman, Victoria had to submit to the constraints of publicity, which were the equivalent, in modern times, of the courtly ceremonials of the past.

At this point it is difficult not to think of Marie-Antoinette, who, a half-century earlier, in totally different circumstances, true, had also been a young, beautiful, and admired queen, but one who was unaware of her political obligations and who manifested her celebrity through narcissism instead of transforming it into popularity. Victoria, without knowing it, incarnated Mirabeau's and Barnave's dream, that of a constitutional sovereign agreeing to be popular, contributing in that way to the sensitive affection and emotion that political liberalism was lacking. The comparison between Marie-Antoinette and Lady Di is not so absurd, either, the moment Victoria becomes the missing link between the two.

With Garibaldi, we have a third figure, one who is not a candidate using his popularity to impress voters or the queen accepting "vulgar sovereignty" in order to firm up the national popularity of the monarchy. He was a great international media figure, capable of giving an identifiable face to the revolutionary aspirations of Italian nationalists, crowned with prestige following his romantic exploits and his vaunted idealism. He was, in a way, the first international revolutionary icon.

On the eve of the 1848 revolt in Rome, Garibaldi was already an internationally known public figure. The exploits of his "Italian legion" in the service of Uruguay against Argentina made a great impact in Italy and in the numerous Italian immigrant communities around the world, but even more so with all those were interested in international news. Giuseppe Mazzini and his friends, who believed in the role of the printed word and political propaganda, greatly contributed to creating the image of Garibaldi as a national hero, an embodiment of Italian virtues, the symbiosis of physical courage and moral generosity. This image of him was widely distributed after his participation in the revolution of 1848. A group of portraits was published in the Italian press, then in *L'Illustration* in Paris, and in the *Illustrated London News*, thick black beard, beret, red billowy tunic, belted at the waist.[88] For at least twenty years, this exotic and picturesque silhouette would become a familiar political icon. At the height of the revolution, the *Illustrated London News*, which at the time had a print run of more than sixty thousand copies, even sent its own illustrator to Rome commissioned to reproduce the most striking scenes of the Rome revolution and, in particular, new portraits of Garibaldi.[89] The death of the revolutionary's wife Anita during a retreat across central Italy gave him a touch of romantic tragedy. Many paintings and engravings represented the hero carrying his dying wife in his arms.

With the Expedition of the Thousand, the liberation of Sicily and the kingdom of the Two Sicilies, the celebrity of Garibaldi grew incredibly. The Italian and international press that reported on the war focused on his personality. Biographical stories multiplied, mixing avowed facts with pure fiction, transforming his life into a soap opera, a popular entertainment.[90] Starting in 1850, Giovanni Battista Cuneo, a close friend of Mazzini and comrade in arms of Garibaldi, published a biography that in the following years served as a model. Garibaldi himself published his autobiography in the United States in 1859, later translated into several European languages. In France, Alexandre Dumas did the translation, rewriting certain passages in his own style, in this way blurring the line between popular revolutionary and literary celebrity. Dumas, who had already, in 1850, written an elegy for Garibaldi, went to Sicily in 1860, guaranteeing a sort of war reportage on the side of the Redshirts, identifying their leader with the Count of Monte Cristo.[91] This commitment by one of the most celebrated writers of his time could only contribute to the impact of the affair in France. It is very possible that Garibaldi was aware of all this. His sense of publicity leaves no doubt; even at the height of military operations, he always reserved the best welcome for journalists.

In spite of the success of his picturesque personality, in spite of the fascination raised by the heroic feat of the Redshirts in liberating the south of Italy, Garibaldi remained controversial. Conservatives were hostile to him. For a long time the European public did not know whether to see him as a soldier, a brigand, a dangerous revolutionary, or an Italian patriot. Historians emphasized the heroism that characterized him and it gave the national cause a popular feel. There was immense and elaborate praise for him at this time in France and England, but also in the United States, in Switzerland and in Germany, as well as the Netherlands. *Le Siècle* exclaimed:

> Garibaldi! What a man! What prestige! He has the ability to excite all those who see him, who follow him, all those who get close to him. His name is on everyone's lips, in everyone's heart. He is present everywhere and in everyone's home. The farmers as well as the rich have a copy of his portrait, engraved or lithographed, in their salons or on the farm. Everyone is happy to see close up the hero of the hour, with his lively and piercing eyes seemingly focused on something in the distance.[92]

This "something" was victory for liberated Italy, the country he loved and fought for. But for conservative Catholics, Garibaldi seemed to be somewhere between a dangerous revolutionary and a highway robber. What is striking is the plasticity of his public image. If the orchestration

252

of his celebrity was the object of great political focus, including help from Garibaldi himself, who was always prompt to welcome journalists, it rapidly acquired its own logic, independent of propaganda, and did not necessarily testify to real popularity. Infatuation with the person of Garibaldi was not always a sign of political support for his battles, which no doubt explains in one sense his failures after 1860, even when his celebrity was at its zenith.

Retired on the Isle of Caprera, the hero of the Redshirts carefully managed his withdrawal from political and military combat and took up the role of the new Cincinnatus, which had already done so much for Washington's renown. But the times had changed and Caprera was both a private retirement area and a place that was intensely scrutinized by the public. The *Illustrated London News* hurried to send the artist Frank Vizitelli to the island, where he offered readers on-the-spot graphic accounts and gave them edifying images of Garibaldi fishing at night or feeding his dog. Political exploitation of private retirement became the advertising of intimacy.[93]

One of the most spectacular manifestations of Garibaldi's international celebrity took place when he visited London in 1864. A century earlier, in 1768, Pascal Paoli had been welcomed in London by curious crowds, thanks to the publicity Boswell orchestrated in support of the Corsican.[94] But the arrival of the Italian revolutionary created an enthusiasm unheard of up till then, according to newspapers and other witnesses. A crowd of five hundred thousand people thronged to welcome him, spectators blocked the streets, hung out of windows, climbed up on parapets and roofs in the hopes of seeing him. The Duke of Sutherland's carriage, in which Garibaldi was riding, was blocked, unable to advance for several hours as the crowd was so dense. For the next two weeks, the hero of the Expedition of the Thousand made some public appearances, notably at the opera, and numerous visits to his friends in exile (Mazzini, Herzen) as well as to representatives of the socio-political English elite, from Gladstone to the Prince of Wales, and all the while biographies, songs, portraits, or statues of him made their way through London. The conservatives were worried, the radicals rejoiced, everyone was surprised.

There were many workers in the crowds acclaiming Garibaldi. But a political meaning cannot immediately be attributed to this enthusiasm. Londoners had celebrated Queen Victoria with as much fervor a few years before, at the time of the World's Fair. Besides, interest aroused by Garibaldi could not be reduced to militant socialists or to the most anti-papal Protestants. Not only did the middle class, attracted by reading newspapers, want to see the hero from Caprera, but polite London society was infatuated with his person (being shown around by the Duke of Sutherland and some other great families) and they were "out of their minds" with enthusiasm, according to Lord Granville, the president of the House of Lords.[95] As Garibaldi was leaving, several ladies wrote him passionate letters. This female infatuation amused the newspapers, who saw in it one reason for the excitement aroused by the handsome Italian warrior with his red shirt and his explosive virility. When he visited the opera, according to *The Scotsman*, excitement from the female public was openly erotic.[96]

The international enthusiasm provoked by Garibaldi during the course of his adventures was sometimes referred to in terms of the "cult hero," or even "myth." But this vocabulary is imprecise, more suggestive than descriptive, and no doubt inaccurate. At this point, it should be clear that there is another way to account for the vast renown of someone who was as much contested as passionately defended. If, for a minority of revolutionaries, Garibaldi was a political model to be imitated, he was also a celebrity whose exploits, disappointments, and eventful life permanently captured the attention of a large European public. The essential aspects of his celebrity were to be found in the theatrical and spectacular nature of his feats and in the seduction exercised by his unique persona. Here again, as in the examples of Jackson and Victoria, although very different, the fundamentally heterogenic character of popularity is clear: it comes from political adhesion that can mean political action (votes, loyalty, armed struggle), but also sympathy or curiosity, or even a darker interest, more related to the power of fascination exercised on the public by media visibility and the multiplicity of narratives.

"Celebrities of the Hour"

Celebrity focuses the public curiosity on singular individuals. The success of virtuosos was proof of it: the public no longer came to hear a symphonic orchestra or an opera, but a piano soloist or a diva in recital. It was the same thing for a celebrated writer hassled by readers or a popular hero acclaimed by the crowd. The dissymmetry which ensued was flagrant, but perhaps illusory, because the perspective could be reversed.

Stars are never alone in the public sphere. Each reader, each spectator, has several celebrated persons in mind who form a group of individuals whose common point is their notoriety. This collective dimension is perfectly expressed by the modern, if paradoxical, expression "people," used to designate celebrated persons. "People" are not "the people," but they are numerous; they constitute at least the plural incarnation of a moment, if not a social or elite group. Their existence, their appearance and their disappearance, is in rhythm with media time, that of the news, an infinite renewal of the present. Beyond the desire for intimacy at a distance, linking a group of fans to a particular star, the curiosity of the public almost always seems to lean indistinctly toward a group of celebrities. The term "celebrity," which now designates an individual and no longer a condition, was first used in the plural. The Émile Littré dictionary presents this usage as a neologism even today and offers as an example: "celebrities of the hour." This expression focuses both on the plurality of celebrities and on their capacity to mark the passage of time by their turnover. To share a common curiosity for a group of public figures, exhibited individually, gives the feeling of being part of one's time, a way to be modern.

The expression "celebrities of the hour" could be found in newspapers of that era, emphasizing even more strongly the sometimes fleeting newsworthiness of some celebrated figures. This was the title that Louis Jourdain and Taxile Delord, two republican journalists, gave to a collection of portraits and biographies they published in 1860 and in which Garibaldi figured alongside Abd el-Kader and other European sovereigns, but also George Sand, Lamartine, Delacroix, and Rossini.[97] Once again, editorial layouts put political men and artists on the same level, with the common goal of arousing public curiosity. The expressions – "contemporary celebrities," "celebrities of the hour" – clearly express the idea that these persons, although very individualized, are perceived as a group, with rather blurry edges. The media system of celebrity not only produced an affective attachment to a particular figure, it also fed a collective curiosity of low or medium intensity. To be interested in the life of "celebrities of the hour," sometimes distractedly, sometimes with more excitement, was to be a contemporary, to be caught up in the rhythm of the news , which dealt with the marriage of an actress, as well as the outbreak of war, rumors of a scandal, or parliamentary debates.

This same principle was found in group biographies of contemporaries, those then in vogue. Whereas in the preceding century biographical dictionaries only referred to the dead, the Revolution gave free rein to satirical publications, like the *Almanach de nos grands hommes* by Rivarol, which made fun of the unjustified celebrity of mediocre writers, as he saw it, or *Dictionnaires des girouettes*, which railed against politicians who rallied to successive regimes.[98] In the first half of the nineteenth century, group biographies increased in response to the "great avidity" with which the public read biographies having to do with "contemporaries."[99] These collections aroused fierce editorial competitiveness. The *Biographie nouvelle des contemporains* undertook to draw up a list of celebrated men who, since the Revolution, "had acquired celebrity through their writing, their feats, their virtue or their crimes." Later,

Gustave Vaporeau was successful with his *Dictionnaire universel des contemporains*, which he published, he said, to satisfy the "legitimate curiosity" of the public. Next to these substantial works, others were happy just to surf along on the satirical wave, such as *Le Rivarol de 1842, ou Dictionnaire satirique des célébrités contemporaines*.[100]

In the same way, portraits of celebrities were often collected in a volume, in the form of a gallery of celebrated people, thus highlighting the plurality of social usages to which celebrity was put. Far from simply being support for imagined affective relationships – as in the symbolic though fictive case of Modeste Mignon – they more often fed curiosity, allowing a group of faces to be looked at together, constituting, in a real sense, an *imaginary* collective. Those who scrutinized the faces of celebrities were seeking less to penetrate secrets than to feel they belonged to a public by appropriating this imaginary museum of public figures.

The taste for caricature was part of this group relationship to celebrities. If newspaper readers during the July Monarchy loved caricatures so much, it was because it permitted them to have a playful relationship with a group of political, literary, and artistic persons whose faces were known. Besides a distant relationship with celebrities, the caricature was based on the principle of minimal deformation of a previously known image. The case of Byron is again striking. The massive reproductions and imitations of the first portraits familiarized the public with the more or less accurate theme of a young man wearing a long white scarf and sporting abundant black hair. This image created numerous derivatives, notably in the form of caricatures or even hidden faces, a game then in fashion in which the face of Byron was concealed in the middle of a landscape, in the leaves of a tree, or in the clouds.[101] The portrait was no longer merely used as an aid for a subjective projection, but the symbol of a shared cultural vision where an image was immediately associated with a contemporary.

With these collections of caricatures, another line was crossed. Each figure was highly individualized and integrated into a background that changed continually and which gave it meaning. At the beginning of the Second Empire, Félix Nadar was the uncontested master of this caricature gallery, bringing together all the celebrities of the day. In the *Journal pour rire*, he published his "magic lantern," where authors, musicians, artists, all the "illustrations" (performers) of the cultural world paraded, as the saying went. Every photo plate had several figures along with a biographical commentary, the celebrity figures shown as popular spectacle, similar to panoramas and other dioramas, which greatly amused the Parisians.[102] They were both individualized and presented collectively, the attraction deriving from gathering the celebrities together in the same temporal space as the curious pubic.

256

After this success, Nadar, in 1852, started the project that would make him the most famous, that of the Nadar Panthéon, four large lithographs combining the eight hundred best-known cultural personalities (writers, musicians, journalists, artists, etc.), "eight hundred full-length portraits of all our celebrities,"[103] according to the write-up in one pamphlet. In the end, only the plate with writers and journalists was published, but it was a real graphic exploit; Nadar had brought together on one page two hundred and fifty personalities expected to go down in history. His Panthéon was written about in every newspaper, vaunted by publicists, promoted by a campaign of publicity handouts and eye-catching announcements, and even given as presents to readers of the *Figaro.* The work was too luxurious and difficult to be a commercial success, but it brought critical acclaim. Unlike the Montagne Sainte-Geneviève Panthéon, Nadar's Panthéon was explicitly a paean to the present, with "illustrations" of the nineteenth century drawn by a contemporary and worthy of all the great men of the past. This gathering together of the celebrities of the hour, even with all the skewed traits that Nadar gave them, leaned toward collective narcissism.

In the following years, the caricatures continued to have success, in spite of the beginnings of photography. Nadar published a series called "Contemporary Faces," a collection of biographical parodies ornamented with portraits drawn from the Nadar Panthéon, before collaborating with Philippon's *Journal amusant* and publishing a series called "Nadar Contemporaries" (1858–62). Each newspaper carried a full-page portrait on the cover, followed by a biography inside, often written with the help of the models themselves. For the first time, full-length portraits of celebrities made the front page of a newspaper.

Toward a New Age of Celebrity

With Nadar's contemporary caricatures, all grouped together, as with the media visibility of Garibaldi or Jenny Lind's grand tour of the United States, a period was reached which corresponded to some extent with the years 1850–60. All the themes of celebrity were accentuated and appeared to announce a new age, one in which the existence of public figures who drew public attention like a magnet was viewed not as intriguing or shocking but as a characteristic trait of modern society. Every periodization has its arbitrary aspects insofar as many transformations are slow, irregular, and incomplete. Garibaldi in many ways was the archetypal romantic hero and his worldwide celebrity echoed that of Washington and Napoleon, and even that of Byron, whose struggle for the liberty of Greece so greatly marked the romantic generation.

Nonetheless, the impressive newspaper coverage of the 1860 war, the appearance of photography, the role of the telegraph in transmission of the news, were all signs of transformations that were taking Europe and America into a new era of mass communication and which would rapidly expand the system of celebrity.

The press above all accelerated the change. The existence of illustrations had already in the 1840s allowed for better diffusion of celebrity images. In the second half of the century, print runs exploded because of the massive literacy rate among populations, the distribution by railroad, and the appearance of new technologies, in particular the rotary cylinder invented in England in the 1850s and introduced into France in 1867. The revolution in journalism also affected new publishing practices in market capitalism. If a symbol of this entrance of the press into the era of mass culture is necessary, *Le Petit Journal* by Moses Millaud offers a suitable example. Founded in 1863, he sold his paper at five centimes each, which broke with the more expensive cost of newspapers in the first half of the century, but Millaud also broke with the practice of subscriptions. His was a non-political newspaper with entertaining news items, quickly selling two hunded and fifty thousand copies a day, then a million in 1891. It favored current news, petty crime, and the life of celebrities, news stories capable of drawing the largest possible readership. The model was imitated, then replaced by *Le Petit Parisien* (1876), *Le Matin* (1883), and the *Journal* (1892).

In 1914, French dailies, Parisian and provincial, sold a total of 5.5 million copies every day.[104] They became an object of daily consumption, even among the working class, and profoundly changed relationships to the news, which was presented in a more spectacular, more emotional way. Politics was given less space, except for the Parisian columns, which attracted readers. Next to the miscellaneous news items, the lives of celebrities successfully filled columns like "Rumors from Paris" in the *Figaro*: "Indiscretion is elevated to an art form; one reads the rumors to be in the know about the scandal sheets," someone said at the time.[105] In the United States, where a veritable press for the masses on a national scale developed in the last third of the century, along the lines of the *New York Herald*, founded early in 1835 but which had an exponential growth, newspapers dedicated more and more space to the lives of celebrities. In the 1890s, new forms of journalism appeared, focused on making the lives of celebrated people public, dedicated to giving readers the feeling that they were sharing an intimacy: reports, interviews, indiscretions.[106]

Nothing after that seemed to escape publicity. Mme de Girardin, who successfully started one of the first social columns in 1836, could claim to marvel at the moral potential of such visibility: "The public will be the earthly judge who we always have before our eyes like pious souls have before them the sacred Judge who must condemn or absolve; yes, for non-believer souls, publicity will replace confession."[107] The ideal of publicity, inherited from the Enlightenment, was enlarged to include the life of celebrities, with the guarantee of morality. Mme de Girardin's successors in the second half of the century had a hard time showing themselves to be so fanciful in the face of an increase in indiscretions and scandals; newspaper columns about the life of celebrities remained marked by tension, more or less explicit, between the desire to feed public curiosity – and thus increase sales – and the assertion that they were moral censors. Mme de Girardin added a second justification in which the publicizing of private life appeared to be an inherent constraint on the status of celebrities:

> Oh, what a mystery! Everyone dreams of celebrity, and everybody fears publicity. Explain this inconsistency; one is but sister of the other, and they must sooner or later be joined in spite of what you think; and it is just because they are inseparable that we must get in the habit of their alliance and understand that it is silly to be alarmed, since this alliance threatens only those one can sweet talk. Because, in the end, we simply talk about what interests the public.

It is in this context that Gabriel Tarde developed his theory of the public, insisting on the importance of the newspaper reader and the effects of imitation at a distance, often not consicously, which constituted a public. For Tarde, who was reacting to the very negative talk at the time about "crowds," a public was the collective group form characteristic of modern societies, governed by fashion-imitation rather than by custom-imitation, by the influence of contemporaries, in the short run; it was governed by news rather than the authority of the past, the long run of tradition. Or, in other words, it was "the habit, which is becoming daily more general, of taking examples that are near at hand, in the present, instead of those that belong exclusively to the past."[108] The public was neither an instance of critical discussion nor an irrational crowd, but a collective made up of fluctuating desires and beliefs, itself fed by the power of the media. It was both a purely spiritual community, in the sense that it only existed by the influence that each person exercised over others from a distance, and a commercial clientele, where the desire of each person was fed by the desire of the other person.[109] The theoretical elaboration that runs through all of Tarde's work was not only a sociological undertaking, it was also a demonstration of contemporary reflexivity in regard to new forms of modern media, the effects of which began to be visible at the turn of the century. It happened precisely at the moment when social sciences, at the turn of the twentieth century, took the place of literature and philosophy as a means of studying the complexity of the world.[110]

The development of photography was contemporary with the rise of newspapers for the masses. Daguerrotype, invented in 1839, only produced one copy at a time. But with the invention of collotype, and then other kinds of negatives, photography entered into the era of reproduction and diffusion. The impact of photography on the image of celebrities was firstly linked to the success of the portrait "visiting card" (3 × 3"), invented by André Disdéri in Paris in 1854, a vogue that swept through all of Europe as well as the United States after 1860. The principle was based on the cheap production of photographs printed on a plate of eight images, then marketed as single units on little cardboard cards. Infatuation with visiting cards was widespread. In Paris, by the end of the 1850s, people rushed to photography studios existing along the boulevards, Disdéri's on Boulevard des Italiens, but also that of Pierre Petit or even Nadar, who had slowly given up caricature in favor of photography. In London, Vienna, St. Petersburg, New York, and Philadelphia, photography studios became fashionable places for both society and show business.

The photo "visiting card" was immediately put to use in massive reproductions of celebrity images. These served as a marketing strategy for photography studios, which showed them in the window, and they were also a commercial product, printed and reproduced en masse. Heads of state and political personalities were the first in line. Disdéri sold photos of Napoleon III; John Mayall, in his *Royal Album* of 1860, published a photograph collection of Victoria and Prince Albert that was so successful he could not fill the demand and was quickly overwhelmed by a flood of imitations.[111] Gustave Le Gray, one of the first Parisian photographers, made a trip to Palermo with Dumas, at the time of the Expedition of the Thousand, to photograph Garibaldi.[112] All the stars of the period, writers, actors, artists, had a photo "visiting card," often sold by the thousands. These photographs were easy to collect in a series. Certain publishers gathered them together, offering a *Galerie des hommes du jour*, made up of photographs by Pierre Petit, or the *Galerie contemporaine*, a weekly publication that included in each issue a photo portrait and a biography.[113] Photographs that sold individually were often collected in albums to be leafed through like the one that entertained Maxime and Renée, characters in Zola's *La Curée* (*The Kill*) (1872):

> Maxime also brought these ladies photographs. He had actresses' photographs in all his pockets, and even in his cigar-case. From time to time he

cleared them out and placed these ladies in the album that lay about on the furniture in the drawing room, which already contained the photographs of Renée's friends. There were men's photographs there too, Monsieur de Rozan, Simpson, de Chibray, and de Mussy, as well as actors, writers, and deputies, who had come somehow to swell the collection. A strangely mixed society, a symbol of the jumble of people and ideas that moved through Renée's and Maxime's lives.

Celebrated actresses and writers were side by side with kept women and politicians, but also friends: public figures were in this way made familiar, they were part of a heroic life, in a minor way at least, of diverse interest, cyclical and of low intensity. It was boredom that motivated leafing through the album: "Whenever it rained or they felt bored, this album was their great subject of conversation. They always ended up looking at it. Renée opened it with a yawn, for the hundredth time perhaps. Then her curiosity would reawaken, the young man came and leant behind her." Both of them scrutinize details of the figures, for example the hair of one "skinny, red-haired celebrity nicknamed the Crayfish,"[114] and imagine spending the night with so and so, various represented people, from the archbishop of Paris to fashionable actresses. Besides this worldly or bourgeois usage of the albums, there existed a more popular consumption of celebrity photographs encouraged by the massive increase in cheap imitations. In England, three or four million photographs of Victoria were sold between 1860 and 1862.

From the moment of its invention, photography became an industry. In 1868, Paris already had 365 photography studios.[115] The photo "visiting card" was a paradoxical object: it spread the image of celebrities far and wide, but it also made portraits more accessible for a part of the urban middle class that rushed to photography studios. The celebrity image both increased and became banal at the same time, which soon caused violent criticism, photography attacked as a vulgar representation of reality, an unworthy rival to art, and the taste for portrait photos the sign of public vacuity and a desire for visibility by celebrities. As early as 1859, Baudelaire criticized photo portraits in "Le public moderne et la photographie." Eight years later, Barbey d'Aurevilly was even more vituperative about the "vain knicknackery of a cheap junk century." He acerbically denounced "shop window celebrity," the desire for exhibitionism, to have one's portrait visible in the public sphere: "The intelligent and charming glory of photography, to attain shop window celebrity, an ugly name written under an ugly face, badly reproduced by a horrid procedure, what a godsend! The delight of misplaced vanity."[116]

This profusion of images gave a new twist to the visual culture of celebrity. The first court decision, considered today to be the origin of individual rights concerning the private image, was rendered in 1858 in order to forbid the publication of a photograph of the French actress Rachel on her death bed.[117] For a whole generation of writers, the development of photography created a dividing line between those who seized on the tool to multiply their image, using it as a means to visibility, like Hugo and Dumas, and those, to the contrary, who chafed against it. Hugo cleverly played with the new techniques to stay visible in Paris in spite of his exile. Certain photos, like those of Nadar and then Carjat, introduced into the public sphere an immediately recognizable representation of the great writer, the tired face framed with a thick beard and white hair. Endlessly reproduced in every medium, these photos played an important role in the immense popularity of Hugo during the last years of his life, when he returned from exile, incarnating the triumph of the republic.[118] On the other hand, Dickens, who, in the early 1860s, was the most photographed Englishman after the royal family, tried in vain to supervise the reproduction of his image.[119]

Gustave Flaubert had a visceral rejection of photography, which included a criticism of the principle behind this new technique, similar to Baudelaire's, and a refusal to let images of himself be circulated, hardly surprising for an author who had made the invisibility of the author a key to his novel aesthetic. One journalist described the consequences of this attitude: "Journalists do not know his face. He thinks it is enough to give his writings to the public and he has always held himself apart from the popularity game, disdaining the noisy publicity of hawked flyers, unofficial advertising and photography exhibits in the windows of cigarette shops, next to a famous criminal, a prince so-and-so, and a girl celebrity."[120] After refusing for a long time to have his photo taken ("I will never consent to having my photo taken," he proudly wrote to Louise Collet), Flaubert ended by giving in, but only gave his photo to his close friends and family, and always refused to have it published ("My features are not for sale"). To readers who asked for a photo, he refused to concede. "Everybody has a passing whim. Mine is to refuse all photographs of myself," he wrote in 1877 to an admirer.[121]

Guy de Maupassant, faithful to the Flaubertian model, refused for a long time, in his turn, to be photographed. "I have made an absolute rule to never let my portrait be published as long as I can stop it. Exceptions will only be made by accident. Our works belong to the public, but not our faces."[122] This was a suggestive sentence that Mercier would not have disavowed a century earlier, one that sounds like a rear-guard action but that a few rare authors in the twentieth century brought up to date. After finally accepting, Maupassant repented after a rapid-fire circulation of his photo. He threatened to sue the publisher Charpentier in 1880, before finally resigning himself to its dissemination. But the idea of a photographic image returned to haunt his work, notably *Le Horla*, creating anxiety about the publication of any biographical aspect of his life.

The invention of photography had a considerable impact in the long run, because it allowed for reproduction on a grand scale of the face of celebrities, giving the impression of absolute veracity. It transformed the image of celebrities and at the same time assured the resemblance between the images and an individual, whereas the profusion of engraved drawings in the preceding years had led to an increase in images that sometimes had no resemblance at all to the person. However, the immediate effects of photography should not be exaggerated, since reproduction on a grand scale was quite difficult for some time. It was not until 1891, for example, that newspapers published the first printed illustrations directly from photographs. And up until World War I, news drawings continued to occupy a large place in press illustrations.[123] It was not until the period between the two wars that photography really took over the press, thanks to offset printing, in the same way the appearance of numerous photographs of Garibaldi, starting in 1860, contributed to fix the image of the de Caprera hero but did not fundamentally change the visual theme of his celebrity, already established in the preceding decade by numerous portraits and reports with graphics published in illustrated newspapers.[124] The example of Nadar is significant: he did not go abruptly from drawing to photography, but continued to market his portrait engravings and did not stop working at producing his Panthéon, even after becoming a celebrated photographer.[125]

This visibility of celebrity was now used in publicity campaigns. Starting in 1891, Angelo Mariani, inventor of the famous "coca wine," published albums called "Contemporary Faces," where each portrait was accompanied by several promotional lines written by a star promoting the wine that Mariani was successfully marketing. These *Albums Mariani* were enormously popular and were even sold in the form of cheap postcards.[126] They referenced the collected portraits and biographies of contemporary celebrities but with an explicit view toward marketing. Artists, politicians, writers, all praised the merits of Mariani's wine. The image of celebrities helped sell things, and they themselves profited through increased notoriety, a case of wine, and, it seems, a financial reward.

The rise of mass media, the success of photography, and new marketing strategies were only some of the most salient aspects of a group of social and cultural transformations, to which must be added the rise of more modern forms of advertising, as well as the increase in urban spectacles. These shows fed a collective fascination for the new way of life of elites and a shared consciousness about the prestige of "modern life."

The Grévin Museum, which opened its doors in Paris in 1882, was both a place of highly popular spectacles, a sort of real-life newspaper where various current news items were represented in the form of wax mini-plays, and also a shrine to celebrity culture. The principal attractions of the museum, in the first room, were currently fashionable celebrities. At first titled "High Society at Grévin's," it was quickly changed to "Salons of Parisian celebrities."[127] Visitors could walk around among the most celebrated people of the day, as though they knew them. Shows like those proposed by the Grévin Museum, in common with the press and photography, offered intense media-hyped representations of celebrities, as well as very realistic ones. The effect of reality was well researched: people could touch the figures in the same way they could observe in photographs details of the face, even if the models remained at a distance and inaccessible.

Sarah Bernhardt perfectly embodied this increased visibility of stars in the second half of the nineteenth century. By the end of the 1860s, she was enormously successful, at a time when the French theater, great popular entertainment, also became a culture consumer product, largely exported throughout Europe and into America.[128] During the Comédie-Française tours in London in the 1870s, it was Bernhardt whom the public came to see, at the same time her eccentricities and her desire for freedom were in the headlines. In 1880, she broke with the Comédie-Française and made a tour of the United States, which was a great triumph. Thirty years after Jenny Lind, the French tragedian aroused excitement that persisted long after her return to France and which led her to return to America several different times. She embodied a new model of femininity, mixing classicism, sentimentalism, romanticism, Parisian charm, exuberance, and eroticism. In the eyes of American society at the end of the nineteenth century, during the "Gilded Age" of economic growth and leisure society, Bernhardt was the symbol of a new era full of promise.[129]

In spite of her international success, which led her to undertake several world tours, from Australia to Latin America, Bernhardt was also a patriotic celebrity. She sought to embody France, displaying her strong anti-German feelings, hardly original, at the start of her career, in the middle of the War of 1870, and then by her choice of favorite roles (*La Fille de Roland*, *L'Aiglon*). Her immense success in foreign countries was linked to the fact that she embodied French culture and theater.[130] She was as successful in classical roles, *Phèdre* or *Andromaque*, as in popular pieces like *Fédora* by Victorien Sardou, written especially for her.

Bernhardt's success aroused not only admiration from the crowds, but also a flood of criticism, caricatures, and ridicule. Maupassant, allergic, as we have seen, to the dynamics of celebrity, attacked her virulently as well as the enthusiasm she aroused in her public the minute she arrived in Le Havre in 1881, after her American tour. He denounced her excessive self-promotion in his *Gaulois* column, both the advertisement and the spectacle, which used every possible theatrical and inauthentic way to create a public figure, summarized by the writer as "ham acting."

> Really, really, this is too much; we must have lost our sense of the grotesque and our ability to laugh not to have danced up and down with hilarity at what the newspapers reported about the fantastic details of Sarah Bernhardt's arrival in Le Havre. "Hip, hip, hurrah!" they cried all along the jetty; never has ham acting, a French vice, this crazy excitement, this particular madness of the crowds, the gullible enthusiasm of bourgeois suckers offered to the world such an example of the ridiculous. [...] It's stupefying. These people were moved, these people were really moved: women cried real tears.[131]

The column is funny, but completely on the attack. The irony in no way encourages debate; it simply contrasts lost good sense to "crazy excitement," and to the advertising and ham acting that constitutes celebrity culture. "Ham acting is king," deplored Maupassant, pell-mell denouncing the credulous sentimentality of the public, the absence of authenticity of the stars, and the commercial interests of the press. By disdaining the "stupidity of the crowds" and the "gullible bourgeoisie," Maupassant associated himself with the artistic position inherited from Flaubert and Baudelaire, but he also showed that critics and criticism had surpassed popular superstition or bourgeois money. Above all, it was a matter of a common culture, from which the writer withdrew in order to better pummel it with contempt. This common culture was neither wise nor popular, but a mass culture produced by the media and by the culture industry. Its consumers made up the public, the same public that Baudelaire compared to a dog that "one should never present with delicate perfumes which annoy it, but instead carefully chosen garbage."[132] We should not see in Bernhardt's popularity or in the satire of ham acting something radically new. Neither the American tours made by European stars, nor the enthusiasm of the crowds, nor the increase in images were a new phenomenon: Jenny Lind, Byron, Liszt, had already experienced the celebrity culture in the first half of the century. And before them, Garrick, Rousseau, and Talma had been welcomed by curious and enthusiastic audiences, even if the celebrity system was still in its early phase. The irony of Maupassant, who seems so modern to us, with his denunciation of the creation of celebrities through publicity, adds nothing to the analysis that Heine made forty years earlier of "Lisztomania." In certain ways, Maupassant was even somewhat behind Samuel Johnson or Louis Sébastien Mercier, not to mention Rousseau, whose subtle analysis had shed light on the intensely ambivalent relationship that celebrities had to their public. In this area, the dividing lines were never straightforward and profound, the historical points always blurry. The essential thing is not to precisely date the changes but to see that roughly a century before, starting from the middle of the eighteenth century, social and cultural systems caused a celebrity culture to emerge that was both a group of practices and a series of discourses, platitudes, and debates. After the 1860s, this culture took on a new dimension, stimulated by what has conveniently been called the birth of mass culture. The second stage of celebrity will effectively start at the beginning of the twentieth century, symbolized, of course, by the movies.

CONCLUSION

The cinema was born at the same time as the twentieth century, and it turned out to be a formidable popular entertainment, as well as a dream factory. No doubt everything has been said about the ability of the movie industry to create new celebrities, those figures who are intensely showcased but nonetheless ephemeral: stars. Sarah Bernhardt embodied the transition from stage celebrity to screen star, making several movies after 1900, including a documentary about her life on Belle Isle. Between the two wars, a new generation of actors and actresses emerged who did not start in the theater and who would reach the top of the star-system: Mary Pickford, "America's sweetheart," but also Douglas Fairbanks, Lilian Gish, Charlie Chaplin, Rudolph Valentino, Greta Garbo. The death of Valentino in 1926 caused a media storm and a collective outcry: according to the newspapers, more than a hunded thousand people gathered in front of the hospital where he died and several women were driven to suicide by their despair. How can such a collective and apparently irrational phenomenon be understood? Thinking of the magic aroused by Garbo's face, Roland Barthes said: "Garbo still belongs to that moment in cinema when capturing the human face still plunged audiences into the deepest ecstasy, when one literally lost oneself in a human image as one would in a philtre."[1] It is tempting to emphasize the particularity of the cinema, the close-ups that make a face so present and produce, as never before, an impression of intimacy, while the star remains in the distance, inaccessible. Many authors, since Edgar Morin, like to imagine that the cinema invented modern forms of celebrity, giving spectators new gods and inventing a mythology out of whole cloth. But it was not like this at all. If, from the start, movies could arouse such enthusiasm for the stars, it was not because of the new character of films as spectacle, but because the culture of celebrity had been growing for the last century and a half.

Cinema not only made stars. Many movies, some of them works of art, were about celebrity. Not only a popular entertainment, cinema was also a form of artistic expression: from *Limelight* to *Sunset Boulevard*, from *La Dolce Vita* to *Celebrity*, great directors portrayed the pitiless world of stars and the dizzying heights of celebrity. Who can forget the look of Norma Desmond, convinced that the newspaper cameras that are there when she is arrested are studio lights meant to capture her return to the screen? Or Sylvia's night walk, happy even for a few minutes to escape the paparazzi in Rome? As an epilogue, I would like to focus on one of these films, less well known than the others, perhaps: *A Face in the Crowd*, directed by Elia Kazan in 1957, a year after the success of *On the Waterfront* and the same year as Roland Barthes' text about Garbo.

The film tells the story of a drifter from Arkansas, Larry "Lonesome" Rhodes, noticed by the woman producer of a local radio station looking for someone unknown. Rhodes' performance is a great success and marks the beginning of a spectacular rise: after he is given a radio show, he goes on television, first in Memphis, then on a national channel. He becomes one of the most popular moderators in the country, accumulating riches and celebrity. His success is quick, unexpected, exhilarating. He uproots in a matter of weeks from misery and homelessness and is propelled into the upper echelons of New York society. His weekly show is watched by millions, a close-up of his face is on the cover of magazines, marketing agencies snap up his services. This spectacular rise, as in all good Hollywood stories, is soon followed by a fall no less spectacular: having become a megalomaniac, angry and paranoid, Rhodes isolates himself, takes refuge in grandiloquence and cynicism, and collapses when the young woman who launched his career reveals his real personality. The end of the film pathetically shows Rhodes ruined, alone and unhappy, fleeing the symbols of his success.

Beyond this classic story of a rise and fall, the film brilliantly describes the mechanisms and the stakes of celebrity in the American consumer society of the 1950s, transformed by the magnitude of the new audio-visual media forms of radio and television. The marketing issues are omnipresent. Rhodes acts in publicity spots, his celebrity, from the beginning of the film, at the service of announcers. Kazan, doing research for the film, met with publicity agents from Madison Avenue, and he amused himself by making a fictive series of commercials which appeared in the movie.[2] The film cleverly mixes two dimensions of advertising: the advertisement itself, communication aimed at marketing, and the way in which an anonymous individual, a "face in the crowd," according to the title, becomes a public figure, known by everyone. One aspect of Rhodes' success is his way of making fun of the products he is supposed to be promoting, this iconoclastic freedom guaranteeing the notoriety of the brand, and, ultimately, an increase in sales. It then becomes difficult to say if Rhodes' celebrity as a show host is manipulated by the announcers or if it is a result of this exposure.

If the program audience is made up of consumers, it is also made up of voters. *A Face in the Crowd* was the most overtly political of all Kazan's movies. In the second part, Rhodes becomes the consultant to a senator who wants to run for president. Rhodes advises him with frank brutality to create a media persona in order to become popular. When the senator invokes the "respect" due a politician, Rhodes responds that ordinary people buy beer because they like it not because they respect it. This way of reducing politics to the immediate satisfaction of the consumer is meant to show Rhodes' vulgarity, but it also reveals a future for democracy based on advertising which the rise in political marketing has only confirmed. It corresponds to the feeling of power that overwhelms the media host, persuaded that through power he can get anything he wants from his public. Wanting to transform his cathodic celebrity into political popularity, he even at one point dreams of a political career. The film shows a certain vague anxiety in the face of transformations taking place in politics, less threatened by classical Caesarism than by a new form of populism, that of marketing, reducing politicians to the status of commercial products aimed at the simple tastes of ordinary people and giving popular stars an unprecedented power to manipulate public opinion. What assures Rhodes' success is his average-man identity, that he talks like the people and addresses himself to them, offering a form of "grass-root wisdom," as proclaimed on the cover of a magazine, shown in close-up.

Could his success be a metaphor for a new democratic era, the precursor of which began to be felt at the end of the 1950s in America? Did Kazan anticipate the success of Ronald Reagan, a former actor putting his fame and his television mastery at the service of a conservative political message, organized around the simplicity of the people? The Kazan film explicitly laid out the menace of popular opinion controlled by a demagogue. Rhodes repeats: "I am a force," to the point that he worries those close to him and they end by betraying him in the name of the public good. Celebrity is shown not only as illegitimate in the cultural domain; it becomes dangerous when undue power is exercised in the public sphere. Political criticism of the effects of celebrity and the dangers of media-constructed democracy is the most explicit ideological thread in the film.

Kazan's worry in 1957 was a response to the growing takeover by new audiovisual media, with a consequent confusing of commercial, cultural, and political issues, given the influence of publicity. A critical discourse began to take shape, denouncing the destructive effects of various kinds of media, its capacity to create from whole cloth factitious stars and put them on show before a passive and alienated public. In the decade that followed, this criticism found some of its strongest formulations in Daniel Boorstin (1961) and Guy Debord (1967), while Andy Warhol enunciated his famous prophesy in 1968 about the fifteen minutes of fame that would be promised to everyone.[3] And it is in this context that one finds nostalgia for the golden age of Hollywood, as visible in Barthes as in Morin (1957), and for the bourgeois public sphere developed by Habermas in 1962. It is this critical agitation that we inherited and that comes up again when we are stunned by the abuses of reality television or when new celebrities appear out of nowhere on the internet. Most of the dangers that threaten us regularly (celebrity politics, the influence of advertising, the rapid and ephemeral success of pseudo-stars) were already strongly denounced a half-century ago.

This criticism of celebrity, however, has often remained ambiguous, as seen in the Kazan film. Who is to blame? The overly ambitious stars? The media? The public itself? Rhodes, in the end, is more pathetic than really dangerous. When he thinks he is manipulating opinion, he is himself manipulated by the "General," a rich patrician who calls on him to launch the campaign of a senator in the same way one launches a brand name. Rhodes is only a tool, adapted to the new media, controlled by the political power of traditional elites. Though his visibility seems to give him power, it is only *trompe-l'oeil*, false and ephemeral. His celebrity is used by others: managers, producers, industrialists, press barons, journalists. And they replace him as fast as they welcome him.[4] Even if Kazan is careful to make Rhodes unlikeable, the film suggests, just beneath the surface, that he is primarily the victim of a profound psychological imbalance. His celebrity shows him an outsized image of himself, all the while pushing him to greatly individualize the seduction he exercises up to the point of forgetting that his success is the result of collective work. Like numerous public figures, Rhodes is confronted by an immense and curious public that maintains a long-distance intimacy with him, as well as a weakening of the social and affective bonds with his closest friends. Rather than embodying the demagogue he thinks he is who influences his public, he is the plaything of a public that takes a shine to him but can, from one day to another, move on to other entertainers, other stars, leaving him beaten and hopeless, deprived of prestige that was only a mirage. As the film shows, Rhodes is selling his own image, but he is also, consequently, a consumer product, perishable and quickly out of date.

This ambivalent type of critique is always present in most of the current discourse about the excesses of a media-hyped society. It is explained by the complexity of the celebrity system that challenges some of the essential values of modern society: the desire for social climbing, legitimacy of the public and its verdicts, the role of media in organizing a democratic public sphere. As we have seen throughout this book, the various issues inherent in this system did not suddenly appear in the 1950s. They took on a new form, more radical no doubt, more focused on the presumed capacity of audiovisual media to sell the public stars they have fabricated. But if the intensity and the layout of the debates have varied, the essential issues were identified in the second half of the eighteenth century. The capacity of the press to raise public figures to a sometimes ephemeral celebrity, the exposure of private lives, the sometimes superficial, sometimes excessive curiosity of the public, the leveling of cultural values, the dangers of political popularity and vulgar sovereignty: all these elements that constitute a criticism of celebrity were progressively brought into play between 1750 and 1850.

My objective in writing this book was not to recount the lives of celebrities in the eighteenth century as a study in itself, or even to write a history of celebrity, but to show that the phenomena that are considered to be the result of recent technological and cultural revolutions, even annoying symbols of our postmodern vacuity, have roots that were sown two centuries before the invention of television, and were abundantly thought about, analyzed, discussed. Concepts that we use today, like the idea of a public, are themselves inherited from these debates, even if the social sciences have since co-opted them. There is no room here to deplore this situation; it is in the condition of the historian, when he gives up the privilege of a fictive distance or an artificial language, to work only with words that carry in them traces of the history he is studying. Given this handicap, he is free to make a strength out of it, to draw from it a surplus of ideas to think about. I forced myself as I wrote this book to hold firmly to two distinct demands: to construct celebrity as an analytical tool, capable of designating and qualifying certain forms of notoriety; and to understand the way in which the term itself, and the phenomena it designated, had been thought about by contemporaries, through moral essays, newspaper columns, aphorisms, memoirs, and unclassifiable texts, as well as through dramatic works like *Rousseau Judge of Jean-Jacques*.

Since the time of Rousseau and Garrick, or even Liszt and Bernhardt, up until our own day, many things, given the evidence, seem to have changed. The genealogical search that I made did not lead me to reject these changes, to neglect those introduced by the cinema, by television and by mass culture. But it did allow for nuances concerning the rupture too generously attributed to them. Throughout this book, I have tried to address the parallels with our current situation, less anachronistic than they might seem. Rousseau and Sarah Siddons, when they denounced

271

the constraints of celebrity, did they not use arguments quite similar to those used by stars today who complain about indiscretions by admirers and threats to their private life? Newspapers that denounced these complaints as too glib and used the public nature of celebrity life to give themselves permission to expose the private lives of celebrities, did this not foreshadow yellow journalism? The crowd welcoming Jenny Lind in New York or Sarah Bernhardt in Le Havre, was this that much different from the welcome shown Madonna or George Clooney today? Scandalized moralizers of our day, targeting the effects of this excessive and displaced curiosity, are they really saying anything other than what was said by Mercier, Chamfort, or Johnson? Criticism of the star-system that accompanied the success of film or theater stars in the twentieth century, was it not already prepared for by Maupassant denouncing universal ham acting or when Heine made fun of Liszt's public? For a long hundred years, starting in the middle of the eighteenth century, the mechanisms of celebrity progressively imposed themselves, little by little, as culture in the cities developed, along with spectacles, newspapers, images, and new marketing methods. The culture of celebrity created a topic, a group of commonplaces, icons, examples, all of them allowing the new phenomenon to be thought about.

Chronological displacement was not the only result of my study. This is only interesting in that it allows us to see what might have remained invisible, masked by the evidence of our contemporary certitudes. Notably, it reveals the ambivalence of celebrity as a value, both desirable and feared, valued and contested. And although celebrity was not a form of grandeur characteristic of democratic and media-driven modern societies, as glory had been in aristocratic societies, it did, however, have certain advantages. Fundamentally democratic, because anyone could attain it; perfectly adapted to modern individualism, encouraging empathy with the individual more than a social type; based entirely on the vote of the majority – did celebrity not possess all the necessary elements needed to become the modern form of social prestige? Some, indeed, consider that this is what it has become, that visibility is now the new capital accumulated by international elites, by celebrities. But the reality is that celebrity as a value has always been suspect and often attacked. We know the accusations by heart: ephemeral, arbitrary, causing excessive and irrational reactions; celebrity is accused pell-mell of producing false idols, participating in the marketing of culture, encouraging public voyeurism, and deforming democratic debate.

Perhaps it is the nature of every modern value to be challenged, creating adhesion only through an ironic distance. But there is more to it in the case of celebrity. Because it is independent of the criteria of assessment for every sphere of activity, celebrity seems illegitimate in regard to each

272

one. The writer who is seen on television every week, the philosopher known for his immaculate shirts, the politician who lays out his love life in public, all seem, more or less, to transgress the standards proper to literary life, to the intellectual world, to political activity. Media visibility has never been thought of, much less defended, as a value in itself, such as a manifest greatness, which implies a specific talent and, often, considerable sacrifice. So many called and so few chosen, one could say.

Far from being thought of as the greatest modern good, par excellence, celebrity continues to arouse the same suspicions, the same criticisms, as it did at the beginning. Notably, it has met with determined resistance around the ideal of authenticity. This in part comes from an old Christian ideal and in part from reaction to new forms of media. Rousseau strongly defended the idea that a true *moi* (self) exists and cannot be reduced to images of oneself circulated in the public sphere to which one has allegiance, and this idea has survived for a long time, either through diverse neo-romantic currents, or though more subtle forms that, while noting the impossible disjunction between the self and the world, seek to save a morality founded on avoiding the advertising injunction.[5] Celebrity, perceived as the undoing of social bonds linked to the excesses of modern media, is denounced commensurately with the fascination it exercises.

The ambiguities of celebrity, a source of prestige and an object of criticism, are inseparable from the ambiguities surrounding images of the public. In its modern configuration, the public is a group of individuals united by the act of reading the same books, by sharing the same emotions and the same interests, an authority invested with a certain legitimacy to make judgments. But it is also not altogether prestigious and is sometimes accused of every evil. In the cultural domain, the very specific economy of symbolic goods often discredits the public in the eyes of critics and peers, and elites, in general.[6] Public tastes and judgments are perceived as mediocre, too influenced by the media and advertising. Commercial and public success is often sought yet also disdained, frequently hoped for even by those who profess contempt for it. In the political realm, the public is only an approximation of a political community, as shown by the very complex status of public opinion, decried for its passivity and its capacity to be manipulated, or for its excessive and aimless passions, but it is difficult not to take public opinion into account in a democratic system. Criticism aimed at the public, found in theories about mass culture as well as in ordinary discussions, sometimes targets its size, sometimes its passivity, often both. In the first instance, the effects of imitation, the role of emotions, and the standardization of taste are denounced. The underlying idea on which these criticisms are based is the autonomous individual, liberal or romantic, whose judgments, even when informed by conversations and discussions, display in the end the personal use of reason or authentic subjectivity. In the second case, aimed at its passivity, the public is perceived as an indistinct mass of consumers subject to powerful advertising devices, in the culture industry and in the media.

Inversely, one can consider that the massive size of the public guarantees the socialization of opinions and judgments. Cultural consumption is open to active interpretation, sometimes leading to particularly creative forms.[7] As large or insignificant as certain traits of the star-system might appear to social players in the legitimate culture, they are often, for fans, important resources that help them create their own self-awareness within a collective framework, allowing them to develop a privileged rapport, although media-based, with a prestigious public figure and the sense of belonging to a public. Readers who avidly follow the life of their favorite celebrities, in the press or on the internet, watching their films, listening to their songs, and following their matches, are no more naïve or alienated than were the readers of *La Nouvelle Héloïse* who wrote enthusiastic letters to Rousseau, or, for those who had not read it, rushed out to catch a glimpse of Jean-Jacques. Like stars, whose public exposure is a prestige factor or at times a burden, so it is with the public, whose curiosity can be superficial or acquire a more profound cultural significance. The mechanisms of celebrity are fundamentally ambivalent.

The law is an excellent way to discover the unresolved contradictions which organize our understanding of celebrity. Jurisprudence is very hesitant about image rights and the protection of private life where it concerns celebrities. When the actress Rachel died in 1858, the judges refused to publish a photograph of the actress on her death bed. This judgment, often considered the origin of right-to-privacy laws, stipulated that "No one without formal consent of the family may reproduce and deliver for publicity the features of a person on her death bed, no matter how celebrated the person nor how much publicity the person received when alive." But the follow-up to this decision remained uncertain; universalizing it was difficult. Neither the right to privacy, when it is a matter of public figures, nor image rights laws in the juridical sense of marketing law concerning representation of the self, have been actually made official. Given their weak legal formalization, these two areas are subject to fluctuating jurisprudence.[8] If judges recognize a "right to escape collective curiosity," they often set it against the opposing principle of the "public's legitimate right to information."[9]

In the United States, being a public figure implies the loss of image rights. Publishing the portrait of a public person does not require prior authorization. In France, several judgments have tended in this direction by focusing on the public life of certain people and then justifying an exception to the image rights law: "Such people not only accept but seek

274

publicity," one judge declared as early as 1965, in an affair concerning Brigitte Bardot. This position was reaffirmed recently in regard to Eric Cantona: "Public personalities tacitly consent to having their photos taken in public places, by the exercise of their public activities." This exception to image rights law obviously refers only to images taken in "public places" and does not refer to privacy laws. So, the difficulties are immense. How can one precisely specify a public space, a public activity? What degree of media exposure is needed for one to be considered a "public personality"? What does it mean exactly to exercise activities "in public"? The essential issue here, more than a wish to accommodate the public interest and the private life of stars, rests on the assumption that underlies jurisprudence: celebrities seek notoriety, they must therefore accept all the "servitude of celebrity." Media visibility is both an injury, when it is imposed without the consent of the individual, and a privileged status with certain constraints, especially the submission to public curiosity.

A few years after the release of *A Face in the Crowd*, in the middle of the Trente Glorieuses in France, when the influence and criticism of the media were intensifying, Georges Brassens intoned these ironic words in "Les Trompettes de la renommée" ("The Trumpets of Fame"):

> People of good counsel managed to make me see
> That to the man in the street, I'd some debts to pay
> And, for fear of falling in complete oblivion,
> I must freely reveal all my little secrets
> Trumpets of the Goddess "Fame," you are so badly out of tune![10]

By lampooning the servitude associated with renown, so contrary to his temperament, by being ironic in this way about public curiosity and journalists, Brassens ingeniously renewed an old subject, that of the modest troubadour more in love with tranquility than glory. But he denounced above all what appeared to him to be a new phenomenon: the nosiness of the "gazettes," the general exposure of "female celebrities" and "stars," public avidity about the sexual life of stars, the excessive demands made in the name of "publicity." As we now know, all these elements and the criticism that accompanies them appeared two centuries earlier in the great cities of the Enlightenment and developed throughout the nineteenth century. Celebrity has a history much longer and more complex than one might suppose from accepted discourse about the society of the spectacle and modern forms of voyeurism.

POSTFACE

Why go back to the eighteenth century to study celebrity? Isn't this anachronistic by its very nature, even provocative? Obviously stars today, given reality television and the internet, have nothing to do with famous writers in the age of the Enlightenment. Is this not just another example of the irritating tendency of historians to look for antecedence in the past?

I am certainly aware of the specific nature of our hypermedia world and contemporary mass culture. And yet I do believe that a historical view which takes into account the entire duration of a phenomenon makes it possible to avoid clichés and platitudes. The subject of this book can be easily summed up. Celebrity is not a recent phenomenon, a vulgar derivative of postmodernism, as the most common response has it. It has been developing since the eighteenth century and its first golden age was in the nineteenth. It is a particular form of notoriety, distinct as much from the glory of heroes, universal and ageless, as from mere reputation, which is always concentrated in a particular time and place. Its development is linked to the economic and cultural changes which have affected European society since the eighteenth century. The explication that I have developed rests on three elements: technological (the development of the printing press and the reproduction of images), cultural (romance literature, an interest in private life), and economic (the rise of privately sponsored shows and the beginning of consumerism). In studying these elements, I have relied on the work of numerous historians and have tried to show how the conjunction of these factors in the eighteenth century gave birth to a new public figure: the celebrity, who aroused the curiosity of an immense public.

Why is it important to date the development of celebrity from the eighteenth century? Because our contemporary myopia makes us think

276

that the phenomenon of celebrity is a radically new one. Discussions about celebrity, especially in public debate, but also in the intellectual world, usually rest on the idea that it is a novel phenomenon that relates to an ethical decline in the public sphere, where heroes have been replaced by stars and then by simple celebrities. There are numerous versions of these moralizing critiques. Conservatives find that the celebrity culture promotes banal individuals and confuses the hierarchies of meritocracy. For progressives, it dumbs down the people and distracts from political issues. Criticism of the society of the spectacle and the media industry are the common denominators for all adversaries of modernity, the cliché of cultural criticism. In reality, all these discussions that oppose celebrity to real merit were already common in the eighteenth century, and knowing this helps us revise our relationship to the present. Isn't this why history is useful?

By studying the culture of celebrity from its beginnings, going back to the very moment when the issues that we continue to raise today were identified and formulated for the first time, we can improve our understanding of the contemporary culture of celebrity at the beginning of the twenty-first century. Given that celebrity appeared in the eighteenth century at the same time as the democratization of Western societies and the ideals of the Enlightenment, its actual development points not to a crisis in the public sphere, but rather to a deepening of its internal contradictions. This book is in line with a number of works undertaken recently by cultural sociologists or specialists in media studies[1] concerning the contemporary nature of celebrity. It adds a historical dimension that covers a longer period of time.

The modern public sphere, as it has developed since the eighteenth century in Europe and the United States, rests on several factors: an optimal and free access to information where each person is welcome to give an opinion about current events; a society that defends equality and where every individual can hope to achieve success or prestige; media development that has profoundly transformed social interactions. Whereas societies during the Ancien Régime were founded on powerful class inequalities, a strict control of information, and face-to-face interactions, modern societies are characterized by a wide circulation of information, social mobility, and a great deal of long-distance communication. Of course, negative forces exist, like censorship or large social inequalities. But the most powerful forces are not exterior and hostile to this development, they are internal. The problem is less about censorship and more about the economic organization of media and the limited attention span of the public. We are not without access to information. To the contrary, we are drowning in it.

277

Celebrity culture is the direct consequence of these developments where individual renown is concerned. In the era of WikiLeaks, reality TV, and the internet, it has never been easier for an unknown person to become a celebrity, or for the public to know everything about the lives of celebrities. Celebrities embody most modern promises of democracy: anybody can become a celebrity, whatever their birth and sometimes whatever their merit, and achieve an enviable way of life. On the other hand, the public has a right to know about the life of prestigious people: celebrities can no longer hide in castles or palaces, but are now in the spotlight.

Has the internet revolution greatly changed the mechanisms of celebrity? This question is raised in *Birdman*, a film by Alejandro González Iñárritu. The film recounts the fate of a cinema star whose superhero roles have made him famous and who is now trying to make it as a Broadway actor. It is a parable about the effects of notoriety, opposing Hollywood stardom, which is big but not much valued, and the artistic reputation symbolized by the theater. No matter how different the two seem, they both come across as artificial, inauthentic worlds run by arbitrary rules, but which both offer great narcissistic pleasures. At one point, the young daughter of the hero contrasts these two forms of recognition, by the public and by the critic, and suggests that a new form of celebrity is rising: visibility online, popularity in the world of social media. With biting irony, she assaults her father by insisting that real celebrity is elsewhere now: "Things are happening in a place that you willfully ignore, a place that has already forgotten you. I mean, who the fuck are you? You hate bloggers. You make fun of Twitter. You don't even have a Facebook page. You're the one who doesn't exist."

It could be, however, that the internet is simply accentuating the mechanisms of celebrity by emphasizing its most ridiculous effects and speeding up the rotation of celebrities. But one can also see it as a profound mutation of the celebrity culture through social media, now that new media forms are producing not unilateral distribution, from broadcasters to the public, but a much more diffuse dissemination in which consumers themselves are producers.

Celebrity is a major aspect of our mediatized societies, but it is not easily defined by the usual sociological categories. Celebrity is not a status. Celebrities do not make up an elite in the traditional sense of the term, with implications of power or the ideology of superiority. Stars and celebrities do not possess power, they do not have a position in institutions. They are admired, sometimes, but they are also mocked, criticized, sometimes detested. Since the eighteenth century, celebrity has fed on scandal. Above all, it is not stable: it is fragile,

278

often ephemeral, because it only exists as long as the public stays interested. And this interest, as Samuel Johnson already noted, is fluctuating and limited.

This is no doubt the reason that angry feelings toward elites in our democratic societies touch celebrities very little. The public sees in their way of life not the symbol of an unequal caste system, but rather an object of fascination, potentially available to everyone and which only depends on the goodwill of the public. And perhaps this is why stories about fallen stars are so successful. The public takes pleasure in seeing stars suffer. Their weakness is the public's power. Celebrity is not capital possessed by only a certain number of people; it is above all a relationship, fundamentally asymmetric, between an individual and the public.

One of the principal results of this book on celebrity is that as an experience and a value, celebrity appears ambivalent. It has been ambivalent since the outset and has never ceased to be so. Avidly sought after, it is a sign of prestige and success, the guarantee of access to an enviable way of life. But it is also often a very painful experience. It is paid for by the absence of a private life, being permanently on display, and, often, psychological instability. From Marilyn Monroe to Kurt Cobain or Britney Spears, one can no longer count the stars who are depressed, closed in on themselves, sometimes pushed to suicide. Sarah Siddons or Lord Byron, at the beginning of the nineteenth century, already described the upsetting effects of celebrity, which at times seemed like a burden or a curse.

Celebrity is also ambivalent for the public, which is both fascinated by the life of celebrities and ironic in regard to them. Much of the press that focuses on celebrities adopts a playful and distanced view of them. The interest that the public has in the life of celebrities also takes a variety of forms, from simple and superficial curiosity to emotional identification. The reader who is amused by tabloid revelations is countered by the teenager who is writing passionate letters to her favorite star. These two extremes exist. As Joshua Gamson has rightly pointed out,[2] spectators (celebrity watchers) are rarely incredulous or cynical; their response is generally half-way between these two reactions, an amused commitment, a benign skepticism.

The history of celebrity forces us to look at one of the principal mysteries of modern societies: the linking of mass culture and individualism. How do mediatized interactions encourage the affirmation of individual subjectivities? Celebrity is at the heart of this change. In modern societies, anonymous individuals who constitute the "public" are regularly confronted with the image and the name of people they will never meet but whom they know a lot about. At the same time, "private" life is

279

contrasted with our public image, the way in which others perceive us. Privacy, the intimate self, is founded on a new principle of personal affirmation, that of individual subjectivity, interior feelings. These two changes, when studied separately, can appear to be contradictory; actually, they are the two sides of modernity. This explains why public curiosity carries over into the private life of celebrities, including their emotional life or the most ordinary details of their existence, while the glory of illustrious men was a matter of public feats or accomplishments. Celebrities must be both distant and close: they must be ordinary people living extraordinary lives. The paradox of modern celebrity is this: the more a person is a public figure, the more his or her private life becomes interesting for a great number of people.

In this way, celebrity culture exercises a double function in society. It permits the public to be aware of itself. It is part of what is happening. It is current events, the news, whose principal value is linked to its ephemeral nature, and the coordination of time which is permitted between members of the same society. But the life of celebrities also highlights the changes happening at the very core of society. Since the fifties, stars in show business, from Elvis to Madonna, have embodied sexual freedom. They are not the cause of it, but they go along with it, accelerate it, and make visible the phenomenon that is taking place. More recently, homosexuality, notably female homosexuality, openly displayed by certain stars, accompanies the public recognition of gay rights. The public exposure of celebrities allows them to make visible little transgressions which accompany societal changes and furnish their fans with new models. The death of David Bowie brings this to mind: the successive characters that he embodied allowed him to expose the metamorphosis in masculinity that marked the changes in Western societies since the seventies. For many of his fans, Bowie was not simply a singer or a star; he was an important person who was part of their personal life.[3]

There is obviously an enormous distance between the detached curiosity and irony that come with following the peripatetic life of stars, and the powerful emotional attachment of the public for certain celebrities. This tension is inherent even in the curiosity excited by a celebrity, with its highs and lows. It was the same in the eighteenth century, as this book has shown. Rousseau's celebrity was amusing and surprising for some, even the subject of bitter irony. Others felt deep emotion for him; he became a model of morality and they followed his example.

Rousseau's case might be seen as problematic, perhaps, because he was celebrated for his writings while celebrities today are the result of media production, without merit in their own right. From Rousseau to Paris Hilton, from Lord Byron to Kim Kardashian, the gap seems enormous.

280

It is true that show business, more than in the eighteenth century, has a tendency today to be independent and to produce its own stars. Celebrity most often seems to come to those who are already known for their way of life and their ability to expose it publicly. But certain celebrities in the eighteenth century were actors, courtesans, or bandits. Inversely, many famous personalities today have gained success for their talents before becoming real celebrities: David Beckham and Cristiano Ronaldo, George Clooney and Julia Roberts, Jay Z and Beyoncé have respectively proven themselves on soccer fields, in films, and in concert halls, even if their fame today goes beyond their initial activity. As in the eighteenth century, certain writers and artists have become true celebrities: Michel Houellebecq, Andy Warhol, or Jeff Koons. One can argue about the way they constructed a public persona, which fed their work and became in itself an advertising tool, but one cannot deny that they enjoy a kind of recognition in their respective areas, beyond their celebrity.

Most of the examples I have cited show the importance of the economic stakes in celebrity culture. The culture industry has become extremely powerful today and certain authors talk about a celebrity industry itself coming out of the entertainment industry. The image of famous people is a consumer product and new professions arose out of this consumerism: managers, press agents, paparazzi, who live off of this industry. Certainly, the change that accompanied the mass entertainment culture is much different from the celebrity I have investigated in this book. However, here again, returning to the past can teach us a lot, because the mechanisms of celebrity preceded the development of the culture industry. The culture industry and celebrity fed each other: the culture industry encouraged celebrity, but celebrity at the same time encouraged the culture industry.

The rise of celebrity in the eighteenth century was linked to the first developments of a consumer society: spectacles independent of court subsidies, the rise of publishing entrepreneurs, as well as the spectacular ascendancy of fashion. Many historians today are rediscovering the enormity of capitalist changes that accompanied the development of public space in the eighteenth century. This merchandising tended to blur social hierarchies and individual identities. People were no longer subjected to class differences; they could freely choose their clothes, their books, their entertainment, their stars. The consumer revolution is dialectical: it allows for freedom but also has the potential to be alienating. From the eighteenth century onward, the possibility of consumer abuse as we know it today was evident, but also the possibility of freedom from the society of the Ancien Régime. Curiosity around celebrities works the same way: it can be solely the effect of social imitation, benefiting mostly the entertainment industry, but it can also be a resource for those who find that through attaching themselves to a star they can affirm and deepen their self-awareness and individual tastes.

It is necessary, then, to give up the idealistic and intellectual notion of the public sphere that was meant to be, in theory, a place for rational, dispassionate argumentation, like a philosophy seminar. In reality, the modern public sphere in capitalist, mediatized societies is, by its nature, full of passion and desire. It is a complex place, subjected to media flux and part of other emotionally charged forms (images, sounds, text), which produce both emotional and symbolic communities as well as separate individuals.

In this light, political celebrity must be reconsidered. Political celebrity is in great evidence today. Film and television stars can have political careers, and political figures are treated like celebrities, their names turned into brands and their private life exposed in the press. Donald Trump's recent election has shown how a businessman and former reality TV star could successfully use the worst devices of celebrity self-fashioning in favor of his political ambition. But here again, a historical investigation shows that this evolution has its roots in earlier periods, even if there has been a radical acceleration since the development of "infotainment." Consequently, the principle of political representation, since the time of democratic revolutions in France, the United States and England, has raised questions about popularity: John Wilkes, Ben Franklin, Mirabeau, were the first "political celebrities." Democratic policy is not simply a question of rational debate, but is also the embodiment of symbols: celebrity, which is based on a fiction of intimacy, seems to promise a closeness between the people and politicians, a fundamentally ambivalent closeness because it can easily be manipulated. Even so, this kind of celebrity, which does not always translate into votes, must not be confused with the cult of personality that is orchestrated by totalitarian regimes. The importance of celebrity in modern political life is not an aberration from the democratic ideal: since the beginning of modern political representation, it has been at the heart of it. Does this mean that it is not dangerous? Certainly not. All aspects of political representation that derive from the aesthetic, emotional, and affective dimension are particularly susceptible to being used to the detriment of rational discourse. They can veer off into despotism or toward a fanaticism that is incomprehensible to the elites. But these dangers at the heart of the democratic principle have been identified and discussed since the Atlantic revolutions at the end of the eighteenth century. We cannot take refuge in a nostalgia for an ideal democracy that has never existed. We must face the congenital fragility of what we have inherited.

282

Celebrity is a cultural phenomenon that is difficult to study, certainly in our societies, where it seems to penetrate every domain of social life. On the one hand, celebrity is seen as nothing but superficiality, spectacle, theater, for the profit of the media industry: given this, it arouses amused curiosity and cynical irony. On the other hand, it plays an important role in the aesthetic and symbolic organization of our public sphere. These effects merit the greatest attention on the part of social scientists. Historians, up until now, have kept a distance. Things are changing. This book has tried to make a contribution.

NOTES

INTRODUCTION: CELEBRITY AND MODERNITY

1   Quoted by Martial Poirson, "Marie-Antoinette, héroïne paradox-
    ale d'une fiction patrimoniale contrariée," in Laurence Schiffano
    and Martial Poirson (eds), *Filmer le dix-huitième siècle* (Paris:
    Desjonquère, 2009), pp. 229–52. See also Yves Citton, "Du bon
    usage de l'anachronisme (*Marie-Antoinette*, Sofia Coppola et
    Gang of Four)," in *L'Écran des Lumières: Regards cinéma-
    tographiques sur le XVIIIe siècle* (Oxford: Voltaire Foundation,
    2009), pp. 231–47.
2   In the United States, celebrity studies has its own anthology:
    Peter David Marshall, *The Celebrity Culture Reader* (New York/
    London: Routledge, 2006). The bibliography, especially in English,
    is now very large. For a French version see Nathalie Heinich, "La
    culture de la célébrité en France et dans les pays Anglophones: Une
    étude comparative," *Revue française de sociologie*, 52:2 (2011),
    pp. 353–72.
3   Leo Braudy, *The Frenzy of Renown: Fame and Its History* (New
    York: Oxford University Press, 1986).
4   Within a large bibliography, a book by Joshua Gamson stands out:
    Claims to Fame: Celebrity in Contemporary America (Berkeley:
    University of California Press, 1994).
5   Daniel J. Boorstin, *The Image: A Guide to Pseudo-Events in
    America* (New York: Vintage Books, 1961).
6   Edgar Morin, *The Stars*, trans. Richard Howard (New York:
    Grove Press, 1961), p. 71. In this pioneering book, Morin brings
    together three themes: a semiotic interpretation of stars as myth;
    an anthropological interpretation of "cult" which would charac-
    terize them; and an economic interpretation of the capitalist

star-system, giving priority to the interpretation of stars as modern myth.

7 Chris Rojek, *Celebrity* (London: Reaktion Books, 2001).

8 Concerning the idea of "figure" as a collection of characteristics which define the social appearance of an individual, not only the face, but also all the various elements by which one's identity is known to those in contact with the person, direct or indirect, see Barbara Carnevali, *Le Apparenze sociali: Una filosofia del prestigio* (Bologna: Il Mulino, 2012).

9 Alan Bowness, *The Conditions of Success: How the Modern Artist Rises to Fame* (London: Thames & Hudson, 1989); Alessandro Pizzorno, *Il Velo della diversità: Studi su razionalità e riconoscimento* (Milan: Feltrinelli, 2007). For an overview of different current approaches to reputation as a social phenomenon, see Gloria Origgi (ed.), "La reputation," *Communications*, 93:2 (2013).

10 Jürgen Habermas, *The Structural Transformation of the Public Sphere: An Inquiry into a Category of Bourgeois Society*, trans. Thomas Burger and Frederick Lawrence (Cambridge, MA: MIT Press, [1962] 1989).

11 The actual goal of the Habermas book, which idealizes the eighteenth century in order to better denounce the cultural and political state of contemporary societies (starting with the early 1960s), is evident in the last part of the book, which proposes an extremely negative view of occidental societies in light of their own democratic ideals. For the theoretical and historical basis of the book see Stéphane Haber, "Pour historiciser *L'Espace public* de Habermas," in Patrick Boucheron and Nicolas Offenstadt (eds), *L'Espace public au Moyen Âge: Débats autour de Jürgen Habermas* (Paris: PUF, 2011), pp. 25–41. In the same volume, Stéphane Van Damme, "Farewell Habermas?" recognizes the importance that the idea of public space has played in eighteenth-century studies over the last twenty years (pp. 43–61).

12 Gabriel Tarde, "The Public and the Crowd" (1898), in *On Communication and Social Influence: Selected Papers*, ed. Terry N. Clark (Chicago: University of Chicago Press, 1969), pp. 277–94, here p. 277.

13 John B. Thompson, *The Media and Modernity: A Social Theory of the Media* (Stanford: Stanford University Press, 1995).

14 This chronology is close to that explored in the collection edited by Tom Mole, *Romanticism and Celebrity Culture, 1750–1850* (Cambridge: Cambridge University Press, 2009), which contains some useful case studies, but is limited to Britain. See also Fred

Inglis, *A Short History of Celebrity* (Princeton: Princeton University Press, 2010), which hypothesizes that the birth of celebrity took place in the eighteenth century, but only dedicates a few pages to this period and, again, only for Britain.

15 Nathalie Heinich, *De la visibilité: Excellence et singularité en régime médiatique* (Paris: Gallimard, 2012).

CHAPTER 1   VOLTAIRE IN PARIS

1 Paul Bénichou, *The Consecration of the Writer, 1750–1830*, trans. Mark K. Jensen (Lincoln: University of Nebraska Press, 1999).

2 In the great biography edited by René Pomeau, the chapter entitled "Le triomphe." After invoking the triumph of the Roman emperors, Pomeau adds: "Sanctified king of poets by other poets themselves, promulgated by his contemporaries to immortality, Voltaire was present at his own apotheosis." *Voltaire en son temps*, Vol. V: *On a voulu l'enterrer, 1770–1791* (Oxford: Voltaire Foundation, 1997), pp. 283–98, here p. 298. Jean-Claude Bonnet, in *Naissance du Panthéon: essai sur le culte des grands hommes* (Paris: Fayard, 1989), pp. 236–8, also invokes a triumph and an "apotheosis while still alive." On the pantheonization of 1791, see Antoine de Baecque, "Voltaire; or, The Body of the Philosopher King," in *Glory and Terror: Seven Deaths under the French Revolution*, trans. Charlotte Mandell (New York/London: Routledge, 2001), pp. 37–60.

3 The literary correspondence of Grimm and Meister offers a long story that is often retold, and Wagnère, Voltaire's secretary, also had his version.

4 Darrin McMahon, *Enemies of the Enlightenment: The French Counter-Enlightenment and the Making of Modernity* (New York: Oxford University Press, 2001), p. 5.

5 Louis Sébastien Mercier, *Tableau de Paris* (Paris: Mercure de France, [1783] 1994), "Triomphe de Voltaire: Janot," pp. 264–9, here p. 266.

6 "Monsieur Brizard brought a crown of laurels that Madame Villette put on the head of the great man, but he took it off immediately, though the public insisted on seeing it by clapping and shouting, making an unheard-of ruckus." *Correspondance littéraire, philosophique et critique par Grimm, Diderot, Raynal, Mesiter, etc.*, ed. M. Tourneux (Paris: Garnier, 1880), Vol. XII, p. 70.

7 The memory of this event was always present. Titon du Tillet recalled it in 1734 in his *Essai sur les honneurs et sur les*

monuments accordés aux illustres savants. Mercier dedicated a chapter to it in *Mon bonnet de nuit*, and the triumph of Corine at the Pantheon is implicitly referred to in Madame de Staël's 1807 eponymous novel. See Bonnet, *Naissance du Panthéon*, p. 330.

8 Graham Gargett, "Oliver Goldsmith et ses *Mémoires de M. de Voltaire*," in Christophe Cave and Simon Davies (eds), *Les Vies de Voltaire: discours et représentations biographiques, XVIIIe–XXIe siècle* (Oxford: Voltaire Foundation, 2008), pp. 203–22.

9 Anne-Sophie Barrovecchio, *Voltairomania* (Saint-Étienne: Presses Universitaires de Saint-Étienne, 2004).

10 Nicholas Cronk, "Le pet de Voltaire," in Alexis Tadié (ed.), *La Figure du philosophe dans les lettres anglaises et françaises* (Nanterre: Presses Universitaires de Paris X, 2012), pp. 123–36.

11 Charles Burney, *The Present State of Music in France and Italy* (London, 1773), p. 56.

12 Voltaire à Étienne Noël Damilaville, *Correspondance, Œuvres complètes de Voltaire* (Oxford: Voltaire Foundation, 1968–77), Vol. CXV, pp. 23–4.

13 François Louis Claude Marin à Voltaire, le 3 mars 1766, ibid., Vol. CXIV, pp. 125–7.

14 *Correspondance littéraire*, February 1778, Vol. XII, pp. 53–4.

15 Lettre de Jean Robert Tronchin à Jean Jacob Vernet, 21 September 1757, ibid., Vol. CII, pp. 170–4.

16 Gustave Desnoiresterres, *Iconographie voltairienne* (Paris, 1879); Garry Apgar, " 'Sage comme une image' : Trois siècles d'iconographie voltairienne," *Nouvelles del'estampe*, July 1994, pp. 4–44.

17 Garry Apgar, *L'Art singulier de Jean Huber* (Paris: Adam Biro, 1995).

18 *Correspondance littéraire*, Vol. X, p. 96.

19 Ibid., p. 98.

20 To the point where Huber had great fun reproducing thirty versions of Voltaire's face on the same piece of paper. Voltaire remained perfectly recognizable in all thirty versions. Houdon was inspired by these drawings for his *Voltaire Seated*.

21 http://gallica.bnf.fr/ark:/12148/btv1b6947967d.r=voltaire+huber+lever.langfr.

22 Apgar, *L'Art singulier*, p. 92.

23 *Mémoires sur M. de Voltaire et sur ses ouvrages par Longchamp et Wagnère, ses secrétaires* (Paris: Aimé André, 1826), Vol. I, p. 121.

24 *Correspondance littéraire*, February 1778, Vol. XII, pp. 53–4.

25 *Journal de Paris*, February 16, 1778, p. 187. On the changing attitude of provincial newspapers, at first enthusiastic and then

more and more critical, see James A. Leith, "Les trois apothéoses de Voltaire," *Annales historiques de la Révolution française*, 51: 236 (1979), pp. 161–209.

26   "Aux auteurs du *Journal de Paris*," *Journal de Paris*, February 20, 1778, p. 204.
27   Letter from Mme du Deffand to Horace Walpole, February 12, 1778, *Horace Walpole's Correspondence* (New Haven: Yale University Press, 1939), Vol. VII, p. 18. A few days later, she adds: "It is not respect which he inspires today, but a kind of worship that we think we owe him" (March 8, 1778, p. 25).
28   According to the Marquis of Saint-Marc, cited by William Marx, "Le couronnement de Voltaire ou Pétrarque perverti," *Histoire, économie & société*, 20:2 (2001), pp. 199–210. Mercier proposes a more literal and ironic interpretation of this symbolic murder: "The visits and the high praise to which his vanity wished to respond soon used up all his energy; his career was cut short by his good friends; apotheosis killed the poet" (*Tableau de Paris*, p. 266).
29   Chosen as the opening speech at the Académie Française (Paris: Demonville, 1808), p. 209, cited by Bonnet, *Naissance du Panthéon*, p. 373.
30   *Correspondance littéraire*, Vol. XII, pp. 68–73.
31   *Mémoires secrets pour servir l'histoire de la République des lettres en France depuis MDCCLXII jusqu'à nos jours* (London: John Adamson, 1780), Vol. XIV, p. 330, December 30, 1779.
32   *Correspondance littéraire*, Vol. XII, p. 254
33   Mercier, *Tableau de Paris*, Vol. IV, p. 268.
34   Stéphane van Damme, *À toutes voiles vers la vérité: Une autre histoire de la philosophie au temps des Lumières* (Paris: Le Seuil, 2014), pp. 81–4.
35   *Annales politiques, civiles et littéraires*, Vol. IV, 1779, pp. 34–5.
36   *Affiches, annonces et avis divers*, 1779, p. 40 (broadsheet March 1779).

CHAPTER 2   SOCIETY OF THE SPECTACLE

1   Jean-Marie Apostolidès, *Le Roi-machine: Politique et spectacle* (Paris: Minuit, 1981), p. 136; Louis Marin, *Portrait of the King*, trans. M. Houle (London: Palgrave Macmillan, 1988); Richard Sennett, *The Fall of Public Man* (New York: Alfred A. Knopf, 1974); Habermas, *The Structural Transformation of the Public Sphere*.

2 Jean-Jacques Rousseau, "J.-J. Rousseau, Citizen of Geneva, to M. D'Alembert," in *The Collected Writings of Rousseau*, Vol. 10, eds Allan Bloom, Charles Butterworth, and Christopher Kelly (Hanover, NH/London: University Press of New England, 2004), pp. 251–352. Among the most recent critiques see Blaise Baschoffen and Bruno Bernardi (eds), *Rousseau, politique et esthétique: sur la "lettre à d'Alembert"* (Lyon: ENS, 2011).

3 Guy Debord, *Society of the Spectacle*, trans. Freddy Perlman et al. (Detroit: Black & Red, [1967] 1977), para. 60.

4 Neil McKendrick, John Brewer, and John H. Plumb, *The Birth of a Consumer Society: The Commercialization of Eighteenth-Century England* (Bloomington: Indiana University Press, 1982); James van Horn Melton, *The Rise of the Public in Enlightenment Europe* (Cambridge: Cambridge University Press, 2001), p. 160; John Brewer, *The Pleasures of the Imagination: English Culture in the Eighteenth Century* (London: HarperCollins, 1997).

5 Brewer, *The Pleasures of the Imagination*.

6 Louis Henry Lecomte, *Histoire des théâtres de Paris – Les Variétés Amusantes* (Paris: Daragon, 1908); Robert Isherwood, *Farce and Fantasy: Popular Entertainment in Eighteenth-Century Paris* (Oxford: Oxford University Press, 1989); Michele Root-Bernstein, *Boulevard Theater and Revolution in Eighteenth-Century Paris* (Ann Arbor: UMI Research, 1984); Laurent Turcot, "Directeurs, comédiens et police: relations de travail dans les spectacles populaires à Paris," *Histoire, économie & société*, 23:1 (2004), pp. 97–119.

7 Felicity Nussbaum, "Actresses and the Economics of Celebrity, 1700–1800," in Mary Luckhurst and Jane Moody (eds), *Celebrity and British Theatre, 1660–2000* (New York: Palgrave, 2005), pp. 148–68; Danielle Spratt, "Genius Thus Munificently Employed!!!: Philanthropy and Celebrity in the Theaters of Garrick and Siddons," *Eighteenth-Century Life*, 37:3 (2013), pp. 55–84.

8 Dominique Quéro, "Le triomphe des Pointu," *Cahiers de l'Association internationale des études françaises*, 43 (1991), pp. 153–67. See also Henri Lavedan, *Volange, comédien de la Foire (1756–1803)* (Paris: J. Tallandier, 1933).

9 Lauren Clay, "Provincial Actors, the Comédie-Française, and the Business of Performing in Eighteenth-Century France," *Eighteenth-Century Studies*, 38:4 (2005), pp. 651–79.

10 *Mémoires secrets*, Vol. I, p. 19.

11 Rahul Markovits, *Civiliser l'Europe: Politiques du théâtre français au XVIIIe siècle* (Paris: Fayard, 2014); "L'Europe française, une

domination culturelle? Kaunitz et le théâtre français à Vienne au XVIIIe siècle," *Annales HSS*, 67:3 (2012), pp. 717–51. See also Mélanie Traversier, "Costruire la fama: la diplomazia al servizio della musica durante il Regno di Carlo di Borbone," *Analecta Musicologica*, 52 (2015), pp. 171–89.

12 Judith Milhous, "Vestris-Mania and the Construction of Celebrity: Auguste Vestris in London, 1780–1781," *Harvard Library Bulletin*, 5:4 (1994), pp. 30–64.

13 On the other hand, the celebrity of Vestris would lead directors of the theater the next year to hire the ballet master Noverre, inventor of *ballet d'action*, in order to take advantage of the craze initiated by the visit of the young dancer.

14 After his benefit evening, the *Public Advertiser*, February 28, 1781, wrote: "A dancer makes sixteen hundred pounds a night! An honest tradesman labours twice sixteen years and thinks himself happy to retire with such a sum. Those in low life work hard from the cradle to the grave and perhaps never possess sixteen shillings that they can call their own. How chequered is the Book of fate!" (quoted in Milhous, "Vestris-Mania and the Construction of Celebrity," p. 41).

15 See in particular the seminal article by Sherwin Rosen, "The Economy of the Superstars," *American Economic Review*, 71:5 (1981), pp. 845–58, and the synthetic reflections by Pierre-Michel Menger, "Talent et réputation: Les inégalités de réussite et leurs explications dans les sciences sociales," in *Le Travail créateur* (Paris: Gallimard-Seuil, 2009), chapter 6.

16 Spratt, "Genius Thus Munificently Employed!!!"

17 The *Mémoires secrets* alludes several times to the youthful indiscretions of the "celebrated Guimard," for instance December 31, 1770, Vol. III, p. 247, where an engraving is described that makes reference to her multiple affairs.

18 The pioneering book of this approach, with a feminist perspective, is Kristina Straub, *Sexual Suspects: Eighteenth-Century Players and Sexual Ideology* (Oxford/Princeton: Princeton University Press, 1992. The bibliography which addresses English actresses from this angle, and mostly concerning the creation of their public image, is now abundant. See notably Robyn Asleson (ed.), *Notorious Muse: The Actress in British Art and Culture, 1776–1812* (New Haven/London: Yale University Press, 2003); Gill Perry, *Spectacular Flirtations: Viewing the Actress in British Art, 1768–1820* (New Haven: Yale University Press, 2007); Felicity Nussbaum, *Rival Queens: Actresses, Performance, and the Eighteenth-Century British Theater* (Philadelphia: University

of Pennsylvania Press, 2010); Laura Engel, *Fashioning Celebrity: Eighteenth-Century British Actresses and Strategies for Image Making* (Columbus: Ohio State University Press, 2011). On France, see Lenard Berlanstein, *Daughters of Eve: A Cultural History of French Theater Women from the Old Regime to the Fin-de-Siècle* (Cambridge, MA: Harvard University Press, 2001).

19 Joseph Roach, "Nell Gwyn and Covent Garden Goddesses," in Gill Perry (ed.), *The First Actresses: Nell Gwyn to Sarah Siddons* (London: National Portrait Gallery, 2011), pp. 63–75.

20 Steven Parissien, *George IV: The Grand Entertainment* (London: John Murray, 2001); Christopher Hibbert, *George IV, Prince of Wales, 1762–1811* (London: Longman, 1972).

21 Claire Brook, *The Feminization of Fame, 1750–1830* (Basingstoke: Palgrave Macmillan, 2006).

22 Paula Byrne, *Perdita: The Life of Mary Robinson* (London: HarperCollins, 2004), and above all Tom Mole, "Mary Robinson's Conflicted Celebrity," in Mole (ed.), *Romanticism and Celebrity Culture*, pp. 186–206.

23 *Memoirs of the Late Mrs Robinson* (London, 1801), Vol. II, p. 127.

24 "I scarcely ventured to enter a shop without experiencing the greatest inconvenience. Many hours have I waited till the crowd disperse, which surrounded my carriage, in expectation of my quitting the shop," ibid., p. 68.

25 Olivia Voisin, "Le portrait de comédien ou la fabrique d'une aura," in *La Comédie-Française s'expose: catalogue de l'exposition du Petit Palais* (Paris: Les Musées de la Ville de Paris, 2011), pp. 93–148; Perry (ed.), *The First Actresses*.

26 *Mémoires secrets*, March 1780, Vol. XV, p. 82. The entire tone of the passage is very hostile to Volange, or rather to "Jeannot," because the editor himself used the name of the character to designate the actor.

27 Patrick Barbier, *The World of the Castrati: The History of an Extraordinary Operatic Phenomenon*, trans. Margaret Crosland (London: Souvenir Press, 2010). If castrati often came from Naples, they practiced their art throughout all of Europe. See, for example, Elizabeth Krimmer, " 'Eviva Il Coltello?' The Castrato Singer in Eighteenth-Century German Literature and Culture," *PMLA*, 120:5 (2005), pp. 1543–9. Musically, their success was prepared for them because the very high voices were valued in Italian music, starting in the eighteenth century, which allowed for the fame of the first professional female singers, sought out for their expressionism: Susan McClary, "Soprano as Fetish: Professional Singers

in Early Modern Italy," *Desire and Pleasure in Seventeenth-Century Music* (Oakland: University of California Press, 2012).

28 Thomas McGeary, "Farinelli and the English: 'One God' or the Devil?," *Revue LISA/LISA e-journal*, 2:3 (2004), https://lisa.revues.org/886.

29 Thomas Gilbert, "The World Unmask'd" (1738), quoted in ibid.

30 Nicolas Morales, *L'artiste de cour dans l'Espagne du XVIIIe siècle: Étude de la communauté des musiciens au service de Philippe V, 1700–1746* (Madrid: Casa de Velazquez, 2007), pp. 238–50; Thomas McGeary, "Farinelli in Madrid: Opera, Politics, and the War of Jenkins' Ear," *Musical Quarterly*, 82 (1998), pp. 383–421.

31 See his correspondence (Carlo Broschi Farinelli, *La Solitudine Amica: Lettere al conte Sicinio Pepoli*, eds Carlo Vitali and Francesca Boris [Palermo: Sellerio, 2000]), which shows a certain worry about the reactions of the London public.

32 Burney, *The Present State of Music in France and Italy*, p. 221.

33 Helen Berry, *The Castrato and His Wife* (Oxford: Oxford University Press, 2011).

34 *La Gazette littéraire de l'Europe*, for instance, made fun of Mme Tenducci, who "really only married a beautiful voice," and asked readers to decide if she was right to remain faithful to him (May 1768, Vol. XXV, p. 170), while the *Mercure de France* regretted having made "such fun of the affair" instead of finding it pathetic (Paris: Lacombe, 1768, Vol. 2, July 1768, p. 117).

35 At least if one believes Fréron's *L'Année littéraire*, which devoted a long article to the event in the form of a letter allegedly from an Italian salesman living in London, addressed to a Dutch correspondent, in which he makes fun of Tenducci's marriage, which caused "outbursts of laughter" when a child was born (Paris, Delalain, 1771, Vol. III, pp. 275–88).

36 *The Complete Memoirs of Jacques Casanova de Seingalt* (1725), trans. Arthur Machen (London, 1894), Vol. III: "He laughed at people who said that a castrato could not procreate. Nature had made him a monster that he might remain a man; he was born triorchis, and as only two of the seminal glands had been destroyed the remaining one was sufficient to endow him with virility."

37 Luc Boltanski, Elisabeth Claverie, Nicolas Offenstadt, and Stéphane Van Damme (eds), *Scandales, affaires et grandes causes: de Socrate à Pinochet* (Paris: Plon, 2007).

38 Max Gluckman, "Gossip and Scandal," *Current Anthropology*, 3:4 (1963), pp. 307–16; Damien de Blic and Cyril Lemieux, "Le scandale comme épreuve: Éléments de sociologie pragmatique," *Politix*, 18:71 (2005), pp. 9–38.

39 Éric de Dampierre, "Thèmes pour l'étude du scandale," *Annales ESC*, 9:3 (1954), pp. 328–36, here p. 331.

40 For a later comparison, the Oscar Wilde trial, see Ari Adut, *On Scandal: Moral Disturbances in Society, Politics and Art* (Cambridge: Cambridge University Press, 2008), pp. 38–72. James B. Thompson has suggested a general reflection on contemporary scandals, focused on his conception of long-distance media and on the new political visibility that this produces: *Political Scandal: Power and Visibility in the Media Age* (Cambridge: Polity, 2000).

41 Berry, *The Castrato and His Wife*, pp. 203 and 205.

42 Shearer West, "Siddons, Celebrity and Regality: Portraiture and the Body of the Ageing Actress," in Mary Luckhurst and Jane Moody (eds), *Theatre and Celebrity, 1660–2000* (York: University of York Press, 2005), pp. 191–213; Heather McPherson, "Picturing Tragedy: Mrs Siddons as the Tragic Muse Revisited," *Eighteenth-Century Studies*, 33:3 (2000), pp. 401–30, and "Siddons Rediviva," in Mole (ed.), *Romanticism and Celebrity Culture*, pp. 120–40.

43 McPherson, "Picturing Tragedy," p. 406.

44 William Hazlitt, "Mrs Siddons," *The Examiner*, June 15, 1816, in *A View of the English Stage* (London: Stedart, 1818), p. 305.

45 William Hazlitt, "Mrs Siddons's Lady Macbeth, June 7, 1817," ibid., pp. 446–8.

46 Hazlitt, "Mrs Siddons," p. 305.

47 Ibid., p. 304. Here one sees that although in this article Hazlitt is talking about Siddons' new performance of Lady Macbeth, he emphasizes, in spite of the quality of the play, the double distance which separates him, as a spectator, from the actress: spatial distance because of the large crowd that pushes him to the back of the room, but also, and especially, temporal distance, which separates him from his memory of the first performance.

48 *Exposé de la conduite et des torts du Sieur Talma envers les comédiens français* (Paris: Prault, 1790); *Réponse de François Talma au mémoire de la comédie française, Garnéry* (Second Year of Liberty); *Réflexions de M. Talma et pièces justificatives* (Paris: Bossange, 1790); *Pétition relative aux comédiens français, adressée au conseil de ville, par un très grand nombre de citoyens*, (Archives of the Comédie-Française, Talma collection, carton 3 – hereafter: ACF, Talma 3).

49 Letter from Talma to Louis Ducis, 1811, cited by Mara Fazio, *François-Joseph Talma* (Paris: CNRS, 2011), p. 147.

50 Fazio, *François-Joseph Talma*, p. 117.

51 *Courrier des spectacles*, September 23 and 24, 1822, ACF, Talma 2.

52 Germaine de Staël, *Germany*, ed. O.W. Wright (Ann Arbor: University of Michigan Press, 2005), chapter XXVII.

53 Stendhal, *Memoirs of an Egotist*, trans. David Ellis (London: Chatto & Windus, [1832] 1975), p. 120. See also Florence Filippi, "L'artiste en vedette: François-Joseph Talma (1763–1826)," doctoral dissertation, Nanterre, 2008.

54 Letter from Michel François Talma to his son, October 6, 1796, ACF, Talma 7.

55 Letter from Talma to the "editor of the *Annales*," August 21, 1817, ACF, Talma 7.

56 The article was published in the *Globe and Traveller* (September 25) then "reprinted in all the English newspapers," according to its author, who sent it to Talma (ACF, Talma 2).

57 Emmanuel Fureix, *La France des larmes: Deuils politiques à l'âge romantique, 1814–1840* (Paris: Champ Vallon, 2009).

58 *La Pandore*, 1250, October 20, 1826.

59 *Courrier de Paris*, 295, October 18, 1826.

60 *Courrier de Paris*, 295, October 20, 1826.

61 *Courrier de Paris*, 295, October 22, 1826.

62 *Le Constitutionnel*, 293, October 20, 1826.

63 Sociologists of contemporary celebrity who have highlighted this phenomenon are Richard Schickle, *Intimate Strangers: The Culture of Celebrity in America* (New York: Ivan R. Dee, 1985); Joshua Gamson, *Claims to Fame: Celebrity in Contemporary America* (Berkeley: University of California Press, 1994); Heinich, *De la visibilité*.

64 Thompson, *The Media and Modernity*, develops this point at length, starting with the pioneering works of social psychologists Donald Horton and R. Richard Wohl, who talked about "parasocial interactions" ("Mass Communication and Para-Social Interactions: Observations on Intimacy at a Distance," *Psychiatry*, 19 [1956], pp. 215–29).

65 Hans-Robert Jauss, *Pour une herméneutique littéraire* (Paris: Gallimard, 1984).

66 Philippe Le Guern (ed.), *Les Cultes médiatiques: Culture fan et oeuvres cultes* (Rennes: Presses Universitaires de Rennes, 2002).

67 Robert Darnton, "Readers Respond to Rousseau: The Fabrication of Romantic Sensitivity, " in *The Great Cat Massacre and Other Episodes in French Cultural History* (New York: Basic Books, 1984), pp. 215–56; Jean-Marie Goulemot and Didier Masseau, "Naissance des lettres adressées à l'écrivain," *Textual*, "Écrire à l'écrivain," 27 (February 1994), pp. 1–12; Judith Lyon-Caen, *La*

Lecture et la Vie: Les usages du roman au temps de Balzac (Paris: Tallandier, 2006).

68 Letter of June 8, 1775, quoted by Cheryl Wanko, "Patron or Patronized? 'Fans' and the Eighteenth-Century English Stage," in Mole (ed.), *Romanticism and Celebrity*, pp. 209–26, here p. 221.

69 Anonymous letter, September 1825, ACF, Talma 2.

70 Anonymous letter, no date, ACF, Talma 1.

71 "Talma admired by a person full of prejudices against him," ACF, Talma 2.

72 Letter, June 3, 1800, ACF, Talma 2.

73 Anonymous letter, ACF, Talma 2.

74 ACF, Talma 1.

75 Letter from Ouvrard, November 14, 1824, ACF, Talma 1.

76 Letter from Mme Bavoist-Hauguet, 1817, ACF, Talma 6.

77 *The Reminiscences of Sarah Kemble Siddons, 1773–1785*, ed. William Van Lennep (Cambridge: Wineder Library, 1942), pp. 15–16.

78 Ibid., p. 22.

CHAPTER 3   A FIRST MEDIA REVOLUTION

1 ACF, Talma 1.

2 Maria Ines Aliverti, *La Naissance de l'acteur moderne: L'acteur et son portrait au XVIIIe siècle* (Paris: Gallimard, 1998), pp. 98–9. See also: Leigh Woods, *Garrick Claims the Stage: Acting as Social Emblem in Eighteenth-Century England* (London: Greenwood Press, 1984); Heather McPherson, "Garrickomania: Garrick's Image," *Folger Shakespeare Library*, http://folgerpedia.folger.edu/ Garrickomania:_Garrick%27s_Image.

3 Heinich, *De la visibilité*.

4 See notably Hannah Barker and Simon Burrows (eds), *Press, Politics and the Public Sphere in Europe and North America, 1760–1820* (Cambridge: Cambridge University Press, 2002); Gilles Feyel, *L'Annonce et la Nouvelle: La presse d'information en France sous l'Ancien Régime (1630–1788)* (Oxford: Voltaire Foundation, 2000); Jeremy D. Popkin, *News and Politics in the Age of Revolution: Jean Luzac's Gazette de Leyde* (Ithaca, NY: Cornell University Press, 1989); Brendan Dooley (ed.), *The Dissemination of News and the Emergence of Contemporaneity in Early Modern Europe* (Farnham: Ashgate, 2010).

5 Dror Wahrman, *Mr Collier's Letter Racks: A Tale of Arts and Illusion at the Threshold of the Modern Information Age* (New York: Oxford University Press, 2012).

6 Marin, *Portrait of the King*.

7 Mireille Huchon, *Rabelais* (Paris: Gallimard, 2011).

8 Therefore, Mme de Sévigné "resisted" as much as she could when her friends wanted to make a copy of her daughter's portrait by Mignard. See Emmanuel Coquery, "Le portrait vu du Grand Siècle," in *Visages du Grand Siècle: Le portrait français sous le règne de Louis XIV, 1660–1715* (Paris: Somogy, 1997), p. 25. Amazingly, this exhibition catalogue includes almost exclusively aristocratic or anonymous portraits, with the notable and very special exception of portraits of the painters.

9 See Horst Bredekamp, *Stratégies visuelles de Thomas Hobbes*, trans. Denise Modigliani (Paris: Éditions de Maison des Sciences de l'Homme, 2003), p. 168; also Horst Bredekamp, "Thomas Hobbes's Visual Strategies," in Patricia Springborg (ed.), *The Cambridge Companion to Hobbes's Leviathan* (Cambridge: Cambridge University Press, 2007), pp. 29–60.

10 Patricia Fara, *Newton: The Making of a Genius* (London: Macmillan, 2002), pp. 36–7.

11 Roger Chartier, "Figures de l'auteur," *Culture écrite et société: l'ordre des livres (XIVe–XVIIIe siècle)* (Paris: Albin Michel, 1996), p. 67.

12 Louis de Rouvroy, duc de Saint-Simon, *Mémoires*, ed. Y. Coirault (Paris: Gallimard, 1983), Vol. I, p. 336.

13 Udolpho van de Sandt, "La fréquentation des salons sous l'Ancien Régime, la Révolution et l'Empire," *Revue de l'art*, 73 (1986), pp. 43–8.

14 David Solkin, *Painting for Money: The Visual Arts and the Public Sphere in Eighteenth-Century England* (New Haven/London: Yale University Press, 1993).

15 Charlotte Guichard, *Les Amateurs d'art à Paris* (Seyssel: Champ Vallon, 2008), pp. 317–29.

16 Étienne La Font de Saint-Yenne, *Sentiments sur quelques ouvrages de peinture*, cited by Édouard Pommier, *Théories du portrait: De la Renaissance aux Lumières* (Paris: Gallimard, 1998), pp. 316–17.

17 "Lettre sur les peintures, sculptures et gravures de messieurs de l'Académie royale, exposées au salon du Louvre, le 25 août 1769," *Mémoires secrets*, 1784, Vol. XIII, pp. 43–4. Criticism of unknown models for portraits is a recurring theme; *Mémoires secrets* returns to it in 1775, once again in order to make an exception for great men and celebrated men. "I don't understand why the busts of the

King, and the Queen, and the Ministers, great authors, celebrated artists are banned, when we should be multiplying their images in order to give at least an idea of them to those who are unable to see these august masters in person, these interesting personages, these famous men in every field."

18 Marcia Pointon, "Portrait! Portrait!! Portrait!!!," in David Solkin (ed.), *Art on the Line: The Royal Academy Exhibitions at Somerset House, 1780–1836* (New Haven: Yale University Press, 2001), pp. 93–105.

19 Mark Hallet, "Reynolds, Celebrity and the Exhibition Space" in Martin Postle (ed.), *Joshua Reynolds: The Creation of Celebrity* (London: Tate Publishing, 2005), pp. 49–60.

20 Peter M. Briggs, "Laurence Sterne and Literary Celebrity in 1760," in Thomas Keymer (ed.), *Lawrence Sterne's Tristram Shandy: A Casebook* (Oxford: Oxford University Press, 2006), pp. 79–107, here pp. 85 and 86; Frank Donoghue, *The Fame Machine: Book Reviewing and Eighteenth-Century Literary Careers* (Stanford: Stanford University Press, 1996), pp. 56–81.

21 Martin Postle, "The Modern Appelles," in Postle (ed.), *Joshua Reynolds*, pp. 17–33; Martin Postle,, " 'Painted Women': Reynolds and the Cult of the Courtesan," in Robin Asleson (ed.), *Notorious Muse: The Actress in British Art and Culture, 1776–1812* (New Haven/London: Yale University Press, 2003), pp. 22–55.

22 On the celebrity of Georgiana Cavendish, see Amanda Foreman, *Georgiana, Duchess of Devonshire* (London: HarperCollins, 1998).

23 Postle, " 'Painted Women'," p. 46.

24 Tim Clayton, "Figures of Fame: Reynolds and the Printed Image," in Postle (ed.), *Joshua Reynolds*, pp. 48–59.

25 McPherson, "Garrickomania."

26 Marianne Grivel, *Le Commerce de l'estampe à Paris au XVIIe siècle* (Geneva: Droz, 1986); Pierre Casselle, "Le Commerce des estampes à Paris dans la seconde moitié du XVIIIe siècle," thesis from École des Chartes, 1976.

27 L.S. Mercier, *Tableau de Paris*, Vol. VI, p. 56, "Graveurs." Mercier was well aware of the iconoclastic nature of his discourse and evokes both the enthusiasm of the consumers and the numerous intermediaries interested in this profusion of images: "No doubt our simple image hobbyists will not miss a chance to turn me into an iconoclast. Armies of drawers, engravers, intaglio printers, illuminators, booksellers, peddlers and image makers of every sort, from every level, will sound the alarm about my heterodoxy."

28 Casselle, "Le Commerce des estampes à Paris," pp. 64–5.

29 Paris archives, unclaimed funds, D4 B6, box 108, file 7709: "État actif et passif des créances des Srs Esnault et Rapilly," February 20, 1790.
30 Katie Scott, "Imitation or Crimes of Likeness," chapter 3 of a book to appear soon about copyright issues in the visual arts. I thank Katie Scott for allowing me to read her text, notably dealing with the proceedings brought against Esnault and Rapilly.
31 Casselle, "Le Commerce des estampes à Paris," p. 122.
32 Ibid., p. 169.
33 Louis Boilly, *L'Atelier d'un sculpteur, ou Jean-Antoine Houdon modelant le buste de Laplace dans son atelier* (Paris: Musée des Arts Décoratifs, 1803). See Annie Scottez-De Wambrechies and Florence Raymond (eds), *Boilly (1761–1845)* (Lille: Palais des Beaux-Arts in Lille, 2011), pp. 178–83.
34 On the career of Sophie Arnould, her success in the opera, but also on the world stage, and her reputation as a libertine, see Edmond and Jules de Goncourt, *Sophie Arnould, d'après sa correspondance et ses mémoires inédits*, Paris, 1893, and, more recently, Colin Jones, "French Crossing IV: Vagaries of Passion and Power in Enlightenment Paris," *Transactions of the Royal Historical Society*, 23 (2013), pp. 3–35.
35 Guilhem Scherf, "Houdon au-dessus de tous les artistes," in Anne L. Poulet and Guilhem Scherf (eds), *Houdon, sculpteur des Lumières*, exhibition catalogue (Versailles: Château de Versailles, 2004), pp. 20–1.
36 Métra, April 16, 1778, cited by Ulrike Mathies, "Voltaire," in Poulet and Scherf (eds), *Houdon, sculpteur des Lumières*, p. 154.
37 Guilhem Scherf, *Houdon, 1741–1828: statues, portraits sculptés* (Paris: Louvre edition, 2006), p. 75.
38 Julius von Schlosser, "History of Portraiture in Wax" (1901), trans. James Michael Loughridge, in Robert Panzanelli (ed.), *Ephemeral Bodies: Wax Sculpture and the Human Figure* (Los Angeles: Getty Research Insttitute, 2008), pp. 171–303.
39 Jean Adhémar, "Les musées de cire en France: Curtius, le 'banquet royal', les 'têtes coupées'," *Gazette des beaux-arts*, Vol. XCII, 1978, pp. 203–14. In the middle of the eighteenth century, the memory of Benoist was still very fresh, as testified by this entry on "Wax" from the *Encyclopédie*: "Everybody knows the name of Monsieur Benoît and that the ingenious invention of circles made up of wax figures was, for many years, much admired by the court and the city This professional painter found the secret for making faces look alive, even the most beautiful and the most delicate, and

without any danger to either health or beauty, by making molds in which he formed the wax masks, to which he gave a life-like quality, in color and in the enamel eyes that looked absolutely natural. These dressed figures so much conformed to the quality of the persons represented, they so much resembled them, sometimes one thought they were alive."

40 Von Schlosser, "History of Portraiture in Wax," p. 204.
41 Mercier, *Tableau de Paris*, Vol. II, "Spectacles des boulevards," p. 42.
42 Pamela M. Pilbeam, *Mme Tussaud and the History of Waxworks* (London: Hambledon, 2006).
43 Von Schlosser, "History of Portraiture in Wax," p. 266.
44 Benedetto Croce, *I Teatri di Napoli, dal Rinascimento alla fine del secolo decimottavo* (Milan: Adelphi, [1891] 1992), p. 278.
45 *Mémoires secrets*, December 30, 1779, Vol. XIV, 1780, p. 331.
46 It is difficult to know the exact numbers in the absence of a catalogue and owing to the rarity of the sources. See Samuel Taylor, "Artists and Philosophes as Mirrored by Sèvres and Wedgwood," in Francis Haskell, Anthony Levi, and Robert Shackleton (eds), *The Artist and the Writer in France: Essays in Honour of Jean Seznec* (Oxford: Oxford University Press, 1974), pp. 21–39.
47 Neil McKendrick, "Josiah Wedgwood and the Commercialization of the Potteries," in McKendrick et al., *The Birth of a Consumer-Society*, pp. 100–45.
48 *Letters of Josiah Wedgwood*, ed. Katherine Farrar (Manchester: Morten, 1903), letter of July 28, 1778, p. 27.
49 *A catalogue of cameos, intaglios, medals, and bas-reliefs; with a general account of vases and other ornaments, after the antique, made by Wedgwood and Bentley; and sold at their rooms in Great Newport-Street, London, London: printed in the year M.DCC. LXXIII and sold by Cadel, in the Strand* (Robson, New Bond-Street and Parker, Print-Seller, Cornhill, 1773).
50 *Catalogue of cameos, intaglios, medals, bas-reliefs, busts and small statues; with a general account of tablets, vases, ecritoires, and other ornamental and useful articles. The whole formed in different kinds of Porcelain and Terra Cotta, chiefly after the antique, and the finest models of modern artists.* By Josiah Wedgwood, F.R.S. and A.S. Potter to Her Majesty, and to His Royal Highness the Duke of York and Albany. Sold at his rooms in Greek Street, Soho, London, and at his manufactory, in Staffordshire, Etruria, 1787.
51 Catalogue *de camées, intaglios, médailles, bas-reliefs, bustes et petites statues* [...] *par Joisah Wedgwood* (London, 1788).

52 Joyce Chaplin, *The First Scientific American: Benjamin Franklin and the Pursuit of Genius* (New York: Basic Books, 2006).

53 The first portrait is in the permanent collection at the Metropolitan Museum of New York, the second is at the National Portrait Gallery in Washington.

54 BNF, stamp office, 60 B 2655.

55 Letter, June 3, 1779, in *The Papers of Benjamin Franklin* (New Haven/London: Yale University Press, 1992), Vol. XXIX, pp. 612–13.

56 *Mémoires secrets*, January 18, 1777, Vol. X, p. 11.

57 Vic Gatrell, *City of Laughter: Sex and Satire in Eighteenth-Century London* (London: Atlantic Books, 2006). See also Diana Donald, *The Age of Caricature: Satirical Prints in the Reign of George III* (New Haven/London: Yale University Press, 1996), and concerning the theater, Heather McPherson, "Painting, Politics and the Stage in the Age of Caricature," in Asleslon (ed.), *Notorious Muse*, pp. 171–93.

58 Kate Williams, *England's Mistress: The Infamous Life of Lady Hamilton* (London: Random House, 2006).

59 Friedrich Rehberg, *Drawings Faithfully Copied from Nature at Naples* (London: 1794); James Gillray, *A new edition considerably enlarged, of attitudes faithfully copied from nature: and humbly dedicated to all admirers of the grand and sublime* (London: H. Humphreys, 1807).

60 Jane Moody, "Stolen Identities: Character, Mimicry and the Invention of Samuel Foote," in Luckhurst and Moody (eds), *Theatre and Celebrity*, pp. 65–89.

61 *Gentleman's Magazine*, 43, February 1773, p. 101, cited in Moody, "Stolen Identities," p. 76.

62 Moody, "Stolen Identities," p. 76.

63 Marcia Pointon, "The Lives of Kitty Fisher," *British Journal for Eighteenth-Century Studies*, 27:1 (2004), pp. 77–98. For a wider perspective on "sexual celebrity" of English courtesans in the eighteenth century, see Faramerz Dabhoiwala, *The Origins of Sex: A History of the First Sexual Revolution* (Princeton: Princeton University Press, 2012).

64 *The Public Advertiser*, March 27, 1759.

65 *The Gentleman's Magazine in the Age of Samuel Johnson, 1731–1745* (London: Pickering & Chatto, 1998).

66 *The Town and Country Magazine. Universal repository of knowledge, instruction, and entertainment* (London: Hamilton, 1780), Vol. XII.

67 John Brewer, *A Sentimental Murder: Love and Madness in the Eighteenth Century* (New York: Farrar, Straus and Giroux, 2004), pp. 37–41.

68 Jeremy Popkin and Bernadette Fort (eds), *The Mémoires secrets and the Culture of Publicity in Eighteenth-Century France* (Oxford: Voltaire Foundation, 1998); Christophe Cave (ed.), *Le Règne de la critique: L'imaginaire culturel des Mémoires secrets* (Paris: Honoré Champion, 2010). See also the critical edition: *Mémoires secrets pour servir à l'histoire de la république des lettres en France, depuis 1762 jusqu'à nos jours*, eds Christophe Cave and Suzanne Cornand (Paris: Honoré Champion, 2009–10), 5 vols.

69 See Yves Citton, "La production critique de la mode dans les *Mémoires secrets*," in Cave (ed.), *Le Règne de la critique*, pp. 55–81, which focuses on the ambivalence of fashion, which is an object of criticism, but also perceived as a creative principle.

70 *Mémoires secrets*, Vol. XVI, p. 25, October 24, 1780.

71 Jeremy Popkin, "The 'Mémoires secrets' and the Reading of the Enlightenment," in Popkin and Fort (eds), *The Mémoires secrets*, pp. 9–36, here p. 28.

72 So, when the *Mémoires secrets* recount an accident that Beaumarchais supposedly had, run over by a carriage, it adds: "It is even thought that [Beaumarchis] in some small way exaggerated his accident before the public in order to create more of a sensation and to get himself talked about, something he loved most of all" (*Mémoires secrets*, Vol. IX, December 8, 1777, p. 307).

73 These numbers are drawn from the *Table alphabétique des auteurs et des personnages cités dans les 'Mémoires secrets'*, published in Brussels in 1866. See Popkin and Fort (eds), *The Mémoires secrets*, pp. 182–3 and 108–9. The index not being totally complete, the numbers fall slightly short of the total

74 Pamela Cheek, "The *Mémoires secrets* and the Actress," in ibid., pp. 107–27.

75 Elizabeth Barry, "From Epitaph to Obituary: Death and Celebrity in Eighteenth-Century British Culture," *International Journal of Cultural Studies*, 11:3 (2008), pp. 259–75. See also Nigel Starck, *Life after Death: The Art of Obituary* (Melbourne: Melbourne University Press, 2006).

76 *Nécrologe des hommes célèbres de France* (Paris: Desprez, 1768), p. vi.

77 Armando Petrucci, *Le Scritture ultime* (Turin: Einaudi, 1995).

78 Sabina Loriga, *Le Petit X: De la biographie à l'histoire* (Paris: Le Seuil, 2010), p. 18.

79   Guido Mazzoni, *Teoria del romanzo* (Bologna: Il Mulino, 2012), especially pp. 151–93.

80   Hélène Merlin, *Public et littérature en France au XVIIe siècle* (Paris: Les Belles Lettres, 1994).

81   Denis Diderot, "Éloge de Richardson," in *Œuvres* (Paris: Gallimard, 1951), pp. 1059–74; Roger Chartier, "Les larmes de Damilaville et la lectrice impatiente," in *Inscrire et effacer: Culture écrite et littérature (XIe–XVIIIe siècle)* (Paris: Gallimard/Seuil, 2005), pp. 155–75; Lynn Hunt, *Inventing Human Rights: A History* (New York: Norton, 2007), pp. 35–69.

82   The impact of the romance novel on historiography in the eighteenth century is still unknown. Nonetheless, see Mark Salber Phillips, "Reconsiderations on History and Antiquarianism: Arnaldo Momigliano and the Historiography of Eighteenth-Century Britain," *Journal of the History of Ideas*, 57:2 (1996), pp. 297–316, and "Histories, Micro- and Literary: Problems of Genre and Distance," *New Literary History*, 34 (2003), pp. 211–12.

83   Samuel Johnson, *The Rambler* (1750–2), in *The Yale Edition of Samuel Johnson* (New Haven: Yale University Press, 1969), October 13, 1750.

84   Giorgio Manganelli, *Vie de Samuel Johnson* (Paris: Le Promeneur, [2008] 2010), p. 46.

85   James Boswell, *An Account of Corsica, the Journal of a Tour to that Island, and Memoirs of Pascal Paoli* (Glasgow: Dilly, 1768). On the voyage of Boswell, see Joseph Foladare, *Boswell's Paoli* (Hamden, CT: Archon Books, 1979), pp. 19–76. The distrust of Paoli was reported by himself to Miss d'Arblay, cited by George Birkbeck Hill, *Boswell's Life of Johnson* (New York: Harper, 1889), Vol. I, p. 6.

86   Beginning with his first visit in 1762, at twenty-two, he kept a journal about his life in London, and for several years, from 1776 to 1783, he wrote numerous articles under a pseudonym for the *London Magazine*. See Frederick Pottle, *James Boswell: The Early Years* (London: Heinemann, 1966); Frank Brady, *James Boswell: The Later Years (1769–1795)* (New York: McGraw-Hill Books, 1984); Peter Martin, *The Life of James Boswell* (London: Weidenfeld and Nicolson, 1999).

87   Cheryl Wanko, *Roles of Authority: Thespian Biography and Celebrity in Eighteenth-Century Britain* (Lubbock: Texas Tech University Press, 2003).

88   See Roger Chartier, *Figures de la gueuserie* (Paris: Montalba, 1982).

89   Christian Biet, "Cartouche et le mythe de l'ennemi public no. 1 en France et en Europe," introduction to Marc-Antoine Legrand,

Cartouche ou les Voleurs (1721), texts edited and commented on by Christian Biet (Vijon: Lampsaque, 2004).

90 Ibid.

91 For a political reading along these lines, see Patrice Péveri, "De Cartouche à Poulailler: l'héroïsation du bandit dans le Paris du XVIIIe siècle," in Claude Gauvard and Jean-Louis Robert *Être parisien au XVIIIe siècle* (Paris: Publications de la Sorbonne, 2004), pp. 135–50. For examples of mass resistance through word of mouth, see Arlette Farge and Jacques Revel, *Logiques de la foule: Les enlèvements d'enfants à Paris en 1750* (Paris: Hachette, 1988).

92 *Histoire de la vie et du procès de Louis-Dominique Cartouche, et de plusieurs de ses complices* (Brussels: Le Trotteur, 1772). There are numerous editions of this text, some of them with the title *Histoire de la vie et du procès du fameux Louis-Dominique Cartouche*. This is the case, for example, of the Rouen edition of 1722. Hans-Jürgen Luserbrink, *Histoires curieuses et véritables de Cartouche et de Mandrin* (Paris: Arthaud, 1984).

93 Madeleine Pinault-Sorensen, "Le thème des brigands à travers la peinture, le dessin et la gravure," in Lise Andries (ed.), *Cartouche, Mandrin, et autres brigands du XVIIIe siècle* (Paris: Desjonquères, 2010), pp. 84–111.

94 Biet, "Cartouche et le mythe de l'ennemi public no. 1."

95 Lise Andries, "Histoires criminelles anglaises," in Andries (ed.), *Cartouche, Mandrin, et autres brigands*, pp. 253–5.

96 *Histoire de Louis Mandrin, depuis sa naissance jusqu'à sa mort: avec un détail de ses cruautés, de ses brigandages, et de son supplice* (Chambéry/Paris: Gorrin/Delormel, 1755); *Abrégé de la vie de Louis Mandrin, chef de contrebandier en France* (1755); Lagrange, *La Mort de Mandrin* (Paris: Société des Libraires, 1755).

97 *Histoire de la vie et du procès de Louis-Dominique Cartouche*, p. 4.

98 *Vie privée et criminelle d'Henri-Augustin Trumeau* (Paris, 1803), cited in *Dictionnaire des vies privées (1722–1842)*, eds Olivier Ferret, Anne-Marie Mercier-Faivre, and Chantal Thomas (Oxford: Voltaire Foundation, 2011), p. 409.

99 A political interpretation has been developed several different times by Robert Darnton. See *The Devil in the Holy Water, or the Art of Slander from Louis XIV to Napoleon* (Philadelphia: University of Pennsylvania Press, 2010). In spite of his disagreement with Darnton on numerous points, Simon Burrows' *Blackmail, Scandal, and Revolution: London's French Libellistes, 1758–1792*

(Manchester: Manchester University Press, 2006) has a similar perspective. For a more global view of this genre, see *Dictionnaire des vies privées*. I will revisit political interpretations in chapter 5, dealing with Marie-Antoinette.

100 Merlin, *Public et littérature*; *De la publication, entre Renaissance et Lumières*, texts combined by Christian Jouhaud and Alain Viala (Paris: Fayard, 2002).

101 Habermas, *The Structural Transformation of the Public Sphere*. There is now a large bibliography. See notably, Roger Chartier, *Les Origines culturelles de la Révolution française* (Paris: Seuil, 1991).

102 P.G. Contant d'Orville, *Précis d'une histoire générale de la vie privée des Français dans tous les temps et dans toutes les provinces de la monarchie* (Paris: Moutard, 1779); Pierre Jean-Baptiste Legrand d'Aussy, *Histoire de la vie privée des Français, depuis l'origine de la nation jusqu'à nos jours* (Paris, 1782), 3 vols.

103 Antoine Lilti, *The World of the Salons: Sociability and Wordliness in Eighteenth-Century Paris*, trans. Lydia G. Cochrane (Oxford: Oxford University Press, [2005] 2015).

104 Pierre Kayser, *La Protection de la vie privée* (Aix-en-Provence: Presses Universitaires d'Aix-Marseille/Economica, 1984).

105 Emma Spary, *Utopia's Garden: French Natural History from Old Regime to Revolution* (Chicago: University of Chicago Press, 2000), pp. 27–9.

106 Joseph Aude, *Vie privée du comte de Buffon* (Lausanne, 1788), p. 2.

107 Ibid., p. 5.

108 Ibid., pp. 18 and 50.

109 Marie Jean Hérault de Séchelles, *Visite à Buffon* (Paris: 1785).

110 Sara Maza, *Private Lives and Public Affairs: The Causes Célèbres of Prerevolutionary France* (Berkeley: University of California Press, 1993).

111 *Vie de Joseph Balsamo, connu sous le nom de Count Cagliostro* (Paris, 1791), p. iii.

CHAPTER 4   FROM GLORY TO CELEBRITY

1 Jean-François Marmontel, "Gloire," *Encyclopédie ou dictionnaire raisonné de arts et des métiers* (Paris: Briasson, 1757), Vol. VII.

2 On this point, see Robert Morrissey, *The Economy of Glory: From Ancien Régime to the Fall of Napoleon*, trans. Teresa Lavendar Fagan (Chicago/London: University of Chicago Press, [2010] 2014).

3   Paul Bénichou, *Morales du Grand Siècle* (Paris: Gallimard, 1948); A.O. Hirschman, *The Passions and the Interests: Political Arguments for Capitalism before Its Triumph* (Princeton: Princeton University Press, 1977).

4   Letter to Thiériot, July 15, 1735, Voltaire, *Correspondence and Related Documents*, ed. Theodore Besterman (Oxford: Voltaire Foundation, 1969), Vol. III, p. 175.

5   John R. Iverson, "La gloire humanisée: Voltaire et son siècle," *Histoire, économie & société*, 20:2 (2001), pp. 211–18. Also, there is the continual success of the re-editions of *Vies des hommes illustres de Plutarque* throughout the century.

6   Darrin McMahon, *Divine Fury: A History of Genius* (New York: Basic Books, 2013).

7   Bénichou, *Morales du Grand Siècle*.

8   Jean-Pierre Vernant, "La belle mort et le cadavre outragé" (1982), in *L'Individu, la Mort, l'Amour* (Paris: Gallimard, 1989), pp. 41–79; Gregory Nagy, *The Best of the Achaeans: Concepts of the Hero in Archaic Greek Poetry* (Baltimore, MD: Johns Hopkins University Press, 1999). *Achéens:. La fabrique du héros dans la poésie grecque archaïque* (Paris: Éditions du Seuil, [1979] 1994).

9   Once greatly lauded, this emulation is now criticized "Men born for glory have sought it where opinion has placed it. Alexander always had his eyes on the fable of Achilles; Charles XII, the story of Alexander: hence this emulation, which made two ruthless warriors of two kings full of valor and talents." (Marmontel, "Gloire"). However, it is not the principle of emulation that is contested; it is the character of the models.

10   The parallel became a commonplace that is found, for example, in Montesquieu (*Mes Pensées*, 1729). It is at the beginning of an *Histoire d'Épaminondas* when the Abbé de Saint-Pierre published his "Discours sur la différence entre l'homme illustre et le grand homme" (1739).

11   *Essai sur les éloges ou histoire de la littérature et de l'éloquence appliquée à ce genre d'ouvrages, Œuvres de M. Thomas* (Paris: Moutard, 1773), Vols 1–2. On this transformation from the eulogy and the figure of the great man, see Bonnet, *Naissance du Panthéon*.

12   William Hazlitt, "On the Living Poets," in *Lectures on the English Poets* (London: Taylor & Hessey, 1819 [2nd edition]), pp. 283–331.

13   Cicero said of glory that it "follows virtue as if it were its shadow," a definition that would often be used during the Renaissance

("gloria [...] virtutem tamquam umbra sequitur"), from *Tusculanarum Disputationum*, I. 45. In the *Somnium Scipionis* ("Dream of Scipio"), Scipio Aemilianus, after having criticized the earthly forms of *fama*, limited in time and space, reveals the blissful state reserved for great men – politicians, but also artists, philosophers, and musicians – who benefit, after death, from a sort of eternal life that allows them to admire the beauty of the universe from the Milky Way.

14 Petrarch, *Letters of Familiar Matters*, quoted in Birger H. Headstrom, "The Historical Significance of Petrarch's Letters," *The Open Court*, 40:1 (1926), pp. 1–13, here p. 10. The letter, addressed to his friend Tommaso da Messina, was actually written in 1350, ten years after the death of Tommaso, at the moment when Petrarch was composing his collection of letters. By placing it earlier, at the head of the collection, he gave it the force of a manifesto.

15 Barbara Carnevali, "Glory: Réputation et pouvoir dans le modèle hobbesien," *Communications*, 93:2 (2013), pp. 49–67.

16 The phrase is Petrarch's. On his ambivalence concerning a desire for literary glory, confronted with Christian condemnation, see his *Secretum*, where he creates a dialogue between himself and Saint Augustine. Petrarch, *Secretum* (New York: Peter Lang, 1989).

17 Letters from Diderot to Falconet from August 1766, *Correspondance* (Paris: Robert Laffont, 1997), pp. 664 and 680; Denis Diderot, "Essai sur les règnes de Claude et de Néron," in *Œuvres* (Paris: Robert Laffont, 1994), Vol. I, p. 115.

18 Patricia Fara, *Newton, the Making of a Genius* (London: Macmillan, 2002); Thomas Gaehtgens and Gregor Wedekind (eds), *Le Culte des grands hommes en France et en Allemagne* (Paris: Éditions de la Maison des Sciences de l'Homme, 2010); Eveline G. Bouwers, *Public Pantheons in Revolutionary Europe: Comparing Cultures of Remembrance, c. 1790–1840* (Basingstoke: Palgrave Macmillan, 2012), p. 35.

19 Hervé Drévillon and Diego Venturino (eds), *Penser et vivre l'honneur à l'époque moderne* (Rennes: Presses Universitaires de Rennes, 2011).

20 Medievalists debated the respective role of local sociability and legal practices. See Claude Gauvard, "La 'fama', une parole fondatrice," *Médiévales*, 24 (1993), pp. 5–13; Julien Théry, "Fama: l'opinion publique comme preuve judiciaire. Aperçu sur la révolution médiévale de l'inquisitoire (XIIe–XIVe siècle)," in Bruno Lesmesle (ed.), *La Preuve en justice de l'Antiquité à nos jours* (Rennes: Presses Universitaires de Rennes, 2003), pp. 119–47;

Thelma Fenster and Daniel Lord Smail (eds), *Fama: The Politics of Talk and Reputation in Medieval Europe* (Ithaca, NY/London, Cornell University Press, 2003).

21 Bernard Guenée, *Du Guesclin et Froissart: La fabrication de la renommée* (Paris: Tallandier, 2008), pp. 75–103.

22 Charles Duclos, *Considérations sur les moeurs de ce siècle* (Paris, 1751; and Paris: Prault, 1764). The book was reprinted five times the first year, eight after an expanded edition in 1764 and up until the Revolution. On the appearance of the text and the challenges, see the critical edition by Carole Dornier (Paris: Honoré Champion, 2005), which goes back to the 1764 text. In the following, I am quoting from the 1751 edition, sometimes comparing it with later editions.

23 Ibid., p. 2

24 Ibid., p. 97.

25 Ibid., p. 18.

26 Ibid., pp. 74 and 102.

27 Ibid., pp. 108, 129, 112, 100.

28 Ibid., pp. 110–11.

29 Duclos tried to resolve this question by introducing a new term, "consideration," which dealt with something the word "reputation" could not: the appropriateness of virtue and esteem: "Consideration is a form of personal respect that a man inspires." But this attempt to base an economy of respect on personal merit falls short: "If one acquires consideration, one also usurps it."

30 Duclos, *Considérations*, 1764 edition, pp. 115–52.

31 Ibid., 1751, p. 97; 1764, p. 116.

32 Ibid., 1751, pp. 104–5; 1764, pp. 123–4.

33 Brewer, *The Pleasures of the Imagination*.

34 Samuel Johnson, *The Rambler*, Vol. III, p. 118, May 29, 1750: "If we consider the distribution of literary fame in our own time, we shall find it a possession of very uncertain tenure; sometimes bestowed by a sudden caprice of the public, and again transferred to a new favourite, for no other reason than that he is new."

35 Ibid., August 10, 1751, Vol. V, pp. 13–17.

36 Ibid.

37 Ibid.

38 Ibid., May 12, 1750, Vol. IV, pp. 86–91.

39 Ibid.

40 Montesquieu, *Persian Letters: With Related Texts*, trans. Raymond N. MacKenzie (Cambridge, MA/Indianapolis: Hackett, [1721] 2014), letter 144, p. 226.

41 The usage frequency is 0.13 for 10,000 words in these two decades, then a new high of 0.10 in 1810–20. In following years, even if the usage grew, it never again attained such a relative frequency.

42 Results obtained with Ngram Viewer software, October 22, 2012.

43 Charles Palissot Demontenoy, *Petites lettres sur de grands philosophes* (1757), *Œuvres* (Liège, 1777), Vol. II, p. 107.

44 François Antoine Chevrier, *Le Colporteur, histoire morale et critique* (London: Jean Nourse, 1762), p. 67.

45 Letter from Julie de Lespinasse on May 22, 1773, *Correspondance entre Mlle de Lespinasse et le comte de Guibert* (Paris: Calmann-Lévy, 1905), p. 5.

46 Denis Diderot, *Œuvres* (Paris: Gallimard, 1951), p. 729.

47 Mme Dufrénoy, *La Femme auteur ou les inconvénients de la célébrité* (Paris, 1812), 2 vols.

48 Francis Bacon, *Essays* (Oxford: Clarendon Press, [1597] 2000); *The Advancement of Learning* (Oxford: Clarendon Press, [1605] 2000).

49 Vittorio Alfieri, *Del principe e delle lettere* (Kehl, 1795); *Du prince et des lettres* (Paris: Eymery and Delaunay, 1818), p. 85.

50 Enrique Vila-Matras, *Bartleby & Co.*, trans. Jonathan Dunne (New York: Harvill, [2000] 2004), pp. 69–71.

51 Nicolas de Chamfort, *Maximes et pensées: Caractères et anecdotes*, ed. Jean Dagen (Paris: Garnier-Flammarion, 1968), p. 66.

52 Ibid., p. 121.

53 Pierre Bourdieu, *The Rules of the Art: Genesis and Structure in the Literary Field*, trans. Susan Emanuel (Cambridge: Polity, [1992] 1996).

54 Nicolas de Chamfort, *Œuvres complètes* (Lyon: Chaumerot, 1825), Vol. V, p. 274.

55 On the literary career of Mercier, see Jean-Claude Bonnet (ed.), *Louis Sébastien Mercier: Un hérétique en littérature* (Paris: Mercure de France, 1995). On the status of the description, a study of both mores and moral considerations, see Joanna Stalnaker, *The Unfinished Enlightenment: Description in the Age of the Encyclopedia* (Ithaca, NY: Cornell University Press, 2010).

56 Louis Sébastien Mercier, *De la littérature et des littérateurs* (Yverdon, 1778), p. 40.

57 Gregory S. Brown, *A Field of Honor: The Identities of Writers, Court Culture and Public Theater in the French Intellectual Field from Racine to the Revolution* (New York: Columbia University Press, e-Gutenberg, 2005).

58 L.S. Mercier, "L'Auteur! l'Auteur!," *Tableau de Paris*, 1788, Vol. XI, pp. 136–7.

CHAPTER 5 LONELINESS OF THE CELEBRITY

1 Jean-Jacques Rousseau, *Rousseau Judge of Jean-Jacques: Dialogues: The Collected Writings of Rousseau*, Vol. 1, eds Roger D. Masters and Christopher Kelly (Hanover, NH/London: University Press of New England, [1782] 1990, pp. 128–9.

2 Jeremy Caradonna, *The Enlightenment in Practice: Academic Prize Contests and Intellectual Culture in France (1670–1794)* (Ithaca, NY: Cornell University Press, 2012).

3 Letter from Mme Graffigny to Devaux, October 29, 1751, *Correspondance de Mme de Graffigny*, ed. J.-A. Dainard (Oxford: Voltaire Foundation, 2008), Vol. XII, p. 151.

4 Jean-Jacques Rousseau, *Correspondance complète* (CC), ed. R. A. Leigh (Oxford: Voltaire Foundation, 1965–98), 52 vols, Vol. II, p. 136.

5 "If I do not have the celebrity of rank and birth, I do have another one which is more my own and which I purchased more dearly; I have the celebrity of misfortune" (draft of the *Confessions, Œuvres complètes* [OC] [Paris: Gallimard, 1959], Vol. I, p. 1151).

6 Sean Goodlett, "The Origins of Celebrity: The Eigtheenth-Century Anglo-French Press Reception of Jean-Jacques Rousseau" (PhD, University of Oregon, 2000).

7 The condemnation of the *Contrat Social* took place in the framwork of a ferocious political confrontation between the Advisory Council and the representatives, ending in a quasi-revolutionary climate in which Rousseau was both an actor and the subject. See notably Richard Whatmore, "Rousseau and the Representants: The Politics of the *Lettres écrites de la montagne*," *Modern Intellectual History*, 3:3 (2006), pp. 385–413.

8 Quoted in Goodlett, "The Origins of Celebrity," p. 127.

9 *The Public Advertiser*, January 13, 1766, CC, Vol. XXIX, p. 295.

10 Letter of Hume to the Marquise de Barbentane, February 16, 1766, CC, Vol. XXVII, p. 309.

11 On Rousseau's visit to England, see Claire Brock, *The Feminization of Fame, 1750–1830* (Basingstoke: Palgrave Macmillan, 2006), pp. 28ff.

12 Raymond Birn, "Fashioning an Icon: Jean-Jacques Rousseau and the *Mémoires secrets*," in Popkin and Fort (eds), *The Mémoires secrets*, pp. 93–105.

13 *Mémoires secrets*, Vol. II, p. 253.

14 *Mémoires secrets*, Vol. V, p. 162.

15 Elizabeth A. Foster, *Le Dernier Séjour de J.-J. Rousseau à Paris, 1770–1778* (Northampton/Paris: H. Champion, 1921); Jacques Berchtold and Michel Porret (eds), *Rousseau visité, Rousseau visiteur: Les dernières années (1770–1778), actes du colloque de Genève (1996), Annales de la société Jean-Jacques Rousseau* (Geneva: Droz, 1999).

16 *Correspondance littéraire*, July 1770, Vol. IX, p. 229.

17 Letter from Mme du Deffand to Horace Walpole, July 15, 1770, *Horace Walpole's Correspondence*, Vol. IV, p. 434.

18 *Les Mémoires secrets* proposed an even less favorable explanation, but which pointed out to what extent the question of Rousseau's relationship to his own celebrity had become an obsessive issue: "Monsieur Jean-Jacques Rousseau, after sometimes being seen at the Café de la Régence, where his vanity was flattered by proving that he still caused a sensation as before and that his renown continued to attract crowds that followed him, wrapped himself in his modesty; he returned to his obscurity, satisfied by this momentary burst, until another event gives him more celebrity" (p. 167).

19 Jean-Baptiste La Harpe, *Correspondance littéraire adressée à son altesse impériale Mgr le grand-duc, aujourd'hui empereur de Russie, et à M. le comte Schowalow* (Paris: Migneret, 1804), Vol. I, p. 204.

20 *Journal inédit du duc de Croÿ* (Paris: Flammarion, 1906–21), Vol. III, p. 12.

21 Jacques Louis Ménétra, *Journal de ma vie*, ed. D. Roche (Paris: Montalba, 1982), p. 222. Ménétra also wrote a letter to Rousseau that showed he knew the titles of his principal works and that he had no doubt read them.

22 Vittorio Alfieri, *Ma vie*, ed. M. Traversier (Paris: Mercure de France, [1803] 2012), p. 175.

23 Quoted in *CC*, Vol. I, pp. 30–1.

24 *Gazette de Berne*, November 13, 1776, *CC*, Vol. XL, p. 104; *Courrier d'Avignon*, December 20, 1776: M. Jean-Jacques Rousseau has died from the after-effects of his fall. [...] There is every reason to believe that the public will not be deprived of his life story and that even the name of the dog who killed him will be found" (quoted in *OC*, Vol. I, p. 1778).

25 Bronislaw Baczko, *Job, mon ami* (Paris: Gallimard, 1997), pp. 177–254; Raymond Birn, *Forging Rousseau: Print, Commerce and Cultural Manipulation in the Late Enlightenment* (Oxford: Voltaire Foundation, 2001); Roger Barny, *Prélude idéologique à la Révolution: Le rousseauisme avant 1789* (Paris: Les Belles Lettres, 1985); Barny, *Rousseau dans la Révolution: Le personnage de*

Jean-Jacques et les débuts du culte révolutionnaire, 1787–1791 (Oxford: Voltaire Foundation, 1986); Carla Hesse, "Lire Rousseau pendant la Révolution française," in Céline Spector (ed.), "Modernités de Rousseau," *Lumières*, 15 (2011), pp. 17–32.

26 *Journal helvétique*, July 1757, CC, Vol. III, pp. 334–5.

27 Louise Alexandrine Julie Dupin de Chenonceaux to Rousseau, CC, Vol. XXIII, p. 108.

28 Alexandre Deleyre to Rousseau, August 6, 1765, CC, Vol. XXVI, pp. 149–53.

29 Niklaus Anton Kirchberger to Rousseau, CC, Vol. XX, pp. 115–17.

30 *Mémoires secrets*, Vol. II, p. 288.

31 Jean-Jacques Rousseau, "Letter on French Music," in *The Collected Writings of Rousseau*, Vol. 7, ed. John Scott (Hanover, NH/ London: University of New England Press, 1990), pp. 141–74. Here is a sample: "I believe I have shown that there is neither meter nor melody in French Music, because the language is not susceptible to them; that French song is but a continual barking, unbearable to any ear not prepared for it; that its harmony is crude, expressionless, and uniquely feels its Schoolboy padding; that French arias are not at all arias; that the French recitative is not at all recitative. From which I conclude that the French do not at all have a Music and cannot have any; or that if they ever have any, it will be so much the worse for them" (p. 174).

32 *Correspondance littéraire*, January 1, 1754, Vol. I, p. 312.

33 *Mémoires secrets*, Vol. 1, p. 92.

34 Memoirs of Princess Czartoryska, quoted by François Rosset, "D'une princesse fantasque aux Considérations: faits et reflets," in Berchtold and Porret (eds), *Rousseau visité, Rousseau visiteur*, p. 22.

35 Paul Charles Thiébault, *Mémoires* (Paris: Plon, 1893), Vol. I, p. 136, quoted by Raymond Trousson, *Lettres à Jean-Jacques Rousseau sur La Nouvelle Héloïse* (Paris: Honoré Champion, 2011), p. 30. For an overall view of the reception of *La Nouvelle Héloïse*, see Yannick Seité, *Du livre au lire: La Nouvelle Héloïse, roman des Lumières* (Paris: Honoré Champion, 2002).

36 Letter from Charles Joseph Panckoucke of February 10, 1761, CC, Vol. VIII, p. 77–9.

37 Rousseau's correspondence inspired several works: Daniel Roche, "Les primitifs du Rousseauisme: une analyse sociologique et quantitative de la correspondance de J.-J. Rousseau," *Annales ESC*, 26: 1 (1971), pp. 151–72; Claude Labrosse, *Lire au XVIIIe siècle: "La Nouvelle Héloïse" et ses lecteurs* (Lyon: Presses Universitaires de Lyon, 1985); Darnton, "Readers Respond to Rousseau."

38 Letter from a stranger, April 6, 1761, CC, Vol. VIII, pp. 296–7.
39 Letter from Jean-Louis Le Cointe, March 27, 1761, ibid., pp. 292–5.
40 Letters from Manon Phlipon to Marie Sophie Caroline Cannet, respectively November 4, 1777, November 17, 1777, and March 21, 1776, in *Lettres de Mme Roland* (Paris: Government Printing Office, 1902), pp. 145, 165, and 46–7.
41 Darnton, "Readers Respond to Rousseau," p. 234.
42 Ibid., pp. 252 and 251.
43 In his "Éloge de Richardson," Diderot exclaims: "Who has not read the words of Richardson without wanting to know this man, to have him for a brother or a friend? [...] Richardson is no more. What a loss for humanity. This loss has moved me as if he had been my brother. He is in my heart though I never saw him; I knew him only through his works" (pp. 1063 and 1069).
44 Jean Staborinski, *Accuser et séduire: Essais sur Jean-Jacques Rousseau* (Paris: Gallimard, 2012), p. 20, who clearly understands the experience of intimacy created by the work and the person of Rousseau, but classically interprets it as a form of religious or political conversion.
45 Quoted in Darnton, "Readers Respond to Rousseau," pp. 236 and 237.
46 Letter from Baron de Bormes, March 27, 1761, CC, Vol. VIII, pp. 280–2.
47 Letter from Jean Romilly, May 23, 1763, CC, Vol. XVI, pp. 222–36.
48 Letter of September 16, 1762, p. 138, and letter of July 25, 1770, Jean-Jacques Rousseau and Mme de La Tour, *Correspondance*, ed. G. May (Arles: Actes Sud, 1998), p. 295.
49 Letter of August 11, 1765, ibid., p. 255.
50 In spite of repeated requests from Mme de La Tour, Rousseau did not really want to meet her. They saw each other only two or three times and never alone.
51 *Lettre à l'auteur de la Justification de J.-J. Rousseau dans la contestation qui lui est survenue avec M. Hume* (1762); "*Réflexions sur ce qui s'est passé au sujet de la rupture de J.-J. Rousseau et de M. Hume*": Jean-Jacques Rousseau vangé par son amie, ou Morale pratico-philosophico-encyclopédique du coryphée de la secte (Au temple de la vérité, 1779).
52 Lilti, *The World of the Salons*, pp. 178–91.
53 Letter from David Hume to the Countess of Boufflers, August 12, 1766, in *The Letters of David Hume, Vol. II: 1766–1776*, ed. J.Y.T. Greig (Oxford: Oxford University Press, 2011), p. 77.

54 See the files compiled by the publisher of the *Correspondance complète de Rousseau: CC*, Vol. XXX, pp. 401ff., and Vol. XXXI, pp. 336ff.

55 Jean Starobinski, *Jean-Jacques Rousseau: Transparency and Obfuscation*, trans. Arthur Goldhammer (Chicago: University of Chicago Press, [1971] 1988), pp. 134–7.

56 *CC*, Vol. XXX, p. 29.

57 *Justification de Jean-Jacques Rousseau dans la contestation qui lui est survenue avec M. Hume* (London, 1766), p. 2.

58 Ibid., pp. 25–6.

59 Dena Goodman, "The Hume–Rousseau Affair: From Private *Querelle* to Public *Procès*," *Eighteenth-Century Studies*, 25:2 (1991–2), pp. 171–201.

60 Letter from d'Alembert to David Hume, July 21, 1766, *CC*, Vol. XXX, p. 130.

61 Letter from Holbach to Hume, July 7, 1766, ibid., pp. 20–1.

62 Letter from Turgot to Hume, July 23, 1766, ibid., p. 149.

63 *Justification*, p. 23.

64 Jean-Jacques Rousseau, *The Confessions and Correspondence, including the Letters to Malesherbes: The Collected Writings of Rousseau*, Vol. 5, trans. Christopher Kelly (Hanover, NH/ London: University Press of New England, 1995), p. 5.

65 Benoît Mély, *Jean-Jacques Rousseau, un intellectuel en rupture* (Paris: Minerve, 1985); Jérôme Meizoz, *Le Guex philosophe (Jean-Jacques Rousseau)* (Lausanne: Antipodes, 2003); Lilti, *The World of the Salons*.

66 Pierre Hadot, *Exercices spirituels et philosophie antique* (Paris: Études augustiniennes, 1981); Hadot, *Philosophy as a Way of Life: Spiritual Exercises from Socrates to Foucault*, trans. Michael Chase (Oxford: Blackwell, 1995); Julius Domaszi, *La Philosophie, théorie ou manière de vivre? Les controverses de l'Antiquité à la Renaissance* (Paris: PUF, 1996).

67 Jean-Jacques Rousseau, "Reveries of the Solitary Walker," in *The Collected Writings of Rousseau*, Vol. 8, ed. Christopher Kelly (Hanover, NH/London: University Press of New England, 2000), p. 18.

68 Jean-Jacques Rousseau, *The Collected Writings of Rousseau*, Vol. 4, ed. Roger D. Masters and Christopher Kelly (Hanover, NH/ London: University Press of New England, 1994), p. 10.

69 Rousseau, *The Confessions and Correspondence*, p. 303.

70 Yves Citton, "Retour sur la misérable querelle Rousseau–Diderot: position, conséquence, spectacle et sphère publique," *Recherches sur Diderot et sur l'Encyclopédie*, 36 (2004), pp. 57–94.

71 Antoine Lilti, "Reconnaissance et célébrité: Jean-Jacques Rousseau et la politique du nom propre," *Orages: Littérature et culture*, 9 (March 2010), pp. 77–94. On Holbach, see Alain Sandrier, *Le Style philosophique du baron d'Holbach* (Paris: Honoré Champion, 2004). On Voltaire, see Olivier Ferret, "Vade mecum. Vade Retro. Le recours au pseudonyme dans la démarche pamphlétaire voltairienne," *La Lettre clandestine*, 8 (1999), pp. 65–82.

72 Quoted by Ourida Mostefai, *Le Citoyen de Genève et la République des lettres: Étude de la controverse autour de la Lettre à d'Alembert de Jean-Jacques Rousseau* (New York: Peter Lang, 2003), p. 115.

73 Ibid., p. 114.

74 See Christopher Kelly, *Rousseau as an Author: Consecrating One's Life to the Truth* (Chicago: University of Chicago Press, 2003).

75 Jean-Jacques Rousseau, "Letter to Beaumont," in *The Collected Writings of Rousseau*, Vol. 9, eds Christopher Kelly and Eve Grace (Hanover, NH/London: University Press of New England, 2001), pp. 17–101, here at p. 23.

76 On the political and theoretical issues in this long-underestimated text by Rousseau the critic, see Bruno Bernardi, Florent Guénard, and Gabriella Silvestrini, *Religion, liberté, justice: Sur les Lettres écrites de la montagne de J.-J. Rousseau* (Paris: J. Vrin, 2005) and Whatmore, "Rousseau and the Representants."

77 Jean-Jacques Rousseau, "Letters Written from the Mountain," in *The Collected Writings of Rousseau*, Vol. 9, pp. 131–306, here at p. 219.

78 Ibid.

79 Ibid., p. 218.

80 Ibid.

81 Letter of April 15, 1758, CC, Vol. V, pp. 70–1.

82 *Julie, Or the New Heloise: Letters of Two Lovers who Live in a Small Town at the Foot of the Alps: Collected Writings of Rousseau*, Vol. 6, eds Philip Stewart and Jean Vaché (Hanover, NH/London: University Press of New England, 1997), p. 19.

83 Rousseau for example wrote to his publisher in 1762: "Let the crazies and the mean-spirited burn my books as much as they want, it won't stop the fact that they are alive and dear to all good people. When they are no longer printed, they will nonetheless be there for posterity and will bless the memory of the only Author who has ever written solely for the good of society and for the true happiness of men" (letter of October 8, 1762 to Marc Michel Rey, CC, Vol. XIII, pp. 182–4).

84 Letter from Rousseau to Daniel Roguin, December 12, 1761, CC, Vol. IX, pp. 309–11. In the end, Rousseau resigned himself to traveling under the name Dudding.

85 *L'Année littéraire*, 1754, Vol. I, pp. 242–4; *Correspondance littéraire*, June 15, 1762, Vol. V, p. 100.

86 Letter from Mme du Deffand to the Duchesse de Choiseul, July 22, 1766, in *Correspondance complète de Mme du Deffand avec la duchesse de Choiseul*, ed. M. de Sainte-Aulaire (Paris: Michel Levy, 1866), Vol. I, p. 59.

87 *Lettres et Pensées du prince de Ligne*, ed. Raymond Trousson (Paris: Tallandier, 1989), p. 289.

88 Rousseau, *The Confessions and Correspondence*, p. 240.

89 Ibid., pp. 304–5.

90 Jean-Jacques Rousseau, "My Portrait," in *The Collected Writings of Rousseau*, Vol. 12, ed. Christopher Kelly (Hanover, NH/London: University of New England Press, 2006), pp. 36–44, here at p. 39.

91 Ibid.

92 Ibid. Rousseau here adds a curious note: "That is plausible, but I do not feel it clearly." Is this vanity (*amour-propre*) once again from someone who thinks that the public will never grow tired of talking about such a singular and interesting person? Or is it intuition about an idea which Rousseau will eventually develop, that celebrity is a trap no one can escape once caught in it?

93 Rousseau, *The Confessions and Correspondence*, p. 304.

94 Ibid., p. 511.

95 Ibid., p. 512.

96 Letters from Rousseau to Mme Thérèse Guillemette Périé, Comtesse de La Rodde de Saint-Haon, CC, Vol. XL, pp. 63–71.

97 Henri Bernardin de Saint-Pierre, *La Vie et les Ouvrages de Jean-Jacques Rousseau*, ed. Raymond Trousson (Paris: Honoré Champion, 2009), p. 319.

98 Barbara Carnevali, *Romantisme et reconnaissance: Figures de la conscience chez Rousseau* (Geneva: Droz, 2012).

99 Ibid.

100 Rousseau, *The Confessions and Correspondence*, p. 317.

101 Ibid., p. 290.

102 Ibid., p. 318.

103 Nicolas Paige, "Rousseau's Readers Revisited," *Eighteenth-Century Studies*, 42:1 (2008), pp. 131–54; James Swenson, *On Jean-Jacques Rousseau Considered as One of the First Authors of the Revolution* (Stanford: Stanford University Press, 2000).

104 Charles Taylor, *Sources of the Self: The Making of the Modern Identity* (Cambridge, MA: Harvard University Press, 1989);

Alessandro Ferrara, *Modernity and Authenticity: A Study of the Social and Ethical Thought of Jean-Jacques Rousseau* (Albany: State University of New York Press, 1993).

105 Rousseau, *The Confessions and Correspondence*, pp. 97–8.
106 Ibid., p. 98.
107 Ibid., p. 458.
108 Ibid., p. 438.
109 Ibid., p. 5.
110 Contrast between the two terms is frequent with Rousseau. See, for example, Rousseau, *Rousseau Judge of Jean-Jacques*, p. 11.
111 Rousseau, *The Confessions and Correspondence*, p. 587.
112 Also, think about the episode of the young beggar in *Reveries of the Solitary Walker*, who called him "Monsieur Rousseau" to show that he knew him, showing, in fact, that he did not known him (otherwise he would have known that Rousseau did not like to be called "Monsieur").
113 Johnny Halliday, "L'idole des jeunes," 1962.
114 Jean-Marie Schaeffer, "Originalité et expression de soi: Éléments pour une généalogie de la figure moderne de l'artiste," *Communications*, 64 (1997), pp. 89–115.
115 Rousseau, "Reveries of the Solitary Walker," p. 54.
116 Rousseau, *The Confessions and Correspondence*, p. 550.
117 On the critical reception of the text, see James F. Jones, *Dialogues: An Interpretative Essay* (Geneva: Droz, 1991); Anne F. Garetta, "Les Dialogues de Rousseau: paradoxes d'une réception critique," in Lorraine Clark and Guy Lafrance (eds), *Rousseau et la critique* (Ottawa: Association nord-américaine des études Jean-Jacques Rousseau, 1995), pp. 5–98; Jean-François Perrin, *Politique du renonçant: Le dernier Rousseau des dialogues aux rêveries* (Paris: Kimé, 2011), pp. 280–9.
118 Rousseau, *Rousseau Judge of Jean-Jacques*, p. 218.
119 Ibid., p. 3.
120 Ibid, pp. 41–2.
121 Ibid., p. 251.
122 Ibid., p. 248.
123 On the paradoxes in the paranoid writing of Rousseau and the puzzling text that theorized and depicted its difficult reception, see Antoine Lilti, "The Writing of Paranoia: Jean-Jacques Rousseau and the Paradoxes of Celebrity," *Representations*, 103 (2008), pp. 53–83.
124 Michel Foucault, "Introduction," in *Rousseau juge de Jean-Jacques: Dialogues* (Paris: Armand Colin, 1962), pp. vii–xxiv.
125 Rousseau, *Rousseau Judge of Jean-Jacques*, p. 6.

126 Ibid., p. 92. See Yves Citton, "Fabrique de l'opinion et folie de la dissidence: le 'complot' dans Rousseau juge de Jean-Jacques," in *Rousseau juge de Jean-Jacques: Études sur les Dialogues* (Ottawa: Presses de l'Université d'Ottawa, 1998), pp. 101–14.

127 Rousseau, *Rousseau Judge of Jean-Jacques*, pp. 30 and 83.

128 "Among the peculiarities that distinguish our century from all others is the methodical and consistent spirit that has guided public opinions for twenty years. [...] Ever since the philosophic sect organized itself into a body with leaders, these leaders – who have become the arbiters of public opinion through the art of intrigue to which they have applied themselves – are through that the arbiters of the reputation, and even the destiny of individuals and through them of that of the State" (ibid., pp. 236–7). On the idea of public opinion about Rousseau and his link with the political theory of general will, see Bruno Bernardi, "Rousseau et la généalogie du concept d'opinion Publique," in Michel O'Dea (ed.), *Jean-Jacques Rousseau en 2012* (Oxford: Voltaire Foundation, 2012).

129 Rousseau, *Rousseau Judge of Jean-Jacques*, p. 181.

130 Rousseau, "Letters Written from the Mountain," p. 138: "No one can escape from this Judge, and for myself, I do not make any appeal from it."

131 Rousseau, "My Portrait," p. 38.

132 Ibid., pp. 38–9.

133 Rousseau, *Rousseau Judge of Jean-Jacques*, p. 217.

134 Ibid., p. 232.

135 Ibid., p. 233.

136 Ibid., p. 92.

137 Ibid., p. 252.

138 Letter from Rousseau to the Comte de Saint-Germain, February 26, 1770, *CC*, Vol. XXXVII, pp. 248–71.

139 Rousseau, *Rousseau Judge of Jean-Jacques*, p. 252.

140 Paul Audi, *Rousseau, une philosophie de l'âme* (Lagrasse: Verdier, 2008).

141 Rousseau, *Rousseau Judge of Jean-Jacques*, p. 252.

142 Ibid., p. 5.

143 Rousseau, *The Confessions and Correspondence*, p. 132.

144 Rousseau, "My Portrait," p. 44.

145 Letter from Rousseau to Abbé Raynal, July 25, 1750, *CC*, Vol. II, pp. 132–6, here p. 133.

146 Rousseau, *Rousseau Judge of Jean-Jacques*, pp. 231–2.

147 Letter from Rousseau to Louise Alexandrine Julie Dupin de Chenonceaux, *CC*, Vol. XX, pp. 112–14.

148 Rousseau, *Rousseau Judge of Jean-Jacques*, p. 197.
149 "Déclaration de Rousseau relative à l'impression de ses écrits," January 23, 1774, CC, Vol. XXXIX, p. 305.
150 Geoffrey Benington, *Dudding: Des noms de Rousseau* (Paris: Galilée, 1991).
151 Rousseau, *Rousseau Judge of Jean-Jacques*, p. 234.
152 Ibid.
153 Rousseau, *The Confessions and Correspondence*, p. 513.
154 Douglas Fordham, "Allan Ramsay's Enlightenment or Hume and the Patronizing Portrait," *Art Bulletin*, 88:3 (2006), pp. 508–24.
155 To the contrary, Diderot criticized a pastel of Rousseau by Quentin de La Tour, in 1753, because it made him look too worldly. "I was looking for the letter censor, the Caton and the Brutus of our age; I expected to see Epictetus shabbily dressed, wig all helter-skelter, his severe look frightening writers, great men and society people: I only see the author of *Devin du village*, well dressed, hair carefully combed, well powdered and ridiculously seated on a straw chair"(*Essai sur la peinture, Œuvres* [Paris: Gallimard, 1951], p. 1134).
156 See, for example, the judgment by Bernardin de Saint-Pierre, in *Essai sur Jean-Jacques Rousseau, Œuvres complètes* (Lequien, 1831), Vol. XI, p. 286.
157 Letter from Mme Riccoboni to Garrick, October 1, 1770, quoted by Angelica Goodden, *Rousseau's Hand: The Crafting of a Writer* (Oxford: Oxford University Press, 2013), p. 146.
158 Letter from Mme de La Tour, in Rousseau and La Tour, *Correspondance*, p. 280.
159 Rousseau, *Rousseau Judge of Jean-Jacques*, p. 91.
160 Denis Diderot, "Salon de 1767," in *Salons*, ed. Michel Delon (Paris: Gallimard, 2008), p. 252.
161 Rousseau, *Rousseau Judge of Jean-Jacques*, p. 92.
162 Rousseau, *The Confessions and Correspondence*, p. 3.
163 Michel Foucault, *The Courage of Truth: The Government of Self and Others II*, trans. Graham Burchell (London: Palgrave Macmillan, [2008] 2011).
164 Louisa Shea, *The Cynic Enlightenment: Diogenes in the Salons* (Baltimore, MD: Johns Hopkins University Press, 2010), pp. 94–104; David Mazella, *The Making of Modern Cynicism* (Charlottesville: University of Virginia Press, 2007), p. 110.
165 Jacques Berchtold, "L'identification nourrie par l'iconographie? Rousseau et le Diogène à la lanterne," in Frédéric Eigeldinger, *Rousseau et les arts visuels: Actes du colloque de Neuchâtel 2001,*

Annales de la Société Jean-Jacques Rousseau, Vol. XLV (2003), pp. 567–82.

166 George Remington Heavens, *Voltaire's Marginalia on the Pages of Rousseau* (Columbus: Ohio State University Press, 1933), p. 21. See also Henri Gouhier, *Rousseau et Voltaire: portraits dans un miroir* (Paris: J. Vrin, 1983), p. 58.

167 Rousseau, *Rousseau Judge of Jean-Jacques*, p. 132.

168 Rousseau, *The Confessions and Correspondence*, p. 308.

169 Rousseau, "Reveries of the Solitary Walker," p. 3.

CHAPTER 6 THE POWER OF CELEBRITY

1 Germaine de Staël, *Considerations on the Principal Events of the French Revolution*, ed. Aurelian Craiutu (Indianapolis: Liberty Fund, [1818] 2008), pp. 429–30.

2 The *Considerations* were published in 1818, after the death of Mme de Staël, by the Duc de Broglie and the Baron de Staël. It would seem that Mme de Staël wrote them around 1812.

3 See the letter to Niethammer, October 13, 1806, after the Battle of Jena (*Hegel: The Letters*, trans. Clark Butler and Christiane Seiler (Bloomington: Indiana University Press, 1984), pp. 114–15). On Napoleon as a great man, a "World-Historical person," like Alexander the Great and Ceasar, see Hegel, *The Philosophy of History*, trans. J. Sibree (Mineola, NY: Dover Publications, [1832] 2012), p. 21.

4 Robert Morrissey, *The Economy of Glory: From Ancien Régime France to the Fall of Napoleon*, trans. Teresa Lavandar Fagan (Chicago/London: University of Chicago Press, [2010] 2014).

5 George Rudé, *Wilkes and Liberty: A Social Study of 1763 to 1774* (Oxford: Clarendon Press, 1962); John Brewer, *Party Ideology and Popular Politics at the Accession of George III* (Cambridge: Cambridge University Press, 1981); John Sainsbury, *Wilkes, the Lives of a Libertine* (Aldershot: Ashgate, 2006); Anna Clark, *Scandal: The Sexual Politics of the British Constitution* (Princeton: Princeton University Press, 2004), pp. 19–52.

6 Simon Burrows, Jonathan Conlin, Russell Goulbourne, and Valerie Mainz et al. (eds), *The Chevalier d'Éon and His Worlds: Gender, Espionage and Politics in the Eighteenth Century* (London: Continuum, 2010), and in particular the contribution by Burrows, "The Chevalier d'Éon, Media Manipulation and the Making of an Eighteenth-Century Celebrity," pp. 13–23. See also Gary Kates,

Monsieur d'Éon is a Woman: A Tale of Political Intrigue and Sexual Masquerade (New York: Basic Books, 1995).

7   Letter from the Commissioner to the Directories with the army in Italy in Carnot, quoted by Luigi Mascilli Migliorini, *Napoléon*, trans. Jean-Michel Gardair (Paris: Perrin, [2002] 2004), p. 500.

8   David A. Bell, *The First Total War: Napoleon's Europe and the Birth of Warfare as We Know It* (New York: Houghton Mifflin Company, 2007), pp. 195–207; Annie Jourdan, *Napoléon, héros, imperator, mécène* (Paris: Aubier, 1998), pp. 70–101; Patrice Gueniffey, *Bonaparte: 1769–1802*, trans. Steven Rendall (Cambridge, MA: Harvard University Press: Gallimard, [2013] 2015), see in particular pp. 355–63; Wayne Hanley, *The Genesis of Napoleonic Propaganda, 1796–1799* (New York: Columbia University Press, 2005).

9   Chantal Thomas, *La Reine scélérate: Marie-Antoinette dans les pamphlets* (Paris: Seuil, 1989).

10 Antoine de Baecque, *Le Corps de l'histoire: Métaphores et politique* (Paris: Calmann-Lévy, 1993); Jacques Revel, "Marie-Antoinette dans ses fictions: la mise en scène de la haine" (1995), in *Un Parcours critique: Douze essais d'histoire sociale* (Paris: Galaad, 2006), pp. 210–68; Lynn Hunt, *The Family Romance of the French Revolution* (Berkeley: University of California Press, 1993); Dena Goodman (ed.), *Marie-Antoinette: Writings on the Body of a Queen* (New York: Routledge, 2003); Darnton, *The Devil in the Holy Water*, pp. 397–421.

11 See especially the *Anecdotes sur Madame la comtesse du Barry* (1775) and the *Vie privée de Louis XV* (1781), which were very successful in the category of clandestine literature.

12 Simon Burrows, *Blackmail, Scandal and Revolution: London's French Libellistes, 1758–1792* (Manchester: Manchester University Press, 2006). See also Viviane R. Gruder, "The Question of Marie-Antoinette: The Queen and Public Opinion before the Revolution," *French History*, 16:3 (2002), pp. 269–98.

13 *Essai historique sur la vie privée de Marie-Antoinette d'Autriche, reine de France* (London, 1789), pp. 4–5.

14 Linda Colley, *Britons: Forging the Nation 1707–1837* (New Haven: Yale University Press, [1992] 2003), pp. 195–236; Ernest A. Smith, *George IV* (New Haven: Yale University Press, 1999); Clark, *Scandal*.

15 Thomas Laquer, "The Queen Caroline Affair: Politics as Art in the Reign of George IV," *Journal of Modern History*, 54:3 (1982), pp. 417–66; Anna Clark, "Queen Caroline and the Sexual Politics of

Popular Culture in London, 1820," *Representations*, 31 (1990), pp. 47–68.

16 Letter from Marie-Thérèse to Mercy d'Argenteau, July 2, 1772, *Correspondance de Marie-Antoinette, 1770–1793*, ed. Evelyne Lever (Paris: Tallandier, 2005), p. 113.

17 Jeanne Louise Henriette Campan, *Mémoires sur la vie privée de Marie-Antoinette, reine de France et de Navarre* (Paris: Baudouin, 1822), p. 142.

18 Ibid., p. 228.

19 Gabriel Sénac de Meilhan, *Des principes et des causes de la Révolution en France* (London, 1790), pp. 30–1.

20 *Mémoires pour l'instruction du Dauphin*, quoted by Norbert Elias, *The Court Society*, trans. Edmund Jephcott (Dublin: University College Dublin Press, [1969] 2006), p. 128.

21 Ibid., *The Court Society*, pp. 127–57.

22 Fanny Cosandey, *La Reine de France: Symbole et pouvoir, XVe–XVIIIe siècle* (Paris: Gallimard, 2003).

23 Campan, *Mémoires*, p. 164.

24 Ibid., p. 167.

25 Letter from Marie-Thérèse to Marie-Antoinette, March 1775, that advised her to be careful of the height of her hair and not outrage fashion instead of modestly following it, *Correspondance de Marie-Antoinette*, p. 206.

26 Clare Haru Crowston, *Credit, Fashion, Sex: Economies of Regard in Old Regime France* (Durham, NC: Duke University Press, 2013), pp. 246–82.

27 On Thomas, see Colin Jones, "Pulling Teeth in Eighteenth-Century Paris," *Past and Present*, 166 (2000), pp. 100–45.

28 Daniel Roche, *The Culture of Clothing: Dress and Fashion in the Ancien Régime*, trans. Jean Birrell (Cambridge: Cambridge University Press, 1996).

29 Carolyn Weber, *Queen of Fashion: What Marie Antoinette Wore to the Revolution* (New York: Henry Holt, 2006).

30 *Essai historique*, p. 62.

31 A copy of the painting is in the National Gallery of Arts in Washington. See *Marie-Antoinette* (Paris: Réunion des musées nationaux, 2008), pp. 307–9. On this episode, see Mary Sheriff, "The Portrait of the Queen," in Goodman (ed.), *Marie-Antoinette*, pp. 45–72.

32 Élisabeth Vigée-Lebrun, *Memoirs*, trans. Lionel Strachey (London: Grant Richards, 1904), p. 175, who says that the portrait was hung on stage at the Vaudeville theater.

33 Letter of July 25, 1791, *Correspondance de Marie-Antoinette*, p. 561.
34 Letter of September 9, 1791, ibid., p. 605.
35 Mona Ozouf, *Varennes: La mort de la royauté, 21 June 1791* (Paris: Gallimard, 2010), pp. 72–81; Ozouf, "Barnave pedagogue: l'éducation d'une reine," in *L'Homme régéneré: Essais sur la Révolution française* (Paris: Gallimard, 1989), pp. 93–114.
36 See, for example, François Furet, "Mirabeau," in François Furet and Mona Ozouf (eds), *A Critical Dictionary of the French Revolution*, trans. Arthur Goldhammer (Cambridge, MA: Harvard University Press, 1989), pp. 265–72. We will mention nonetheless that Furet did see Mirabeau as having an ideological coherence and a theory consistent with the liberal monarchy.
37 Georges Guibal, *Mirabeau et la Provence* (Paris: E. Thorin, 1887–91), Vol. I, p. 231.
38 Letter from the marquis to the bailiff, November 22, 1782, ibid., p. 405.
39 *Mémoires secrets*, Vol. XXVII, p. 99.
40 Dumont, who met him in the spring of 1788, wrote that his "reputation" was "at its lowest point possible," and that they advised him not to frequent him.
41 Letter from Chamfort to Mirabeau, January 3, 1789, *Mémoires biographiques, littéraires et politiques de Mirabeau* (Paris: Auffray, 1834–5), Vol. VII, p. 210.
42 Letter from Mirabeau to Mauvillon, August 11, 1788, *Lettres du comte de Mirabeau à un de ses amis en Allemagne* (n.p.: 1792), p. 372.
43 Letter from the Marquis de Mirabeau, January 18, 1789, quoted by François Quastana, *La Pensée politique de Mirabeau, 1771–1789: "républicanisme classique" et régénération de la monarchie* (Aix-en-Provence: Presses Universitaires d'Aix-Marseille, 2007), p. 537.
44 Monique Cubbels, *Les Horizons de la liberté: Naissance de la Révolution en Provence, 1787–1789* (Aix-en-Provence: ÉDISUD, 1987), pp. 64–5.
45 Étienne Dumont, *Souvenirs sur Mirabeau*, ed. J. Bénétruy (Paris: PUF, 1951), p. 58.
46 Timothy Tackett, *Becoming a Revolutionary: The Deputies of the French National Assembly and the Emergence of a French Revolutionary Culture (1789–1790)* (University Park: Pennsylvania State University Press, 1996).
47 Dumont, *Souvenirs sur Mirabeau*, p. 158.
48 Ibid.

49 Paul Friedland, *Political Actors: Representative Bodies and Theatricality in the Age of the French Revolution* (Ithaca, NY: Cornell University Press, 2002), p. 182.

50 Dumont, *Souvenirs sur Mirabeau*, p. 146.

51 *Le Patriote français*, Vol. XXXI, September 1, 1789, p. 3.

52 Dumont, *Souvenirs sur Mirabeau*, p. 146.

53 Gérard Fabre, *Joseph Boze, portraitiste de l'Ancien Régime à la Restauration, 1745–1826* (Paris: Zomogy, 2004), p. 174.

54 Dumont, *Souvenirs sur Mirabeau*, p. 148.

55 Jean-François Feraud, *Dictionnaire critique de la langue française* (Marseille: Mossy, 1787–8). In English, the term appears in the 1785 edition of the *Dictionary* by Johnson, with a double meaning.

56 "Sur la popularité," *L'Ami des patriotes ou le Défenseur de la Révolution*, XI (1791), pp. 295 ff.

57 Pierre Rosanvallon, *Le Peuple introuvable: Histoire de la représentation démocratique en France* (Paris: Gallimard, 1998), p. 19.

58 Jean-Claude Monod, *Qu'est-ce qu'un chef en démocratie? Politiques du charisme* (Paris: Le Seuil, 2012). On the intellectual and political context for reflection about "leaders" in which is found the Weberian theory of charisma, see Yves Cohen, *Le Siècle des chefs: Une histoire transnationale du commandement et de l'autorité, 1890–1940* (Paris: Amsterdam, 2013).

59 Lloyd Kramer, *Lafayette in Two Worlds: Public Cultures and Personal Identities in an Age of Revolution* (Chapel Hill: University of North Carolina Press, 1996); François Weil, " 'L'hôte de la nation': le voyage de La Fayette aux États-Unis, 1824–1825," in Philippe Bourdin (ed.), *La Fayette entre deux mondes* (Clermond-Ferrand: Presses Universitaires Blaise Pascal, 2009), pp. 129–50.

60 Germaine de Staël, *Du caractère de M. Necker et de sa vie privée* (Paris, 1804), p. 76.

61 Pierre Jean Georges Cabanis, *Journal de la maladie et de la mort de Mirabeau* (Paris: Grabit, 1791); re-edited by Carmela Ferrandes (Bari: Adriatica, 1996), p. 119.

62 Dumont, *Souvenirs sur Mirabeau*, p. 170. Cabanis, for his part, notes: "The patient never ceased receiving, conversing with, and listening to the public that surrounded his bed and his house."

63 *Le Patriote français*, April 6, 1791.

64 Haïm Burstin, *Une révolution à l'oeuvre: Le faubourg Saint-Marcel* (Seyssel: Champ Vallon, 2005), pp. 220–1.

65 On Corsica, all the ships were draped in mourning (*Moniteur*, May 29, 1791), while in Rouen the city authorities and the Jacobins organized the funeral ceremonies (Joseph Clarke, *Commemorating*

the Dead in Revolutionary France [Cambridge: Cambridge University Press, 2007], pp. 97–106).

66 *Journal de Paris*, April 5, 1791.

67 Antoine de Baecque, "Mirabeau; or, The Spectacle of a Public Corpse," in *Glory and Terror*, pp. 15–36, insists on the tragic dimension of the funeral rites and on the ideal of political transparency that impels them.

68 Jules Michelet, *Histoire de la Révolution française* (Paris: Gallimard, 1976), Vol. II, p. 558.

69 See notably Jacques Julliard (ed.), *La Mort du roi: Autour de François Mitterrand, essai d'ethnographie comparée* (Paris: Gallimard, 1999).

70 *La Feuille villageoise*, 29, 1791.

71 See Jeremy D. Popkin, *Revolutionary News: The Press in France, 1789–1799* (Durham, NC, and London: Duke University Press, 1990), who talks about a "media revolution in 1789" (an impressive argument with the number of titles, print runs, liberty of the press).

72 Ernst Kantorowicz, *The King's Two Bodies: A Study in Mediaeval Political Theology* (Princeton: Princeton University Press, 1957); Ralph E. Giesey, *The Royal Funeral Ceremony in Renaissance France* (Geneva: Librairie E. Droz, 1960).

73 On Marat, see Jean-Claude Bonnet (ed.), *La Mort de Marat* (Paris: Flammarion, 1992), and Alain Boureau, *Le Simple corps du roi: L'impossible sacralité des souverains français, XVe–XVIIIe siècle* (Paris: Les Éditions de Paris, 2000), pp. 10–11.

74 *Mémoires biographiques*, Vol. VIII, p. 511.

75 *L'Ami du peuple*, 419, April 11, 1791.

76 *Mirabeau, jugé par ses amis et par ses ennemis* (Paris: Couret, 1791).

77 De Baecque, "Voltaire; or, The Body of the Philosopher King," pp. 25–9.

78 Cabanis, *Journal*, p. 137.

79 On Manuel, author and subject of "private lives," see Darnton, *The Devil in the Holy Water*, pp. 50–79.

80 Mirabeau's adversaries played on the same curiosity about his private life. They republished his libertine novel, *Ma conversion*, as an autobiography, a form now well known, about his private life: *Vie privée, libertine et scandaleuse de Feu Honoré-Gabriel-Riquetti, ci-devant Comte de Mirabeau, Député du Tiers-État des Sénéchaussées d'Aix et de Marseille, membre du département de Paris, commandant de bataillon de la milice bourgeoise au district de Grange-Batellière, président du club Jacobite, etc.* (Paris, 1791).

81   The documents are collected in the *Actes de la commune de Paris pendant la Révolution*, ed. S. Lacroix (Paris: Service des travaux historiques de la ville, 1894–1955), Series 2, Vol. VIII, citations pp. 571 and 574.

82   *Ibid.*, p. 576.

83   In the end, the transfer did not take place until September 21, 1794, after Thermidor. "It was a sad autumn day, in this tragic year of 1794, when France, having almost exterminated herself, after having killed the living she began to kill the dead, tearing out the heart of her most glorious son" (Michelet, *Histoire de la Révolution française*, Vol. II, p. 562).

84   Étienne Barry, "Discours sur les dangers de l'idolâtrie individuelle dans une République," in *Discours prononcés les jours de décadi dans la section Guillaume Tell* (Paris: Massot, 1794), quoted by Gueniffey, *Bonaparte*, p. 292; Michel Vovelle, *La Mentalité révolutionnaire: Sociétés et mentalités sous la Révolution française* (Paris: Éditions sociales, 1985), pp. 125–40; Bronislaw Baczko, *Ending the Terror: The French Revolution after Robespierre* (Cambridge: Cambridge University Press, 1994).

85   Guillaume Mazeau, *Le Bain de l'histoire: Charlotte Corday et l'attentat contre Marat, 1793–2009* (Seyssel: Champ Vallon, 2009).

86   Barry Schwartz, *George Washington: The Making of an American Symbol* (Ithaca, NY: Cornell University Press, 2007), p. 13.

87   *Ibid.*, p. 162.

88   Joseph Ellis, *His Excellency: George Washington* (New York: Random House, 2004), pp. 110–46.

89   Schwartz, *George Washington*, p. 136.

90   *London Chronicle*, April 16, 1778.

91   *Mémoires secrets*, Vol. XIX, p. 244.

92   Gilbert Chinard, *George Washington as the French Knew Him* (Princeton: Princeton University Press, 1940).

93   *Nouveau voyage dans l'Amérique septentrionale, en l'année 1781, et Campagne de l'armée de M. le Comte de Rochambeau* (Philadelphia/Paris: Moutard, 1782), p. 61.

94   *Ibid.*, p. 64.

95   Jacques Pierre Brissot, *Nouveau voyage dans les États-Unis de l'Amérique septentrionale, fait en 1788* (Paris: Buisson, 1791), Vol. II, p. 265. When Brissot published the work in 1791, Washington had been elected president.

96   John Ferling, *The Ascent of George Washington: The Hidden Political Genius of an American Icon* (New York: Bloomsbury Press, 2010).

97 Born into a rich family of Virginia planters, Washington issued from a second marriage, and, with the death of his father, although just eleven years old, he inherited a small plantation. It was with the help and then the death of his half-brother Lawrence, as well as the protection of Lord Fairfax, that he was able to become part of the colonial elite by inheriting the Mount Vernon property.

98 Letter from John Rush to John Adams, April 22, 1806, *The Spur of Fame: Dialogues of John Adams and Benjamin Rush, 1805–1813* (ed.) D. Adar and J. Schutz (Indianapolis: Liberty Fund, 2001), p. 67.

99 Ellis, *His Excellency*, p. 151.

100 Letter from George Washington, January 15, 1785, *The Papers of George Washington (Digital Edition)*, Virginia University Press, rotunda.upress.virginia.edu.

101 Letter from David Humphreys, July 17, 1785, ibid.

102 Letter from George Washington, July 25, 1785, ibid.

103 The parts written by Humphreys were not published until 1991, along with comments by Washington, by Rosemarie Zagarri, *David Humphreys' Life of General Washington* (Athens/London: University of Georgia Press, 1991).

104 Todd Estes, *The Jay Treaty Debate: Public Opinion and the Evolution of Early American Political Culture* (Amherst: University of Massachusetts Press, 2003). On the role of the press: Jeff Pasley, *"The Tyranny of Printers": Newspaper Politics in the Early American Republic* (Charlottesville: University Press of Virginia, 2001).

105 This is also the result of recent work by historians. See notably Estes, *The Jay Treaty Debate*.

106 François Furstenberg, *In the Name of the Father: Washington's Legacy, Slavery, and the Making of a Nation* (New York: Penguin, 2006).

107 Letter of February 25, 1808, *The Spur of Fame*, p. 113.

108 "Those who trumpeted Washington in the highest strains at some times spoke of him at others in the strongest terms of contempt. Indeed I know of no character to which so much hypocritical adulation has been offered" (letter of January 25, 1806, ibid., p. 49; here, Adams notably targets Alexander Hamilton).

109 As he writes pleasantly in 1790, "the history of our revolution will be one continued lie from one end to the other. The essence of the whole will be that Dr Franklin's electrical rod smote the earth and out sprang General Washington" (quoted by Schwartz, *George Washington*, p. 87).

110 Letter of July 23, 1806, *The Spur of Fame*, p. 65.

111 Douglas Adair, "Fame and the Founding Fathers," in *Fame and the Founding Fathers* (New York: W.W. Norton, 1974), pp. 3–24.

112 Nathaniel Hawthorne, *Passages from the French and Italian Note Books* (Boston: Osgood and Company, 1876), Vol. I, pp. 258–9.

113 See, for example, the letter by Washington to James Craik, March 25, 1784: "I will frankly declare to you, My dear Doctor, that any memoirs of my life, distinct & unconnected with the general history of the war, would rather hurt my feelings than tickle my pride whilst I lived. I had rather glide gently down the stream of life, leaving it to posterity to think & say what they please of me, than by an act of mine to have vanity or ostentation imputed to me."

114 Letter of January 13, 1800.

115 After 1806, the title was: *The Life of George Washington: With Curious Anecdotes, Equally Honourable to Himself and Exemplary to His Young Countrymen*. For details about the editorial history, see the introduction by Marcus Cunliffe in the 1862 edition (Cambridge, MA: Belknap Press), as well as Christopher Harris, " 'Mason Locke Weems's 'Life of Washington'. The Making of a Bestseller," *Southern Literary Journal*, 19:2 (1987), pp. 92–101.

116 Furstenberg, *In the Name of the Father*.

117 The book successively compares Washington to all the classical heroes (Hercules, Achilles, Alexander) and even Jupiter and Mars. It was a matter of giving the nation a hero at the moment when, in Europe, nations were looking for legendary and historical heroes. On this point, see Anne-Marie Thiesse, *Les Créations des identités nationales en Europe, XVIIIe–XXe siècle* (Paris: Seuil, 1999). On the research done in the same years, about the American epic tradition, see John P. McWilliams, *The American Epic: Transforming a Genre, 1770–1860* (Cambridge: Cambridge University Press, 2009). The same year as Weems published his book, John Blair Linn published *The Death of Washington: A Poem in Imitation of the Manner of Ossian* (Philadelphia: J. Ormrod, 1800).

118 When Washington died, Bonaparte organized an important public ceremony orchestrated by Talleyrand, with a grand speech by Fontanes. A statue of the first American president was placed in the gallery of the Tuileries alongside statues of other great men. See Bronislaw Baczko, *Politiques de la Révolution française* (Paris: Gallimard, 2008), pp. 594–618.

119 François René de Chateaubriand, *Mémoires d'outre-tombe*, book VI, chapter VIII, ed. J.-P. Clément (Paris: Gallimard, 1997), Vol. I, pp. 414–18.

120 The publishing history of the *Mémorial* is complex. The manuscript was seized by Governor Hudson Lowe in 1816, then returned to Emmanuel de Las Cases in 1821. He published it at the beginning of 1823, in a self-censored puritanical edition. It was followed by several other editions, the most important of which are the ones of 1823–4 (complete and corrected), 1828, 1830–1 (complete once again, but this time without fear of censorship), and 1842 (more triumphant and Bonapartiste). I used the 1831 edition, the critical edition published by Seuil in 1968.

121 Jean Tulard, "Un chef-d'oeuvre de propagande," preface to the *Mémorial* (Paris: Seuil, 1968), pp. 7–11; Didier Le Gall, *Napoleon et le mémorial de Sainte-Hélène: Analyse d'un discours* (Paris: Kimé, 2003).

122 The exact title of the *Mémorial* is: *Mémorial de Sainte-Hélène ou Journal où se trouve consigné, jour par jour, ce qu'a dit et fait Napoleon durant dix-huit mois.*

123 As shown by Morrissey in *The Economy of Glory*, pp. 147–78.

124 Cited in ibid., p. 158; *Mémorial*, p. 195.

125 *Mémorial*, p. 20.

126 Bonnet, *Naissance du Panthéon.*

127 The direct influence of Boswell on Las Cases is not explicit in the *Mémorial*, but it can be hypothesized. The *Life of Samuel Johnson* appeared in 1791 in London, where it had enormous success, and Las Cases lived in England from 1793 to 1802, a period during which he returned to being a man of letters and a scholar. He was fond of the English language and gave courses in English to Napoleon while on the island. Therefore, it is fairly likely that he was aware of the *Life of Samuel Johnson*. As for Napoleon, he surely knew about *An Account of Corsica* by Boswell.

128 *Mémorial*, p. 206.

129 Laure Murat, *The Man who Thought He was Napoleon: Toward a Political History of Madness*, trans. Dukin Dusinberre (Chicago: University of Chicago Press, [2011] 2014).

130 *Mémorial*, p. 80.

131 Ibid., p. 120.

132 Ibid., p. 206.

133 In December 1815, Napoleon and Las Cases read *La Nouvelle Héloïse* out loud together the whole morning and then again at night, and they talked about the novel at lunch. They did the same thing again in June 1815. Then "Jean-Jacques" was the subject of conversation for the emperor in August 1816 (*Mémorial*, pp. 112, 303, and 429): "He discussed Jean-Jacques for a long time and in

the most interesting way, his talent, his influence, his eccentricities, his private depravaties" (p. 429).

134 Ibid., p. 112.

135 Ibid., p. 194.

136 Ibid.

137 The episode is reported in a less romantic way in the *Journal d'un voyage autour du monde de Camille Roquefeuille*, published the same year as the first edition of *Mémorial* (Paris: Ponthieu, 1823). The meeting between Roquefeuille and Taméaméa took place on January 10, 1819. After the salutations, "he wanted to know the news from Europe and about the health of various potentates. Two of his wives who were present seemed to take an interest in affairs of the civilized world, the most well-known figures of which were unknown to them. One of them asked several questions about Napoleon" (p. 345).

138 *Mémorial*, p. 635.

139 Ibid., p. 36.

140 Giorgio Agamben, *The Kingdom and the Glory: For a Theological Genealogy of Economy and Government*, trans. Lorenzo Chiesa (with Matteo Mandarini) (Stanford: Stanford University Press, [2008] 2011).

141 Bernard Manin, *The Principles of Representative Government* (Cambridge: Cambridge University Press, [1995] 1997), in particular pp. 94–131.

142 *Mémorial*, p. 419. Mme de Staël is often brought up in conversation by Napoleon on Saint Helena. He reads her novels, comments on them, and complacently tells anecdotes about her, sometimes repeating himself: "In the day's conversations, the emperor returned to the subject of Mme de Staël, and said nothing new about her" (*Mémorial*, p. 575).

143 Chateaubriand, *Mémoires d'outre-tombe*, Vol. II, p. 3.

CHAPTER 7 ROMANTICISM AND CELEBRITY

1 Alain Vaillant, "Pour une histoire globale du romantisme," in *Dictionnaire du romantisme* (Paris: CNRS Éditions, 2012).

2 José-Luis Diaz, *L'Écrivain imaginaire: Scénographies auctoriales à l'époque romantique* (Paris: Honoré Champion, 2007).

3 Stendhal, *Racine et Shakespeare* (Paris: Honoré Champion, [1825] 2006), p. XXV, quoted in Vaillant, "Pour une histoire globale."

4 Frances Wilson (ed.), *Byromania: Portraits of the Artist in Nineteenth- and Twentieth-Century Culture* (Basingstoke/London: Palgrave Macmillan, 1999), p. 3.

5 Hervé Mazurel, *Vertiges de la guerre: Byron, les philhellènes et le mirage grec* (Paris: Les Belles Lettres, 2013), pp. 460–9.

6 Clark, *Scandal.*

7 Wilson (ed.), *Byromania*, p. 10.

8 Tom Mole, *Byron's Romantic Celebrity: Industrial Culture and the Hermeneutics of Intimacy* (Basingstoke: Palgrave MacMillan, 2007).

9 Thomas Moore, "Notice of the Life of Lord Byron," in *Letters and Journal of Lord Byron* (London: J. Murray, 1833), p. 258.

10 Nicholas Mason, "Building Brand Byron: Early Nineteenth-Century Advertising and the Marketing of *Childe Harold's Pilgrimage,*" *Modern Language Quarterly*, 63 (2002), pp. 411–41.

11 Mole, *Byron*, p. 81; Annette Peach, "The Portraits of Byron," *Walpole Society*, 62 (2000).

12 Mole, *Byron*, pp. 74–5.

13 Quoted by Edmond Estève, *Byron et le romantisme français: Essai sur la fortune et l'influence de l'oeuvre de Byron en France de 1812 à 1850* (Paris: Boivin, 1929), p. 57.

14 Letter from Mme de Rémusat to her son, November 11, 1819, quoted by Estève, ibid., p. 66.

15 *Conversations of Lord Byron: noted during a residence with his Lordship at Pisa, in the years 1821 and 1822, by Thomas Medwin* (London: New Burlington Street, 1824), p. 11.

16 For a detailed account of the preparation and then the success of the book, see Jean-Claude Berchet, *Chateaubriand* (Paris: Gallimard, 2012), chapter IX of which is appropriately called "A Star is Born" (pp. 309–49). The following year, his celebrity increased with the popular triumph of the *Génie du christianisme*.

17 Mathieu Molé, *Souvenirs de jeunesse* (Paris: Mercure de France, 2005), p. 156. According to Molé, even Chateaubriand's passions were aimed at getting himself talked about: "Seeking in love the chatter and the renown of success, he bucked all social decorum in order to let it be known that he was the object of a great passion. Success was the heart throb for which he had sacrificed everything" (p. 164).

18 Berchet, *Chateaubriand*, p. 566.

19 F.R. de Chateaubriand, *Mémoires d'outre-tombe*, book XIII, chapter VI. This chapter, written in 1837, was revised in 1846. All the following citations come from that edition.

20 F.R. de Chateaubriand, "Sur les Annales littéraires ou De la littérature avant et après la Restauration" (1819), in *Mélanges politiques et littéraires* (Paris: Firmin-Didot, 1846), pp. 493–501, quoted p. 499.

21 John Clare, "Popularity and Authorship," *European Magazine*, I:3 (November 1825), pp. 300–3, Edited by John Birtwhistle, http://www.johnclare.info/birtwhistle.htm.

22 Johann Wolfgang von Goethe, *Poetry and Truth: Parts One to Three*, trans. Robert R. Heitner, eds Thomas P. Saine and Jeffrey L. Sammons (New York: Suhrkamp, [1811] 1987), pp. 286 and 195.

23 According to remarks made at Stroganov and quoted by Marie-Anne Lescouret, *Goethe: La fatalité poétique* (Paris: Flammarion, 1998), p. 374.

24 *Conversations de Goethe avec Eckermann* (Paris: Gallimard, 1988), p. 92.

25 When an admirer of Eugène Sue wrote an account of her "visit" to a celebrated writer in 1842, she symbolically mentioned a statue of the "Geneva philosopher." See Lyon-Caen, *La Lecture et la Vie*, p. 91, which gives other examples of this reference to Rousseau.

26 Letter of April 3, 1823, in George Paston and Peter Quenell (eds), *"To Lord Byron": Feminine Profiles Based upon Unpublished Letters, 1807–1824* (London: J. Murray, 1939), pp. 263–4.

27 Ghislaine McDayter, *Byromania and the Birth of Celebrity Culture* (Albany: State University of New York Press, 2009).

28 *Conversations of Lord Byron*, p. 253.

29 Corin Throsby, "Flirting with Fame: Byron's Anonymous Female Fans," *Byron Journal*, 32 (2004), pp. 115–23.

30 Lyon-Caen, *La Lecture et la Vie.*.

31 Honoré de Balzac, *Modeste Mignon* (Paris: Gallimard, [1844] 1982), p. 83.

32 Ibid., pp. 86–7.

33 Ibid., p. 255.

34 Brenda R. Weber, *Women and Literary Celebrity in the Nineteenth Century: The Transatlantic Production of Fame and Gender* (Farnham: Ashgate, 2012), p. 3.

35 Martine Reid, *Signer Sand: L'oeuvre et le nom* (Paris: Belin, 2003). On the importance of anonymity and masculine pseudonyms in the nineteenth century, see Christine Planté, *La Petite Soeur de Balzac: Essai sur la femme auteur* (Paris: Seuil, 1989), pp. 30–5.

36 George Sand, *Histoire de ma vie* (Paris: Gallimard, 1971), Vol. II, pp. 182–3.

37 Louis Jourdain and Taxile Delord, *Les Célébrités du jour, 1860–1861* (Paris: Le Siècle, 1860), p. 307.

38 Rachel Meschel, "A Belle Époque Media Storm: Gender, Celebrity and the Marcelle Tinayre Affair," *French Historical Studies*, 35:1 (2012), pp. 93–121.

39 *Rachel, une vie pour le théâtre, 1821–1858* (Paris: Musée d'Art et d'Histoire du Judaïsme, 2004); Anne Martin-Fugier, *Comédienne: De Mlle Mars à Sarah Bernhardt* (Paris: Le Seuil, 2001).

40 Marie-Hélène Girard, "Tombeau de Rachel," in Olivier Bara and Marie-Ève Thérenty (eds), "Presse et scène au XIXe siècle," Médias 19, http://www.medias19.org/index.php?id=2988.

41 Jeffrey Kahan, *The Cult of Kean* (Aldershot: Ashgate, 2006).

42 McMahon, *Divine Fury*, p. 92.

43 Letter from Mozart to his father, May 1, 1778, in *The Letters of Mozart and His Family*, trans. and ed. Emily Anderson (London: Macmillan, 1938), Vol. II, pp. 786–7. See also Lilti, *The World of the Salons* , p. 135.

44 William Weber, *Music and the Middle Class: The Social Structure of Concert Life in London, Paris and Vienna* (London: Croom Helm, 1975).

45 Henrich Heine, "Lettres sur la scène française," April 20, 1841, reissued in *Mais qu'est-ce que la musique? Chroniques*, ed. Rémy Stricker (Arles: Actes Sud, 1997), pp. 68–9.

46 Tia DeNora, *Beethoven and the Construction of Genius: Musical Politics in Vienna, 1792–1803* (Berkeley: University of California Press, 1997). See also commentaries by Menger, "Comment analyser la grandeur artistique: Beethoven et son génie," in *Le Travail créateur*, pp. 367–427.

47 Esteban Buch, *Beethoven's Ninth: A Political History* (Chicago: University of Chicago Press, 2003), pp. 111–55.

48 Stendhal, *Life of Rossini*, trans. Richard N. Coe (London: Calder, [1824] 1956), p. 1. On the celebrity of Rossini in Paris in 1824, see Benjamin Walton, *Rossini in Restoration Paris: The Sound of Modern Life* (Cambridge: Cambridge University Press, 2007).

49 According to the music critic Eduard Hanslick, quoted by Dana Gooley, "From the Top: Liszt's Aristocratic Airs," in Edward Berenson and Eva Giloi (eds), *Constructing Charisma: Celebrity, Fame and Power in Nineteenth-Century Europe* (New York: Berghahn Books, 2010), pp. 69–85.

50 Franz Liszt, "De la situation des artistes et de leur condition dans la société" (1835), in *L'Artiste et la Société* (Paris: Flammarion, 1993), pp. 54 and 48.

51 Bruno Moysan, *Liszt: Virtuose subversif* (Lyon: Symétrie, 2009).

52 Alan Walker, *Franz Liszt: Vol. I: The Virtuoso Years, 1811–1847*, revised edition (Ithaca, NY: Cornell University Press, 1987).

53 Dana Gooley, *The Virtuoso Liszt* (Cambridge: Cambridge University Press, 2004), pp. 156–200.

54 Ibid., p. 221.

55 Laure Schnapper, *Henri Herz, magnat du piano: La vie musicale en France au XIXe siècle (1815–1870)* (Paris: EHESS, 2011).

56 Famous for his boxing matches at the end of the 1780s, Mendoza had a talent for provoking his adversaries, announcing the matches in advance, and opening boxing up to the advertising world, whereas it had previously been kept secret. He attempted to capitalize on his celebrity by having shows in theaters, by founding a gentlemen's boxing club, and by publishing a treatise glorifying himself, *The Art of Boxing*. Peter Briggs, "Daniel Mendoza and Sporting Celebrity," in Mole, *Romanticism and Celebrity Culture*, pp. 103–19.

57 Gooley, *The Virtuoso Liszt*, pp. 78–116.

58 The expression is by Théophile Gautier, quoted by Moysan, *Liszt*, p. 245.

59 Legouvé, "Concert de Liszt à l'Opéra," quoted in ibid., p. 246.

60 William Weber, "From the Self-Managing Musician to the Independent Concert Agent," in William Weber (ed.), *The Musician as Entrepreneur, 1700–1914: Managers, Charlatans and Idealists* (Bloomington: Indiana University Press, 2004), pp. 105–29; James Deaville, "Publishing Paraphrases and Creating Collectors," in Christopher Gibbs and Dana Gooley (eds), *Franz Liszt and His World* (Princeton: Princeton University Press, 2006), pp. 255–90.

61 Heine had already developed this idea in a more general way, but with Liszt in mind, in a previous letter, where he went after the "tireless industry" with which virtuosos "played on our credulousness," aided by the press. He mentioned a virtuoso who gave successful concerts for the profit of an old and ruined gothic church, for a widow, for a "seventy-year-old school teacher who had lost his only cow, etc.," all the while letting his own father suffer in poverty (Heine, *Mais qu'est-ce que la musique?*, March 20, 1844, p. 104).

62 Letter of April 25, 1844, ibid., pp. 127–33.

63 Franz Liszt, "Sur la mort de Paganini," in *L'Artiste et la Société*, p. 258.

64 Franz Liszt, "Lettre d'un bachelier ès musique," *Gazette musicale*, 1838, reprinted in ibid., p. 127.

65 Paul Metzner, *Crescendo of the Virtuoso: Spectacle, Skill and Self-Promotion in Paris during the Age of Revolution* (Los Angeles: University of California Press, 1998).

66 Franz Liszt, "De la situation des artistes," in *L'Artiste et la Société*, p. 42.

67 Heinrich Heine, letter of April 25, 1844, in ibid., p. 135. After a series of concerts throughout Europe, Ole Bull returned several times to the United States and had enormous success, to the point of almost founding a Norwegian colony there in 1852. On the success of Fanny Elssler, see Lawrence Levine, *Highbrow/Lowbrow: The Emergence of Cultural Hierarchy in America* (Cambridge, MA: Harvard University Press, 1990), pp. 108–9.

68 Quoted by Thomas N. Baker, *Sentiment and Celebrity: Nathaniel Parker Willis and the Trials of Literary Fame* (New York: Oxford University Press, 1999), p. 11.

69 Karian Akemi Yokota, *Unbecoming British: How Revolutionary America Became a Postcolonial Nation* (Oxford: Oxford University Press, 2011).

70 Robert Bogdan, *Freak Show: Presenting Human Oddities for Amusement and Profit* (Chicago: University of Chicago Press, 1995).

71 Adams Bluford, *E Pluribus Barnum: The Great Showman and the Making of US Popular Culture* (Minneapolis: University of Minnesota Press, 1997).

72 Quoted by Sherry Lee Linkon, "Reading Lind Mania: Print Culture and the Construction of Nineteenth-Century Audiences," *Book History*, 1 (1998), pp. 94–106.

73 Charles Rosenberg, *The Life of Jenny Lind: Her Life, Her Struggles, and Her Triumphs* (New York: Stringer & Townsend, 1850); Nathaniel P. Willis, *Memoranda of the Life of Jenny Lind* (Philadelphia: Robert E. Peterson, 1851).

74 William Porter Ware and Thaddeus Lockard, Jr, *P.T. Barnum Presents Jenny Lind: The American Tour of the Swedish Nightingale* (Baton Rouge: Louisiana State University Press, 1980).

75 Levine, *Highbrow/Lowbrow*, p. 19.

76 Ibid., p. 100.

77 James W. Cook, "Mass Marketing and Cultural History: The Case of P.T. Barnum," *American Quarterly*, 51:1 (1999), pp. 175–86.

78 Quentin Deluermoz, *Le Crépuscule des révolutions, 1848–1871* (Paris: Le Seuil, 2012), p. 62.

79 Sudhir Hazareesingh, *The Legend of Napoleon* (London: Granta Books, 2005); Bernard Ménager, *Les Napoleons du peuple* (Paris: Aubier, 1988).

80 Daniel Walker Howe, *What Hath God Wrought: The Transformation of America, 1815–1848* (New York: Oxford University Press, 2007), pp. 328–45.

81 Lynn Hudson Parsons, *The Birth of Modern Politics: Andrew Jackson, John Quincy Adams, and the Election of 1828* (New York: Oxford University Press, 2009); see especially pp. xi–xv for an account of the ceremonial investiture, and pp. 135–6 for the role of the press.

82 John Plunkett, *Queen Victoria: First Media Monarch* (Oxford: Oxford University Press, 2003).

83 Ibid., pp. 36–7.

84 Ibid., p. 72.

85 Thompson, *The Media and Modernity*.

86 Plunkett, *Queen Victoria*, pp. 133–4.

87 Elizabeth Barrett-Browning, *Letters to Mary Russell Mitford* (Waco, TX: Browning Institute and Wellesley College, 1983), quoted in ibid., p. 124.

88 Lucy Riall, *Garibaldi: Invention of a Hero* (New Haven: Yale University Press, 2007), pp. 95–6.

89 *Garibaldi, arte et storia* (Rome: Museo centrale di Risorgimento, 1982).

90 Riall, *Garibaldi*, pp. 198–206.

91 The articles by Dumas were published in his own newspaper, *Le Monte Cristo*, and reprinted in volumes as: Alexandre Dumas, *Les Garibaldiens* (Paris: Michel Lévy frères, 1861); Dumas, *Viva Garibaldi! Une odyssée en 1860*, ed. Claude Schopp (Paris: Fayard, 2002). See the preface to the Italian edition: Gilles Pécout, "Una crociera nel Mediterrano con Garibaldi," in *Viva Garibaldi!* (Turin: Einaudi, 2004), pp. vii–xxxi.

92 *Le Siècle*, June 2, 1859, 8819, p. 1, http://gallica.bnf.fr.

93 Riall, *Garibaldi*, pp. 198–206.

94 Foladare, *Boswell's Paoli*, p. 77.

95 In a letter to Victoria of April 21,1864, quoted by Derek Beales, "Garibaldi in England: The Politics of Italian Enthusiasm," in John A. Davis and Paul Ginsborg (eds), *Society and Politics in the Age of the Risorgimento* (Cambridge: Cambridge University Press, 1991), pp. 184–216, here p. 187.

96 *The Scotsman* wrote: "Women, more or less in full dress, flew upon him, seized his hands, touched his beard, his poncho, his trousers, any part of him that they could reach..." (quoted by Beales, "Garibaldi in England," p. 187).

97 Jourdain and Delord, *Les Célébrités du jour*.

98 Jean-Luc Chappey, *Ordres et désordres biographiques: Dictionnaires, listes de noms, réputation, des Lumières à Wikipédia* (Seyssel: Champ Vallon, 2013).

99 *Biographie des hommes vivants* (Paris: Michaud, 1816), "avertissement," p. i.

100 A.V. Arnaud, A. Jay, E. Jouy, J. Norvins, *Biographie nouvelle des contemporains ou dictionnaire raisonné de tous les hommes qui, depuis la Révolution française, ont acquis de la célébrité par leurs actions, leurs écrits, leurs erreurs ou leurs crimes* (Paris: Librairie historique, 1820–5); Gustave Vaporeau, *Dictionnaire universel des contemporains* (Paris: Hachette, 1861); *Le Rivarol de 1842, ou Dictionnaire satirique des célébrités contemporaines* (Paris: Feuilleton mensuel, 1842). On the texts, see Loïc Chotard, "Les biographies contemporaines au XIXe siècle," in *Approches du XIXe siècle* (Paris: Presses Universitaires de Paris-Sorbonne, 2000), pp. 7–20; Chotard, "Les grands hommes du jour," *Romantisme*, 28:100 (1998), pp. 105–14; and for the context of editorial competition around "contemporary works," Chappey, *Ordres et désordres biographiques*, p. 268.

101 Mole, *Byron*, pp. 89–97.

102 Walter Benjamin, "Paris, Capital of the Nineteenth Century" (1935), in *The Arcades Project*, trans. Howard Eiland and Kevin McLaughlin (Cambridge, MA: Harvard University Press, 1999); Jonathan Crary, *Techniques of the Observer: On Vision and Modernity in the Nineteenth Century* (Cambridge, MA: MIT Press, 1992); Vanessa Schwartz, *Spectacular Realities: Early Mass Culture in Fin-de-Siècle Paris* (Berkeley: University of California Press, 1998).

103 Adeline Wrona, "Des panthéons à vendre: le portrait d'hommes de lettres, entre réclame et biographie," *Romantisme*, 1 (2012), pp. 37–50, here p. 38.

104 *Histoire générale de la presse française, Vol. II: 1815–1871* (Paris: PUF, 1972); Dominique Kalifa, *La Culture de masse en France, Vol. I: 1860–1930* (Paris: La Découverte, 2001), pp. 9–11; Judith Lyon-Caen, "Lecteurs et lectures: les usages de la presse au XIXe siècle," *in* Dominique Kalifa, Philippe Régnier, Marie-Ève Thérenty, and Alain Vaillant (eds), *La Civilisation du journal: Histoire culturelle et littéraire de la presse française au XIXe siècle* (Paris: Nouveau Monde, 2011), pp. 23–60.

105 Ibid., p. 286.

106 Charles L. Ponce de Leon, *Self-Exposure: Human-Interest Journalism and the Emergence of Celebrity in America, 1890–1940* (Chapel Hill: University of North Carolina Press, 2002). See also

Michael Schudson, *Discovering the News: A Social History of American Newspapers* (New York: Basic Books, 1978). On the development in France of the interview in the same years at the end of the century: Marie-Ève Thérenty, *La Littérature au quotidien: Poétiques journalistiques au XIXe siècle* (Paris: Le Seuil, 2007), pp. 330–52.

107 Letter of April 12, 1837, Mme de Girardin, *Lettres parisiennes du vicomte de Launay*, ed. A.-M. Fugier (Paris: Mercure de France, 1986), pp. 133–4.

108 Gabriel Tarde, *The Laws of Imitation*, trans. Elsie Worthington Clews Parsons (Charleston, SC: Bibliolife, [1890] 2010), p. 307.

109 Ibid.. The primary text "The Public and the Crowd," was first published in 1898.

110 Bruno Karsenti, *D'une philosophie à l'autre: Les sciences sociales et la politique des modernes* (Paris: Gallimard, 2013).

111 Plunkett, *Victoria*.

112 Riall, *Garibaldi*, p. 253.

113 Jean Sagne, "Portraits en tout genre, l'Atelier de photographie," in Michel Frizot (ed.), *Nouvelle histoire de la photographie* (Paris: Bordas, 1995), pp. 103–30. On the contemporary gallery, see Wrona, "Des panthéons à vendre."

114 Émile Zola, *The Kill (La Curée)*, trans. Brian Nelson (Oxford: Oxford University Press, [1872] 2004), pp. 105 and 104.

115 Elisabeth Anne McCauley, *Industrial Madness: Commercial Photography in Paris, 1848–1871* (New Haven: Yale University Press, 1994).

116 Jules Barbey d'Aurevilly, "Le portrait photographique," *Le Nain jaune*, January 3, 1867.

117 The judgment was rendered on June 16, 1858 by the Court of the Seine (Kayser, *La Protection de la vie privé*, p. 68).

118 Pierre Georgel (ed.), *La gloire de Victor Hugo* (Paris: RMN, 1985).

119 Joss Marsh, "The Rise of Celebrity Culture," in Sally Ledger and Holly Furneaux (eds), *Charles Dickens in Context* (Cambridge: Cambridge University Press, 2011), pp. 98–108.

120 "Gustave Flaubert," *La République des Lettres*, October 23, 1876, quoted by Yvan Leclerc, "Portraits de Flaubert et de Maupassant en photophobes," *Romantisme*, 105 (1999), pp. 97–106.

121 Leclerc, "Portraits de Flaubert et de Maupassant en photophobes," p. 103.

122 A signed manuscript note, BM Rouen, quoted ibid., p. 105.

123 Anne-Claude Ambroise-Rendu, "Du dessin de presse à la photographie (1878–1914): histoire d'une mutation technique et

culturelle," *Revue d'histoire moderne et contemporaine*, 39:1 (1992), pp. 6–28.

124 Wladimiro Setinelli, *Garibaldi: l'album fotografico* (Florence: Alinari, 1982).

125 Loïc Chotard, *Nadar: Caricatures et photographies* (Paris: Paris-musée, 1992), p. 105–9.

126 Wrona, "Des panthéons à vendre," p. 50.

127 Schwartz, *Spectacular Realities*, pp. 92–9.

128 Christophe Charle, *Théâtres en capitales: Naissance de la société du spectacle à Paris, Berlin, Londres et Vienne, 1860–1914* (Paris: Albin Michel, 2008).

129 Jackson Lears, *Rebirth of a Nation: The Making of Modern America* (New York: HarperCollins, 2009), p. 251.

130 Kenneth E. Silver, "Celebrity, Patriotism and Sarah Bernhardt," in Berenson and Giloi (eds), *Constructing Charisma*, pp. 145–54.

131 Guy de Maupassant, "Enthousiasme et cabotinage," *Le Gaulois*, May 19, 1881, reprinted in *Chroniques* (Paris: Le Livre de Poche, 2008), pp. 392–7.

132 Charles Baudelaire, "Le chien et le flacon," *Petits poèmes en prose: Œuvres complètes* (Paris: Robert Laffont, 1980), p. 166.

CONCLUSION

1 Roland Barthes, *Mythologies*, trans. Annette Lavers (London: Jonathan Cape, [1957] 1972), p. 56.

2 *Kazan on Kazan: Interviews with Michel Ciment* (London: Secker & Warburg, 1973).

3 The original sentence ("In the future, everyone will be world-famous for 15 minutes") appeared in 1968, in an exhibition catalogue, but was perhaps said in 1966. Annette Michelson (ed.), *Andy Warhol* (Cambridge, MA: MIT Press, 2002).

4 In one of the last scenes, we see Rhodes' agent launching the career of a new star.

5 A recent example: Pierre Zaoui, *La Discrétion ou l'art de disparaître* (Paris: Autrement, 2013).

6 Pierre Bourdieu, "The Economy of Symbolic Goods," in *Practical Reason: On the Theory of Action*, trans. Randal Johnson et al. (Cambridge: Polity, [1994] 1998), pp. 92–123.

7 Michel de Certeau, *The Practice of Everyday Life*, trans. Steven Rendall (Berkeley: University of California Press, [1980] 1984).

8 David Lefranc, *La Renommée en droit privé* (Paris: LGDJ, 2003), p. 98.

9 Ibid., p. 80.
10 Georges Brassens, "Trompettes de la renommée." See "The Songs of Georges Brassens with English Translation," http://brassenswithenglish.blogspot.co.uk/2008/11/les-trompettes-de-la-renommee-his.html.

POSTFACE

1 In particular see Richard Dyer, *Stars* (London: BFI Publishing, 1998); Gamson, *Claims to Fame*; Peter David Marshall, *Celebrity and Power: Fame in Contemporary Culture* (Minneapolis: University of Minnesota Press, 1997); Graeme Turner, *Understanding Celebrity* (London: Sage, 2004); Sue Homes and Sean Redmond, *Framing Celebrities: New Directions in Celebrity Culture* (London: Routledge, 2006). A recent synthesis can be found in P. David Marshall and Sean Redmond, *A Companion to Celebrity* (Oxford: Wiley, 2015).
2 Gamson, *Claims to Fame*.
3 Simon Critchley, *On Bowie* (London: Serpent's Tail, 2016).

ILLUSTRATION CREDITS

Figure 1: © Bridgeman Images
Figure 2: © Tate, London 2016
Figure 3: © Getty Images
Figure 4: © RMN-Grand Palais (Château de Blérancourt)/Christian Jean
Figure 5: © RMN-Grand Palais (Musée du Louvre)/René-Gabriel Ojéda
Figure 6: © RMN-Grand Palais (Château de Blérancourt)/Gérard Blot
Figure 7: © TopFoto/Roger-Viollet
Figure 8: © The Gilbert Collection/Victoria and Albert Museum, London
Figure 9: © Victoria and Albert Museum, London
Figure 10: Wedgwood Medallion with Portrait of Benjamin Franklin, after 1766. Ceramic, white on black jasper dip. 5½ × 4 inches. American Philosophical Society. Gift of the estate of Isaac Minis Hays, 1967
Figure 11: Courtesy of the State Museum of Pennsylvania, Pennsylvania Historical and Museum Commission
Figure 12: © National Portrait Gallery, London
Figure 13: © Fine Art/Contributor/Getty Images
Figure 14: Courtesy of the National Gallery of Art, Washington
Figure 15: © Bibliothèque nationale de France
Figure 16: © Bibliothèque nationale de France

INDEX

342

pose, 230
scandal, 220–1
seduction of women, 219–20, 229

Cabanis, Pierre Jean Georges, 186,
190
Caesar, Julius, 88, 161, 192, 195
Caffieri, Jean-Jacques, 59, 63
Cagliostro (Giuseppe Balsamo), 59,
84–5
Calonne, Charles de, 178, 179
Campan, Madame, 167, 172
Cantona, Eric, 275
Caraman, Comte de, 179–80
Carey, Mathew, 203
caricatures, 19, 65–7, 256–7
Carjat, Étienne, 262
Caroline, Queen, 166
Cartouche, Louis-Dominique, 77–8,
79
Casanova, Giacomo, 34
castrati, 32–6, 234
Catherine II, 19, 58
Cavendish, Georgiana, 56
celebrity
authenticity and, 273
curse, 100–1, 133–43
definition, 3–10
economics, 3, 26–32, 40–1, 276,
277, 281
eighteenth-century concept,
92–102
first media revolution, 50–85
glory and, 5, 6, 7, 86–108, 184
loneliness, 109–59
mechanisms, 9
merit and, 105–8, 280–1
modernity and, 12
politics see politics
reputation and, 5, 6–7
Romanticism see Romanticism
servitude, 275
society of the spectacle, 1, 3, 13
terminology, 5, 102–5, 255
theater see theater
Voltaire see Voltaire
censorship, 68–9, 77–8, 277

ceramic figurines, 61–2, 63, **fig. 7,
fig. 10, fig. 11**
ceremonials, 2, 24, 169–72, 175–6,
251
Chalier, Joseph, 192
Chamfort, Nicolas de, 105–7, 142,
159, 179, 272
Chaplin, Charlie, 267
charisma, 13, 169, 185–6, 213
Charles II, 30, 53
Charlotte, Queen, 37
Charmois, Monsieur de, 46
Charpentier, Georges, 262
Chateaubriand, François-René de
Atala, 223–4, 226
Byron and, 223
celebrity, 223–8
Essai sur les révolutions, 223
fan mail, 229
Génie du christianisme, 228
Mémoires d'outre-tombe, 205, 216,
224–8, 229
Napoleon and, 205–6, 215–16
publicity demon, 224
Rousseau and, 227–8
seduction of women, 228–9, 231
on Washington, 205–6
Chaumont, Jacques-Donatien Le Ray
de, 63
Chénier, Marie-Joseph, 39–40
Chenonceaux, Julie Dupin de, 110,
115, 152
Chevrier, François Antoine, 103
Choiseul, Duchesse de, 133
Cicero, Marcus Tullius, 89, 91, 225
Cincinnatus, 195, 197, 200, 201, 253
cinema, 266, 267–70
circles of recognition, 6
Clairon, Hippolyte, 27, 71
Clara the Rhinoceros, 136
Clare, John, 225
Clive, Kitty, 30
Clooney, George, 272, 281
Cobain, Kurt, 159, 279
Cobbett, William, 202
Cochin, Charles Nicolas, **fig. 11**
Collet, Louise, 262

Lamb, Caroline, 222
Las Cases, Emmanuel de, 206–13
Lauragais, Duc de, 60
Laurès, Antoine de, 72
Lauzun, Duc de, 172
Lawrence, Thomas, 37
Le Beau, Pierre Adrien, 64, fig. 6
Le Gay, Nicole, 176
Le Gray, Gustave, 260
Le Peletier, Louis-Michel, 192
Le Ray de Chaumont, Joseph
    Donatien, 63
Lécluse, Louis, 27
Legrand, Marc-Antoine, 77–8
Leibniz, Gottfried Wilhelm, 53
Lekain (Henri-Louis Cain), 27, 71
Lemaître, Frédérick, 233
Lemoyne, Jean-Baptiste, 59
Léonard (hairdresser), 173
lesbianism, 32, 164
Lespinasse, Julie, 103
Leszczyńska, Marie, 169
Leszczyński, Stanisław, 110, 116
Levasseur, Thérèse, 76, 113
Ligne, Prince de, 113, 133
Lind, Jenny, 13, 242–5, 257, 264,
    265, 272
Linguet, Simon, 22, 58, 61, 71
Liszt, Franz, 12, 234–41, 265, 272
literacy, 51, 258
Louis I of Bavaria, 90
Louis XIV, 2, 60, 66, 164, 168–9,
    215
Louis XV, 167, 169, 174, 175
Louis XVI, 2, 169, 175, 176
Lowe, Hudson, 207
Ludwig I, 90
Luxembourg, Madame de, 124, 125,
    140–1
Luxembourg, Maréchal de, 137

Macaire, Robert, 233
Madonna, 272, 280
Malibran, Maria, 233
Mandrin, Louis, 79
Manuel, Pierre, 191, 192
Marat, Jean-Paul, 189, 190, 192, 193

Marchand, Jean-Henri, 16
Maria Theresa, Empress, 167, 169,
    172
Mariani, Angelo, 263
Marie-Antoinette, Queen
    celebrity and, 170–1, 214, 251
    court, 166–72
    disguises, 170, 172
    fashion, 163, 173–4
    film, 1–2
    lavish spending, 175, 176
    Mlle Raucourt and, 32, 173
    narcissism, 251
    necklace affair, 71, 175–6
    pamphlet campaign against, 164–6
    portraits, 64, 174–5, fig. 14
    Princess Diana and, 1, 251
    revolution, 176
    Sophie Arnould and, 60
Marie de Médicis, 174
Marin, François, 17
Marivaux, Pierre de, 102
Marmontel, Jean-François, 86–7, 91
Marron, Madame de, 72
Mars, Mademoiselle, 233
Martel, Thomas de, 53
Maupassant, Guy de, 262–3, 264–5,
    272
Maupeou, René Nicolas Charles
    Augustin de, 71
Mayall, John, 260
Mayeur de Saint-Paul, Françoise-
    Marie, 77
Mazzini, Giuseppe, 251, 252, 253
media communication
    first media revolution, 50–85
    biography, 73–85
    caricatures, 65–7
    idols and puppets, 62–7
    periodicals, 67–73
    public figurines, 57–62
    public/private sphere, 73–85
    techniques, 50–62
    visual culture of celebrity, 52–7
    French Revolution, 255–6
    long-distance intimacy, 44
    media monarchs, 248–51

171/2
185 - Charisma
202 Fame v. celebrity
204
208
214
234
241
259
262
⭐ 276ff

Plato: "I loved for
        Dion"
        —

Horace & Brave men
   before Agamemnon